Applying Artificial Intelligence in Cybersecurity Analytics and Cyber Threat Detection

Applying Artificial Intelligence in Cybersecurity Analytics and Cyber Threat Detection

Edited by

Shilpa Mahajan
The NorthCap University, India

Mehak Khurana
The NorthCap University, India

Vania Vieira Estrela
Fluminense Federal University, Brazil

WILEY

Published by John Wiley & Sons, Inc., Hoboken, New Jersey.
Published simultaneously in Canada.

Library of Congress Cataloging-in-Publication Data Applied for:

Hardback ISBN: 9781394196449

Cover Design: Wiley
Cover Image: © Yuichiro Chino/Getty Images

Set in 9.5/12.5pt STIXTwoText by Straive, Chennai, India

This work is dedicated to the cybersecurity professionals, academicians, researchers, and enthusiasts who strive to make the digital world a safer place for all. Dedicated to those on the front lines of cybersecurity, tirelessly safeguarding our digital landscapes, and to the relentless pursuit of knowledge that fuels our collective defense against evolving threats. Their commitment inspired the editors to push their boundaries of understanding and fortify the resilience of interconnected society.

Contents

About the Editors

Dr. Shilpa Mahajan is a distinguished Certified Ethical Hacker (CEHv11) and Cisco Certified Instructor with a notable career spanning over 16 years in research and education. She is currently serving as an Associate Professor at the NorthCap University. Dr. Mahajan holds a Ph.D. in Wireless Sensor Networks from Guru Nanak Dev University, Amritsar, and graduated with distinction from Punjab Engineering College, Chandigarh. Her extensive contributions include authoring numerous papers published in prestigious international journals, books, conferences, and holding patents. In her current role, she guides doctoral scholars and successfully supervises M.Tech and B.Tech projects. Dr. Mahajan has designed courses focusing on Computer Networks, Network Security, and Cryptography. She actively participates in various academic activities, serving as a resource person for Faculty Development Programs (FDPs), workshops, guest lectures, invited talks, and panel discussions. Dr. Mahajan's expertise is underscored by her proactive involvement in chairing sessions at conferences, highlighting her standing within the academic community. Notably, she coordinated the ATAL FDP on Web Security in 2022 and organized EDPs for CCNA Modules. Remarkably, she has contributed as an editor for esteemed publishers including Springer, CRC Press, Wiley, and several others. Her contributions extend to the establishment of a Cisco lab at the NorthCap University, Gurgaon, in January 2014. Recognized by Cisco Networking Academy for her active participation over five years, Dr. Mahajan's dedication and expertise continue to shape the academic landscape in the fields of Cybersecurity and Information Security.

Dr. Mehak Khurana is an accomplished and dedicated Certified Ethical Hacker (CEHv11) with an illustrious career spanning over 13 years in the fields of research and teaching. Dr. Mehak Khurana is currently leveraging her extensive expertise as an Associate Professor at the NorthCap University, contributing to the academic and practical realms of Cybersecurity and Information Security. Her academic journey is marked by exceptional achievements, including the attainment of a Ph.D. degree specializing in Information Security and Cryptography. Complementing this, she was honored with a silver medal for her M.Tech degree in Information Technology from USICT, GGSIPU. Her specialization lies in Cybersecurity, Information Security, and Cryptography. She has left an indelible mark on academia through her prolific publications in renowned journals, conferences books, and patents. She demonstrated her commitment to aligning education with industry best practices; she introduced and designed cutting-edge courses in Penetration Testing, Secure Coding, Software Vulnerabilities, and Web and Mobile Security. Her mentorship extends to guiding B.Tech., M.Tech. projects, and Ph.D. scholars, nurturing the potential of future leaders in the field. She convened the International Conference on Cyber Security and Digital Forensics in collaboration with Springer in 2021. She served as a valuable resource person for various Faculty Development Programs (FDPs), workshops, guest lectures, invited talks, panelists, etc. Her active involvement in chairing sessions at various conferences underscores her expertise and prominence in the academic community. She edited books for esteemed publishers such as Springer, CRC Press, Wiley, and edited many more. Furthermore, her role as a reviewer for reputable journals and a Technical Program Committee (TPC) member for various international conferences highlights her commitment to fostering excellence. Her contributions have earned her recognition as the Emerging Women Leader in Cybersecurity Sector in 2023 by StarDiVvaz Women Awards, presented by Dr. Rajshri Singh, IPS, IGP Haryana State Crime. Likewise, her selection as one of the top three finalists for the Cyberjutsu award by Womencyberjutsu in Virginia, US, underscores her standing as a prominent Cyber Educator.

Dr. Vania Vieira Estrela has ample experience teaching postgraduate and undergraduate courses. She holds a B.Sc. degree from the Federal University of Rio de Janeiro (UFRJ) in Electrical and Computer Engineering (ECE), an M.Sc. from the Technological Institute of Aeronautics (ITA), Brazil, and M.Sc. in ECE at Northwestern University, USA, and a Ph.D. in ECE from the Illinois Institute of Technology (IIT), Chicago, IL, USA. She has taught at DePaul University, USA, and Universidade Estadual do Norte Fluminense (UENF), Brazil. She was a visiting professor at the Polytechnic Institute of Rio de Janeiro (IPRJ)/State University of Rio de Janeiro (UERJ) in Brazil. She works at Universidade Federal Fluminense's (UFF) Department of Telecommunications. She has proposed and participated in various pedagogical projects for the specialities of "Computer Engineering" at UENF, "Computer Technology" at Universidade Estadual da Zona Oeste (UEZO)/UERJ, and "Material Science and Engineering with Emphasis on Polymers" also at UEZO/UERJ. Research interests include Cyber-Physical Systems, Signal/Image/Video Processing, Multimedia, Biomedical Engineering, Neuroscience, Electronic Instrumentation, Computer Architecture, Unmanned Aerial Systems, Modeling/Simulation, Sustainable Projects, Smart Designs, Inverse Problems, Communications, Motion Estimation and Understanding, Artificial Intelligence, and Geoprocessing. She edits and reviews for several prestigious publishers. She is engaged in Humanitarian Engineering, Technology Transfer, STEAM Education, Environmental Issues, Digital Inclusion, and all UN Sustainable Development Goals (SDGs). She has served as editor of more than 15 books and special issues. She has served on a plethora of technical and organizational committees and is a member of IEEE.

List of Contributors

Nikolaos Andreopoulos
Computer Science Department
Technological Institute of Iceland
Reykjavík
Iceland

Joaquim T. de Assis
Instituto Politecnico do Rio de Janeiro
Nova Friburgo
RJ
Brazil

Avi Chakravarti
Amity School of Engineering and Technology
Amity University
Noida
Uttar Pradesh
India

Suman Das
Information Security
Zensar Technologies
Kolkata
India

Anand Deshpande
Electronics and Communication Engineering
Angadi Institute of Technology and Management
Belagavi
India

Chingakham Nirma Devi
Department of Computer Science
Vels Institute of Science
Technology and Advanced Studies (VISTAS)
Chennai
India

Edwiges G.H. Grata
Department of Telecommunications
Federal Fluminense University (UFF)
Niterói
RJ
Brazil

Jahnavi
Department of Computer Science
Dr. B.R. Ambedkar National Institute of Technology
Jalandhar
India

R. Jenice Aroma
Department of CSE
Karunya Institute of Technology and Sciences
Karunya University
Coimbatore
India

Maria A. de Jesus
Department of Telecommunications
Federal Fluminense University (UFF)
Niterói
RJ
Brazil

Ashish Joshi
Information Security
Zensar Technologies
Pune
India

Awais Khan Jumani
Department of Computer Science
Sindh Madressa-tul-Islam University
Karachi
Sindh
Pakistan

Keshav Kaushik
School of Computer Science
University of Petroleum and Energy Studies
Dehradun
Uttarakhand
India

Abdullah A. Khan
Research Lab of Artificial Intelligence and Information Security
Faculty of Computing
Science and Information Technology
Benazir Bhutto Shaheed University
Karachi
Sindh
Pakistan

Asiya Khan
School of Engineering
Computing and Mathematics (Faculty of Science and Engineering)
University of Plymouth
Plymouth
UK

Mehak Khurana
The NorthCap University
Gurugram
India

Dhanashree Kulkarni
Department of Computer Science and Engineering
Angadi Institute of Technology and Management
Belagavi
India

Asif A. Laghari
Sindh Madresstul Islam University
Karachi
Sindh
Pakistan

Ricardo T. Lopes
Federal University of Rio de Janeiro (COPPE/UFRJ)
Nuclear Engineering Laboratory (LIN)
Rio de Janeiro
RJ
Brazil

Shilpa Mahajan
Department of Computer Science
The NorthCap University
Gurgaon
India

Geetika Munjal
Amity School of Engineering and Technology
Amity University
Noida
Uttar Pradesh
India

Paridhi Pasrija
The NorthCap University
Gurugram
India

Vishwas Pitre
Information Security
Zensar Technologies
Pune
India

Tushar Puri
Amity School of Engineering and Technology
Amity University
Noida
Uttar Pradesh
India

Supriya Raheja
Amity University
Noida
India

Kumudha Raimond
Department of Computer Science and Engineering
Karunya Institute of Technology and Sciences
Coimbatore
India

R. Renuga Devi
Department of Computer Science and Applications (MCA)
SRM Institute of Science and Technology
Ramapuram
Chennai
India

Satya Saladi
Information Security
Zensar Technologies
Hyderabad
India

Mohammad Shabaz
Chitkara University Institute of Engineering and Technology
Chitkara University
Rajpura
Punjab
India

Bhawna
Department of Computer Science
The NorthCap University
Gurgaon
India

Utkarsh Sharma
Amity School of Engineering and Technology
Amity University
Noida
Uttar Pradesh
India

Laishram Kirtibas Singh
Department of Computer Science
Vels Institute of Science Technology and Advanced Studies (VISTAS)
Chennai
India

Utkarsh Singh
The NorthCap University
Gurugram
India

Dalmo Stutz
Centro Federal de Educação Tecnológica Celso Suckow da Fonseca (CEFET) at Nova Friburgo
Nova Friburgo
RJ
Brazil

Lin Teng
Software College
Shenyang Normal University
Shenyang
China

Andrey Terziev
TerziA
Sofia
Bulgaria

Diego M.R. Tudesco
Department of Telecommunications
Federal Fluminense University (UFF)
Niterói
RJ
Brazil

Urvashi
Department of Computer Science and Engineering
Dr. B.R. Ambedkar National Institute of Technology
Jalandhar
India

Shoulin Yin
Shenyang Normal University
Shenyang
Liaoning Province
China

Preface

In the ever-evolving digital landscape, the fusion of artificial intelligence (AI) with the realm of cybersecurity has introduced a formidable ally. AI's unique capabilities in processing vast data volumes, recognizing intricate patterns, and swiftly adapting to emerging threats have marked the dawn of a new era in cyber defense. As AI continues to seamlessly integrate into our cybersecurity strategies, it plays a pivotal role in our ongoing battle against the ever-shifting landscape of cyber threats.

The digital landscape is rapidly evolving, and with it, the nature of cyber threats. This book addresses a pressing need – to bridge the knowledge gap between the potent capabilities of AI and its practical applications in fortifying cybersecurity. Our aim is to provide readers with a comprehensive guide to understand, implement, and harness the power of AI in safeguarding digital ecosystems. Collecting insights from seasoned cybersecurity professionals and AI experts, this book seeks to demystify the world of AI in cybersecurity. It aims to serve as a valuable resource for cybersecurity professionals looking to enhance their defenses, students eager to explore the exciting intersection of AI and cybersecurity, and individuals concerned about their online security. Another aim of this book is to empower our readers with knowledge and tools to shield against evolving cyber threats and inspire innovation in the field.

This book offers a comprehensive exploration of the synergy between AI and cybersecurity. It delves into the realm of AI-powered tools, techniques, and practices that empower organizations and individuals to stay ahead of malicious actors. The scope of the book encompasses AI applications in intrusion detection, threat identification, and risk assessment, among others. It provides practical guidance, real-world case studies, and a holistic view of the evolving landscape of cyber threats and the innovative solutions AI offers to mitigate them. While we strive to cover a wide spectrum of AI techniques tailored for cyber defense, it is important to recognize that the field of AI and cybersecurity is dynamic and ever-evolving. This book does not claim to be an exhaustive encyclopedia; rather, it serves as a snapshot of the state of the field at the time of its writing. As technology progresses, new challenges and solutions will arise, and our understanding of the subject will continue to evolve.

This book builds upon the existing body of literature that explores the integration of AI and cybersecurity, acknowledging the pioneering work of researchers and professionals in this field. It provides a comprehensive overview of the current landscape while offering fresh perspectives and insights.

In closing, this collaborative effort reflects the dedication of experts passionate about securing our digital world. The fusion of AI and cybersecurity has the potential to reshape the future of digital security. We hope this book empowers the readers to harness this potential and become a guardian of the digital realm.

Shilpa Mahajan
The NorthCap University, India

Mehak Khurana
The NorthCap University, India

Vania Vieira Estrela
Fluminense Federal University, Brazil

Acknowledgment

Heartfelt gratitude to the contributors and experts whose unwavering dedication has shaped this book. Their invaluable insights and expertise have played an instrumental role in bringing this collaborative effort to fruition.

Disclaimer

Note for Readers

Dear Readers,

This book is a collaborative effort aimed at providing you with a comprehensive understanding of the intricate world of cybersecurity analytics. The intention of the authors/editors is to equip you with insights, strategies, and practical knowledge that will empower you in navigating the complexities of cyberthreats. Throughout these chapters, you'll find a blend of theoretical concepts and hands-on approaches, all crafted to enhance your understanding and proficiency in addressing contemporary cybersecurity challenges. Whether you are a seasoned cybersecurity professional, a student entering the field, or simply someone passionate about the evolving digital landscape, we hope you find this book both informative and inspiring.

Introduction

In the realm of cybersecurity, where digital landscapes are in constant flux, the unceasing evolution of cyber threats poses an ever-growing challenge. Navigating this intricate web of potential risks requires a comprehensive understanding of the various facets of cybersecurity and the implementation of effective detection and mitigation strategies. This book, "Applying Artificial Intelligence in Cybersecurity Analytics and Cyber Threat Detection," takes a deep dive into the dynamic world of cybersecurity analytics, emphasizing the pressing need for innovative approaches to counteract a diverse array of cyber threats. The chapters within this book are carefully curated to offer a nuanced exploration of techniques, methodologies, and practical applications designed to fortify our defenses against malicious activities in the digital space.

As we embark on this exploration, the aim is to equip readers with a profound understanding of the multifaceted landscape of cybersecurity, encompassing not only the traditional forms of threats but also the more contemporary and sophisticated challenges that emerge with technological advancements. Each chapter is crafted to provide insights, analyses, and actionable strategies, offering a holistic view of cyberthreat detection and mitigation. The dynamic nature of the cybersecurity landscape necessitates an adaptive and informed approach. Therefore, this book serves as a compendium of knowledge, drawing on the collective expertise of contributors who bring real-world experience and practical insights to the forefront. It is intended for cybersecurity professionals seeking to enhance their skills, students entering the field, and anyone intrigued by the ever-evolving landscape of digital security.

As we traverse through the following pages, the goal is to shed light on effective strategies, methodologies, and practices that go beyond mere detection. The emphasis lies in understanding the intricacies of cyberthreats, enhancing the analytical capabilities of security practitioners, and fostering a proactive stance against potential risks. In closing, the collective wisdom encapsulated in these chapters aims to empower readers with the knowledge and tools needed to navigate the complexities of cybersecurity analytics. By fostering a deeper understanding of cyber threats and effective detection mechanisms, we can collectively contribute to fortifying the digital realms we inhabit.

Part I

Artificial Intelligence (AI) in Cybersecurity Analytics: Fundamental and Challenges

1

Analysis of Malicious Executables and Detection Techniques

Geetika Munjal and Tushar Puri

Amity School of Engineering and Technology, Amity University, Noida, Uttar Pradesh, India

1.1 Introduction

An instruction set created to harm a system is known as malware, which is short for malicious software [1]. The production of malware is increasing, making it more challenging for security firms to identify it. Traditionally, security firms and antivirus vendors employed antivirus software to distinguish between dangerous and clean data. Most of these tools compare the malicious programs to a database of well-known malware signatures using a signature-based method to identify them [2, 3]. The signature of an executable file serves as its distinctive identifier, and signatures can be generated using static, dynamic, and hybrid methodologies. However, this technique's drawback is that it is ineffective at detecting new malware samples. Due to the continuous increase in the quantity of new malware samples, these signatures must be continually updated [3].

Static analysis, the method that extracts features from a program's binary code by examining it and building models that illustrate the features, was developed to counter these tactics. These techniques are used to distinguish between hazardous and useful files. However, static analysis is easily evaded since malware authors utilize numerous code obfuscation techniques, like metamorphic and polymorphic approaches. Despite providing valuable insight into the behavior of programs, functions, and parameters, static analysis can still be unreliable [1].

Dynamic analysis, on the other hand, implements the software inside a secure environment to observe its behavior. This method exposes the code obfuscation strategies used by malware authors and works well with compressed files. However, dynamic analysis needs to be carried out within a secure environment to prevent system damage and can be time-consuming. Additionally, malware may behave differently in a virtual (secure) environment compared to an actual environment, leading to an incorrect log of behavior [4].

Applying Artificial Intelligence in Cybersecurity Analytics and Cyber Threat Detection, First Edition.
Edited by Shilpa Mahajan, Mehak Khurana, and Vania Vieira Estrela.

Combining static and dynamic analysis techniques can result in a more effective and reliable malware detection strategy. The main categories of executable malicious code (MC) are (i) MC that has been injected, such as worms that use buffer overflow exploits to inject their code into active software processes, (ii) dynamically generated malware (MC), and (iii) obfuscated malware (MC), which includes, viruses, Trojan horses, and worms that cloak their code via data manipulations and obscure computations to avoid detection and analysis. Polymorphic viruses or Trojans are an example of obfuscated malware [1]. Static feature-based analysis seems to be effective and efficient, as it enables network detection when the algorithm is loaded into memory [5, 6]. However, when the malicious file or code is compressed or encrypted, it becomes more challenging to detect. As a result, dynamic feature analysis must first unpack or decrypt the CPU instructions before being executed. Dynamic analysis for detecting network malware may not be practical due to the rapidity of network traffic [1].

Malicious executables are classified into three types based on how malware is transmitted: viruses, Trojan horses, and worms [7]. They infect already-running programs, causing them to become "infected" and spread to other programs when they are run. Worms, on the other hand, are standalone programs that propagate throughout a network, usually by taking advantage of bugs in the software that is operating on networked machines. Trojan horses disguise themselves as legitimate applications while carrying out harmful tasks. Malicious executables aren't really usually easily categorized and can behave in a variety of ways. Virus detection tools, including McAfee Virus Scan are extensively used, and Dell suggests Norton Antivirus for any and all new computers [7]. Although the titles of these programs include the term "virus," some also detect worms and Trojan horses. This approach of looking for recognized patterns of MC, called signature-based detection, is effective in detecting previously known threats [8]. However, it is not always effective against new and unknown threats [9]. In response to these limitations, a new approach to virus detection called behavior-based detection has emerged. Based on their behavior, this strategy employs artificial intelligence (AI) and deep learning (DL) algorithms to discover and categorize new and unknown risks [10].

Behavior-based detection relies on monitoring the actions of a piece of software, looking for signs of malicious behavior [8]. If a piece of software is behaving in a way that is deemed suspicious, it can be classified as a potential threat and further analyzed. This approach is more proactive and effective against new and unknown threats than traditional signature-based detection [11]. In recent years, AI and machine learning (ML) algorithms have become more sophisticated, making it possible to automatically detect malware in real-time and without human intervention [12].

1.2 Malicious Code Classification System

A static analysis approach is proposed to automate the discovery and categorization of the type of file without executing it, using a MC classification model. The classification system takes all files, including MC, normal files, and source files, as input data. During the pre-processing step, the portable executable (PE) information extraction module and the picture production module are used to produce input data that is used in the classification stage. In the subsequent classification step, a variety of algorithms, including convolutional neural network (CNN), random forest, gradient boosting, and decision tree algorithms, are used to decide if the input is malicious. The final classification of MC is achieved by integrating the results from each model. The classification outcomes are stored in a database that includes information about the data along with a single value indicating whether or not the data is harmful. The system uses a learning model that has been developed using different algorithms as a preparation step. The input file is processed and converted into input data for the model by extracting hash values, PE data, and performing image conversion.

Hash Extraction: The input data is first transformed into an eigenvalue from its hash value to determine if the input data is duplicated. In the database update step, the classification outcome of newly entered data is incorporated into the database, and duplicate data is updated using the extracted hash value as a primary key.

Data extraction from PE: The header and sections of the PE structure contain the necessary data for PE files to function correctly in Windows. The capability to identify installed dynamic link libraries (DLLs) as well as the functions they perform using the import address table (IAT) inside the PE Header enables the extraction of malignancy-related data from PE structures without the need to execute MC. If the file contains a PE structure, the header and section portions may be used to extract 55 characteristics, including entropy and packers. The binary file's packing information is located using the Yet Another Reverse Engineering Framework (YARA) rule configuration, using signatures to recognize and categorize MC types. The image creation module visualizes and converts the input file for CNN by transforming the input data into a one-dimensional vector [13].

1.3 Literature Review

In the field of malware detection, two major techniques have been employed: static analysis and dynamic analysis. The application of ML methods has been proposed to improve the performance of malware detection. Schultz et al. [1] introduced a method of using ML to detect new malicious executables by using three distinct byte sequences, readable texts, and PE as static features. The method was tested on 4266 different files and achieved an accuracy of 97.11% using the Bayes algorithm for classification. Usukhbayar et al. [2] presented a framework that utilized three static features, including data from the PE Header, application programming interface (API) function calls made by DLLs, and DLLs. They chose the subset of characteristics using data mining techniques like information gain and tested three different classification methodologies: Svms, Naive Bayes (NB), and J48 where maximum accuracy was obtained by J48 at 98%. Tzu-Yen Wang et al. [3] used data contained in the PE Headers to detect malware. Their dataset consisted of 9771 different programs, including backdoors, email worms, Trojan horses, and viruses. The accuracy rates for viruses, email worms, Trojan horses, and backdoors were 97.19%, 93.96%, 84.11%, and 89.54%, respectively, demonstrating high detection rates for email worms and viruses. With the advancement of dynamic malware analysis, researchers have shifted from static feature extraction to dynamic analysis. Tian et al's use of Weka classifiers to extract dynamic characterestics (API call sequences) out of an executable file operating in a virtual environment to separate malware from trustworthy software and identify the malware family. The dataset included 1824 executables, and the accuracy was 97%. Wang et al. [5] also proposed the use of dynamic analysis for malware detection, using similarity matrices of dynamic extraction technologies on a dataset of 104 files. They achieved an accuracy of 93%. Santos et al. [14] proposed a hybrid strategy that combined the static and dynamic features of an executable file. By using a semi-supervised learning method, in which only 50% of the training data was labeled, they achieved an accuracy of 88%. PE-Miner was suggested by Shafiq et al. [13] as a technique for finding PE malware. They collected 189 characteristics first from PE file segments and used feature selection/reduction methods like principal component analysis (PCA) to choose the most pertinent features. The technique was evaluated using five supervised algorithms Ibk, J48, NB, RIPPER, and SMO on seven distinct types of dangerous executables. The identification of viruses produced the highest results (99% true positive rate and 0.5% false positive rate).

Lo, Pablo, and Carlos [8] investigated the bare minimum requirements for PE malware detection and concluded that by using an assembly classification schema, they could detect malware with 99% accuracy using nine features. However, their base feature pool was created using third-party software, VirusTotal, and the system was not evaluated against various malware detection techniques. PE files are executable files that typically run on the Windows platform and have the .exe or .dll extension. The executable code text part, the data sections (.bss, .rdata, and.data), the resource section (.rsrc), the export section (.edata), and the import section are all portions that make up a PE file (.idata), among others. The PE file format is defined by Microsoft and is documented in the PE and common object file format (COFF) specifications, which can be found in the microsoft developer network (MSDN) library. The point of entry (the starting location of the script to be

Table 1.1 Comparison of existing malware detection approaches.

Features	Kirin	STREAM	SmartDroid	AMDetector
Method used	BNF notation specifications Action strings and static permission labels are equivalent	Emulation of machine learning input using monkey	GUI-based trigger circumstances Activity call graphs and function call graphs	Analysis of an attack tree hybrid
Advantages	Decent performance and ease of implementation	Suited for extensive research. Platform for distributed experimentation	While dynamic analysis looks at sensitive behaviors, static analysis pinpoints activity switch connections. There is a substantial amount of coding for the detection	Rules are arranged through the use of an attack tree to get precise and programmable outcomes. While dynamic analysis verifies the smaller rule set, static analysis looks for possible assaults. triggers depending on components
Drawbacks	Nine rules are not enough. The real behavior of an application cannot be adequately modeled by static authorization features	User interaction is not faithfully simulated by the Monkey tool. The classifiers produce a lot of false positive results	Other than activity, there is no trigger for components such as service and broadcast	Manually developed rules A detailed dynamic analysis takes a long time
Detection result	Ten of the 311 apps did not pass the rules. Five of them are considered dangerous, the other five are seen to be reasonable	Bayes net Logistic TPR: 81.25% 68.75% FPR: 31.03% 15.86%	A UI-based trigger situation that triggers a behavior may be seen on SmartDroid. It is unable to expose trigger circumstances that are logic-based or indirect, though	TPR: 88.14% FPR: 1.80% Accuracy: 96.57%

run), the number of sections, the size of the additional header, and other crucial details about the file are all contained in the PE file header. Information about each portion of the file is provided in the section table, including the name, virtual size, virtual address, and raw data size. The text section contains the executable code of the file, which is machine code that the computer can execute directly. The data sections contain initialized and uninitialized data used by the program. The resource section contains information about the resources used by the program, such as icons, bitmaps, and dialog boxes. The export section contains information about the functions and variables that are exported from the file, allowing other files to call them. Information on the variables and functions loaded from other files is provided in the import section, which is needed by the program. Overall, the PE file format provides a way for Windows to efficiently load and execute programs, making it an important component of the Windows operating system.

Table 1.1 compares four existing malware detection approaches, namely Kirin, STREAM, SmartDroid, and AMDetector. It includes information on the methods used, advantages, drawbacks, and detection results of each approach. The data shows varying levels of performance and limitations in the different approaches.

1.4 Malware Behavior Analysis

The categorization of malicious executable files can be based on a wide range of factors, including execution time, network activity, registry access frequency, number of accessed files, and more. However, the most promising approach is to categorize executable files based on an examination of their behavior. Such a classification will allow for the identification of classes linked to the fundamental concepts driving the functionality and intent of malicious software. To differentiate between these classes, clustering algorithms should feed data that accurately describes the behavior of executable files. It is recommended that this information be obtained by sequencing the calls to WinAPI functions. To analyze the behavior of each file, executables are run in a virtual environment, and the API call logs of each file are saved. These features are then combined after static and dynamic features have been extracted. ML classifiers use the integrated feature set as input to identify files as malicious or benign. The header and sections of the PE structure contain the data necessary for PE files to operate on Windows. The DLL that was loaded and the function being utilized may both be identified using the IAT within PE Header. Thus, information about malignancy may be obtained from PE components without the need to execute the MC [5]. If the information has a PE structure, the header and section parts of a file have been utilized to extract a total of 55 features, including entropy and packers. By using YARA rule setting, the file's packing information can now be found within the binary file. The YARA rule comprises tools that categorize different kinds of malicious programs depending on their signatures and can identify them. The maliciousness of code can be categorized using conventional techniques if the patterns are compared and found to be malicious.

There have been various techniques proposed and implemented to prevent malicious program executions at the client side and on cloud hosts. In this section, we will review some of the most notable techniques and their limitations. Forest et al. [6] introduced a process-level anomaly detection method for buffer overflow and symbolic link attacks. The authors differentiated typical and unusual features using brief System Call sequences produced by an active privileged process. Researchers examined the execution of procedure System Call sequences and identified typical behavior. Lee et al. [15] distinguished between typical and abnormal patterns in UNIX processes. Using a ML approach, they discovered abuses and intrusions in UNIX processes and demonstrated RIPPER, a rule-based training technique, was used by them to analyze information obtained from UNIX sendmail software.

A technique for identifying intrusions based on invasive System Calls was put out by Warrender et al. [16] They captured the kernel's System Call patterns and gained knowledge of over four distinct techniques for locating intrusions based on the System Call sequences, identifying privileged processes, and studying their normal behavior. An artificial neural system was utilized by Ghosh et al. [17] to learn the normal System Call pattern of UNIX program execution. They used the Defense Advanced Research Projects Agency (DARP) dataset to establish profiles for over 150 different programs and trained a neural network for each program to recognize unusual behavior. Liao et al. [18] developed a novel method for identifying typical program behavior by using the frequencies of System Calls and classifying it as ordinary or intrusive behavior using a K-nearest neighbor (KNN) classifier. Qing et al. [10] based their method on rough set theory. They took the System Call sequences produced during a process's regular executions and extracted rules with the smallest possible size to build a model of the process's typical behavior. Then, based on the normal behavioral model of the constructed process, they employed a crude set concept algorithm to detect intrusions. Sun et al. [18] recommended Collabra, which provides a filtration layer within the cloud to protect the cloud and the hosts from illegal access. A technique for automated intrusion assessment in the cloud was put out by Arshad et al. [11]. They categorized all attacks based on three security attributes: availability, confidentiality, and integrity. They used supervised and unsupervised learning techniques to create training datasets and mapped System Calls to these three attributes based on the type of attack. However, a demonstration of the approach is missing.

Using frequent System Call sequences, Hai et al. [12] presented an automated method for cloud-based intrusion detection. They used a Hidden Markov model

(HMM) to detect potential threats and an automated mining algorithm to extract frequently occurring System Call sequences. This approach, however, demands continual learning and detection resources, and the rule extraction process is computationally challenging. Sebastian et al. [19] proposed a method of introspection for detecting kernel rootkits. Based on alterations to the system state, they were able to locate rootkits. The system state was examined using a bottom-up methodology, starting from a binary representation down to the kernel object level. The authors were successful in identifying kernel rootkits using their method. However, the analysis and reporting are complex, and the method is not architecturally independent because it is based on the kernel level. Intrusion detection in cloud environments is a crucial aspect of ensuring the security of cloud-based systems. The traditional approach to intrusion detection involves the use of System Calls and process states to gauge the similarity of the system to itself. However, this approach has several limitations and can be ineffective in detecting slow-moving threats. In this context, measures for self-similarity are used to identify abnormalities in Kwon et al.'s [20] proposed self-similarity-based strategy for intrusion detection within the cloud.

The self-similarity measure is computed using cosine similarity, making it a system-wide strategy. However, this approach is not always accurate enough to identify attacks that occur gradually. Kong et al. [21] proposed an alternative approach, Ad-joint, which uses an Ad-joint to monitor the kernel state of the protected system. This approach provides two layers of security but also increases the demand for additional resources. Despite the efforts made to date, several research gaps still exist in the field of intrusion detection in the cloud. For instance, previous techniques have not been effectively applied to newer systems such as the cloud, which requires a distributed architecture with synchronization, log collection, alerts, and response mechanisms. Additionally, the cost–benefit analysis of using the self-similarity-based approach in cloud infrastructure does not support the solution's effectiveness in identifying anomalous programs.

When it comes to identifying malicious System Calls inside the host operating system, the conventional system call pattern method is difficult and inefficient. It permits the identification of suspect system call patterns without having to look at particular applications or processes. Its efficacy is however constrained by the fact that system call patterns that were recognized as unusual once the training could occasionally occur as part of a typical execution scenario.

By saving processing and data gathering resources, methods that use the rate in System Calls for unexpected behavior detection can achieve respectable efficiency. These techniques might not always catch assaults nevertheless, especially if the attacker uses the same frequency in system call sequences but in a different order to trick the detection system. Additionally, the research on such systems [22] indicated that virtual machine monitor (VMM) layer detection is hypervisor-dependent, rendering distributed solutions susceptible to client-side IDS instance failure [14]. Additionally, system-wide intrusion detection systems are less effective than program-wide intrusion detection systems and cannot detect slow-moving threats, where the probability of unusual system call sequence behavior indicating an intrusion is low. Despite the advances in intrusion detection in the cloud, there is still a need for effective and efficient solutions that can address the limitations of the existing approaches. Further research is necessary to address the research gaps and improve the efficacy of intrusion detection in cloud environments.

1.5 Conventional Detection Systems

Malware scanners [23] are tools that attempt to identify malicious executable files by comparing them to a known set of patterns. They typically search through each line of code in the file, looking for a unique signature represented as a hash code or string. Extracting these signatures is a challenging and time-consuming process, and modern malware can evade scanners by changing their patterns dynamically. To overcome this, scanners are developing more sophisticated algorithms that use ML, such as analyzing machine instructions or API calls [7, 22]. For instance, systems that use machine instructions train classifiers using features derived from op-codes. These systems may use op-code sequences to extract features such as frequency, histogram, and others. By examining op-codes, they typically label any potentially malicious behavior in a cloud application as benign. This may not accurately reflect reality, as the behavior could be legitimate malicious access to databases, root filesystems, or networks in a certain situation. To confirm whether the file is safe, the suspect file is temporarily monitored and isolated in a simulated environment, and marked as safe if its behavior appears reasonable based on established metrics.

Intrusion detection systems are used to prevent external attacks on an organization's computer networks. They categorize malicious communications by monitoring incoming packets for irregularities at the entrance to a local area network [24]. However, these systems often presume that the trusted perimeter is secure and may not detect malicious activity from insiders [23]. They operate similarly to malware scanners by detecting known rules or patterns, with sophisticated systems using ML to detect more advanced network attacks. They rely on inspecting packet headers and, in some cases, packet contents.

From a ML perspective, signature-based mechanisms classify malicious feature vectors by comparing the current feature vector with a labeled set that has already been recorded [25]. As a result, they are ineffective against 0-day attacks. Also, behavior-based mechanisms can be adapted, as they estimate the most recent feature vectors and learn from a provided dataset. There have been many studies in the literature that use ML methods in malicious behavior recognition systems, with most of them focusing on network communications intrusion detection systems [22, 26]. Feature vectors are extracted from various sources, for instance, user command patterns, log entries, information about lower-layer systems, and CPU and memory use [24]. ML-based detection systems often employ attributes such as API calls and machine commands [10]. These systems classify malware into categories such as viruses, worms, backdoors, and Trojan horses.

In the domain of malware analysis, techniques are divided into two types: signature-based and behavior-based [27]. Signature-based techniques search for unique patterns in malicious files, such as distinct raw byte patterns or regular expressions. In contrast, during code execution, behavior-based techniques get particular feature values through runtime actions and logs.

1.6 Classifying Executables by Payload Function

In this research, the focus is on the classification of malicious executables based on their payload functions, rather than on their detection. The goal is to determine if classification techniques can determine the type of malicious executable, such as whether it opens a backdoor, is sent in bulk, or is an executable virus. This aspect of the research is particularly beneficial for computer forensics experts. The first step in the process is the identification and cataloging of the characteristics of malicious executable payloads. A challenge encountered in this process is that many executables fit into multiple categories, making them multi-class examples, which is a common problem in document classification and bioinformatics. For instance, an executable may both log keystrokes and open a backdoor, making it fall into both the keylogger and backdoor categories.

One solution to this issue is to combine compound classes with simple classes, such as backdoor + keylogger. This can be achieved by using one-versus-all classification, where all executables are categorized into groups based on their capabilities. For example, all backdoor-capable executables regardless of any additional features, including keylogging, would be put inside the backdoor class, whereas every other executable would be put inside a non-backdoor class.

The following stage is to develop a detector for something like the backdoor category, and thereafter carry out the same procedure for the other classes. The total prediction of the program may be determined by applying every detector and reporting every classifier's prediction. For instance, if the backdoor or keylogger detectors both identify hits, the executable's overall forecast would've been backdoor + keylogger.

1.7 Result and Discussion

It has been observed that the detection methods used may have simply developed the ability to recognize some obfuscation techniques, such as runtime compression, but as long as these techniques are linked to malicious executables, this does not provide a serious problem. Alternative data extraction techniques were also investigated. One concept was to create an audit of machine instructions and execute the malicious exe files in a "sandbox." However, this strategy was abandoned owing to a number of drawbacks, including a lack of auditing tools, challenges managing a large number of interactive programs, and an inability to identify malicious activity at the conclusion of lengthy programs. Additionally, some dangerous programs have the ability to recognize when they are running inside a virtual machine (VM) and then either stop running or avoid running destructive code.

Our research has practical implications in two areas of commercial applications. The first is the development of a system for detecting malicious executables, similar to the MECS system. This system would require storage of a large set of both known malicious executables and benign executables in server software. The computation-intensive task of creating classifiers from such algorithms for measuring information gain and assessing categorization techniques would need to be used, and the data would need to be processed sequentially, in parallel, or both. To create a prediction, the client program would just need to collect the top n-grams out of an executable and utilize the classifier. Through the internet, the classifier might be remotely updated. It is vital for the server to test several techniques as well as for the client to handle any viable classifiers since the best-performing technique may change with new training data. These methods, when combined with signature-based methods, could provide a more effective way of detecting malicious executables than what is currently possible.

The second system is focused on serving computer forensic experts. Although it is uncertain if the statistical properties of an executable are predictive of its function, there is evidence that high detection rates can be achieved when predicting its function.

In today's digital world, where files and information are exchanged over networks and the internet, network malware detection is of utmost importance. Using the network analysis program BroIDS [16], PE files may be extracted from incoming packets that are routed through the router and into the internal network. Then, the pertinent characteristics are extracted using the feature extraction module. Following the extraction of the features and representation of the file, the file may be passed toward the malware analysis engine, which already has the training learning algorithm stored in memory. If malware is found, a warning will be created and forwarded to the operator.

Table 1.2 Displaying malware families with the specific malware.

Malware family	Spyware	Adware	Cookies	Trapdoor	Trojan Horse	Sniffers	Spam	Botnet	Logic bomb	Worm	Virus
Pattern	✓	✓	✓	✓	✓	✓	✓	✓	✓	✓	✓
Obfuscated	✓	✓	✓	✓	✓	✓	✓	✓	✓	✓	✓
Polymorphic	✓	✓	✓	✓	✓	✓	✓	✓	✓	✓	✓
Toolkit	✓	✓	✓	✓	✓	✓	✓	✓	✓	✓	✓
Network	✓	✓	✓	✓	✗	✓	✓	✓	✓	✗	✗
Remote execution through we	✓	✓	✓	✓	✓	✓	✓	✓	✗	✗	✗
PC	✗	✗	✗	✗	✗	✗	✗	✗	✓	✓	✓
Network	✓	✓	✓	✓	✓	✓	✓	✓	✓	✓	✓
Removable disks	✓	✓	✓	✓	✓	✓	✓	✓	✓	✓	✓
Internet downloads	✓	✓	✓	✓	✓	✓	✓	✓	✓	✓	✓
Breaching confidentiality	✓	✗	✓	✗	✓	✓	✗	✗	✗	✗	✗
Inconveniencing users	✗	✓	✗	✗	✗	✗	✓	✗	✗	✗	✗
Denying services	✗	✗	✗	✓	✗	✗	✓	✓	✓	✓	✓
Data corruption	✗	✗	✗	✓	✗	✗	✓	✓	✓	✗	✓

MC detection techniques may be broadly categorized into two groups: abuse detection and anomaly detection. Misuse detection strategies concentrate on "maliciousness" and seek to recognize the traits and/or runtime behaviors of MC. Anomaly detection strategies, on the other hand, focus on "normalcy" and attempt to spot code traits and/or runtime behaviors that depart from what is thought to be normal, i.e., non-malicious.

Table 1.2 displays a list of malware families and their specific types. This table provides an overview of different types of malware and the families they belong to. It helps to categorize and understand the different types of malware that exist and the potential threats they pose.

1.8 Conclusion

The rising threat of MC has led to an increasing demand for efficient and effective ways to detect and respond to it. In this research, we introduced a system that examines code statically and automatically to assess its maliciousness. This system, called the malicious executable classification system (MECS), extracts various features of code using ML methods, the packer information, the PE metadata, and the hash value to classify it. MECS is different from traditional signature-based classification tools in that it relies on considerations instead of patterns to identify MC. The system also visualizes the code using a visualization method and inputs it into a CNN model, which allows for the classification of both PE and shell-like files.

MECS can find undiscovered harmful executables in the wild by employing retrieval of information and text classification algorithms. After detection, computer forensics experts can further analyze the program's functional characteristics, such as its ability to send mass emails, modify system files, or grant access. This may involve removing obfuscation, such as compression. However, this task can be challenging due to the fact that most malicious executables perform multiple functions, requiring multiple class labels for each training example. Despite its potential, MECS is only one stage of a more comprehensive system for identifying and categorizing malware. Integrating it with other techniques that search for well-known signs can further enhance the security of computers. However, some existing anomaly detection techniques may have limitations, as they only take into account the behavior that was seen when the program is still learning, which is probably only a small part of all of its behaviors. This can lead to false positives and missed detections. Additionally, some antivirus techniques can be bypassed by malicious actors who change the PE Header attributes or add inconsequential strings to the printable strings feature.

In conclusion, the development and implementation of the MECS system offer a promising solution to the challenge of detecting and responding to MC. By automating the analysis process and incorporating various ML techniques, MECS can enhance the efficiency and accuracy of malware detection and classification. It provides a useful tool for computer forensics professionals in their ongoing efforts to protect computer systems from malicious actors. However, it is just one piece of the puzzle. While the MECS system can detect malicious executables, it still requires computer forensic experts to determine the program's functional characteristics and remove any obfuscation such as compression. Additionally, MECS only considers a small portion of all the software's possible behaviors, meaning that false positives can still occur. Moreover, the traditional antivirus techniques have limitations as well. For example, some malware writers can avoid detection by changing the PE Header attributes or adding inconsequential strings. Thus, a more comprehensive approach to detecting and classifying malware is needed, one that combines the strengths of various methods and takes into account the evolving nature of MC. To that end, a strategic approach that employs a combination of methods, such as signature-based detection, runtime monitoring, and behavior-based analysis, would likely be more effective in detecting and classifying malicious executables. By combining these methods, computer forensic professionals can have a better understanding of the program's behavior and can determine the true nature of the code, even if it is obfuscated.

In conclusion, while the MECS system is a valuable tool for computer forensic professionals, it should be seen as just one component of a larger, comprehensive approach to detecting and classifying MC. By combining the strengths of various methods, computer forensic professionals can better protect computer systems and stay ahead of the ever-evolving threat of malicious actors.

References

1 Schultz, M., Eskin, E., Zadok, F., and Stolfo, S. (2001). Data mining methods for detection of new malicious executables. In: *Proceedings of the 2001 IEEE Symposium on Security and Privacy, Oakland, CA, USA*, 38–49.

2 Baldangombo, U., Jambaljav, N., and Horng, S.-J. (2013). A static malware detection system using data mining methods. *International Journal of Artificial Intelligence and Applications* 4 (4): 113–126.

3 Wang, T.-Y., Wu, C.-H., and Hsieh, C.-C. (2009). Detecting unknown malicious executables using portable executable headers. In: *Proceedings of the 5th International Conference on Network and Communication Security*, 278–284.

4 Tian, R., Islam, R., Batten, L., and Versteeg, S. (2010). Differentiating malware from clean ware using behavioral analysis. In: *Proceedings of the 5th International Conference on Malicious and Unwanted Software: MALWARE 2010*, 23–30.

5 Wang, C., Pang, J., Zhao, R., and Liu, X. (2009). Using API sequence and Bayes algorithm to detect suspicious behavior. In: *Proceedings of the International Conference on Communication Software and Networks*, 544–548.

6 Steven, A.H., Stephanie, F., and Anil, S. (1998). Intrusion detection using sequences of system calls. *Journal of Computer Security* 6 (3): 151–180.

7 Lo, T.D., Ordonez, P., and Cepeda, C. (2016). Feature selection and improving classification performance for malware detection. In: *Proceedings of the IEEE International Conferences on Big Data and Cloud Computing, Social Computing and Networking, Sustainable Computing and Communications*, 560–566.

8 Lo, C.T.D., Pablo, O., and Carlos, C. (2016). Feature selection and improving classification performance for malware detection. In: *IEEE International Conferences on Big Data and Cloud Computing (BDCloud), Social Computing and Networking (SocialCom), Sustainable Computing and Communications (SustainCom)*, 560–566.

9 Win32 API Programming with Visual Basic by Roman, Steven–ISBN 10: 1565926315–ISBN 13: 9781565926318–O'Reilly Media–1999–Softcover.

10 Ye, Q., Wu, X., and Yan, B. (2010). An intrusion detection approach based on system call sequences and rules extraction. In: *e-business and information system security (EBISS), 2010 2nd international conference on. Wuhan, China: IEEE*.

11 Arshad, J., Townend, P., and Xu, J. (2011). A novel intrusion severity analysis approach for clouds. *Future Generation Computer Systems*. The International Journal of Grid Computing and eScience 28 (7): 965–1154.

12 Jin, H. et al. (2013). A VMM-based intrusion prevention system in cloud computing environment. *The Journal of Supercomputing* 66 (3): 1133–1151.

13 Shafiq, M.Z., Tabish, S.M., Mirza, F., and Farooq, M. (2009). PE-Miner: mining structural information to detect malicious executables in real-time. *Recent Advances in Intrusion Detection* 121–141.

14 Santos, I., Nieves, J., and Bringas, P.G. (2011). Semi-supervised learning for unknown malware detection. In: *International Symposium on DCAI. AISC*, vol. 91 (ed. A. Abraham, J.M. Corchado, S.R. González, and J.F. De Paz Santana), 415–422. Heidelberg: Springer.

15 Lee, W., Stolfo, J.S., and Chan, P.K. (1997). Learning patterns from unix process execution traces for intrusion detection. In: *Proceedings of AAAI97 workshop on AI methods in fraud and risk management*.

16 Warrender, C., Forrest, S., and Pearlmutter, B. (1999). Detecting intrusions using system calls: alternative data models. In: *IEEE Symposium on Security and Privacy*. IEEE.

17 Ghosh, A.K., Schwartzbard, A., and Schatz, M. (1999). Learning program behaviour profiles for intrusion detection. In: *Proceedings of 1st USENIX Workshop on Intrusion Detection.*

18 Bharadwaja, S. et al. (2011). Collabra: a xen hypervisor based collaborative intrusion detection system. In: *Information technology: New generations (ITNG), 2011 eighth international conference on.* Las Vegas, NV: IEEE.

19 Vogl, S. (2010). A bottom-up approach to VMI-based Kernel-level Rootkit detection. Ph.D. thesis in Computer Science, Technische Unversität München.

20 Kwon, H. et al. (2011). Self-similarity based lightweight intrusion detection method for cloud computing intelligent information and database systems. In: *Third international conference, ACIIDS 2011, Daegu, Korea, April 20–22, 2011, Proceedings, Part II* (ed. N.N. Thanh, K. ChongGun, and J. Adam), 353–362. Berlin, Heidelberg: Springer.

21 Jinzhu, K. (2011). AdjointVM: a new intrusion detection model for cloud computing. *Energy Procedia* 13 (1): 7902–7911.

22 Shafiq, M.Z., Tabish, S.M., Mirza, F., and Farooq, M. (2009). PE-Miner: mining structural information to detect malicious executables in realtime. In: *Recent Advances in Intrusion Detection, vol. 5758 of the Series Lecture Notes in Computer Science*, 121–141.

23 Wang, C., Pang, J., Zhao, R., and Liu, X. (2009). Using API sequence and Bayes algorithm to detect suspicious behaviour. In: *International Conference on Communication Software and Networks*, 544–548.

24 Shalaginov, A., Grini, L.S., and Franke, K. (2016). Understanding neuro-fuzzy on a class of multinomial malware detection problems. In: *IEEE International Joint Conference on Neural Networks (IJCNN)*, 684–691.

25 Tian, R., Islam, R., Batten, L., and Versteeg, S. (2010). Differentiating malware from clean ware using behavioural analysis. In: *Proceedings of the 5th International Conference on Malicious and Unwanted Software: MALWARE, 2010*, 23–30.

26 Wang, T.-Y., Wu, C.-H., and Hsieh, C.-C. (2009). Detecting unknown malicious executables using portable executable headers. In: *NCM, Fifth International Joint Conference on INC, IMS and IDC*, 278–284.

27 Pektas, A. and Acarman, T. (2017). Classification of malware families based on runtime behaviours. *Journal of Information Security and Applications* 37: 91–100.

2

Detection and Analysis of Botnet Attacks Using Machine Learning Techniques

Supriya Raheja

Amity University, Noida, India

2.1 Introduction

Internet access is now considered to be a basic requirement for everyone. The age of cloud computing, which allows users to access and store data over the cloud, is currently upon us. A public, private, and hybrid shared lake of computing resources, such as storage, services, servers, networks, and applications, is what cloud computing represents. It enables convenient, on-demand network access from anywhere. These services can be delivered swiftly and with the least amount of managerial work. The threat of various attacks carried out by harmful software is there nowadays for devices that are linked to the internet. Access to the cloud servers is possible. The more cloud computing is used, the more cyberattacks there will be thanks to the internet.

One of the most significant threats to online security is the botnet. The phrase "botnet," which combines the terms "Bot" and "Network," refers to a collection of hacked, infected, internet-connected devices that are under the direction of a person known as the "Botmaster" or "Botterder." Through a command-and-control server, the botmaster can remotely manipulate these infected devices. Because botnets enable a one-to-many interaction between the command-and-control server and the bots, the botmaster uses them for things like advertising and cyberattacks. As soon as a device is infected with malicious code, it joins a botnet and begins to work for the botmaster without the user's knowledge. Botnet spreads itself periodically by infecting an increasing number of computers, laptops, servers, and mobile devices.

Most internet users today are victims of the numerous cyberattacks that are carried out using botnets. Cybercrimes such as DDoS, click fraud, phishing fraud, key

Applying Artificial Intelligence in Cybersecurity Analytics and Cyber Threat Detection, First Edition.
Edited by Shilpa Mahajan, Mehak Khurana, and Vania Vieira Estrela.

logging, bitcoin fraud, spamming, sniffing traffic, propagating new viruses, and abusing Google AdSense can all be carried out by botmasters. Today, the botnet is being used as the foundation for all online cybercrimes. Drive-by downloads, emails, and pirated software are the most popular ways for a botmaster to infect a user device and turn it into a zombie. Numerous detection methods have been suggested based on prior research.

However, most of them are concentrated on offline botnet detection; we still need to concentrate on the real-time detection. The two primary categories of the currently used botnet detection methods are intrusion detection systems (IDSs) and Honeynets Based Detection Techniques. To identify botnet attacks and shield cloud servers from them, researchers concentrate on cybersecurity and machine learning (ML). ML algorithms are now involved in more and more aspects of everyday life, from what one can read and watch, to how one can shop, to who one can meet, and how one can travel [1–5]. This study presents the performance comparison of different ML algorithms for the detection of Internet of Things (IoT) botnet attacks.

The rest of the work is structured as mentioned. Section 2.2 presents the existing work for detection of Botnet attacks. Section 2.3 discusses about the botnet architecture, botnet life cycle, and different botnet detection techniques. Section 2.4 describes the methodology adopted to perform this work. Section 2.5 discusses the experimental setup followed by results and discussion in Section 2.6. Section 2.7 finally concludes the work.

2.2 Literature Review

Recently, many studies have shown that ML and deep learning are effective in detecting botnet attacks. Some studies also look for the essential attributes of a botnet that may assist to differentiate between normal traffic and an attack. Feizollah et al. [6] evaluated the five classifiers K-nearest neighbor (KNN), multi-layer perceptron (MLP), decision tree (DT), support vector machine (SVM), and Naïve Bayes (NB) for identifying the Android-based malware on the IoT network. They used the three important features among various network-based features. Authors claimed that the KNN classifiers perform better among all five classifiers. Stevanovic and Pedersen [7] investigated how botnet recognition can be accomplished with high exactness by utilizing directed artificial intelligence (AI). They, first and foremost, proposed a botnet identification framework that utilizes stream-based traffic investigation and directed AI as a device for distinguishing botnets. They then, at that point, continue to test exhibitions of eight of the main AI calculations (machine learning algorithms – MLAs) for grouping botnets traffic.

One of the studies examined the utilization and viability of AI in recognizing botnets. Authors examined the security features used in the existing solutions available in the literature and the associated problems with the existing solutions. They analyzed the existing security features with the help of different ML algorithms [8]. In another study, authors utilized these methods for drawing and creating information through an IoT organization. They applied new information to investigate various qualities of an attack, for example, network addresses, physical layer addresses, package size, and so on [9].

Khraisat et al. [10] introduced a hybrid-based system for identifying the IoT attacks. Authors compared the proposed technique with the other existing techniques, and they claimed that the proposed technique gives higher accuracy among all, and it also helped to reduce the false alarm rates.

In contemporary work, authors introduced a new labeled dataset over the IoT botnet network traffic. They utilized up to 83 IoT devices and deployed real malware for generating this labeled dataset. Authors validated the dataset by applying both supervised and unsupervised ML algorithms [11]. They claimed that the dataset is effective and now available as a MedBIoT dataset. In another study, authors used the SVM-based model for detecting the IoT-based botnets. Authors applied the Grey Wolf Optimization (GWO) for optimizing the hyperparameters. Authors claimed the proposed model took less detection time as compared to the existing models [12].

Hariri et al. [13] described a new thread for IoT-based home security systems. Authors discussed few prevention and detection techniques for preventing IoT attacks. Tuan et al. [14] applied the numerous ML techniques for identifying the distributed denial-of-service (DDoS) IoT botnet attacks. They have considered two datasets for their experimental work. Authors claimed that among two datasets KDD99 has shown better performance with all the applied algorithms. Hoang and Vu [15] proposed an assessment on botnet recognition model utilizing AI calculations in contrast with peculiarity-based botnet location strategies. Authors applied different classifiers namely KNN, RF, and NB to make classification among genuine and botnet-created domain names. Authors used the domain-based features to further improve the alarm rates.

2.3 Botnet Architecture

According to their architectural styles, the individual bots that make up a botnet can be divided into three groups [16]. This study discusses a few techniques for categorizing botnet architectures, along with their benefits and drawbacks.

- Centralized architecture: The simplest for the botmaster to control and administer. One central location known as the command-and-control server is where the botmaster controls and manages all the bots in a botnet under centralized architecture (C&C server). In this architecture, all the bots receive commands from a single location known as the C&C server and report to it as illustrated in Figure 2.1. In this botnet architecture, two topologies are employed: star topology and hierarchical topology. The essential internet relay chat (IRC) and hypertext transfer protocol (HTTP) are protocols used in centralized architecture. Because there is only one central location, botnet management and monitoring are relatively simple. Simple and quick direct communication between the botmaster and the bots. The design is simpler and has lower communication latency and survivability in the centralized architecture. The botmaster sends commands to the C&C server, from whence they are distributed to every bot in the botnet. The fundamental drawback of centralized design is that it has a higher probability of failure than other architectures. Because of the central point of control, if the C&C server fails, then all the botnets will fail. Similarly, the detection of botmaster is very easy as compared to decentralized and hybrid architectures.

- Decentralized architecture: In a botnet's decentralized or peer-to-peer architecture, no single organization oversees managing the bots. There are various C&C servers that interact with bots. Decentralized architecture makes it more difficult to detect a botnet than centralized architecture. There is no specific command and control server in a decentralized architecture; instead, all the bots function as both clients and command and control servers. Peer-to-peer architecture is more complex to create than centralized architecture, making it more difficult to identify a botnet with such architecture than one with another. Like

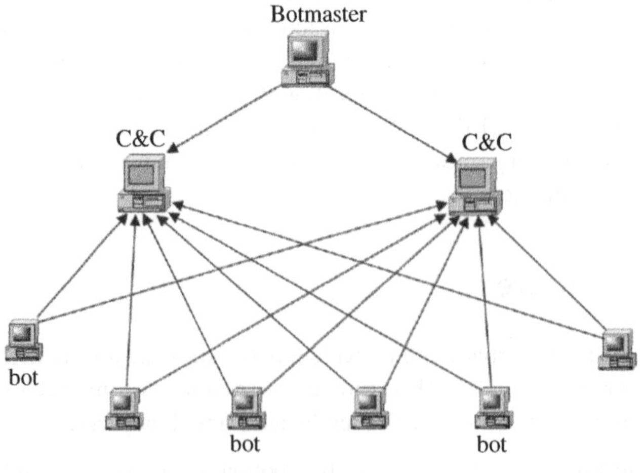

Figure 2.1 Botnet architecture.

this, decentralized botnet architecture has higher message delay and durability. Chances of failure are less in distributed architecture as compared to centralized, as in case of failure of one control server, another command and control server may work on behalf of failed one.

- Hybrid architecture is a combination of both centralized and decentralized architecture. Hybrid architecture may have two different bots: a servant bot and a client bot. Either as a client or a servant, the bots are linked to the hybrid botnet. Although the design is not very sophisticated, monitoring and detection of botnets with hybrid architectures are more difficult than those with centralized and decentralized systems.

2.3.1 Botnet Life Cycle

The botmaster should follow the correct steps, including first infection, secondary injection, connection, transmitting malicious code, maintenance and updating, while attempting to infect another victim device. A botnet first infects a new internet-connected device, after which it uses various protocols, including HTTP, FTP, and P2P, to inject malicious malware. The target device automatically establishes a connection with an already operational command and control server following the successful injection of malicious code. The victim device turns into a zombie once malicious code has been put into it. The botmaster issues orders to the bot army through the command-and-control server in step four. According to the commands that the target device receives from the command, it carries out malicious actions and control servers. The last step is to maintain and update the zombie active all the time, it sends updates to the zombie devices from time to time [17].

2.3.2 Botnet Detection Techniques

Botnet detection is the most crucial task to enhance cybersecurity against the many cyberattacks that happen on the internet today. According to prior research, there are two sorts of botnet detection approaches: intrusion detection techniques and honeynet detection techniques. Sub-categories of IDSs are further separated. Detection system based on honeynets and honeypots: Both honeynets and honeypots stand for end-user devices. The greatest approach to gather important data regarding cyberattacks is through these end-user PCs. Due to its high susceptibility to malicious attacks, this end-user PC is relatively simple for the botmaster to attack and infiltrate. The knowledge regarding botnet attacks gathered by these honeynets will allow the cybersecurity team to develop effective detection methods. According to an earlier study, the botnet periodically changes its signature for security reasons, and honeynets are crucial for comprehending these botnet characteristics. The honeywall, which is used for monitoring, gathering, altering, and managing communication over the honeypots, is crucial to the honeynet detection technique [18].

Intrusion detection system: An IDS is used to keep an eye on network traffic for nefarious activity. If a malicious attack is discovered during traffic, the computer system or the system administrator is immediately notified. IDSs are also equipped to respond to such malicious activity and prevent traffic coming from a machine that has a virus on it. There are two different kinds of IDSs: anomaly-based and signature-based.

A) ***Signature-based detection***: Malware is referred to as packet sequences or the transportation of bytes series in searching networks in signature-based botnet detection technique. The primary benefit of this detection method is how easy it is to create new signatures. if you are aware of the network performance you are looking for. This method is just too straightforward and simple to comprehend and master. To make a botnet attack more secure against PCs that have been infected with bots, the botmaster alters the signatures of each attack over time.

B) ***Anomaly-based detection***: This method mainly focuses on the performance of network. It can consider only those activities and traffic on network which are pre-set by the admin. With this method, each protocol's rule needs to be defined in advance and tested for accuracy. It recognizes events that are unrelated to the feed or the generally recognized performance model. Compared to signature-based detection techniques, anomaly-based detection is slightly more expensive in terms of computing, but it is also more secure. This method also has several drawbacks, with the biggest drawback being the difficulty in defining the rules. Different rules are set for various protocols, which is a more difficult task. Anomaly-based techniques also have some time and bot monitoring restrictions.

2.4 Methodology Adopted

2.4.1 Dataset Used

This study considered dataset of UCI's repository for experiment work (12). The dataset contains 10 attacks which are conducted by 2 botnets namely "gafgyt" and "mirai." These attacks are performed on nine IoT devices namely "Danmini Doorbell," "Ecobee Thermostat," "Ennio Doorbell," "Philips B120N10 Baby Monitor," "Provision PT 737E Security Camera," "Provision PT 838 Security Camera," "Samsung SNH 1011 N Webcam," "SimpleHome XCS7 1002 WHT Security Camera," and "SimpleHome XCS7 1003 WHT Security Camera."

The dataset contains 7062606 instances and 115 attributes. This study used selected instances during experiments for reducing the complexity. However, the created model may work with the entire data as well with more time consumption.

2.4.2 Machine Learning Algorithms Used

ML algorithms are the essential structure for implementing any ML models. These models can be used for classification as well as for regression [19, 20]. These algorithms can be classified as supervised, unsupervised, and reinforcement learning. Five different classifiers were used in this study namely logistic regression (LR), random forest (RF), KNN, DT, and NB [22–28].

- ***Logistic regression***: LR lies in the category of supervised ML algorithms and is mainly used for binary classification like whether an attack lies in the class or not, as shown in Figure 2.2. This algorithm basically predicts the possibility of an input to be classified into a specific class.
- ***Decision tree***: DT lies in the category of supervised ML algorithms. It is basically used for making classifications and performing predictions. Just like a tree, DT also starts with a root that represents a question and then represents branches with respect to answer. These internal branches can again represent another question, and the node can be further branched with respect to answer. This process may continue till the leaf node, or the end of data, as shown in Figure 2.3. This algorithm is commonly used as it can process complex datasets.
- ***Naïve Bayes***: NB also belongs to the category of supervised learning algorithms. This algorithm is used for making predictions for both binary as well as multi-classification. This algorithm works on the Bayes theorem, which runs based on conditional probabilities that are unlikely to each other. However, it represents the prospects of classification as per their joint factors.

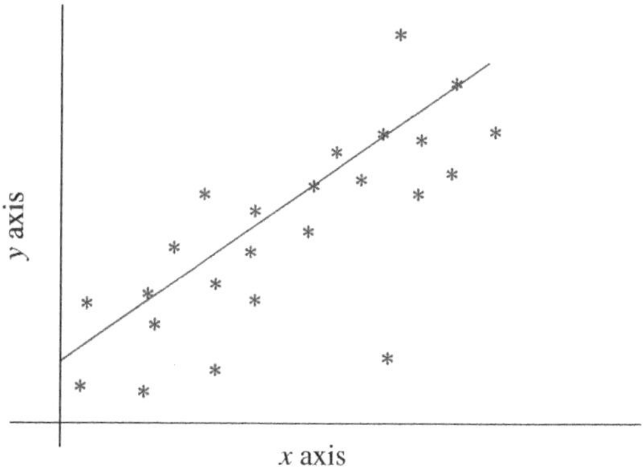

Figure 2.2 Logistic regression classification.

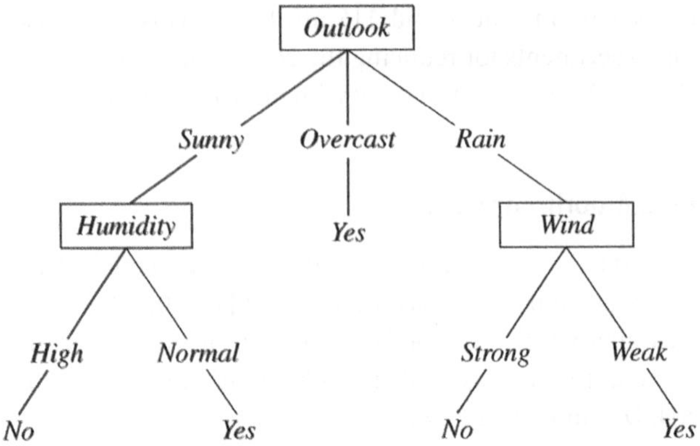

Figure 2.3 Example for decision tree classification.

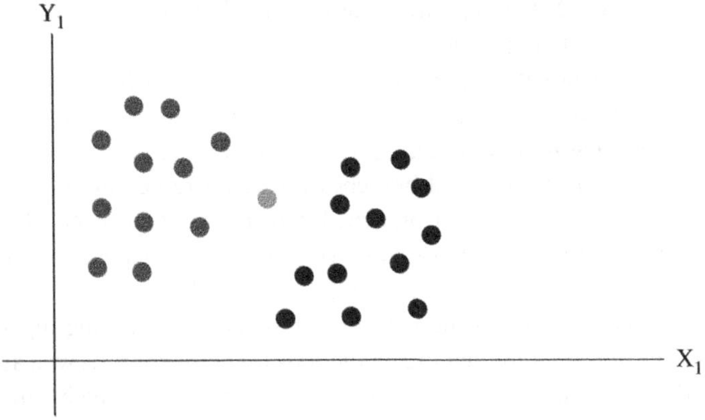

Figure 2.4 *K*-nearest neighbor algorithm.

- ***K-nearest neighbor***: KNN algorithms can solve both classification and regression problems. However, it is majorly used for classification problems by data scientists. This algorithm works on the mass vote of its *k*-neighbors, as shown in Figure 2.4. Such measurements are performed using distance function. For example, you can get the information of a person through his friends and colleagues. However, this algorithm is very expensive to implement.
- ***Random forest***: RF belongs to the category of supervised learning algorithm which is built upon DT algorithms. It is used for solving both classification and regression real-life problems. This algorithm contains a forest of DTs, as shown in Figure 2.5. The forest which is produced by it is making use of bagging or bootstrapping techniques to improve the accuracy of ML algorithms. RF algorithm improves the problem of overfitting of datasets and helps to improve the precision value [21].

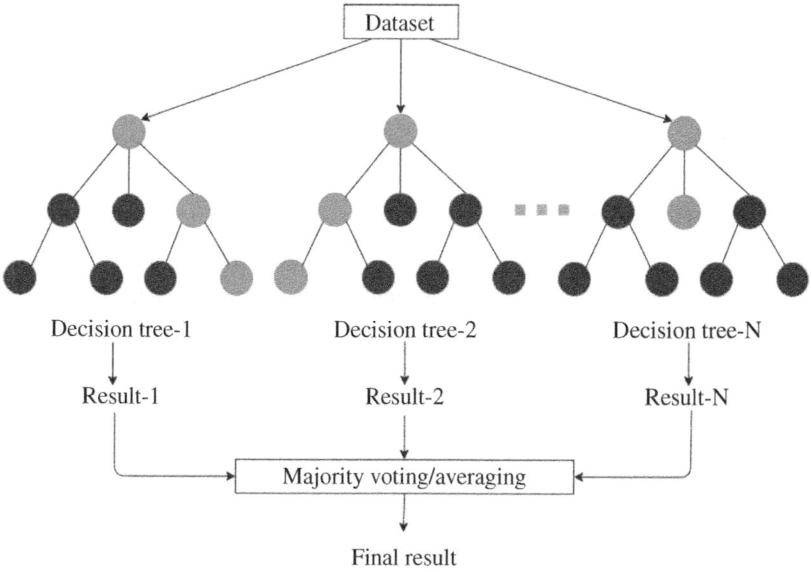

Figure 2.5 Random forest learning algorithm.

2.5 Experimental Setup

The experiments were performed on HP Laptop with Windows 10 Operating System. Jupyter notebook for python with libraries like Scikit learn, NumPy, Pandas, Matplotlib, and other python libraries were used for performing experiments. Five different classifiers, namely LR, NB, KNN, DT, and RF, were executed. The data was imbalanced, so before executing these ML classifiers, the data was prepared to be balanced using z-score standardization. Each ML algorithm was trained on using 75% of the dataset; however, to assess the effectiveness of each algorithm, 25% of the data was used for performing testing of the model. The function code for each classifier is given below:

```
def DT_model():
     dt_class = DecisionTreeClassifier()
     return dt_class.fit(x_train, np.ravel(y_train))
def KNN_model():
     knn_class = KNeighborsClassifier(n_neighbors=5)
     return knn_class.fit(x_train, np.ravel(y_train))
def LR_model():
     lr_class = LogisticRegression(solver='lbfgs',
max_iter=1000)
     return lr_class.fit(x_train, np.ravel(y_train))
def RF_model():
```

```
    rf_class = RandomForestClassifier()
    return rf_class.fit(x_train, np.ravel(y_train))
def NB_model():
    nb_class = GaussianNB()
    return nb_class.fit(X_train, np.ravel(y_train))
```

2.5.1 Evaluation Metrics

Each algorithm is evaluated based on four evaluation metrics namely Accuracy, Precision, Recall, and F1-score. All these metrics are computed using confusion matrix (Table 2.1).

The definition of each metrics is given below:

- *Accuracy*: It represents the proportion of correct predictions to the entire data. Accuracy can be computed as given in Eq. (2.1).

$$Accuracy = \frac{T_P + T_N}{T_P + F_N + F_P + T_N} \tag{2.1}$$

- *Recall*: It represents the proportion of all positive cases which are correctly categorized as positive by model to the total number of positive cases. Recall can be computed as given in Eq. (2.2).

$$Recall = \frac{T_P}{T_P + F_N} \tag{2.2}$$

- *Precision:* It represents the proportion of correctly categorized as positive to the total number of categorized positive cases.
- F1-score: This is the relationship between precision and recall. Higher value of F1-score shows the model is more accurate and robust.

Table 2.1 Confusion matrix.

		Forecasted results	
		+ve	−ve
True	+ve	T_P	F_N
	−ve	F_P	T_N

2.6 Results and Discussions

This section discusses the results in detail for one of the IoT devices (Philips B120N10 Baby Monitor). Figure 2.6 illustrates the classification matrix generated by each classifier.

From Figure 2.7, it can be observed that RF classifier performed best among all classifiers. After RF, DT gives performance at second position for IoT device

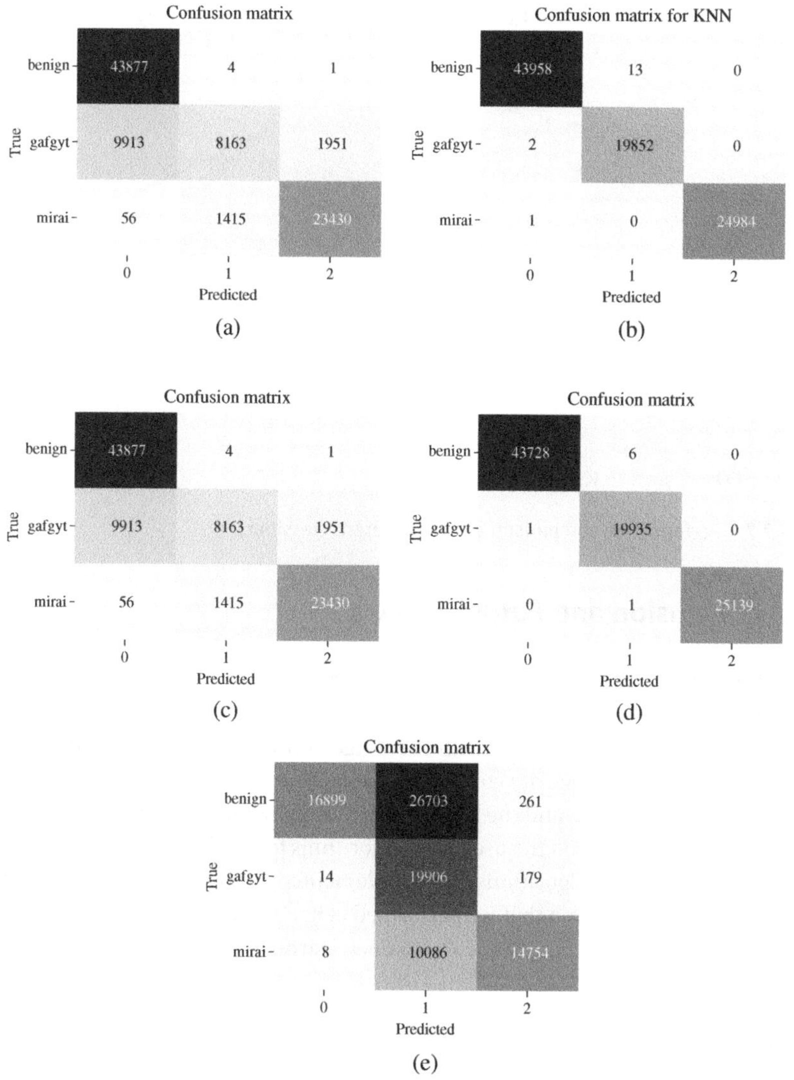

Figure 2.6 Confusion matrix (a) logistic regression, (b) KNN, (c) decision tree, (d) random forest, and (e) Naïve Bayes.

Philips B120N10 Baby Monitor followed by KNN. There is a slight difference in the performance of KNN and LR as compared to the performance of RF and DT. However, among all five classifiers, NB classifier performed least accurately. From Figure 2.7, it can also be noted that the implemented model provides a significantly high attack detection rate, around 99% in most scenarios. Moreover, in many cases, it gives 100% detection rate with RF classifier. All these classifiers except NB provide a very high precision as well as F1-score.

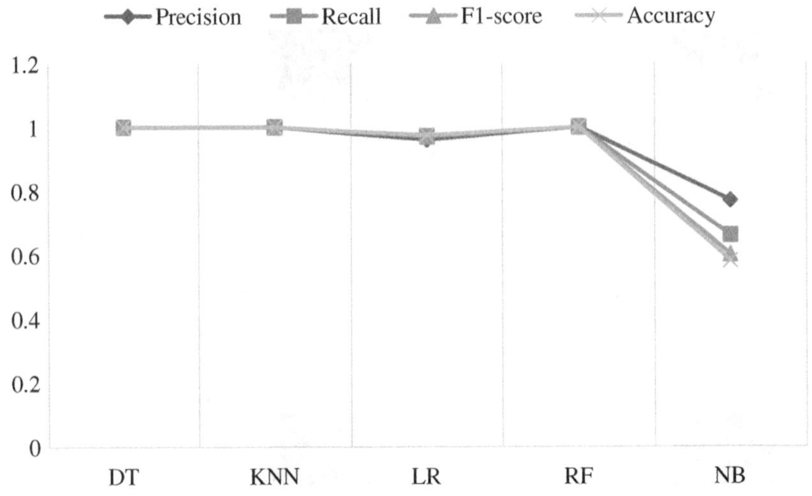

Figure 2.7 Performance comparison among different classifiers.

2.7 Conclusion and Future Work

The IoT has the capacity for universal transformation as it has made it possible to share and store the information from anywhere on the network. It makes human lives comfortable and fast with the usage of intelligent devices. However, these facilities raise the security concerns as well. This study discussed the botnet attacks, their architecture, and the literature review presented on botnet attacks in detail. This work focused on the use of ML algorithms for analysis and detection of botnet attacks. Five ML algorithms were implemented for detection of IoT botnet attacks. Results have proven that RF performed better among all five classifiers. In the future, the study will be extended with deep learning techniques.

References

1 Raheja, S. and Kasturia, S. (2022). Analysis of machine learning techniques for spam detection. In: *Applications of Machine Learning in Big-Data Analytics and Cloud Computing*, 43–62. River Publishers.

2 Gupta, S. and Raheja, S. (2022, January). Stroke prediction using machine learning methods. In: *2022 12th International Conference on Cloud Computing, Data Science & Engineering (Confluence)*, 553–558. IEEE.

3 Raheja, S. (2022). Analysis of psychological distress during COVID-19 among professionals. *International Journal of Software Innovation (IJSI)* 10 (1): 1–17.

4 Raheja, S., Garg, R., and Gururani, B. (2021). Analysis of kernel vulnerabilities using machine learning. In: *Advanced Smart Computing Technologies in Cyber-security and Forensics*, 65–84. CRC Press.

5 Raheja, S. and Datta, S. (2021). *Analysis and Prediction on COVID-19 Using Machine Learning Techniques. Enabling Healthcare 4.0 for Pandemics: A Roadmap Using AI, Machine Learning, IoT and Cognitive Technologies*, 39–57.

6 Feizollah, A., Anuar, N.B., Salleh, R. et al. (2013). A study of machine learning classifiers for anomaly-based mobile botnet detection. *Malaysian Journal of Computer Science* 26 (4): 251–265.

7 Stevanovic, M. and Pedersen, J.M. (2016). On the use of machine learning for identifying botnet network traffic. *Journal of Cyber Security and Mobility* 4 (2 & 3).

8 Dong, X., Hu, J., and Cui, Y. (2018). Overview of botnet detection based on machine learning. In: *2018 3rd International Conference on Mechanical, Control and Computer Engineering (ICMCCE)*, 476–479. IEEE.

9 Vishwakarma, R. and Jain, A.K. (2020). A survey of DDoS attacking techniques and defence mechanisms in the IoT network. *Telecommunication Systems* 73 (1): 3–25.

10 Khraisat, A., Gondal, I., Vamplew, P. et al. (2019). A novel ensemble of hybrid intrusion detection system for detecting Internet of Things attacks. *Electronics* 8 (11): 1210.

11 Guerra-Manzanares, A., Medina-Galindo, J., Bahsi, H., and Nõmm, S. (2020). Using MedBIoT dataset to build effective machine learning-based IoT botnet detection systems. In: *International Conference on Information Systems Security and Privacy*, 222–243. Cham: Springer.

12 Al Shorman, A., Faris, H., and Aljarah, I. (2020). Unsupervised intelligent system based on one class support vector machine and Grey Wolf optimization for IoT botnet detection. *Journal of Ambient Intelligence and Humanized Computing* 11 (7): 2809–2825.

13 Hariri, A., Giannelos, N., and Arief, B. (2020). Selective forwarding attack on iot home security kits. In: *International Workshop on the Security of Industrial Control Systems and Cyber-Physical Systems, International Workshop on Security and Privacy Requirements Engineering, International Workshop on Security, Privacy, Organizations, and Systems Engineering, International Workshop on Attacks and Defenses for Internet-of-Things*, 360–373. Cham: Springer.

14 Tuan, T.A., Long, H.V., Son, L.H. et al. (2020). Performance evaluation of Botnet DDoS attack detection using machine learning. *Evolutionary Intelligence* 13 (2): 283–294.

15 Hoang, X.D. and Vu, X.H. (2022). An improved model for detecting DGA botnets using random forest algorithm. *Information Security Journal: A Global Perspective* 31 (4): 441–450.

16 Ullah, I., Khan, N., and Aboalsamh, H.A. (2013). Survey on botnet: its architecture, detection, prevention and mitigation. In: *2013 10th IEEE International Conference on Networking, Sensing and Control (ICNSC)*, 660–665. IEEE.

17 Rodríguez-Gómez, R.A., Maciá-Fernández, G., and García-Teodoro, P. (2013). Survey and taxonomy of botnet research through life-cycle. *ACM Computing Surveys (CSUR)* 45 (4): 1–33.

18 Thapliyal, M., Garg, N., & Bijalwan, A. (2013). *Botnet Forensics: Survey and Research Challenges*. April.

19 Raheja, S. and Malik, S. (2022). Prediction of air quality using LSTM recurrent neural network. *International Journal of Software Innovation (IJSI)* 10 (1): 1–16.

20 Kumar, M., Rani, A., Raheja, S., and Munjal, G. (2021). Automatic brain tumor detection using machine learning and mixed supervision. In: *Evolving Role of AI and IoMT in the Healthcare Market*, 247–262.

21 Raheja, S. and Asthana, A. (2023). Sentiment analysis of tweets during the COVID-19 pandemic using multinomial logistic regression. *International Journal of Software Innovation (IJSI)* 11 (1): 1–16.

22 Alomari, E., Manickam, S., Gupta, B. B., Karuppayah, S., & Alfaris, R. (2012). Botnet-based distributed denial of service (DDoS) attacks on web servers: classification and art. arXiv preprint arXiv:1208.0403.

23 Ammar, M., Russello, G., and Crispo, B. (2018). Internet of Things: a survey on the security of IoT frameworks. *Journal of Information Security and Applications* 38: 8–27.

24 Raheja, S., Kasturia, S., Cheng, X., and Kumar, M. (2021). Machine learning-based diffusion model for prediction of coronavirus-19 outbreak. *Neural Computing and Applications* 1–20.

25 Vashi, S., Ram, J., Modi, J. et al. (2017, February). Internet of Things (IoT): a vision, architectural elements, and security issues. In: *2017 International Conference on I-SMAC (IoT in Social, Mobile, Analytics and Cloud) (I-SMAC)*, 492–496. IEEE.

26 Da Costa, K.A., Papa, J.P., Lisboa, C.O. et al. (2019). Internet of Things: a survey on machine learning-based intrusion detection approaches. *Computer Networks* 151: 147–157.

27 Arko, A.R., Khan, S.H., Preety, A., and Biswas, M.H. (2019). *Anomaly Detection in IoT Using Machine Learning Algorithms*. Doctoral Dissertation. Brac University.

28 Nižetić, S., Šolić, P., González-De, D.L.D.I., and Patrono, L. (2020). Internet of Things (IoT): opportunities, issues and challenges towards a smart and sustainable future. *Journal of Cleaner Production* 274: 122877.

3

Artificial Intelligence Perspective on Digital Forensics

Bhawna and Shilpa Mahajan

Department of Computer Science, The NorthCap University, Gurgaon, India

3.1 Introduction

Digital forensics is a vast field; it has to deal with systems and data that are associated with it. Intelligent digital forensics serves as a valuable technique for enhancing system security and analysis capabilities. It aids in the proactive management of information and computer vulnerabilities, thereby mitigating potential risks. In digital forensics, the dedicated investigator is required to collect or gather information and evidence while making sure no data or evidence is lost, harmed, or modified. The investigator then would have to make a report of all their findings. Preserving the digital evidence is a very important task in digital forensics, analyzing the digital evidence, and then making an analytic report of the investigation all fall under the field of digital forensics.

Consider the scenario in which Connie Debate, a woman, was fatally attacked in her residence in 2015 [1]. Her spouse, Richard, stated that he had returned home prompted by an alarm notification and recounted that he was rendered immobile upon arrival, enduring further assault by an intruder. He narrated that his wife had been shot and killed by this intruder upon her return from the gym. Subsequent digital inquiries were conducted, revealing a contradiction to Richard's account. Data from Connie's Fitbit, a wearable device capable of tracking GPS location, distance traveled, steps taken, and heart rate, disclosed that she was indeed at home during the time Richard alleged she was at the gym. The Fitbit data indicated that Connie ceased movement one minute before the home alarm was triggered. This instance underscores the potential of digital forensic methodologies, as they allow the collection and synthesis of evidence from diverse sources.

Applying Artificial Intelligence in Cybersecurity Analytics and Cyber Threat Detection, First Edition. Edited by Shilpa Mahajan, Mehak Khurana, and Vania Vieira Estrela.

The continuous expansion of digital storage capacity, coupled with its ubiquitous integration into daily routines, leads to an increased need for such investigations. This, in turn, results in a higher volume of data requiring thorough examination [2]. As observed, conducting forensic inquiries on extensive data and systems can become both labor-intensive and ineffective. This is where artificial intelligence (AI) and machine learning offer valuable assistance. AI endeavors to replicate human cognitive abilities, rendering it particularly advantageous due to its heightened efficiency when contrasted with the manual efforts of human operatives. It can be applied where it is dangerous for humans to enter and perform digital investigations. Machine learning which is a subset of AI can make it more efficient and reliable by applying mathematical algorithms to avoid manual programming which can be extremely inefficient. It helps in increasing the accuracy and reducing the possibility of an error to a great extent. Different techniques are applied to reduce the dimensionality and complexity of the data so that applying machine learning algorithms will be easier and more accurate.

3.2 Literature Survey

Cihan et al. in Intelligence in Digital Forensics Process mention digital forensics corresponds to the modern counterpart of traditional criminal investigations, utilizing digital technologies to expedite the process [3]. In conventional forensics, an investigator's expertise and prior experiences significantly influence the success and efficiency of the investigation. Likewise, harnessing computational resources and intelligence within contemporary contexts enhances the outcomes of digital investigations. This research builds upon existing literature by proposing the integration of machine learning algorithms, specifically those related to clustering and classification, applied to dynamic database files. The goal is to inject a level of intelligence into the digital investigation process. The study culminates in the creation of a comprehensive versatile framework for intelligent forensic investigations.

Forensic examination is commonly an intricate and time-intensive procedure, demanding that forensic analysts gather and scrutinize diverse fragments of evidence to formulate a robust conclusion, Kelly et al. explained in Explainable AI for Digital Forensics: Opportunities, Challenges, and a Drug Testing Case Study [4]. In this chapter, a thorough examination is conducted into the potential opportunities and challenges linked to the advancement of interactive and comprehensible AI systems, recognized as explainable AI (XAI). These systems are designed to provide support to digital forensics by automating the decision-making process. This automation, in turn, expedites the creation of credible evidence suitable for presentation in a court of law, ensuring both speed and reliability.

Jadhav et al. in its paper talked about AI involving endowing machines or computer programs with the capacity to emulate human-like functions. These encompass a wide array of capabilities including visual comprehension, speech discernment, cognitive analysis, decision formulation, experiential assimilation, and the adept resolution of intricate problems. Notably, AI accomplishes these tasks with greater swiftness and a notably diminished error rate in contrast to human performance.

Dr. Mitchell suggests that the application of AI presents a valuable prospect. This field, deeply entrenched in contemporary computer science, excels in managing computationally intricate and expansive issues. Its potential utility in digital forensics is noteworthy, considering the escalating significance of this field [5]. Digital forensics frequently demands astute evaluation of extensive and intricate datasets. Herein lies the potential for AI to serve as a connecting link, effectively addressing these challenges.

Philip Turner's work delves into the amalgamation of digital evidence derived from varying origins [2], as well as the adept utilization of digital evidence bags (DEBs) for targeted and judicious imaging [6]. The application of a forensic methodology to incident response, network analysis, and system administration, facilitated by the implementation of DEBs, is a subject of research [7]. The notion of DEBs is pivotal in this context, providing an encompassing container for diverse digital evidence origins. This approach ensures the preservation of origin information and the consistent thread of investigation across the entirety of its duration. The author advocates for the integration of intelligent methodologies in handling selective information capture scenarios, proposing the use of a selective image approach in conjunction with the DEB. The research delves into significant facets mirroring the effective amalgamation of expert insights from both technical and legal domains and ensuring the comprehensive capture of pertinent information and evidence relating to related crimes within the DEB.

3.3 Phases of Digital Forensics

The digital forensics phases for investigation are discussed as shown in Figure 3.1.

1. Investigation preparation
   This phase involves recognizing the investigation's objective and determining the necessary resources for its execution. The investigator needs to understand the purpose and the goal of the particular case investigation. They need to prepare the essential resources that would be required to facilitate the investigation.

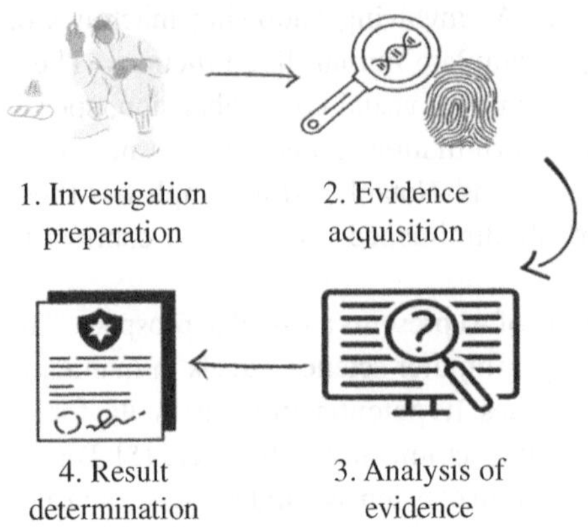

Figure 3.1 Phases of digital forensic investigation.

2. Evidence acquisition
   This step requires identifying the sources of the digital evidence and looking for methods to preserve the digital evidence. This step is extremely crucial, collecting evidence from different possible sources. A single wrong step could lead to the loss of highly important information. The investigator needs to make sure to search areas that are easily missed for hidden data or information. Collecting data or evidence is surely important but thinking and implementing methods to preserve these collected data is equally important.
3. Analysis of evidence
   In this stage, it is necessary to pinpoint the potential tools and methods that could be applied for data processing and the interpretation of analytical outcomes. Analyzing the evidence collected, its relevance in regards to the case, and checking how it can be used to get closer to the result.
4. Result determination
   This step requires making or compiling your findings into a report and then presenting those findings. Compiling all the evidence collected along with your conclusion based on your findings.

3.4 Demystifying Artificial Intelligence in the Digital World

AI constitutes a domain within computer science wherein computer systems are enabled to replicate human intelligence. This discipline encompasses the investigation and construction of computer systems capable of emulating certain human-like forms of intelligence. It encompasses the realm of systems that possess the ability to grasp novel concepts, engage in logical reasoning, formulate deductions, comprehend natural language, and interpret visual scenes.

AI can be categorized into different types based on its capabilities and functionalities.

3.4.1 Artificial Narrow Intelligence

This type of AI is focused on a specific task with specific intelligence [8]. The form of AI referred to as Narrow AI is readily observable in contemporary computing environments. These intelligent systems have acquired the capability to execute specific tasks without direct, explicit programming. This manifestation of intelligence is exemplified by technologies such as voice recognition in Apple's iPhone assistant Siri, the visual recognition system within self-driving cars, and even product recommendation engines. Unlike human cognitive abilities, these systems are confined to mastering and performing designated tasks, hence earning the label of "narrow" AI.

3.4.2 Artificial General Intelligence

This type of AI can perform anything a human is capable of performing. Diverging significantly, General AI embodies a form of adaptive cognition akin to the flexibility seen in human intelligence. It possesses the capacity to learn and proficiently execute a broad spectrum of tasks, ranging from basic activities like hair cutting to complex undertakings such as problem-solving across diverse domains. This ability to engage with various subjects stems from accumulated experiential learning (Figure 3.2).

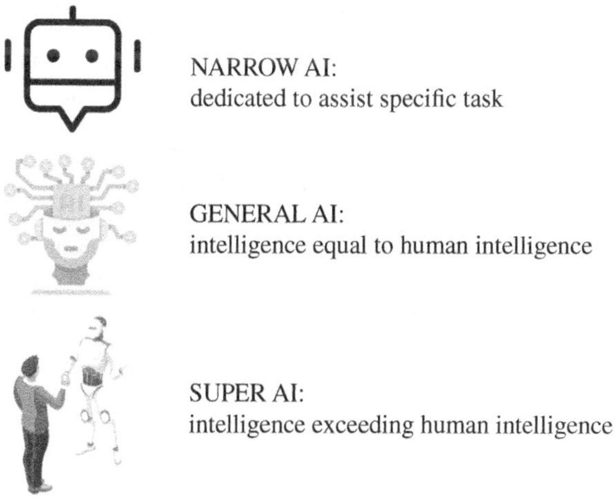
NARROW AI:
dedicated to assist specific task
GENERAL AI:
intelligence equal to human intelligence
SUPER AI:
intelligence exceeding human intelligence

Figure 3.2 Types of artificial intelligence.

3.4.3 Artificial Super Intelligence

These are the AI systems that can outshine human intelligence in every aspect. These are self-learning systems that outshine human intelligence in problem-solving, creativity, and planning. These systems have capabilities to learn itself.

AI is a technique based on algorithms and models and is one of the biggest reasons for the rise in technology and business fields. The AI revelations come with a couple of advantages [9].

- AI provides great reliability.
- Its cost-effectiveness is a real help for companies and businesses.
- It is capable of solving complicated or complex issues and problems.

Table 3.1 The benefits of AI in forensics.

Benefits of incorporating AI into Digital Forensics	
Decrease in personnel hours and reduction of involvement schedules.	AI systems have the capacity to efficiently handle and analyze considerably larger volumes of data in a notably shorter timeframe. As a consequence, the allocation of personnel hours for engagements is decreased, yielding savings for both accounting firms and audited organizations. Furthermore, AI can expedite the process of pinpointing the root cause of fraud, a particularly valuable advantage in cases where fraudulent activities are still ongoing.
Technology related to machine learning and the processing of natural language.	Through the integration of natural language processing technology, AI identifies key attributes and performance indicators in contracts, administrative records, financial statements, and similar documents. Furthermore, AI platforms, operating as machine-learning solutions, provide organizations the flexibility to adapt the systems to their unique requirements using sample documents. These systems continue to enhance their capabilities through usage, without the need for explicit programming [10].
Elimination of human mistakes.	Due to its minimal requirement for human involvement in data processing and analysis, AI substantially diminishes the likelihood of human error stemming from clerical mistakes, typos in equations or figures, and similar issues. Additionally, AI plays a pivotal role in detecting irregularities or incongruities within data sets, aiding in the recognition of human-made errors.
Enhanced data interpretation.	As AI possesses the capability to handle substantial data volumes, the platforms can condense information into user-friendly visuals for presenting findings. This facilitates precise, prompt, and comprehensible data analysis.

- It is capable of providing helpful options and is useful in decision-making.
- AI also makes sure to restrict data from getting lost.
- AI has reinforcement learning which is one of the greatest tools in trying to increase the reliability of applications. It is based on testing in real life the success and failure of applications.

Table 3.1 discusses the benefits of incorporating AI into Digital Forensics.

3.5 Application of Machine Learning in Digital Forensics Investigations

Digital forensics analysts can largely make use or take advantage of machine learning algorithms and models to detect and uncover easily missed (when conducted manually) and hidden evidence in digital sources [11]. Machine learning pattern detection and recognition can be used or applied to carry these forensic investigations out. Regardless of the many works or methods proposed to apply machine learning to digital forensics, there are numerous skepticisms regarding the opacity of AI in digital forensics (Figure 3.3).

The goal of AIML in computer forensics is to be able to analyze and then correlate the data or information stored as evidence in an investigation [12]. It is

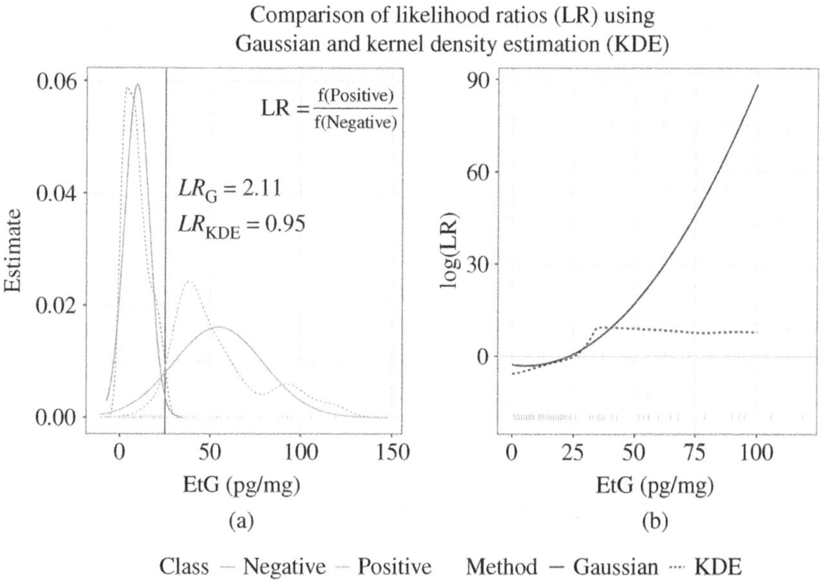

Figure 3.3 Evaluation of Forensics Data (a) using Gaussian Method and (b) Using Kernel Density Estimation Approach.

used to reduce the large amounts of data collected to only required and interesting evidence related to the investigation, in this way data or evidence to be personally analyzed is reduced.

The correlation functionality serves the purpose of identifying connections among evidence that might be disregarded or not noticed by human professionals, primarily due to the substantial volume of data under consideration [13]. This analytical approach has been empirically validated using authentic datasets, yielding notably favorable, and dependable outcomes in comparison to instances where solely human experts undertook analogous manual analysis.

3.6 Implementation of Artificial Intelligence in Forensics

The implementation of AI in the field of forensic or digital security can help different systems analyze the predeterminate approach to handle the errors as well as possible upcoming errors along with possible security breaches and attacks. It can also help us by providing us with different possible approaches that can be taken to predict or analyze the problem, such that the problem is solved before the security of our systems, machines, or applications gets compromised.

When working or analyzing using traditional forensics tools, it is important to get external input from the users to work along with the procedure of the forensic process which is not a need or requirement when using AI tools to analyze forensic data, when using AI tools, it may detect and allocate the threat on the computer system in prior which lets the security program to execute and handle the threat before the breach takes place. However, in case the breach has taken place already, AI can capture the evidence from the source and then maintain a record of the attack to prevent future similar breaches [14].

AI possesses the capability to aid forensic experts by effectively arranging and overseeing data, as well as conducting multi-tiered meta-analysis. This contribution can prove time-saving for forensic investigators during their inquiry processes, thereby safeguarding their dedication to case resolution and elevating the dependability of outcomes to a considerable degree.

3.7 Pattern Recognition Using Artificial Intelligence

AI helps investigators in recognizing patterns which is one of the most important things to find or realize when it comes to forensic investigations. It is important to realize subtle or hard connections to conclude.

Pattern recognition helps in connecting the dots by detecting patterns in emails and messages as well as in the different components of single images. AI is capable of automatically storing previous existing data in databases which makes it easier to match new information with existing information [15]. It assists investigators by making it easier for them to realize if the criminal performing the current breach is possibly someone who has attacked similarly before as well. It would try to fit all the potential data types to obtain a high degree of performance (Figure 3.4).

AI is capable of providing fast and quick solutions to legal communities when it is required in the case of more complex and extensive databases of information.

Miscommunication between important parties involved in a particular forensic investigation could be one of the biggest issues since it would lead to misinterpretation of data, information, or evidence which further would lead to wrong conclusions during the decision-making process and conclude with injustice. AI helps in bridging the gap between forensic statisticians, lawyers, criminal investigators, and other parties involved in a particular forensic investigation.

Forensic investigations require and involve support from strong statistical evidence to prove your narrative and arguments regarding the particular forensic case. AI is capable of building graphical structures and models situations that will help to prove the reliability of the evidence provided and therefore help the law in approving or disapproving arguments to make better judgements and provide justice. AI also makes it easier to understand the statistics of a study while reducing errors with the help of its mathematical and computational tools.

AI can be a good tool to store, analyze, and use the data stored in its online repositories of all the digital investigations. The exponential rate of development of the storage capacities of USBs, optical media, and hard drives has made it hard for forensic science investigators to store and analyze the data that is in those storage

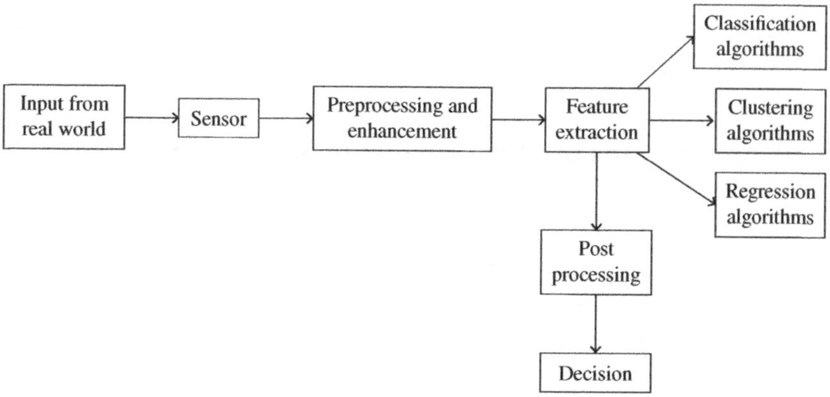

Figure 3.4 Pattern recognition process.

devices [4]. This is where AI comes into play and helps in storing and analyzing all of these large amounts of data.

Data mining is one of the most known fields to use AI. Data mining can aid or facilitate the process of pattern recognition since during data mining, the user can ask for a certain file that contains specific information to be highlighted. It is capable of ignoring obvious patterns or irrelevant patterns focusing on the relevant ones only. It is a combination of statistical and probabilistic AI methods and is used on large or enormously sized data where the normal manual computational methods would prove ineffective and inefficient.

Feature selection and dimensionality reduction help in filtering out relevant, important, quality data from irrelevant, noisy, and redundant data. Both these methods are used in reducing the amount of data, but they are still very different from each other. Feature selection simply selects the most relevant features to increase prediction accuracy while dimensionality reduction fully transforms high-level features to low-level features. A few commonly used methods are PCA which is the principal component analysis, information gain, and random projection.

AI helps by providing fraud detection technologies. It helps in combining structured and unstructured data that is collected from various sources to create or form risk models which are extremely crucial and of great importance for advanced analytics. These advanced analytics are utilized to rank risks that are at firm level layer rather than data layer and further approaches like machine learning and cognitive data analytics are used to further the investigations.

Artificial neural networks are capable of telling us the activities of a web surfer. We will be able to distinguish which surfer is surfing legally and which is surfing illegally – making use of proxy servers and accumulating online traffic over a server to crack it down.

Through remote sensing and satellite facilities artificial neural networks are capable of deciding which phone calls to trace and which not during investigations to aid the investigators.

3.8 Applications of AI in Criminal Investigations

3.8.1 Bombing Scenarios

Bombs are extremely hard to deal with and criminals are also capable of destroying hundreds of lives with just a single bomb. However, with the help of AI, we may be able to detect these bombs [16]. Robots, a creation of AI, may be able to detect the various components used in the making of bombs like aluminum powder, nitroglycerine, passive infrared sensors, tetranitrate, etc. This way we may be able to detect explosives beforehand and avoid loss of lives.

3.8.2 Gun Fires

Sensors linked to a cloud-based program may be placed in municipal infrastructures which will help to correctly identify and pinpoint gunshots. The sensors are capable of recording the time and sound of the gunshots which is information that would help the investigators to pinpoint the location of the shooter or shooters.

Interpretable machine learning classifiers, like decision trees and models based on rules, have frequently found application within digital forensics scenarios. In the realm of elucidating legal cases, the concept of Bayesian Networks (BN) has also garnered attention from the community. AfzaliSeresht and colleagues introduced an approach rooted in explainable AI (XAI), employing event-based rules to generate narratives for detecting patterns in security event logs. This model serves to support forensic investigators. Furthermore, Mahajan and co-researchers leveraged Local Interpretable Model-agnostic Explanations (LIME) for the classification of toxic comments in the realm of cyber forensics. This adoption resulted in not only notable accuracy but also interpretability, surpassing diverse machine learning models.

3.9 Conclusion

This chapter has mentioned the growing rates of criminal attacks in the digital world and how handling these digital attacks manually with limited human labor becomes extensive, unreliable, and extremely hard. Large amounts of data and evidence collected cannot be manually analyzed or handled, and this is the juncture at which the integration of AI becomes pertinent. The utilization of AI simplifies the process for investigators to gather, analyze, and categorize data and evidence. AI technologies like pattern recognition and remote sensing make it easier for investigators to realize the significance of the evidence collected and the correlation between newly collected information and existing information. The forensic sector benefits from AI and considers it a supplementary tool but does not fully depend on it.

References

1 Hoelz, B., Ralha, C., and Geeverghese, R. (2009). Artificial intelligence applied to computer forensics. In: *Proceedings of the ACM Symposium on Applied Computing*, 883–888. https://doi.org/10.1145/1529282.1529471.

2 Turner, P. (2005). Unification of digital evidence from disparate sources (digital evidence bags). *Digital Investigation*, 2(3), 223–228.

3 Adam, I.Y. and Varol, C. (2020). Intelligence in digital forensics process. In: *8th International Symposium on Digital Forensics and Security (ISDFS), Beirut, Lebanon*, 1–6. https://doi.org/10.1109/ISDFS49300.2020.9116442.

4 Kelly, L., Sachan, S., Ni, L. et al. (2020). Explainable artificial intelligence for digital forensics: opportunities, challenges and a drug testing case study. In: *Digital Forensic Science*. IntechOpen https://doi.org/10.5772/intechopen.93310.

5 Mitchell, F. (2014). The use of Artificial Intelligence in digital forensics: an introduction. *Digital Evidence and Electronic Signature Law Review* 7: https://doi.org/10.14296/deeslr.v7i0.1922.

6 Turner, P. (2006). Selective and intelligent imaging using digital evidence bags. *Digital Investigation* 3 (Supplement 1): 59–64.

7 Turner, P. (2007). Applying a forensic approach to incident response, network investigation and system administration using digital evidence bags. *Digital Investigation* 4 (1): 30–35.

8 Solanke, A.A. and Biasiotti, M.A. (2022b). Digital forensics AI: evaluating, standardizing and optimizing digital evidence mining techniques. *Künstliche Intelligenz* 36 (2): 143–161. https://doi.org/10.1007/s13218-022-00763-9.

9 Williams, L. (2023). *What Is Digital Forensics? History, Process, Types, Challenges*. Guru99 Assets| International Journal of Innovative Science and Research Technology. (n.d.).

10 Martens, S. (2022). *The Phases of Digital Forensics*. Reno: University of Nevada https://onlinedegrees.unr.edu/blog/digital-forensics/.

11 Biosa, G., Giurghita, D., Alladio, E. et al. (2020). Evaluation of forensic data using logistic regression-based classification methods and an R shiny implementation. *Frontiers in Chemistry*, 8: 738.

12 Mohsin, K. (2021). *Artificial Intelligence in Forensic Science*. Social Science Research Network https://doi.org/10.2139/ssrn.3910244.

13 News-Medical.net. 2023. '*AI in Forensic Science*'. https://www.news-medical.net/life-sciences/AI-in-Forensic-Science.aspx

14 Chowdhury, M. (2021). *AI in Forensic Investigation and Crime Detection*. Analytics Insight https://www.analyticsinsight.net/ai-in-forensic-investigation-and-crime-detection/.

15 Gupta, S. and Johri, P. (2020). Artificial intelligence in forensic science. *International Research Journal of Engineering and Technology* 7: 7181–7184.

16 Disharoon, J. (2022). *Forensic Auditing and Artificial Intelligence Help Detect Fraudulent Activity*. GRF CPAs & Advisors https://www.grfcpa.com/2019/02/forensic-auditing-and-artificial-intelligence-help-detect-fraudulent-activity/.

4

Review on Machine Learning-based Traffic Rules Contravention Detection System

Jahnavi[1] *and Urvashi*[2]

[1]*Department of Computer Science, Dr. B.R. Ambedkar National Institute of Technology, Jalandhar, India*
[2]*Department of Computer Science and Engineering, Dr. B.R. Ambedkar National Institute of Technology, Jalandhar, India*

4.1 Introduction

The primary goal of developing a traffic rule violation system is to detect numerous offenses committed by defaulters on the road so that severe action can be taken against them to lower the number of fatalities brought on by accidents. Initially, monitoring a large volume of traffic on the roads was done by a single individual, which was problematic as it was more prone to errors due to limited human memory capacity [1]. To solve this issue, a system was introduced that operates 24/7 without the need for human intervention and can accurately detect multiple traffic violations with a high degree of precision. The traffic rule violation detecting system works in conjunction with a surveillance system established along highways and roads. To obtain vital information, these surveillance cameras record images of license plates from vehicles involved in infractions. Computer vision techniques and machine learning algorithms are used to process and analyze the collected photos and videos. This entails collecting relevant information from visual data, such as vehicle position, speed, lane adherence, and traffic signal status [18]. To detect instances of traffic offenses, the processed data is compared to pre-defined rules and laws. Speeding, running red lights, inappropriate lane switching not wearing a helmet, and illegal overtaking are examples of such offenses. The diagram summarizes the operation of the traffic law violation system when connected with the highway CCTV system. To maintain the effectiveness of the traffic rule violation [13]. system, its general operation is constantly reviewed. Reports and analytics can be provided to analyze the frequency and types of infractions, find patterns, and continuously enhance the system's effectiveness (Figure 4.1).

Applying Artificial Intelligence in Cybersecurity Analytics and Cyber Threat Detection, First Edition.
Edited by Shilpa Mahajan, Mehak Khurana, and Vania Vieira Estrela.

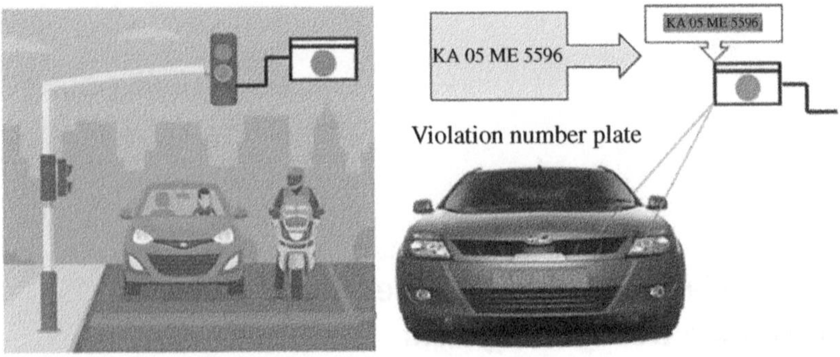

Figure 4.1 Illustration of violation capture process.

Another significant feature of the system is its ability to detect traffic violations caused by two-wheeled vehicles with ease. Studies have shown that the number of two-wheelers on the road is higher compared to other means of transportation, and so it is more common to the fatal accidents due to violation of traffic regulations [15, 18]. To decrease the number of causalities, the system has been designed and trained to detect violations of traffic rules by motorcyclists, such as driving without wearing a helmet [19]. Despite the fact that helmets are mandatory in numerous areas, there are still some riders who do not wear them, and as a result, they face severe accidents. Past observations have revealed that fatalities are increasing at an alarming rate in many developing countries as drivers avoid using helmets. Hence, the designed architecture is multipurpose and can even be extended to other traffic laws such as not wearing helmet, high speed limit, red signal crossing, and many more [9].

The main approach used by the system involves capturing an image of the offending vehicle's number plate in order to retrieve the necessary details of the owner. This can be achieved by utilizing the surveillance systems that are already installed in both urban and rural areas [1]. Once the image is obtained, the violation is analyzed and information about the traffic rule contravention along with the fine to be paid is sent to the registered mobile number of the possessor. To make the interaction more user-friendly, various flexible graphical user interfaces (GUIs) have been designed that enable individuals to track their status easily and quickly.

Figure 4.2 elaborates on the flow of the proposed traffic rule violation detection system in accordance with the vigilance system.

The TRVDS currently in use has resolved numerous issues in terms of human resources, cost, and time. The task of monitoring millions of vehicles has been made effortless, resulting in remarkable outcomes by successfully catching

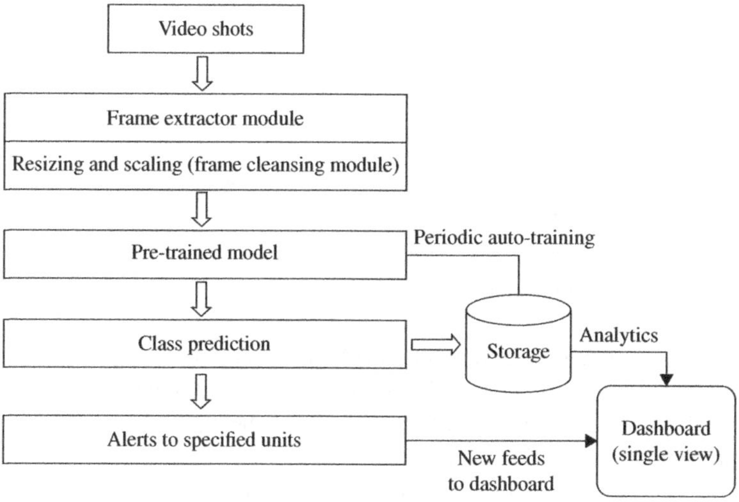

Figure 4.2 Workflow diagram for violation system. Source: Kumar et al. [1]\Blue Eyes Intelligence Engineering and Sciences Publication.

violators. In this chapter, we have focused on different sections, including an introduction, adopted techniques, literature survey, conclusion, and future work.

4.2 Technologies Involved in Smart Traffic Monitoring

4.2.1 Device Involving Sensors

IoT-based sensors are typically configured in such systems, which gather data from assets or target objects and communicate the acquired information to the centralized computer system [4]. The collected statistics play a major role as they help an individual to make better and quicker decisions. The goal of these tiny sensors is to gather all the required real-time data [14]. Some common technologies adopted by the sensor to fetch the required details include the following (Figure 4.3):

- **Infrared Sensors (IR):** The detection of traffic density on the road is accomplished by IR sensors, which signal the traffic light to switch from red to green or vice versa. These sensors work by measuring the infrared radiations present in the environment and tracking the movement of objects. Infrared sensors are divided into two categories: active and passive [16]. Active sensors consist of an LED and a receiver, while passive sensors include infrared filter and a Fresnel lens.
- **VANET:** Vehicular Ad Hoc Network or VANET is a wireless network formed in an ad hoc environment where all the moving vehicles and connected objects

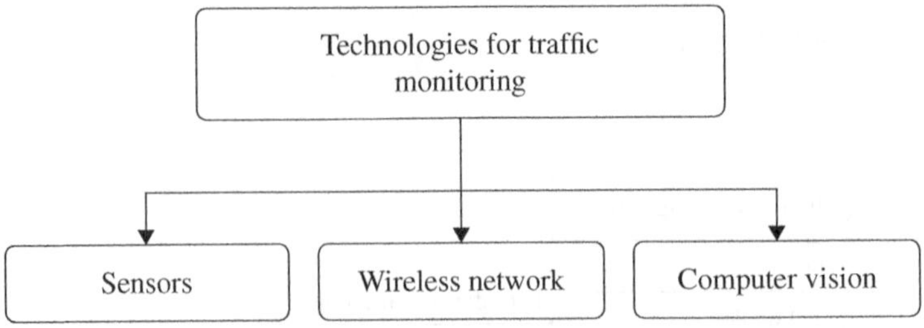

Figure 4.3 Technologies for monitoring traffic congestion.

establish a connection among themselves [13]. Through this connection, they exchange crucial information. Initially, VANET was only designed to provide comfort and safety to drivers, but currently it is also being used to accurately detect traffic violations on the road.

- **RFID:** The wireless approach is supported by RFID sensors that consist of two essential elements, namely tags and readers [2, 15]. The reader device includes antennas that transmit radio waves and receive signals from the tags. These tags transmit information about their identity and other characteristics to nearby objects via radio waves. RFID tags are classified into two types: active and passive. The only distinction between the two is that active tags are battery-powered while passive ones do not require batteries. The automatic tracking and uploading of necessary information onto a centralized system by RFID eliminates the need for manual efforts, saving both time and money [4]. Additionally, the possibility of data duplication and missed items is minimized, as all collected details are electronically recorded. Figure 4.4 [2] shows tags that will be tracked, reader which will detect the RFID tags, antennas, radio waves, and computer wherein all the accumulated data will be stored.

4.2.2 Wireless Network

The term wireless network refers to a network that establishes connections between devices through radio frequencies. The distinguishing feature of wireless networks is that they keep objects connected to the network while allowing them to move around freely, without being encumbered by cables [18]. In contrast, wired networks require a large number of wires to establish a connection to the network. Wireless frequencies like Bluetooth, Wi-Fi, and Zigbee all support the establishment of wireless networks. These networks come with various protocol variants that facilitate data communication over a large coverage area.

Wireless networks also allow for centralized management and oversight of the system, which aids in the detection of traffic offenses. It is feasible to wirelessly

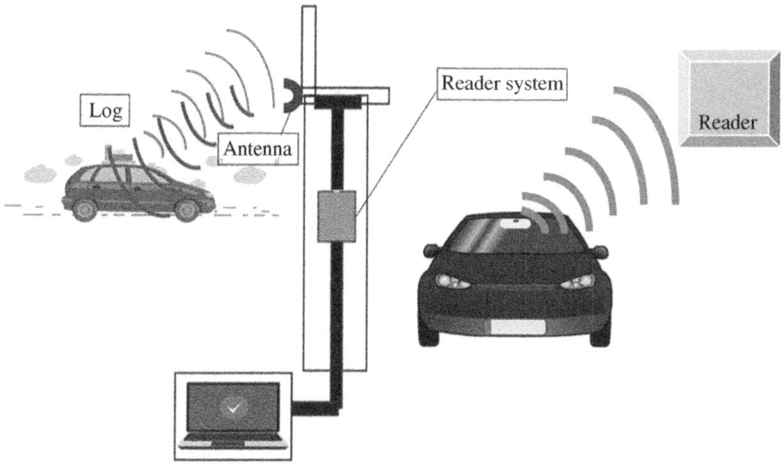

Figure 4.4 RFID system.

transmit data from sensors, cameras, and other equipment positioned throughout the road network to a central control facility. This control center is the key hub for data analysis, processing, and initiating relevant tasks. Because of wireless connectivity, the control unit can immediately identify and fix traffic violations. This can include alerting the necessary parties, automatically billing costs, or dispatching enforcement officials to the offending area [17]. Wireless networks can be compared to a system that aids in the detection of traffic offenses. They simplify data control and analysis, let vehicles to interface with infrastructure, and accelerate data transmission.

In TRVDS, these network plays a major role by initiating a seamless transmission between sensors, cameras, monitoring stations, and other components, enabling quick detection and response to traffic rule violations.

4.2.3 Computer Vision

Computer Vision is the prominent field of Artificial Intelligence that involves training computer systems to comprehend the real world. Many papers utilizing Computer Vision technology rely on the implementation of Convolutional Neural Network (CNN) models [3]. Traffic rule violation systems that adopt this technique begin by extracting video frames from the surveillance system. These frames are then loaded into the CNN model, where four pre-trained layers analyze the features to identify illegal driving activities of the driver on the road. After the video frames are extracted for approximately 0.5 seconds, a DBN model is employed to make the final decision before sending the alert to the violator.

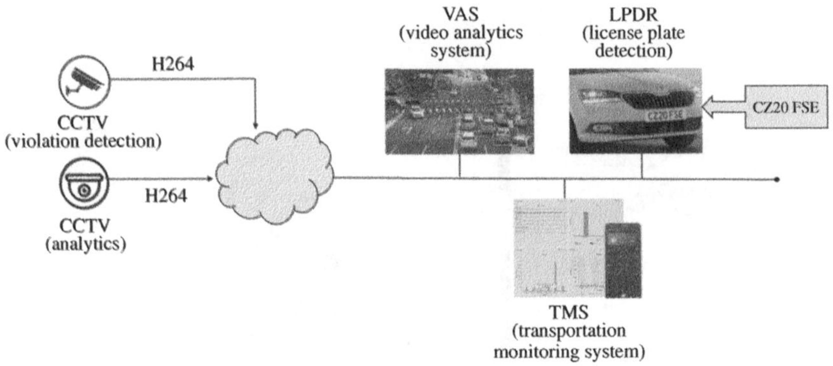

Figure 4.5 Computer vision workflow. Source: Alaydrusl et al. [3]/IOP Publishing/CC BY 3.0.

In this process, the DBN model aids the CNN in deriving all the essential features and defining the feature map, which is the intermediate representation of input data. The current system primarily employs this map, which is extracted from the video frames. To perform the ultimate prediction of the driver's unlawful movement, a set of video frames is utilized for recognition. Its primary function is to collect, process, and interpret information from photos or videos, allowing the system to identify and enforce traffic laws by recognizing various transgressions. One notable feature of CV is its capacity to recognize and track things in real time. Vehicles, pedestrians, and traffic signs are all included. The device may detect possible offenses such as automobiles running red lights or pedestrians jaywalking by utilizing computer vision. Approximately thirteen feature maps are used by CNN for making the predictions. Afterward, the set of maps is condensed into a solitary pattern and fed into the DBN model to obtain the ultimate classification for the traffic law violation system. The workflow for Computer vision technology is summarized in Figure 4.5 [3].

4.3 Literature Review

In [5], the prime objective is to provide drivers with feedback about traffic rule violations committed while driving. The proposed methodology is capable of detecting specific traffic law infringements and recording information about the offender in a local database. They utilized the "Standard Google Earth" tool to visualize the stored data based on rule breakage in a geographical map. The system is designed to work both during the day and at night, with dual high-resolution cameras mounted on the vehicle's roof, with one camera operating during the day and the other at night.

To make it user-friendly, a human interface software was introduced, allowing the driver to visualize the offense committed. Furthermore, the vehicle owner can also receive assistance with various other actions that can help them to avoid violations. The application can be installed on the screen in the vehicle for easy interaction and quick actions. The system can accurately detect various signboards placed along the road to alert individuals about potentially dangerous situations such as high speeds, stop signs, intersections, no-parking zones, and schools ahead. In such cases, the system delivers an audible message through a loudspeaker to the driver.

Initially, the pre-installed camera captures a snapshot from which all the essential statistics are extracted based on the image region. The images are then segmented to focus on the traffic signs, which is achieved through flexible thresholding, ignoring numerous untracked regions that can be disregarded later. Subsequently, the segmented image's shape is analyzed to obtain the area of interest. Shape analysis involves multiple filtering process followed by geometric restrictions. The final stage involves pattern matching on the filtered image to arrive at the ultimate decision.

In [6], a system called "Vehitrack" was developed for Android to detect traffic law violations using RFID technology and sensors. The ultimate objective of the system was to manage volume of the traffic in a specific area. In addition, the creators also developed a mobile application that included a database for saving all the relevant information of the driver and a list of previously violated regulations. The approached aimed to create an integrated system with Android application that would automatically send a message to the vehicle's owner, including the total amount to be paid for breaching the traffic law. The flowchart below describes the working of the system (Figure 4.6).

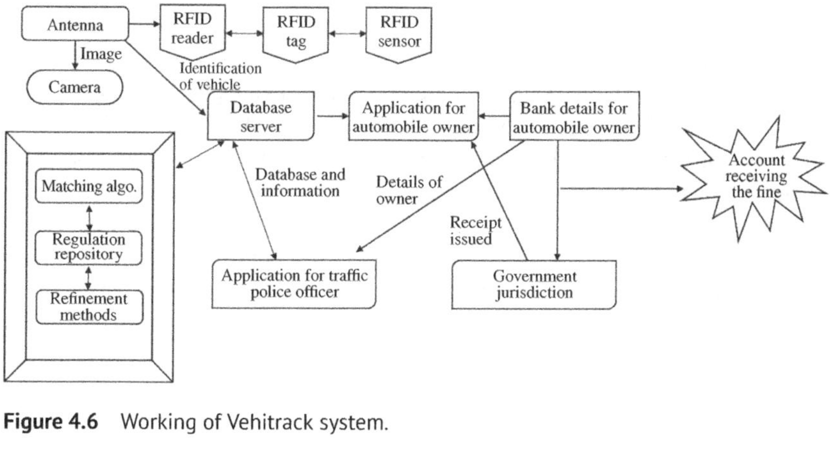

Figure 4.6 Working of Vehitrack system.

The process was segmented into four distinct stages. In the initial step, the identification of the vehicle on the road was carried out through the utilization of RFID, sensors, and tags, with the aid of a camera for capturing an image of the transport. In the second phase, various technologies performed different functions. The sensor detects the RFID number, which is read by the reader, and all the acquired information is transferred to the database. The third module involves the implementation of an Android application that establishes a link between the police officer and the perpetrator. Finally, the offender is automatically issued a fine on their registered mobile number.

The paper discusses the experiment results used to evaluate the performance of the Vehitrack system. According to the authors' demonstration, the system achieves excellent accuracy in identifying traffic law violations. They also emphasize the constraints and difficulties experienced when putting the system into action. The study continues by introducing the Vehitrack system, an Android-based tool for detecting traffic offenses. The research contributes to the field of traffic management and enforcement by providing a mobile platform that uses image-processing techniques for precise and immediate infraction recognition. The Vehitrack system has the potential to improve road safety by quickly detecting and documenting traffic violations, allowing law enforcement to take appropriate action.

Chitra et al. [7] proposed a traffic management approach that includes detecting rule violations. Their traffic management architecture utilizes sensors to monitor traffic flow on a lane. The controller adjusts the duration of the green light based on signals received from the sensors. The circuit built into the system operates when the signal turns red, requiring vehicles to stop. If a vehicle moves during the red signal, the circuit uses an LDR and laser to detect it. Once the signal is disrupted, a buzzer alerts on-site commuters on the lane.

The system is designed with infrared sensors that detect traffic flow and adjust the duration of the green and red signals accordingly. A circuit is installed in the proposed architecture to recognize signal-crossing violations. The traffic infringement circuit operates in two stages, where first stage uses a Light Dependent Resistor (LDR) to switch the buzzer on or off based on the LDR signal. In the second stage, the buzzer sounds whenever a traffic regulation violation occurs, sending a warning to the centralized system. Figure 4.7 elaborates on the working of the traffic violation circuit.

The paper also mentioned a downside of using LDR, noting that it does not function as intended when there is ambient light present. In situations where there is low traffic volume and a vehicle stops in front of the sensor, the green light is automatically activated. To address these problems, sensors can be used instead of LDR. Additionally, instead of relying on a centralized computer, a Raspberry Pi can be employed to operate the surveillance system. To address these issues, the

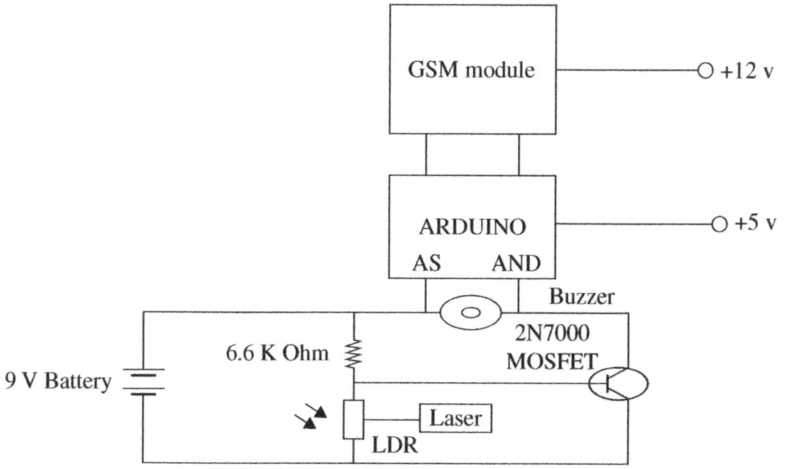

Figure 4.7 Architecture for traffic violation circuit. Source: Chitra et al. [7]\International Journal of Computer Applications.

research report suggests using sensors on top of LDR. With sensors that are less affected by ambient light, the system can detect traffic violations more reliably and correctly. Another suggestion for improvement is to use a Raspberry Pi as the operating system for the surveillance system rather than a centralized computer. The system's effectiveness and performance can be improved through these changes.

In [8], an AI-based traffic sign violation detection system was created in 2020 using deep learning techniques. The research employed YOLO version 3 to recognize law breakage such as signal jumping, seatbelt usage, and speeding on two-wheelers. To identify objects from the input given to the system, YOLOv3 was coupled with CNN. The YOLOv3 primarily comprises a CNN, which consists of layers that enable the visualization of images and videos captured. It belongs to the class of multi-layer perceptron where neurons of one network are linked to those of another network. CNN is a specific type of model used for processing information in a grid-like manner. The model initially extracts features from the image frame by frame. The CNN's layer also has the ability to detect multiple objects simultaneously from a single input. The study highlights potential future work by emphasizing on the need for a system which is capable of monitoring traffic efficiently and can cover a huge area.

The objective is to detect violations from a single input using a parallel computation approach. Moreover, the researchers recommend using larger datasets and training them using GPUs and high-end FPGA kits. The block diagram below explains the working of the traffic rule violation detection system. The CNN layer can differentiate several objects from a single input at the same time. The study

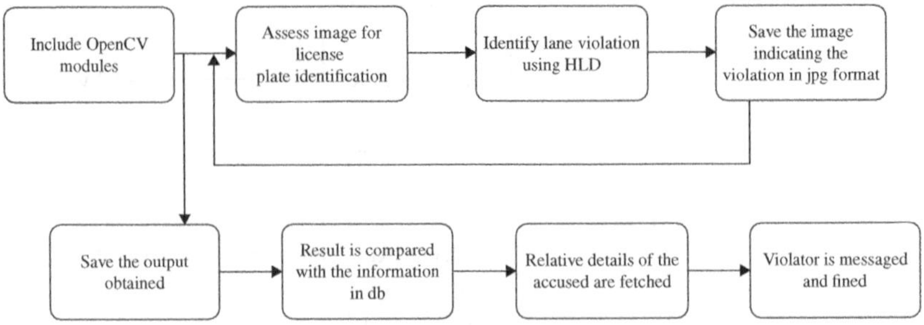

Figure 4.8 Flowchart for proposed traffic monitoring system. Source: Adapted from Arnob et al. [9].

indicates opportunities for future research by emphasizing the need for a system that can successfully monitor traffic across a vast area. The purpose is to discover violations from a single input using a parallel processing method. Overall, the research uses AI and deep learning techniques to improve traffic signal detection. The findings demonstrate how these technologies could enhance traffic safety and enforce traffic laws at signalized crossings.

In [9], a lane-based rule violation detection system was introduced in 2020 using a combination of various algorithms. The prime aim of the authors was to address a problem related to both Raspberry Pi as well as OpenCV. The flowchart below demonstrates the traffic monitoring system in detail (Figure 4.8).

Initially, a pre-processing step was applied using a Gaussian blur filter on the collected video, the image was masked and sent to the canny edge detection algorithm. Subsequently, the accused individual and their vehicle license plates were identified, and if any violation was detected, an alert message was dispatched. The system achieved an accuracy of 78.83%, which was considered sufficient for identifying offenders based on license plate information. The implementation of the Hough line concept involved the use of the OpenCV and NumPy platforms to monitor traffic. A Raspberry Pi was employed, which was constructed on the singleton chip of the computer system. The proposed system was initiated by first booting the Raspberry Pi and installing both OpenCV and its contour. The captured images were converted to grayscale, and a threshold was applied. The surveillance system was used to record videos of vehicles committing offenses. Lane violations are also detected by using combination of canny edge, Gaussian blur, and HLT. Finally, once an offense was recorded, a text message was sent to the user's phone number, which was previously stored in the database.

The camera footage and images captured on highways are often not clear enough to be directly used for the final prediction in the model. To enhance the sharpness of the input and to eliminate noise, a Gaussian blur filter is applied. The filter

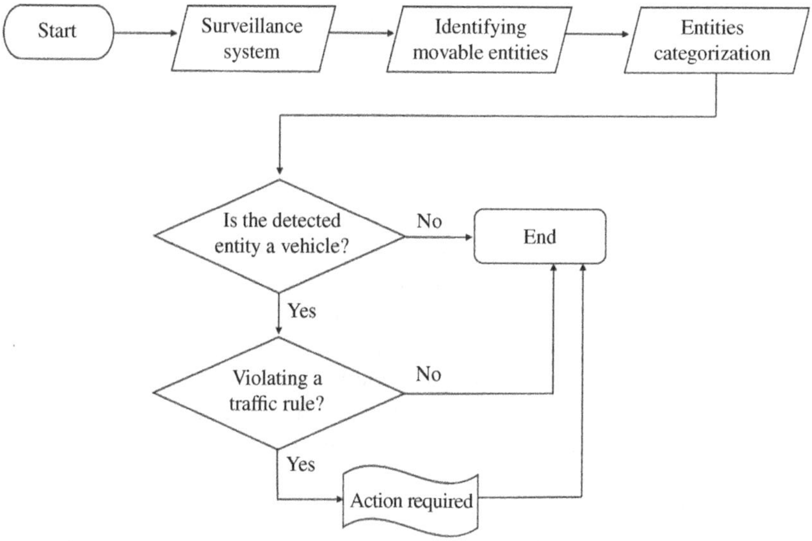

Figure 4.9 System for designing the traffic violation detection system.

utilizes the Gaussian kernel to adjust the height and width of the image or video. By implementing these techniques, the system was able to achieve high accuracy and demonstrate superior performance.

The 2021 [10] research work employed a range of machine learning techniques to construct a system which is capable of automatically identifying offenses in the absence of traffic officers. To achieve the best results and to reduce existing noise, input images underwent gray scaling using the Gaussian blur approach. Furthermore, dilation was employed to fill in any emptied holes. After pre-processing, multiple object detection ML approaches were utilized, and their outcomes were assessed. SVM was initially employed, which revealed that objects could be easily extracted from the given data. However, RCNN gathered features from each region of the image and produced a significantly higher recognition rate. Ultimately, the study found that RCNN was superior to SVM for this purpose (Figure 4.9).

To create a more user-friendly interaction with individuals, the study utilized tkinter as it is a proven to be attractive GUI. This allows even the traffic inspector to review the footage before penalizing an offender. Therefore, the investigation process can be conducted with ease through the use of this technique. Image processing steps include gray scaling and blurring, followed by background subtraction to isolate the area of interest and remove unwanted image elements. To attain high accuracy, it is essential to eliminate existing noise and disturbances, which is achieved through binarization. It is a technique where a gray scaled images are converted into the binary format, where each value is either 0 or 1. The main motive behind adopting it was to simplify the data and to transform it in the way that it can be easily used by the algorithm in use. The proposition employed a model that categorizes vehicles into different types such as 4-wheeler, 2-wheeler, and 3-wheeler. This was accomplished by utilizing a neural network model on the input obtained after the pre-processing stage.

In [11], the author reviewed past research and devised a system that uses a genetic algorithm to obtain a high degree of accuracy. The algorithm's main goal is to optimize the input in order to provide a desirable output. Background subtraction was applied to create the image foreground and to transform the input data into a frame. This procedure is viewed as pre-processing stage, and a genetic set of rules were utilized in order to ascertain whether a violation actually happened. According to the results, deploying a genetic algorithm enhanced the inputted initiatives and generated the best accurate algorithm. The traffic rule contravention detection system employed the Haar tool for identifying and capturing those vehicles that were breaking the rules.

The tool comprised numerous files and folders in XML format. To begin with, positive and negative images were considered, where the positive images contained the required object while negative ones did not. In the next stage, a classifier was trained to identify vector files that had a combination of both types of images. In the final step, a folder was created and loaded with files ranging from 0 to $N-1$. This approach ensured that the classifier used was fully trained and ready to use. The process commenced with the visualization of an image from the footage, followed by the use of a genetic algorithm to determine if a particular vehicle is breaking the law. Prior to feeding the image into the model, the frame in which it was captured is isolated from the main frame, and the image is converted to black and white. These steps enable the genetic algorithm to accurately detect traffic rule violations.

In [12], a study introduced a traffic rule violation detection system based on machine learning. Its purpose was to identify a vehicle's license plate in inclement weather such as smog or rain, as well as to function with low-quality images captured in dim lighting conditions that include low contrast and blurriness. The research involved six stages, starting by obtaining an image from a camera and resizing it to a smaller dimension, followed by the identification of the license plate location, segmentation, and saving the image in a specified format.

The CNN algorithm was used to detect whether motorcyclists were wearing helmets or not, to classify them as motor biker or non-motor biker, and to identify the vehicle number plate. The researchers stated that enhancing the training dataset and improving image quality could further enhance the accuracy level. To begin with, the proposed methodology involves capturing an image and saving it to a database for subsequent pre-processing. The acquired image is transformed into a binary format, followed by localization of the number plate and determination of its width and height. All gaps in the image are filled with numbers to ensure that the license plate appears large enough as compared to the rest portion of the image.

The research involved six stages, starting with obtaining an image from a camera and resizing it to a smaller dimension, followed by identifying the license plate location, segmentation, and saving the image in a specified format. The CNN algorithm was used to detect whether motorcyclists were wearing helmets or not, to classify them as motor biker or non-motor biker, and to identify the vehicle number plate.

The accuracy was 85%, 93%, and 51%, respectively, in each of the three areas. The researchers stated that enhancing the training dataset and improving image quality could further enhance the accuracy level. To begin with, the proposed methodology involves capturing an image and saving it to a database for subsequent pre-processing. The acquired image is transformed into a binary format, followed by localization of the number plate and determination of its width and height. All gaps in the image are filled with numbers to ensure that the license plate appears large enough as compared to the rest portion of the picture. Lastly, the results obtained were saved in the document file with the desired extension. The flowchart illustrates the working of the system (Figure 4.10, Table 4.1).

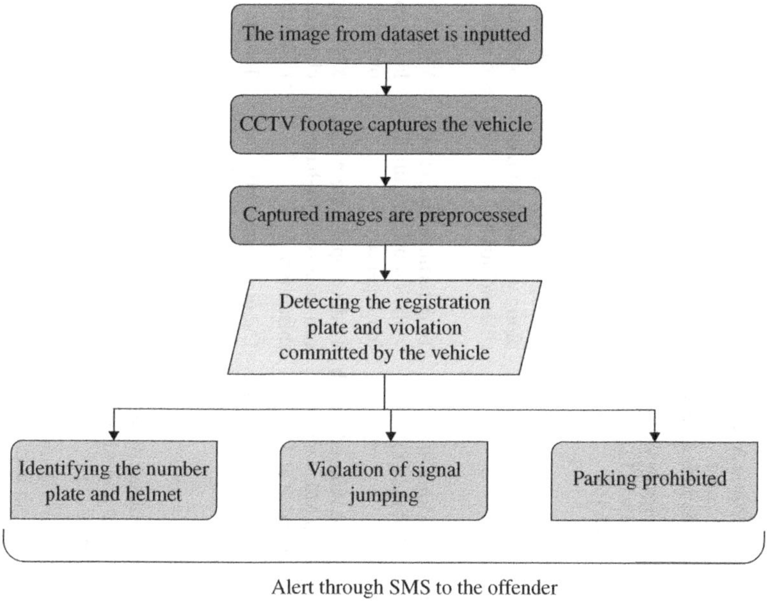

Figure 4.10 Block diagram explaining system architecture.

Table 4.1 Summary of literature review.

Year	Author	Objective	Methodology	Future scope
2014	Nourdine Aliane and Javier Fernandez et al. [5]	To provide feedback to the driver about the offense being committed	Computer vision to detect traffic signs and EDR used to save information related to the particular violation	To further improve the proposed system based on driver's feedback
2017	Dr. Agrawal and Kasliwal Komal et al. [6]	To detect traffic law violation using RFID reader, tag and to capture the image using camera	The RFID reader will collect the tag number, while the surveillance system will capture the image. This data will be transmitted to a server, where it will be saved in a database	—
2020	Chitra and Vanishree et al. [7]	Management of the traffic along with detection of rule violation	Infrared sensors to figure out the density of traffic and battery circuits to send notification to authority at time of infringement	Apply numerous image processing techniques on the image captured to fetch all the necessary details
2020	Fraklin and Mohana et al. [8]	To determine traffic rule violation using artificial intelligence	YOLOv3 is implemented to detect the traffic law breakage such as signal jumping and overspeeding	Develop a system that can cover huge areas and can monitor large traffic through single input
2020	Faed Ahmed Arnob and Md. Azmol Fuad et al. [9]	To develop a system that can discover lane-based infraction	KNN algo. is adopted for extracting nearby character, gaussian blur to remove noise and to make the image smooth	—
2021	Srinivas Reddy and Nishwa et al. [10]	Using different ML techniques to build traffic rule violation detection system	Tensor Flow technique is used to build the proposed system and various libraries have been implemented to perform particular actions	To figure out which vehicle has a greater number of challans, the concept of penalty coins or points can be implemented
2021	Akhilalakshmi T Bhat and Anupama et al. [11]	To detect traffic regulation breach using genetic algo	Used Haar tool to detect the blockage of pedestrian lanes at the time of huge traffic on the road	—
2022	Dr. Yeresime Suresh and Ankitha et al. [12]	Determine traffic rule breach using OpenCV, OCR and Tensor Flow	Implemented ML techniques to figure out traffic regulation infraction under poor weather conditions	To improve the prevailing system by working on other violations such as no parking zone and signal jumping

Table 4.2 Summary of results.

Techniques used	Accuracy obtained
YOLO v3	• Vehicle recognition – 98% • Vehicular speed – 89%
KNN	• Lane-based rule violation – 78.78%
CNN	• Wearing helmet or not – 85% • Classification as motorbike/non-motor biker – 93% • Identify number plate – 51%

4.4 Comparison of Results

The previous research has yielded varying levels of accuracy, employing different techniques. Table 4.2 provides a summary of the methods used and their corresponding precision percentages.

4.5 Conclusion and Future Scope

Enforcing laws is crucial for creating a law-abiding community, and it is essential for the proper functioning of the world. The traffic management system, along with the violation detection system, can assist traffic authorities in identifying violations and in taking strict action against violators. Past studies have shown that by developing such traffic violation architecture around 65% road accidents have been reduced in India. By penalizing a single offender, thousands of people can be alerted, and the number of casualties caused by traffic rule violations can be reduced, thereby saving millions of lives.

The scale of aforementioned figure can be further reduced if systems capable of simultaneously handling multiple violations with high speed are implemented, encompassing various traffic laws such as multiple riders on 2-wheelers and failure to wear seat belts while driving. Therefore, the implementation of a traffic contravention detection system is of utmost importance as it will bring significant societal changes by preventing injuries and effectively managing heavy traffic on roads and highways.

References

1 Kumar, A. et al. (2019). S-TVDS: smart traffic violation detection system for Indian traffic scenario. *International Journal of Innovative Technology and Exploring Engineering (IJITEE)* 8 (4S3): 6–10.

2 Anaza, S.O., Abdulazeez, M.S., Anugboba, I. et al. (2016). A review of radio frequency identification (RFID) system. *International Journal of Electrical and Electronics Research* 79–86.

3 Alaydrusl, A., Putra, W.K., Nugroho, Y., and Surantha, N. (2021). A review of traffic violation detection technology in reporting mechanism. *IOP Conference Series: Earth and Environmental Science* 729 (1): 012005.

4 Bharambe, S., Dixit, O., Wavhal, S. et al. (2017). Automated penalty collection for traffic signal violation using RFID. *International Journal of Engineering Science* 15555.

5 Aliane, N., Fernandez, J., Mata, M., and Bemposta, S. (2014). A system for traffic violation detection. *Sensors* 14 (11): 22113–22127.

6 Agrawal, D.R., Kasliwal, K.S., Gandhi, L.R. et al. (2017). Android based traffic rules violation detection system "Vehitrack". *International Journal of Computer Applications* 163 (8).

7 Chitra, A., Vanishree, J., RaziaSultana, W. et al. (2020). Smart traffic management system with violation detection. *International Journal of Emerging Trends in Engineering Research* 10: 7480–7485.

8 Franklin, R.J. (2020). Traffic signal violation detection using artificial intelligence and deep learning. In: *2020 5th International Conference on Communication and Electronics Systems (ICCES)*, 839–844. IEEE.

9 Arnob, F.A., Fuad, A., Nizam, A.T. et al. (2020). An intelligent traffic system for detecting lane-based rule violation. In: *2019 International Conference on Advances in the Emerging Computing Technologies (AECT)*, 1–6. IEEE.

10 Reddy, P.S., Nishwa, T., Reddy, R.S.K. et al. (2021). Traffic rules violation detection using machine learning techniques. In: *2021 6th International Conference on Communication and Electronics Systems (ICCES)*, 1264–1268. IEEE.

11 Bhat, A.T., Rao, M.S., and Pai, D.G. (2021). Traffic violation detection in India using genetic algorithm. *Global Transitions Proceedings* 2 (2): 309–314.

12 Suresh, Y., Ankitha, R., Chillara, A. et al. (2022). Traffic rules violation detection system. In: *Information and Communication Technology for Competitive Strategies (ICTCS 2020) ICT: Applications and Social Interfaces*, 77–87.

13 Anwer, M.S. and Guy, C. (2014). A survey of VANET technologies. *Journal of Emerging Trends in Computing and Information Sciences* 5 (9): 661–671.

14 Rizwan, P., Suresh, K., and Babu, M.R. (2016). Real-time smart traffic management system for smart cities by using Internet of Things and big data. In: *2016 International Conference on Emerging Technological Trends (ICETT)*, 1–7. IEEE.

15 Costa, F. et al. (2021). A review of RFID sensors, the new frontier of internet of things. *Sensors* 21 (9): 3138.

16 Zappi, P., Farella, E., and Benini, L. (2010). Tracking motion direction and distance with pyroelectric IR sensors. *IEEE Sensors Journal* 10 (9): 1486–1494.

17 Ye, H., Walsh, G.C., and Bushnell, L.G. (2001). Real-time mixed-traffic wireless networks. *IEEE Transactions on Industrial Electronics* 48 (5): 883–890.

18 Pattanashetty, V.B. et al. (2022). Traffic rules violation detection system. In: *Information and Communication Technology for Competitive Strategies (ICTCS 2020) ICT: Applications and Social Interfaces*. Springer Singapore.

19 Raj, K.C.D. et al. (2018). Helmet violation processing using deep learning. In: *2018 International Workshop on Advanced Image Technology (IWAIT)*. IEEE.

5

Enhancing Cybersecurity Ratings Using Artificial Intelligence and DevOps Technologies

Vishwas Pitre[1], Ashish Joshi[1], Satya Saladi[2], and Suman Das[3]

[1] *Information Security, Zensar Technologies, Pune, India*
[2] *Information Security, Zensar Technologies, Hyderabad, India*
[3] *Information Security, Zensar Technologies, Kolkata, India*

5.1 Introduction

As internet has become an essential part of today's lifestyle or generation, all the organizations and businesses have moved to digital frameworks to expand their business so that it can reach each corner of the world. At the same time as majority of the business has moved to digital frameworks, it is has become vulnerable to cyberattacks, which are increasing day by day and business suffers huge reputation as well as revenue. As per reports [1], United States found that nearly a quarter of companies that have experienced a cyberattack have lost between 50,000 and 99,999 US dollars. Among the surveyed companies, another 22% reported losing between 100,000 and 499,999 US dollars. Overall, four percent have lost more than 1 million US dollars in a cyberattack. The count is much more in the global market. Over the past couple of years, particularly, IT companies had developed strategies for assessing their Infrastructure, Digital Systems be it Web Applications or Mobile Applications, Network Devices, Source Code (through DevSecOps implementation) etc., engaging in Red and Blue Teaming activities, to ensure if all their ecosystem is secure enough and is safe to bring those systems over the internet. However, today's IT business doesn't rely only on the internal security assessment or framework that an organization is following. Let's consider an example: Suppose Organization "X" is bidding a project for a banking project from CUSTOMER "Y" which can significantly add to Organization's "X" revenue. As the project is from Banking/Financial sector, it would take significant efforts to convivence Customer "Y" regarding security frameworks that the organization is following w.r.t quality and control measures. Here Cybersecurity Rating platforms

Applying Artificial Intelligence in Cybersecurity Analytics and Cyber Threat Detection, First Edition.
Edited by Shilpa Mahajan, Mehak Khurana, and Vania Vieira Estrela.

come into picture, which can assess the Organization's "X" security in terms of various parameters like "Application Security, Network Security, End Point Security, IP Reputation." The ratings given by these platforms can play a significant role in the business, as achieving a good score or grade through these platforms can help convince customers to engage in project or to sign a deal, particularly in a project which requires greater level of security into consideration. Nowadays, many IT organizations to gain business are enrolling themselves in these Cybersecurity Rating platforms, to gain business and companies put constant efforts to maintain good score/grade or ratings from these platforms. As mentioned above in this section these Cybersecurity Rating platforms [2] tools assess the Organization's security in terms of various parameters like "Application Security, Network Security, End Point Security, IP Reputation," the organization enrolls to these tools, these platforms automatically figure out the scope and run several test cases on constant basis and they report vulnerabilities/misconfiguration details w.r.t above mentioned parameters.

Figure 5.1. illustrates the flow of the same and Figure 5.2 illustrates the scope of work for Cybersecurity Rating Platform.

Once any vulnerabilities are flagged in these platforms, the Security Score gets affected and decreased, and after that some efforts are given to get those identified issues remediated. Generally, IT or Server Operations Team, Application development, need to do most of these things; however, all these efforts are being done Manually, just like Security team monitors these platforms, they report the issue to concerned Digital team, and after that IT/Server Operations team or Application Development team gets involved to close the issues on time; however, the entire

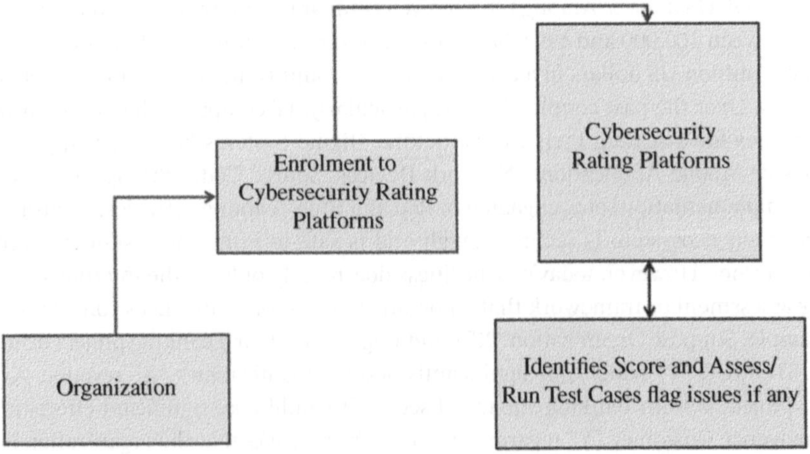

Figure 5.1 Enrolment to Cybersecurity rating platform.

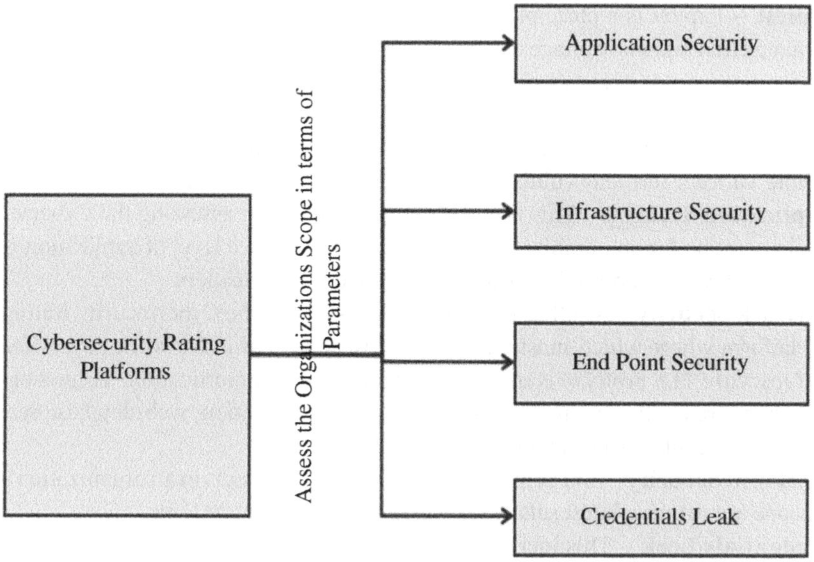

Figure 5.2 Scope and parameters of Cybersecurity rating platform taken into consideration.

process may be time-consuming and there may be lack of skill sets when it comes to close these issues. If these issues are not mitigated or closed on time, organization may negatively impact the organization in terms of business or revenue. As all the efforts to close these vulnerabilities depend on multiple groups within an organization and entire process for closing identified vulnerabilities is being done manually. Authors in this literature have proposed an automated framework to mitigate the Security Vulnerabilities in real time. Authors have leveraged AI and DevOps technologies in this literature for the same.

Before going into the in-depth details of the proposed framework, authors have done a literature survey explained in the next section, where the work done by other authors are mentioned and how this literature is unique.

Below are few key words that will be used quiet often in this literature.

Vulnerability – A vulnerability is a weakness which allows a hacker to compromise the security of a computer or network system.

Threat – A threat is a possible danger that can exploit an existing bug or vulnerability to compromise the security of a computer or network system.

Attack – In terms of hacking attack is defined as an attempt that is done on the computer system or network to gain access to the system with an intent to gain critical or sensitive information.

Exploit – Exploit is a piece of software, a chunk of data, or a sequence of commands that takes advantage of a bug or vulnerability to compromise the security of a computer or network system.

Zero-Day Exploit – A zero-day exploit is an unknown security vulnerability or software flaw that attackers specifically target with malicious code. This flaw or hole, called a zero-day vulnerability, can go unnoticed for years.

Application Security – This is one of the parameters for assessing the Cybersecurity rating for an organization, here mostly the surface level of application is assessed which is hosted over the internet like HTTP Headers.

Network Security – Another parameters for assessing the Cybersecurity Rating Platform where which mostly flagged the issue related to Network Layer, like if insecure TLS protocol is used or configured for communication, Vulnerable ciphers are configured in TLS protocol for communication, web/database service is accessible over the internet, etc.

End Point Security – End point security ensures all the assets in an organization's scope are running latest sets of softwares and Operating systems.

Credentials Leak – This identifies all the leaked credentials particularly those that are maintained at client-side code [JavaScript code], Source Code like GitHub, Bit-bucket public repositories, and in other source code management tools. Developers often mistakenly upload few sensitive information like Access keys, Database Passwords, Admin Credentials, SSH and SSL keys, and details of outdated dependencies over public repositories GitHub, Bit-bucket/Client Side JavaScript codes, etc. which can impact the organization badly. In this literature, authors have proposed a way to crawl the internet for such sensitive information over the internet and report to the business group once such issues are detected. Ideally, most of the Cybersecurity Ratings that are available only perform the activity over website, not at source code level (source code repository scan w.r.t credentials leak doesn't happen). In this literature, authors have proposed a crawler to do the same.

5.2 Literature Review

Daniel Kant and Johannsen Andreas [3], talks about AI Based use cases for enhancing Cybersecurity posture for small- and mid-size organizations, and have done literature survey to identify usable AI-based solution for enhancing cybersecurity defense for small- and mid-sized organization. Poltavtseva et al. [4] proposed an effective approach to formalizing information for Penetration Testing activities from subject domains, quantitative relevance estimates of object characteristics, and estimates of object similarity. AlSadhan, Tina et al. [5] talk about importance and existence of automation in Cybersecurity Operations, and the difficulties and challenges for achieving full-fledged ISCM, Information Security Monitoring capabilities like real-time threat detection and incidence response and risk-based decision-making capabilities. This research talks about redefining ISCM framework to enhance risk-based decision-making embedding security automation. Mohammad, Sikender Mohsienuddin et al. [6] talk about the need of automation in Cybersecurity domain, as this particular fields lack automation compared to other domains, in terms of testing for vulnerabilities, reporting vulnerabilities in real time, and mitigating the same. The authors talk in detail about the need of automation in security and incident management and how security automation can safeguard organization's technological systems. Aguirre, Idoia et al. [7] talk about presenting a collaborative strategy between Security Information and Event Manager from different trusted domains that share notification and the consequently adopted countermeasures. These have been based on traffic patterns related to offered online services. The concept of sharing alarms and adopted measures in domains with similar profiles, intends to enhance a global view of the security, and by this way, facilitates decision-making for security domain administrators. It is clear from this background study that there is a lot of scope for automation in Cybersecurity domain, hence authors have specifically chosen to use AI and DevOps for automation to increase cybersecurity ratings for an organization to grow business.

5.3 Proposed Methodology

Before proceeding to the system architecture and design, authors have first provided the GIST of various parameters and its attributes which are taken into consideration while processing the remediation of vulnerabilities which are taken into consideration by Cybersecurity Rating platforms. Tables 5.1–5.3 show descriptions of each parameter taken into consideration in this literature.

Authors in this literature have provided a unique ID for each of the vulnerabilities to process the mitigation of the issues. System Architecture of the proposed solution in this literature has been shown in Figure 5.3.

There are five main components of the proposed system. Authors have explained in this section in brief about all the modules.

Notification Module: Figure 5.4 shows the workflow of the notification module proposed in this literature, when the case or issue is flagged by Cybersecurity Rating platform, and Figure 5.5 shows the workflow of notification module during closure of the flagged issue or case.

This module will trigger notification to the user/Business owner regarding the issue flagged in the Cybersecurity Rating Platforms. It will generate the detailed notification regarding name of issue like Unique ID for tracking purpose,

Table 5.1 Description of application security parameter.

Application Security:			
Parameters	**Name/ID**	**Severity**	**Description**
Vulnerabilities in CMS	AppSec-V-01	**High**	Identifying Vulnerabilities with known CMS like WordPress, Joomla, Drupal, etc.
Site/IP does not support HTTPS	AppSec-V-02	**High**	Issue arises when Web application is transmitting data over plain text or using HTTP protocol
CSP Missing	AppSec-V-03	**Medium**	Issue arises when Web Application is missing Content Security Policy in HTTP response
Strict Transport Security Misconfigured	AppSec-V-04	**Medium**	Issues arises when application is missing strict transport security header/or hsts header is misconfigured (hsts value set apart from max-age = include Subdomain)
Insecure HTTPS redirect chain	AppSec-V-05	**Medium**	Issue arises when there is an insecure redirect in application either to external site
X-Frame-Options-Missing	AppSec-V-06	**Medium**	Issue arises when X-Frame-Options Header is missing from the Web Application HTTP response, and it makes application potentially vulnerable to Clickjacking and other UI Rendering attacks
Redirect Chain contains HTTP	AppSec-V-07	**Medium**	Issue arises when there is a redirect of request to a website where HTTPS is not implemented
Session Cookie missing HTTP Only flag	AppSec-V-08	**Low**	This issue arises when a cookie session on Set-Cookie attribute is missing HTTP Only flag
Session Cookie missing secure Attribute	AppSec-V-09	**Low**	This issue arises when a cookie session on Set-Cookie attribute is missing Secure flag
X-Content-Type-Option-Missing	AppSec-V-010	**Low**	Issue arises when application is missing X-Content-Type Options from the HTTP Response

Table 5.2 Description of endpoint security parameter.

End Point Security:			
Parameters	**Name/ID**	**Severity**	**Description**
Outdated Operating System Observed	EPSec-V-01	**High**	This issue arises when the any of the asset is running Outdated Operating System
Outdated Web Browser Observed	EPSec-V-02	**High**	This issue arises when the any of the asset is running Outdated Web Browsers in the system

Table 5.3 Description of infrastructure security parameter.

Infrastructure Security:			
Parameters	**Name/ID**	**Severity**	**Description**
Certificate is Revoked	InfSec-V-01	**High**	This issue arises when the TLS certificates used in the application are revoked
Elasticsearch Service and MongoDB Service Observed	InfSec-V-02	**High**	This issue arises when Elasticsearch and MongoDB services get detected over web
Neo4j Database and Oracle Database Server Accessible	InfSec-V-03	**High**	This issue arises when Database like Neo4j and Oracle DB server is accessible over the web
SSH Software Supports Vulnerable Protocol	InfSec-V-04	**High**	This issue arises when SSH Protocol is supporting vulnerable protocol during communication
SSL/TLS Service Supports Weak Protocol	InftSec-V-05	**High**	This issue arises when Application or Services is using TLS protocol less than version 1.2
Apache Cassandra and CouchDB Service Observed	InfSec-V-06	**Medium**	This issue arises when Apache Cassandra and Couch DB Service are observed over internet
Certificate is Expired	InfSec-V-07	**Medium**	This issue arises when any of the service which is running on TLS protocol and the TLS Certificate is expired
Certificate Signed with Weak Algorithm	InfSec-V-08	**Medium**	This issue arises when TLS certificate is using weak Algorithm with inadequate strength
Weak MAC, Microsoft SQL Server, PPTP, PostgreSQL, RDP, Redis, Remote Access, SMB Service, resync Service, VNC Service Observed	InfSec-V-09	**Medium**	This issue arises when the mentioned service is detected over the internet and few of the protocols or services uses weak MAC algorithm
SSH Supports Weak Cipher and Weak MAC	InfSec-V-10	**Medium**	This issue arises when the SSH Service which is using weak cipher keys and mac algorithms over the internet
FTP Service, Telnet Observed	InfSec-V-11	**Low**	This issue arises when FTP service is detected over the internet
IP Camera Accessible	InfSec-V-12	**Low**	This issue arises when any of the device having camera service is accessible over the internet. This is kept out of this literature

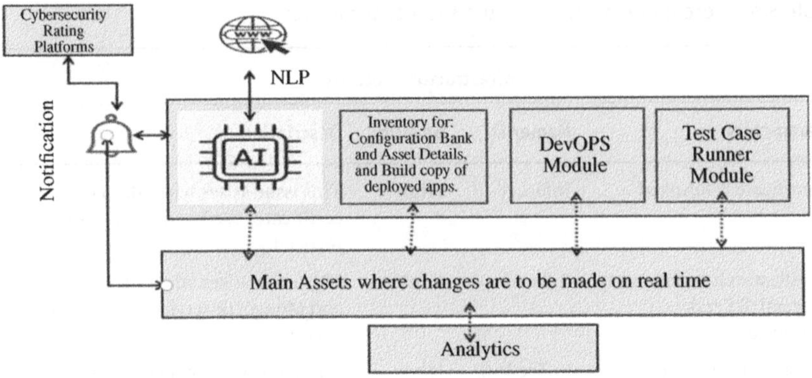

Figure 5.3 System architecture.

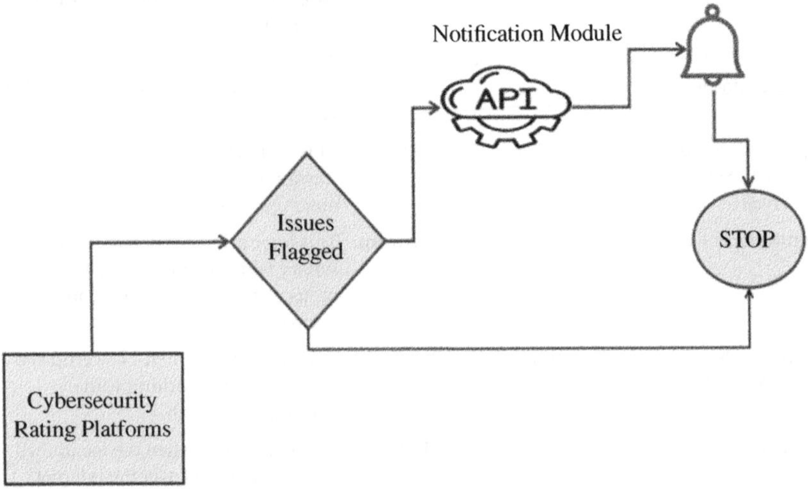

Figure 5.4 Workflow for logging an issue.

IP/DNS/Website the issue is flagged, its severity, and overall score impact for the organization. Figure 5.6 shows the details of Notification in JSON Format.

Later according to the proposed framework, these reported issues will be first evaluated internally by the DevOps module powered by AI to check if the reported issue is true positive or false positive. If it is false positive, evidence will be generated and log will be forwarded against the Issue ID, in Cybersecurity rating platforms, for closing the logged issues. If the issue is true positive, then again, the proposed DevOps module powered by AI will be activated, and it will create a Sand

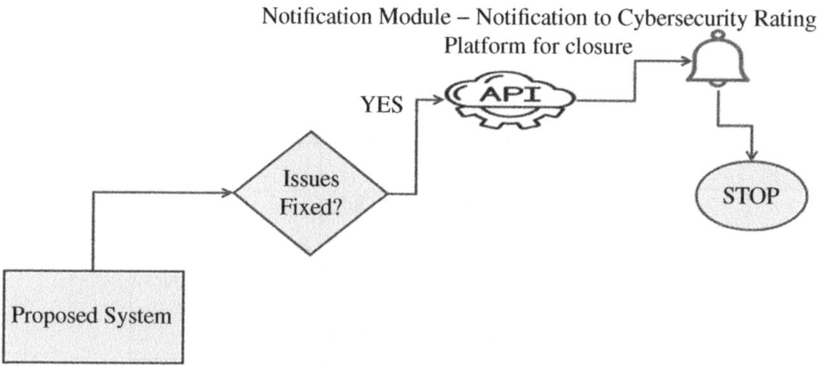

Figure 5.5 Workflow for closure of the issue.

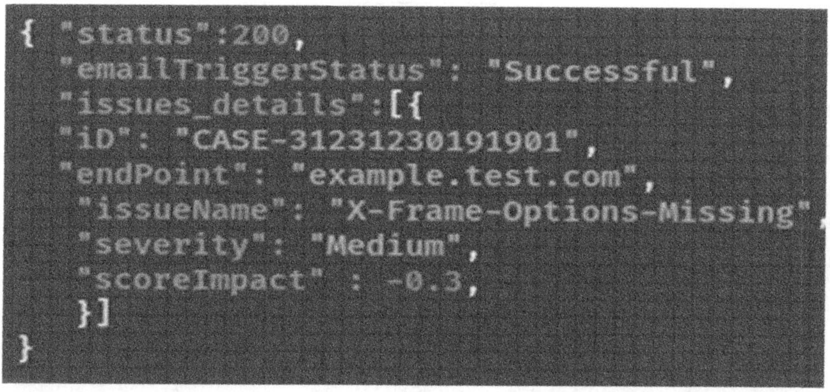

```
{ "status":200,
  "emailTriggerStatus": "Successful",
  "issues_details":[{
  "iD": "CASE-31231230191901",
  "endPoint": "example.test.com",
   "issueName": "X-Frame-Options-Missing",
   "severity": "Medium",
   "scoreImpact" : -0.3,
   }]
}
```


Figure 5.6 Sample of Notification Data/Response in JSON Format.

Box environment (Say a docker-based container), which is explained in detail later in this section.

Workflow of the same is shown below in Figure 5.7.

After successfully applying the patch or remediating the vulnerabilities, the sample response in JSON format for notification purposes is shown in Figure 5.8.

AI Module: This module is used to train the entire system on how to respond and to initiate the mitigation of vulnerabilities on real time, with the help of underlying DevOps platform. DevOps module will do the execution but what sort of commands, and configuration files are to be loaded and which tools are to be used will be defined by this module. It will be in sync with various libraries like (nginx, apache2, httpd, tomcat, sshd, etc.). The idea is to create a set of secure configuration files when it comes to application security where all the findings

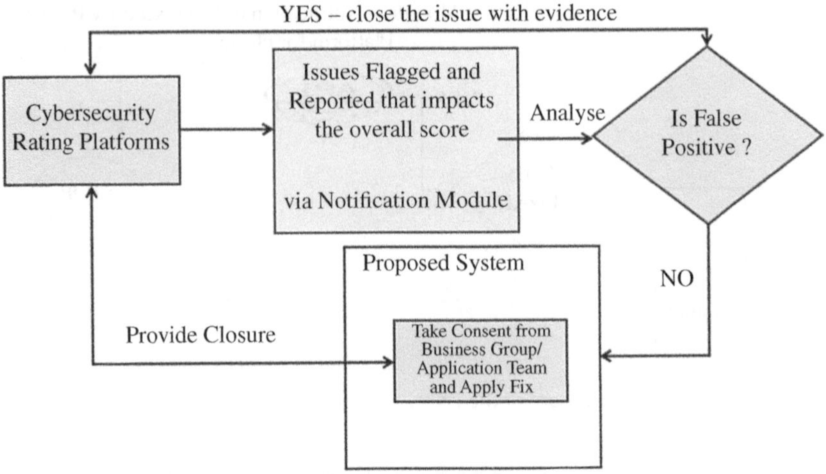

Figure 5.7 Flow for validating the issue and closure of the same.


```
{
    "status": 200,
    "emailTriggeredStatus": "Successful",
    "closureDeatils":[{
     "iD": "CASE-31231230191901",
     "endPoint": "example.test.com",
     "issueName": "X-Frame-Options-Missing",
     "severity": "Medium",
     "scoreImpact" : -0.3,
     "status": "Closed or Fixed",
     "closureEvidence": "X-Frame-Options: SAMEORIGIN value added"
  }]
}
```


Figure 5.8 Sample JSON Data for closure.

are generally related to HTTP Headers, those configs are easily available over the internet, and AI module proposed in this system will leverage the NLP-based module and will create a configuration bank out of that information available over the internet. Authors in this section are committed to make the usage of AI more effectively and work is in progress. Here for experimentation, authors have created arbitrary set of configuration files in the inventory, like nginx.conf[Web Server], apache2.conf[Web Server], sshd.conf [For SSHing to server], server.xml[Tomcat Web Server], server.js[Node.JS], config.php[PHP Framework], commands for uninstalling outdated software's, command for upgrading package or system level kernels, and all these are mostly tested on Linux and Windows Server

Environments as most of the Digital applications in enterprise systems are hosted these platforms only.

Inventory: This is the store for all the commands that our system will going to trigger, all the configuration files that are to be loaded while mitigating the vulnerabilities, SSL Certificates, and build or replica of application that is deployed and running live. Other than that this module will also have an asset mapping file where the public IP, Intranet IP mapping/DNS mapping are being done, and what all services or applications are running on the systems are provided. This file will help in identifying where the patch or remediation will actually going to be applied as the system proposed by the authors will be running over the VLAN of the organization ideally. Further this system is configured in such a way that it can access all the servers or assets running in the system through various DevOps module which authors have taken into consideration.

DevOps Module: This module is about using DevOps [8] technologies to automate every operation. What to execute is something that will be decided by AI Module as per the proposed methodologies by authors; however, here authors have created pre-sets of configurations and have used certain flags for the experimentation purposes. Authors in this environment have majorly used containerized [9] environment to test the execution and also run the test cases against mitigation.

Test Case Runner Module: This is one of the important aspects and feature of the entire proposed system. As for the business, it is very important to ensure whatever the changes that are being made in terms of vulnerability mitigation is not impacting the overall liveliness of the system, as if the system or application is not working as expected after applying the fix it will impact the overall business of an organization and may impact the revenue. So, this module will ensure to apply the patch or remediation to the live system only after testing the same in sandbox or containerized environment and also will run some test cases to ensure production/live system is working as expected.

Authors have given an example to understand the overall workflow of all the modules explained above. Suppose a vulnerability is reported by CSRP saying X-Frame-Options Header is missing from the Application running URL https://test.example.com. Actually, X-Frame-Options Headers are used to prevent applications from Click-jacking and UI Rendering attacks, it is given as Low to Medium Severity in OWASP Category, in this literature it is marked as Medium Severity Vulnerability. Now there will be an internal schema of the above URL, i.e., domain - test.example.com must have been hosted over internet and is assigned some Public IPs which ideally is mapped to some Private IP (Virtual LAN IP of the organization's internal network). Table – Sample Table 1.1 below illustrates the same.

Sample Table 1.1

Domain	Public IP	Internal/Private IP
test.example.com	1.1.1.1	10.X.X.X

All these details will be mentioned in the inventory like which Domain has been assigned which Public IP and which Public IP is mapped to which Internal IP, and the inventory will also hold other details like Web Application details like on which web server Web Application is running, and on which Operating system the Web Application is running, location of the build, etc., so the inventory details will look something like shown in Sample Table 1.2.

Sample Table 1.2

Domain	Public IP	Internal / Private IP	Web server and build details	OS details
test.example.com	1.1.1.1	10.X.X.X	nginx version = 1.22.1 build = call_for_papers.zip	Ubuntu 22.10 LTS

First AI module with some preexisting commands will verify if the reported issue from Cybersecurity Rating Platform is valid or not, if it is invalid it will submit the snap or evidence to close the issue using API Integration that is supposed to be done with Cybersecurity Rating platforms. If the reported issue is true positive then AI will leverage the NLP feature and will fetch the secure nginx configuration file from the internet and will update the inventory with latest set of configurations, only if the existing nginx configuration in the inventory is not addressing the X-Frame-Options-Missing issue. However, in this literature, authors have used a static secure nginx configuration, shown in below Figure 5.9 to address the issue.

A Docker containerized environment will be created with nginx Build image and Web Application build will also be placed, after extracting call_for_papers.zip mentioned in Sample Table 5.1. And later all the test cases will be executed like web servers running status, login module, and after providing credentials, if application is able to navigate to the dashboard page or not, Session details from database can also be captured to check the same. If everything works out well, the same changes will be replicated to the production or live system (10.X.X.X) and later only liveness of web server will be tested to check if the nginx web server is up and running, and Business owner will be notified using notification module and the issue/case flagged by the CSRP will be submitted for closure using evidence, later CSRP can validate and close the issue from their end.

```
server {
 charset utf-8;
 listen  443 ssl;
 ssl_stapling on;
 add_header Strict-Transport-Security "max-age=63072000" always;
 ssl_certificate      /etc/nginx/ssl-new-2022/ssl-bundle.crt;
 ssl_certificate_key  /etc/nginx/ssl-new-2022/keyFile.key;
 ssl_protocols TLSv1.2 TLSv1.3;
 proxy_set_header Host $host;
 proxy_set_header X-Forwarded-For $remote_addr;
 if ( $host !~* ^(test.example.com$ ) {
          return 403;
  }
 if ($http_x_forwarded_host !~* ^(test.example.com)$) {
            return 403;
   }
 location ~/ {
   add_header Cache-Control "no-store";
   add_header "Pragma" "no-cache";
   etag off;
   server_tokens off;
   add_header X-XSS-Protection "1; mode=block";
   add_header X-Frame-Options "SAMEORIGIN";
   add_header Strict-Transport-Security "max-age=63072000" always;
   add_header X-Content-Type-Options nosniff;
   add_header Referrer-Policy "strict-origin";
   add_header Set-Cookie "Path=/; HttpOnly; Secure";
   add_header Permissions-Policy "geolocation=(),midi=(),sync-xhr=(),microphone=(),camera=(),magnetometer=(),gyroscope=(),fullscreen=(self),payment=()";
   add_header Content-Security-Policy "default-src 'self' 'unsafe-inline' test.example.com:9443; script-src 'self' 'unsafe-inline' test.example.com; img-src 'self'
data: https:; frame-ancestors 'self'; object-src 'none';";
   root /var/www/html/build/;
   try_files $uri /index.html;
  }
}
```

Figure 5.9 Secure Nginx configuration file.

If any of the test cases gets failed or liveness of the system is affected, all the operations will be rolled back business owner or Application development team will be notified with the issues, score impact, and some remediation to close the issue.

5.4 Results

5.4.1 First Notification Regarding Issues Flagged by Cybersecurity Rating Platform

5.4.1.1 Whenever Any Issues Are Flagged to the Cybersecurity Rating Platform

APIs are triggered automatically from the Cybersecurity ratings platform – to notify the system proposed, and internally the proposed system notify the business groups and other concerned team regarding the issue.

Authors have developed their APIs to integrate their internal systems with third party Cybersecurity Rating Platforms.

Figures 5.10 and 5.11 show the API request and API Response for notifications.

These issues will be flagged on constant basis and will notify the concerned team.

5.4.2 Checking False Positive and True Positive

5.4.2.1 Validate and Close the Reported Findings – A Case of False Positive Reported Issue

Figures 5.12 and 5.13 show the API request and API Response for validating issues flagged by Cybersecurity Rating Platform, and Figure 5.14 shows the background commands for validating the same.

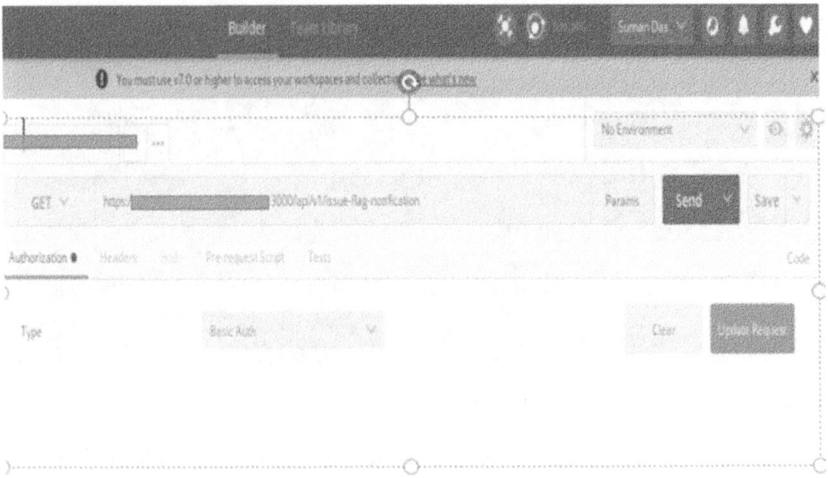

Figure 5.10 API Request for triggering notification for flagging issues.

Figure 5.11 API Response for notification related to flagging issues.

Once this request is submitted, cybersecurity rating platforms will automatically close the issue after validating the same from their end and security rating or grade will again increase.

5.4.2.2 Mitigating Vulnerabilities in Realtime with the Proposed System

Validating the vulnerabilities will be as is as mentioned above. Later applying patch/mitigation will be executed by DevOps module, by referring to the Configuration Bank. Figure 5.15 shows validation of the same, and Figures 5.16 and 5.17 show API request and API Response for applying the fix or mitigation.

Figure 5.12 API Request for validating the issue.

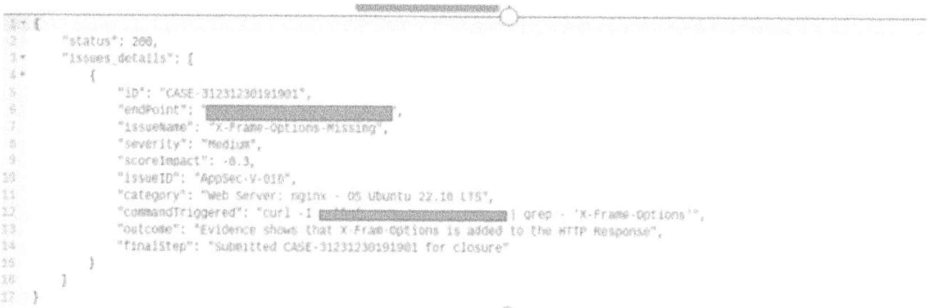

Figure 5.13 API Response for validating the issue.

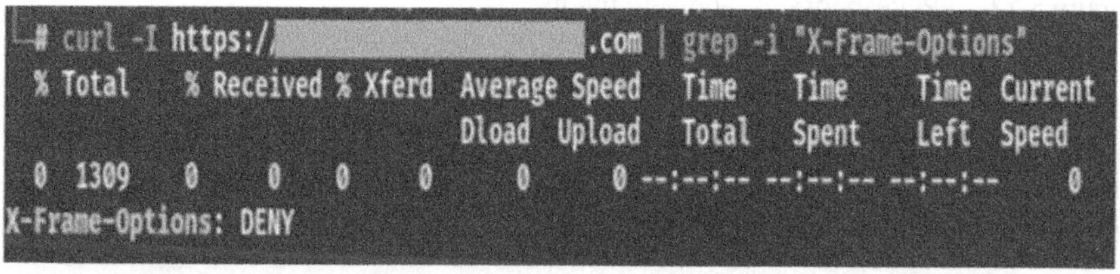
curl -I https://[redacted].com | grep -i "X-Frame-Options"
% Total % Received % Xferd Average Speed Time Time Time Current
Dload Upload Total Spent Left Speed
0 1309 0 0 0 0 0 0 --:--:-- --:--:-- --:--:-- 0
X-Frame-Options: DENY

Figure 5.14 Sample of Background command for validating the issue.

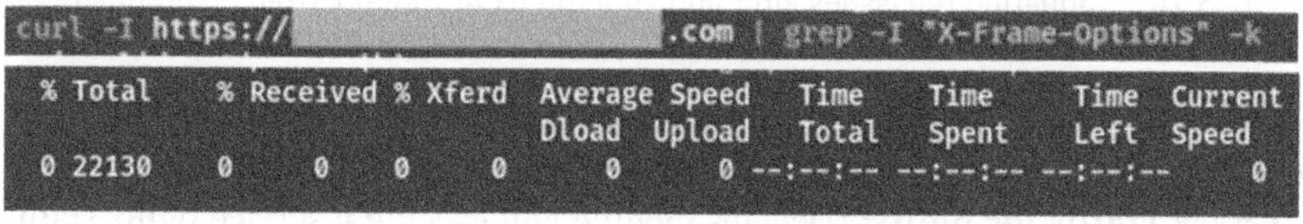
curl -I https://[redacted].com | grep -I "X-Frame-Options" -k
% Total % Received % Xferd Average Speed Time Time Time Current
Dload Upload Total Spent Left Speed
0 22130 0 0 0 0 0 0 --:--:-- --:--:-- --:--:-- 0

Figure 5.15 Shows that X-frame-Options Header is missing from the application.

Check for test cases after applying the fix on containerized/sandbox environment, Figure 5.18 shows the same.

Figure to show that X-Frame-Options Headers are added to the HTTP response.

Nginx Configuration File before applying fix: Figure 5.19 shows the snap of config before applying a fix.

GET
https:/[redacted]:3000/api/v1/apply-fix
Params
Send
Save
Authorization
Type
OAuth 2.0

Figure 5.16 API Request for applying the fix.

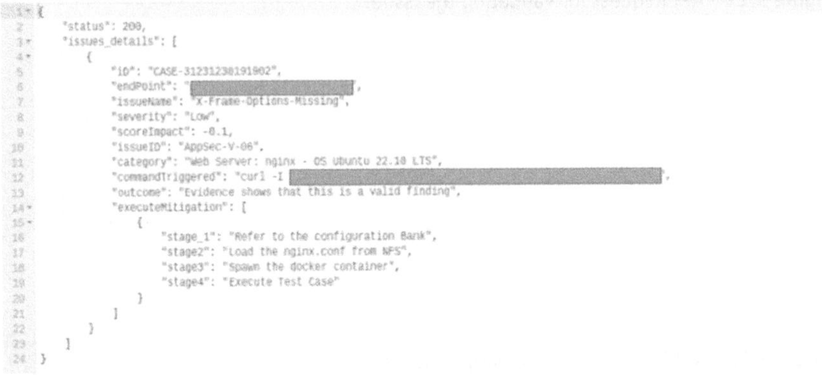
{
"status": 200,
"issues_details": [
{
"ID": "CASE-31231230191902",
"endPoint": "[redacted]",
"issueName": "X-Frame-Options-Missing",
"severity": "Low",
"scoreImpact": -0.1,
"issueID": "AppSec-V-06",
"category": "Web Server: nginx - OS Ubuntu 22.10 LTS",
"commandTriggered": "curl -I [redacted]",
"outcome": "Evidence shows that this is a valid finding",
"executeMitigation": [
{
"stage_1": "Refer to the configuration Bank",
"stage2": "Load the nginx.conf from NFS",
"stage3": "Spawn the docker container",
"stage4": "Execute Test Case"
}
]
}
]
}

Figure 5.17 API Response for applying the fix.

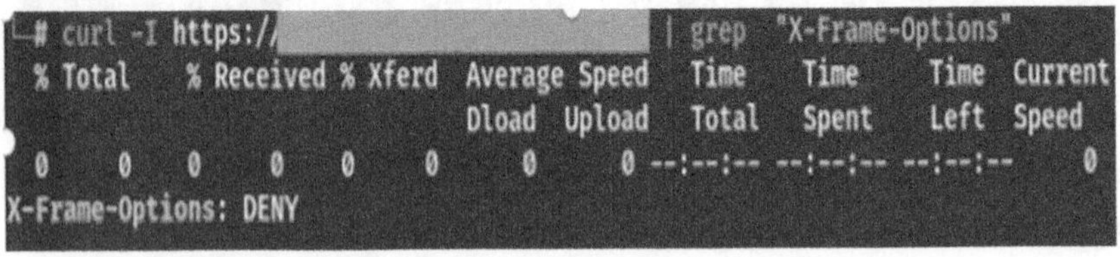
curl -I https:/[redacted] | grep "X-Frame-Options"
% Total % Received % Xferd Average Speed Time Time Time Current
Dload Upload Total Spent Left Speed
0 0 0 0 0 0 0 0 --:--:-- --:--:-- --:--:-- 0
X-Frame-Options: DENY

Figure 5.18 Validating the issues after applying the fix in containerized environment.

Nginx Config file after applying fix: Figure 5.20 shows the snap of config after applying fix.

Check status for nginx: [DevOps module will execute # service nginx status on containerized env] and will show below status. Figure 5.21 shows the live status of nginx web server.

Since status is up and running then commit the changes and mount the configuration file in the actual file and server.

Before that, the system will take approval or consent from Business team/ Application development team to take the consent. As of now, author has created an email-based notification and consent-taking system which will be sent to

```
server {
  charset utf-8;
  listen  443 ssl;
  ssl_stapling on;
  add_header Strict-Transport-Security "max-age=63072000" always;
  ssl_certificate      /etc/nginx/ssl-new-2022/ssl-bundle.crt;
  ssl_certificate_key  /etc/nginx/ssl-new-2022/keyFile.key;
  ssl_protocols TLSv1.2 TLSv1.3;
  proxy_set_header Host $host;
  proxy_set_header X-Forwarded-For $remote_addr;
  if ( $host !~* ^(test.example.com$ ) {
            return 403;
   }
  if ($http_x_forwarded_host !~* ^(test.example.com)$) {
              return 403;
    }
  location ~/ {
    add_header Cache-Control "no-store";
    add_header "Pragma" "no-cache";
    etag off;
    server_tokens off;
    add_header X-XSS-Protection "1; mode=block";
    add_header Strict-Transport-Security "max-age=63072000" always;
    add_header X-Content-Type-Options nosniff;
    add_header Referrer-Policy "strict-origin";
    add_header Set-Cookie "Path=/; HttpOnly; Secure";
    add_header Permissions-Policy "geolocation=(),midi=(),sync-xhr=(),microphone=(),camera=(),magnetometer=(),gyroscope=(),fullscreen=(self),payment=()";
    add_header Content-Security-Policy "default-src 'self' 'unsafe-inline' test.example.com:9443; script-src 'self' 'unsafe-inline' test.example.com; img-src 'self'
data: https:; frame-ancestors 'self'; object-src 'none';";
    root /var/www/html/build/;
    try_files $uri /index.html;
  }
}
```

Figure 5.19 Nginx configuration file before applying fix.

```
server {
  charset utf-8;
  listen  443 ssl;
  ssl_stapling on;
  add_header Strict-Transport-Security "max-age=63072000" always;
  ssl_certificate      /etc/nginx/ssl-new-2022/ssl-bundle.crt;
  ssl_certificate_key  /etc/nginx/ssl-new-2022/keyFile.key;
  ssl_protocols TLSv1.2 TLSv1.3;
  proxy_set_header Host $host;
  proxy_set_header X-Forwarded-For $remote_addr;
  if ( $host !~* ^(test.example.com$ ) {
            return 403;
   }
  if ($http_x_forwarded_host !~* ^(test.example.com)$) {
              return 403;
    }
  location ~/ {
    add_header Cache-Control "no-store";
    add_header "Pragma" "no-cache";
    etag off;
    server_tokens off;
    add_header X-XSS-Protection "1; mode=block";
    add_header X-Frame-Options "SAMEORIGIN";
    add_header Strict-Transport-Security "max-age=63072000" always;
    add_header X-Content-Type-Options nosniff;
    add_header Referrer-Policy "strict-origin";
    add_header Set-Cookie "Path=/; HttpOnly; Secure";
    add_header Permissions-Policy "geolocation=(),midi=(),sync-xhr=(),microphone=(),camera=(),magnetometer=(),gyroscope=(),fullscreen=(self),payment=()";
    add_header Content-Security-Policy "default-src 'self' 'unsafe-inline' test.example.com:9443; script-src 'self' 'unsafe-inline' test.example.com; img-src 'self'
data: https:; frame-ancestors 'self'; object-src 'none';";
    root /var/www/html/build/;
    try_files $uri /index.html;
  }
}
```

Figure 5.20 Nginx configuration file after applying fix.

concerned Application Owner and its development or IT team. Figures 5.22–5.24 show the consent or approval flow for the same.

Notification at Application Development teams end:

Once the request or consent is approved by the team, then only the system will apply the patch or fix in the system.

Closure for the mitigated vulnerabilities: Figure 5.25 shows API Request for closure of the issue against which Patch, or fix is applied and Figure 5.26 shows API Response of the same.

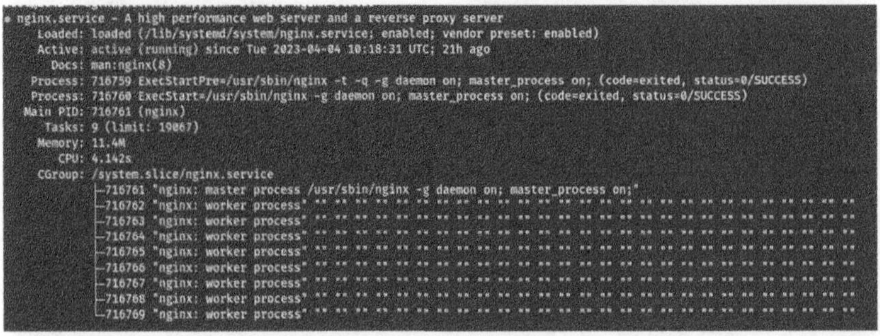

Figure 5.21 Snap of nginx web server is up and running.

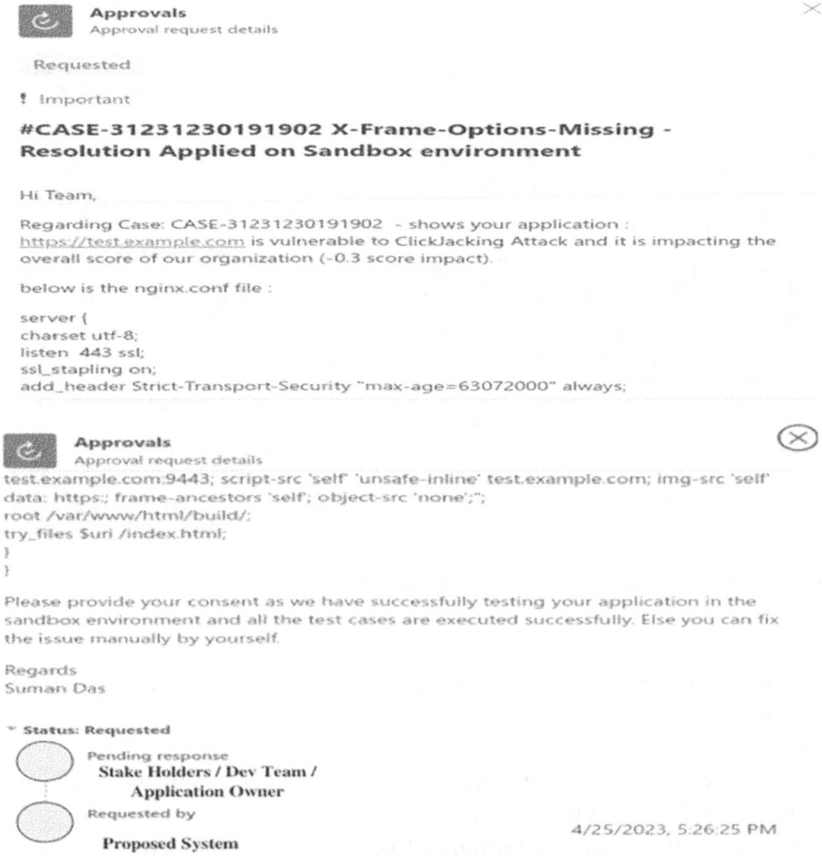

Figure 5.22 Approval or consent workflow generated by the system.

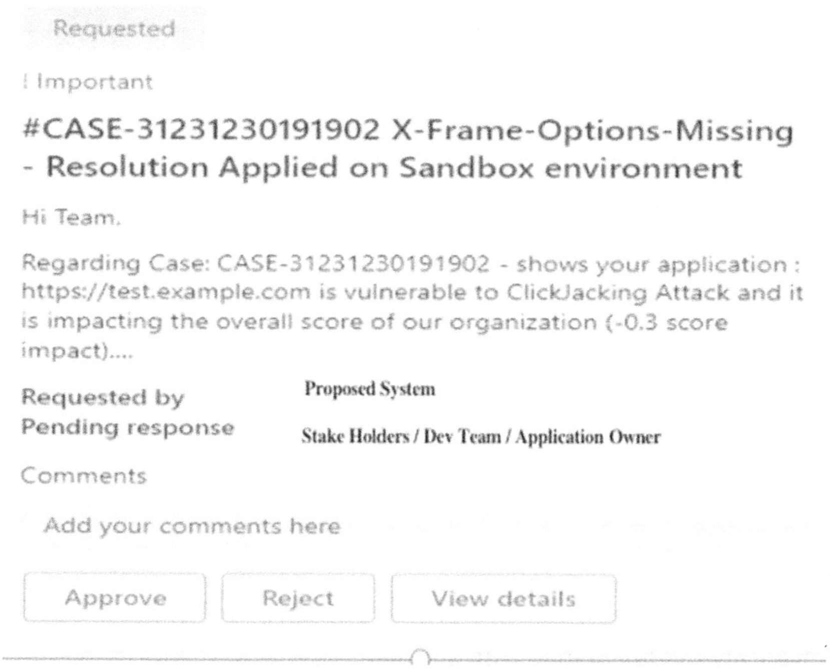
Requested
! Important
#CASE-31231230191902 X-Frame-Options-Missing - Resolution Applied on Sandbox environment
Hi Team.
Regarding Case: CASE-31231230191902 - shows your application : https://test.example.com is vulnerable to ClickJacking Attack and it is impacting the overall score of our organization (-0.3 score impact)....
Requested by
Pending response
Proposed System
Stake Holders / Dev Team / Application Owner
Comments
Add your comments here
Approve
Reject
View details

Figure 5.23 Approval or consent workflow pending at concerned team.

Approved
! Important
#CASE-31231230191902 X-Frame-Options-Missing - Resolution Applied on Sandbox...
Hi Team,
Regarding Case: CASE-31231230191902 - shows your application : https://test.example.com is vulnerable to ClickJacking Attack and it is impacting the overall score of our organization (-0.3 score impact)....
Requested by
Approved by
Proposed System
Stake Holders / Dev Team / Application Owner
View details

Figure 5.24 Consent approved.

GET
https:[redacted]3000/api/v1/closure
Params
Send
Authorization
Type
OAuth 2.0

Figure 5.25 API Request for closure.

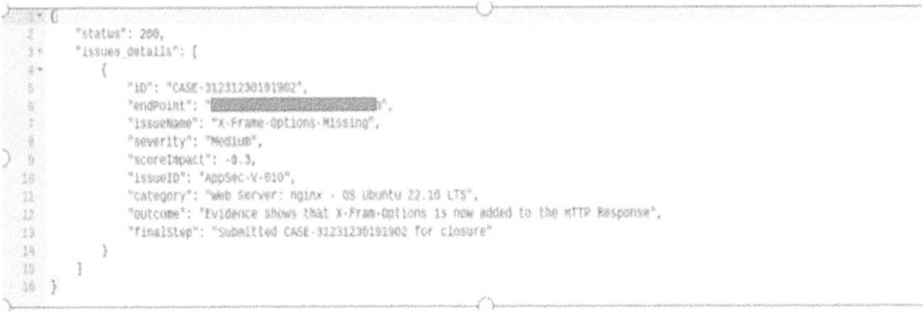
{
"status": 200,
"issues_details": [
{
"ID": "CASE-31231230191902",
"endPoint": "[redacted]",
"issueName": "X-Frame-Options-Missing",
"severity": "Medium",
"scoreImpact": -0.3,
"issueID": "AppSec-V-010",
"category": "Web Server: nginx - OS Ubuntu 22.10 LTS",
"outcome": "Evidence shows that X-Fram-Options is now added to the HTTP Response",
"finalStep": "Submitted CASE-31231230191902 for closure"
}
]
}

Figure 5.26 API Response for closure.

Table of experimentation with outcome:

Tables 5.3–5.5 show the success rate for all the issues flagged (in 30 iterations on various applications and servers), for Application Security, Network Security, and End Point Security, respectively.

Table 5.4 Experimentation on application security issues.

Parameter	Issue ID	Fixed	Expected success rate on 30 iterations in %
Vulnerabilities in CMS	AppSec-V-01	Yes	93.33
Site/IP does not support HTTPS	AppSec-V-02	Yes	90.00
CSP Missing	AppSec-V-03	Yes	80
Strict Transport Security Misconfigured	AppSec-V-04	Yes	100
Insecure HTTPS redirect chain	AppSec-V-05	Yes	83.33
X-Frame-Options-Missing	AppSec-V-06	Yes	100
Redirect Chain contains HTTP	AppSec-V-07	Yes	100
Session Cookie missing HTTP Only flag	AppSec-V-08	Yes	100
Session Cookie missing secure Attribute	AppSec-V-09	Yes	100
X-Content-Type-Option-Missing	AppSec-V-010	Yes	100

Table 5.5 Experimentation on network security issues.

Parameter	Issue ID	Fixed	Expected success rate on 30 iterations in %
Certificate Is Revoked	InfSec-V-01	Yes	80
Elasticsearch Service and MongoDB Service Observed	InfSec-V-02	Yes	100
Neo4j Database and Oracle Database Server Accessible	InfSec-V-03	Yes	100
SSH Software Supports Vulnerable Protocol	InfSec-V-04	Yes	100
SSL/TLS Service Supports Weak Protocol	InfSec-V-05	Yes	93.33
Apache Cassandra and CouchDB Service Observed	InfSec-V-06	Yes	100
Certificate Is Expired	InfSec-V-07	Yes	100
Certificate Signed with Weak Algorithm	InfSec-V-08	Yes	100
Weak MAC, Microsoft SQL Server, PPTP, PostgreSQL, RDP, Redis, Remote Access, SMB Service, resync Service, VNC Service Observed	InfSec-V-09	Yes	100
SSH Supports Weak Cipherand Weak MAC	InfSec-V-10	Yes	100
FTP Service, Telnet Observed	InfSec-V-11	Yes	100
IP Camera Accessible	InfSec-V-12	Yes	NA

Table 5.6 Experimentation on endpoint security issues.

Parameter	Issue ID	Fixed	Expected success rate on 30 iterations in %
Outdated Operating System Observed	EPSec-V-01	Yes	100
Outdated Web Browser Observed	EPSec-V-02	Yes	100

Figure 5.27 GitHub crawling module for identifying sensitive information over GitHub.

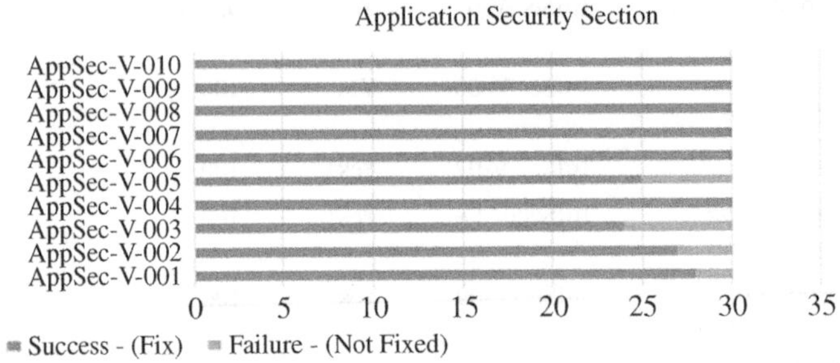

Figure 5.28 Analytical Representation of Application Security Section or Table 5.4.

Credentials Leak: Figure 5.27 shows the crawling modules created for GitHub Dorking.

This module will generate the results in CSV or Excel format and from there some manual checks need to be done for reassuring whether or not the generated results have identified some sensitive information or not. Later this information will be sent out to Development team and business owner for the closure. This module will eventually ensure that before application is going live there is no sensitive information or hard-coded credentials present in the live website/client side JavaScript code.

Analytics: Figures 5.28–5.30 show graphical or analytical representation of Tables 5.4–5.6.

5.5 Conclusion and Future Scope of Work

In this literature, authors have discussed importance of Vulnerability Management in regard to Cybersecurity Rating Platforms, which assess the overall security posture at surface level of an organization and give grade or score.

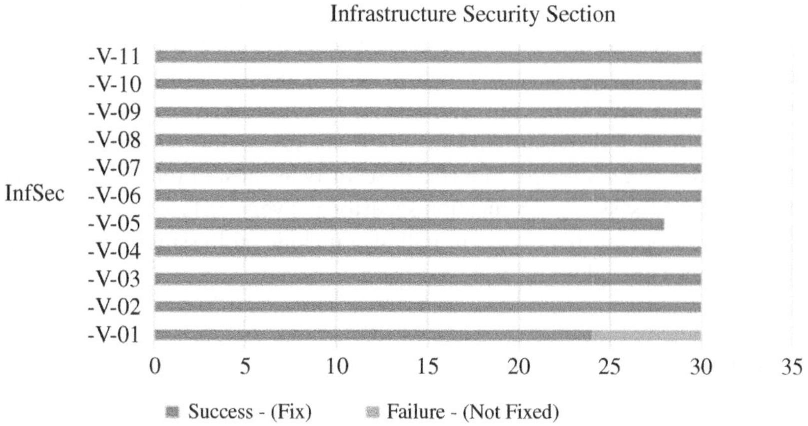

Figure 5.29 Analytical Representation of Network Security Section or Table 5.5.

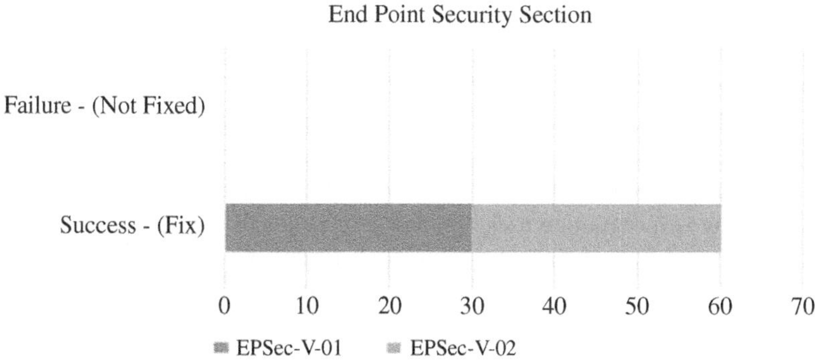

Figure 5.30 Analytical Representation of Endpoint Security Section or Table 5.6.

These scores/grades help the organization to attract business. In this literature, authors have taken into consideration three parameters which are commonly used by Cybersecurity rating (like Application, Network, and End Point Security) platforms for assessing the overall security score for an organization. Authors also have discussed the issues related to the mitigation strategy for the security vulnerabilities reported by Cybersecurity Rating platforms, like lack of awareness, skill set, and automation strategy across organizations, etc. Authors in this literature have proposed a DevOps powered by AI to mitigate and remediate the vulnerabilities reported by Cybersecurity Rating Platforms in real time. Experimentation was also done against each category and subcategory of vulnerabilities and all the vulnerabilities that were taken into consideration were executed successfully. However, AI and NLP which will be the driving force for this work is under progress and is putted under future scope of work for this literature. Here all the experimentation was done based on the preexisting dictionary or configuration sets, which ideally as per the proposal should be fetched from the various authentic sources over the internet. Also, holding a good security score from Cybersecurity rating platforms doesn't necessarily mean the organization has great strength in terms of security as most of the Cybersecurity rating platforms assess the organization security at a very surface level (minimal level). Future scope of this literature will also include addressing or mitigating Zero Day attacks or exploits on real-time basis.

References

1. Statista, *Monetary Loss of Companies in the United States as a Result of Cyber Attacks as of 2022* https://www.statista.com/statistics/1334399/us-common-results-of-cyber-attacks/ (Accessed 2 February 2023).
2. Wikipedia, *Cyber Security Rating*: https://en.wikipedia.org/wiki/Cybersecurity_rating (Accessed 03 February 2023).
3. Kant, Daniel & Johannsen, Andreas. (2022). *Evaluation of AI-based use cases for enhancing the cyber security defense of small and medium-sized companies (SMEs).*
4. Maria, P. and Pechenkin, A. (2017). Intelligent data analysis in decision support systems for penetration tests. *Automatic Control and Computer Sciences* 51: 985–991. https://doi.org/10.3103/S014641161708017X.
5. AlSadhan, Tina & Park, Joon. (2016). *Enhancing Risk-Based Decisions by Leveraging Cyber Security Automation*, 164–167. https://doi.org/10.1109/EISIC.2016.042.
6. Mohammad, S.M. and Surya, L. (2018). Security automation in information technology. *SSRN Electronic Journal* 6: 901–905. https://doi.org/10.1729/Journal.24048.
7. Aguirre, I. and Alonso, S. (2012). Improving the automation of security information management tools. A collaborative approach. *Security & Privacy, IEEE* 10: 1–1. https://doi.org/10.1109/MSP.2011.153.
8. Erich, F., Amrit, C., and Daneva, M. (2017). A qualitative study of DevOps usage in practice. *Journal of Software: Evolution and Process* https://doi.org/10.1002/smr.1885.
9. Biener, Adam & Crawford, Andrea. (2019). *DevOps for Containerized Applications.* Date of Indexing: https://doi.org/10.1007/978-3-319-94229-2_4

Part II

Cyber Threat Detection and Analysis Using Artificial Intelligence and Big Data

6

Malware Analysis Techniques in Android-Based Smartphone Applications

Geetika Munjal, Avi Chakravarti, and Utkarsh Sharma

Amity School of Engineering and Technology, Amity University, Noida, Uttar Pradesh, India

6.1 Introduction

Due to a decline in price and an expansion of features and services, mobile devices like smartphones and tablets have recently gained a lot of popularity. Additionally, the increasing trend of bringing your own device (BYOD) regulations into organizations has facilitated the adoption of these technologies. These policies encourage the use of such technologies for routine communication and to support commercial transactions and enterprise systems, all of which pose new security threats. Operating systems have also been crucial in this situation for the acceptance and growth of mobile devices and apps, allowing for the emergence of harmful malware [1]. This is true of the Android OS, as it has grown to be a significant part of the market for mobile devices as well as an appealing target for hackers because it is an open-source OS.

The Android development community, the Open Handset Alliance manufacturers, and Google have collectively put a lot of effort to increase the security of Android. Yet new security threats continue to appear and develop, and this is a significant concern [2]. This chapter presents some recent results and trends in the study of Android malware analysis and detection. This chapter first provides a quick overview of the security model for Android before moving on to a review of various static, dynamic, and hybrid malware detection and analysis methodologies. Following that, a comparative study between the malware analysis methodologies is provided.

6.1.1 Android Security Architecture

Android is not just an operating system but also a platform made up of the device hardware, Android OS, and application runtime. Firstly, the term "Android device

Applying Artificial Intelligence in Cybersecurity Analytics and Cyber Threat Detection, First Edition.
Edited by Shilpa Mahajan, Mehak Khurana, and Vania Vieira Estrela.

hardware block" refers to the diverse variety of hardware setups on which Android may be used, including smartphones, smart TVs, tablets, watches, and cars [3]. Although Android is a processor-independent OS, it does utilize some security features specific to hardware like ARM eXecute-Never. Secondly, the "Android OS building block" refers to the operating system itself, which is based on the Linux kernel and through which all device resources are accessed. Thirdly, the managed runtime that apps and some system services on Android employ is called the "Android application runtime block" [4]. The fact that apps are created in Java and run on the Android runtime (ART) must be considered in this situation. However, a large number of programs, including the essential services and programs for Android, are native programs or contain native libraries [5]. The same security environment, controlled by the apps sandbox, is used to execute both ART and native programs. Applications now have their own area of the file system where they may store sensitive information like databases and raw files [6].

A number of important security features are offered by Android, including strong OS-level security provided by the Linux kernel, a requirement that all applications run in sandboxes, secure process-to-process communication, application signing, and permissions that are both application-defined and user-granted [7].

The security capabilities made available by the Linux kernel are also utilized by the Android security model. The kernel separates the user resources from each other on a Linux system, which is a multi-user OS, much as it does with processes [8]. As a result, unless expressly permitted, a user cannot access a file owned by another user, and each process runs under the user's identity that initiated it. Since distinct physical users did not need to be registered with the system when Android was first created, the physical user is implicit and UIDs are utilized to differentiate applications instead. This is the foundation for Android's application sandboxing [9].

6.1.2 Android Attack Surface

The qualities of a target that make it susceptible to security attacks are referred to as its "attack surface." The method by which an attacker launches an attack is referred to as an attack vector [10]. The code that an attacker may run and therefore attack is referred to as the "attack surface" in other terms. An attack surface, in contrast to an attack vector, indicates where in-code vulnerabilities could be lurking and waiting to be found, without depending on the attackers' activities or requiring a vulnerability to be present. Generally, the amount of system interfaces a target has closely relates to the size of its attack surface [11].

It is possible to attack or defend a system more efficiently by concentrating on specific dangerous attack surfaces. While determining attack surfaces, several factors are crucial, such as attack vectors, privileged access, memory security, and complexity [12]. It is vital to segregate Android attack surfaces since they are such a broad and complicated array. The attack surfaces for Android devices, as well as certain attack vectors and propagation methods [13], are illustrated in Figure 6.1.

The most appealing attack surface is the remote attack surface. This attack surface is a categorization for attack vectors in which it is not necessary for the malicious attacker to be close to the victim [14]. Rather, attacks are carried out through the network, most often the Internet. Figure 6.1 shows how several characteristics further categorize this surface into separate categories. Depending on how each

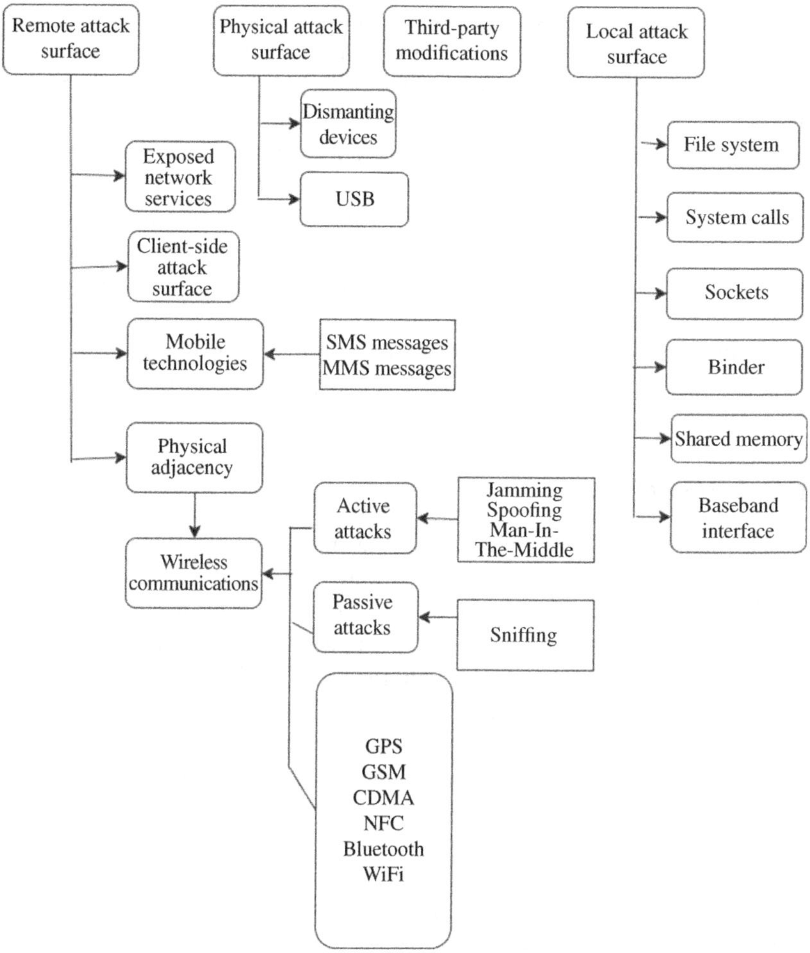

Figure 6.1 The Android attack surface.

endpoint is protected, different access controls are needed to access these attack surfaces [15].

Escalating privileges, either under the root or system user or in the kernel space, is the obvious next step once an attacker has successfully executed arbitrary code on a device. The physical attack surfaces are where attacks that necessitate physically accessing a device are made. As many parties engaged in manufacturing, Android devices usually make significant modifications as a part of their integration process, the term "third-party modification attack surface" refers to the potentially vulnerable endpoints linked with the modified components of an Android application [16].

On top of this complexity, a review of Android's security must additionally include a number of security issues specific to Android, including fragmentation, malware, user behavior, and compartmentalization [17]. The term "fragmentation problem" describes the difficulty brought on by the several Android versions that have been changed and are being used on various devices. The increasing rise in harmful program creation and complexity that targets the Android OS is a concern for malware advocates [18]. The selection of management tools is a problem since it must optimize IT efficiency while avoiding features that overlap or clash with one another. The user behavior issue is the requirement to motivate users to follow appropriate security rules and procedures. The term compartmentalization, which divides a single device into many personal settings, lastly highlights the difficulty of offering dual personal and mobile virtualization [19].

6.1.3 Android Malware

Repackaging, update attacks, and drive-by downloads are the three major social engineering-based tactics for installing malware. Repackaging is the most widely utilized technique by malware developers to insert harmful payloads into software. Basically, malware writers obtain an application file (APK), decompile it, include harmful payloads, recompile, and then publish the modified application to a legitimate or unofficial market. By being persuaded to download and install these malicious software packages, users may become exposed. In the updated attack, the harmful payloads are only included in an update component that will retrieve or download them during runtime rather than the entire payload [20]. It is stealthier than malware installation methods that explicitly contain the complete harmful payload since the malicious payload is in the "updated" program and not the original application. The third method converts the standard drive-by download attack vector for use in Android environments. They are simply luring consumers to download "interesting" or "feature-rich" programs, though still not directly exploiting mobile browser vulnerabilities [21].

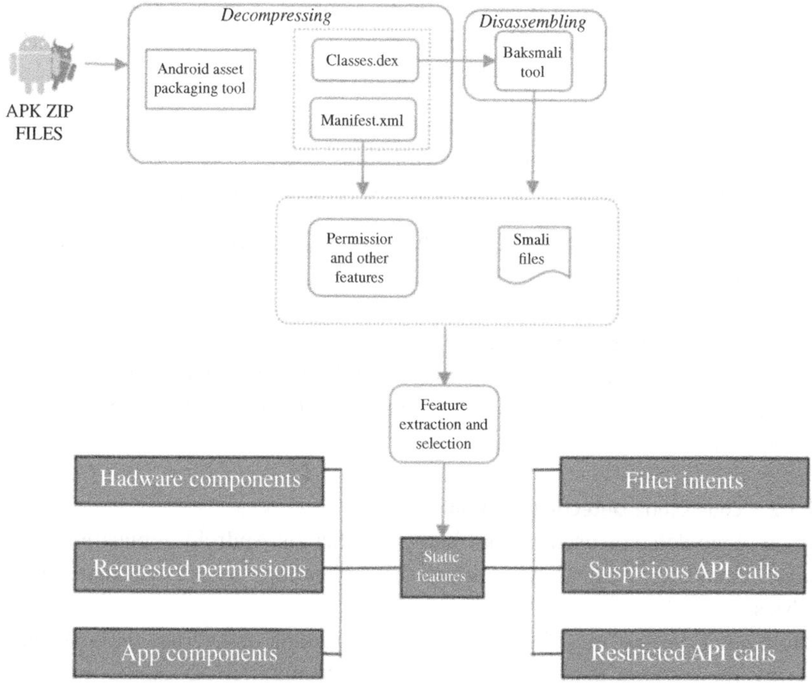

Figure 6.2 Static feature extraction and detection.

6.2 Malware Analysis Techniques

This section describes in detail the techniques used to analyze malware in Android devices. Android Malware Detection Techniques can be broadly classified into three categories: static analysis, dynamic analysis, and hybrid analysis.

6.2.1 Static Analysis

The term "static analysis method" describes the process of studying source code or executable files even without having to run any applications. There are a number of features, including API calls and permissions for static analysis [2]. Figure 6.2 depicts the feature extraction techniques.

Static analysis includes a wide variety of techniques that attempting to ascertain a software's runtime behavior before execution. Naturally, the goal in a security environment is to weed before they are installed and run, programs are screened for potential malware. Static analysis identifies an application as malicious based on an inflated estimate of its runtime actions. Therefore, static analysis techniques increase accurate detection and reduce the likelihood of false positives [12].

Over the 10-year study timeframe, many solutions have been developed to address the problem of malware detection using a static analysis approach. These tools are separated into three groups for the sake of this analysis:

1) Methods relying on code analysis, like bytecode analysis after decompilation,
2) Methods relying on API calls and permissions, and
3) Other methods that are a combination of several factors for detection.

The majority of malware detection techniques use a variety of variables and defy simple classification.

6.2.1.1 Code Analysis Based Tools

Static analysis's first subcategory focuses on analyzing an application code, at the bytecode or source level. We list and analyze the most noteworthy tools that use this method.

6.2.1.2 Code Clone Detection Method

A code clone detector used to spot known malicious Android applications was researched by Chen et al. They examined the applications' source code using static analysis.

The Dalvik virtual machine's bytecode was initially converted to JVM bytecode by the authors using dex2jar. The Java decompiler JD-CORE was then used to decompile the Java bytecode. This made it possible to detect clones in higher-level code.

This technique employs NiCad, an open-source tool that groups code files based on their syntactic similarities and finds related code segments (functions, classes, blocks, etc.) among sets of code files. This method was able to successfully train NiCad to carry out malware detection by employing a training set made up of well-known benign and malicious apps.

This method makes it possible to discover malicious apps that are a part of specific malware families quickly and accurately. In fact, 95% of previously identified malware was found utilizing a dataset comprising 1170 malware-infected apps from 19 different malware families [8].

TinyDroid is a malware detection tool that uses static malware analysis. It first abstracts source code and then uses machine learning.

Every app on TinyDroid is split into one of two categories: benign or malicious. Using a program named Apktool, the APK of the app is decompiled into Smali code (Figure 6.3). Smali can be thought of as a more sophisticated interpretation of Dalvik bytecode, that TinyDroid then further abstracts to symbolic instructions. The classification process used by this method subsequently computes the number of *n*-grams of abstract instructions present in the code. As a result, a collection of *n*-grams is calculated for every app under evaluation and contrasted

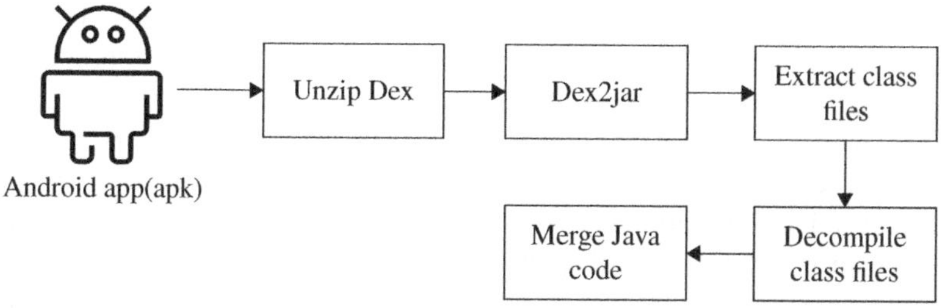

Figure 6.3 APK decompilation process.

with a collection of *n*-grams that were taken from apps that were either known to be benign or malicious. The collection of *n*-grams which best describe an app's behavior if it is determined to be malicious will be uploaded to TinyDroid's database of harmful app *n*-grams.

According to test results, TinyDroid displays a high degree of accuracy. In fact, whereas many antivirus programs have detection rates around 50%, TinyDroid's detection rate (recall) may reach up to 95.6%, outperforming 7 of the 9-antivirus programs it was compared to [9].

NSDroid analyses the call graphs of applications to identify if it resemble known malware since malware groups have similar code.

Using androgexf, first, the tool extracts the call graph of the apps. It then creates a signature for every app to further abstract this information. To produce this signature, do the following:

In order to identify which sensitive API calls are made by each method (i.e., every node that belongs to the function graph), NSDroid first builds a label from the function graph. This label logs two attributes, the sensitive API calls and the type of API calls called by the function. It does so by using a predefined set of 15 sensitive API call categories. Thus, each node is labeled with a 15-bit vector, and this information is registered with a single bit. To produce the signature for this node, each node's label is XORed with those of all of its neighbors (callers and callees). This label serves as the foundation for the detection of code similarity. The classification of four distinct malware datasets totaling 32,190 programs is then carried out using three different classifiers, decision tree, random forest, and support vector machine (SVM), of which the latter produced the best results. The advantage of this scheme is its tremendous efficiency, which allows it to analyze 32,190 apps in just over 90 seconds. The technique is also very efficient, achieving 100% precision, recall, and accuracy across a range of malware types [18].

The objective of Zhou et al.'s systematic detection and analysis of repackaged apps. They developed the DroidMOSS framework for measuring application similarity, which uses a fuzzy hash method to efficiently identify an application's behavior changes. It doesn't require access to source code because it works directly with the Dalvik bytecode. Three main steps make up how DroidMOSS works. The first step is to extract the set of instructions and author information from each application. It is possible to recognize each program separately thanks to these two qualities. Creating a fingerprint for every application in the second phase greatly reduces the length of the sequence. In the third step, which is based on the application fingerprint, the source of the applications is determined and the resemblance between pairs of applications from the same source is measured to identify recompiled applications. This technique depends on the original applications being present in the data collection that relate to them. DroidMOSS may overlook some repackaged programs if the testing database is insufficient. Since the prototype used a white-list strategy, it might not be able to identify potentially harmful alterations to shared libraries or advertising SDKs4 [16].

Finally, like with several other processes mentioned in this section, DroidMoss' evaluation is based on the entirety of the code found in every part of the program. Activities, services, content providers, and broadcast receivers are the four different categories of Android components. While this may seem exhaustive, recent research suggests that malware creators insert dangerous code in the applications' background-running components [18].

6.2.1.3 Methods Based on API Calls and Permissions

This static analysis technique focuses on the examination of the application's numerous API calls and the permissions it requests in the source code.

6.2.1.4 Analysis of API Function Calls and Permissions

This method first looks at the AndroidManifest.xml file to determine the permissions that the application uses. The authors point out that since some apps ask for more permissions than necessary, this may potentially be an overestimate of the permissions that the app uses. In order to build a set of API calls which need permissions and really appear in the app's code, the writers decompile the.dex bytecode into Java source code. The API and permissions utilized in the code are then arranged into feature vectors, and three different machine learning algorithms – Random Forest, SVMs, and Artificial Neural Networks – are employed to classify the data (RNA) [20].

The detection using API method calls performs better than the detection using only permissions, according to experimental results on a dataset with 6260 applications. The approach has a significant processing overhead. Depending on the machine learning algorithm, it achieves an accuracy between 81.68% and 94.41%.

6.2.1.5 Risk Signals-Based Detection

This method seeks to enhance the detection method currently based on permissions by using an alarm system that considers the permissions requested by the app and the permissions that other apps of the same category request. If an app requests a permission and the majority of other apps with related features do the same, it infers that the request is likely necessary for the intended functionality [8].

In order to reduce the cognitive load on users who might not be familiar with the technical workings of the operating system's security architecture, Android consciously tries to restrict the amount of permissions. The efficiency of the strategy under discussion would be enhanced by a more detailed set of permissions, which would also result in more informative alarm messages. On applying a classification using SVMs to a dataset with 158,062 applications obtained through Contagio 5 malware dump repository, this method was able to achieve a detection rate (recall) of 80.99% [1].

6.2.1.6 Other Methods

In a third category, we finally list static analysis tools that do not really come under API or source code examination.

DREBIN is another tool that uses the outcomes of the application's static analysis to detect malware.

The feature set of DREBIN seems to be among the most comprehensive of all the tools examined. It uses information from the decompiled .dex file (which includes chosen network addresses and API call) and the manifest file (which includes permissions, components, and requested hardware) to construct a total of 8 feature sets for each app. Without the need for intricate static analysis like data flow analysis, the full feature set is built in linear time. SVMs are then used for detection. Training is not carried out on the device itself to preserve a minimal footprint on the end device. The classifier is trained offline, then the user is presented with the sole model that was produced [6].

DREBIN's classifier is trained to detect the traits responsible for an application to be classified as malware. The Android Malware Genome Project's 5560 malware samples and 131,611 safe apps from the Google Play Store and two additional marketplaces were used to test DREBIN. It outperformed numerous antivirus programs on the same dataset, with a successful detection of 93% with just 1% false positives [11].

The DroidRanger application can identify the specific characteristics that malware from different harmful families share. It gathers Android applications from already-established Android markets using a crawler and stores them in a central log or repository. DroidRanger extracts the essential attributes of each gathered application (author information, requested permissions, etc.) and stores them in a centralized database.

This tool uses two different detecting methods. The first is dependent on a behavioral footprint based on application permissions. The second method is based on a heuristic assessment of the application's behavior inferred through its manifest file and bytecode. Then, if any suspect applications are actually acting maliciously while in use, they are executed and observed. If yes, the first detection process database will be expanded to include the corresponding behavioral fingerprint [10].

The top downloaded apps from 2011 were used to test this study, and the results were promising. With false negative frequency of 4.2%, DroidRanger only handles free applications and five Android stores [2].

6.2.2 Dynamic Analysis

An option for malware detection that doesn't involve executing the program in order to see how it behaves and how it affects its surroundings is dynamic analysis. It is later compared to static analysis since it only picks up vulnerabilities as they are about to happen. Due to the fact that it only takes into account one possible program execution and not all possible program executions, it also has coverage restrictions [19].

Dynamic analysis tools are divided into four major groups based on the element used for detection:

1) Tools relying on system calls
2) Tools relying on information of system (CPU usage or network communication)
3) Tools relying on information of user space (e.g., API calls)
4) Other methods.

6.2.2.1 System Call Monitoring

This dynamic analysis method uses the study of system calls to detect suspicious system calls that pose potential threats. Following methods are used to detect such system calls (Figure 6.4):

6.2.2.2 Processing of Natural Language

This detection technique, based on examining the Android application's system calls through processing of natural language, is widely used in dynamic analysis. Using sequences of system calls from good and bad applications, tools that employ this technique train two classifiers. The long short-term memory (LSTM) model serves as the foundation for both of these classifiers. In natural language, a system call is viewed as a "word" in their paradigm, and a series of system calls as a sentence. In both the legitimate and the malicious models, a probability is assigned by LSTM to the occurrence of a sentence. Then, if an execution has a higher likelihood of occurring in the malicious model, it is classified as malicious.

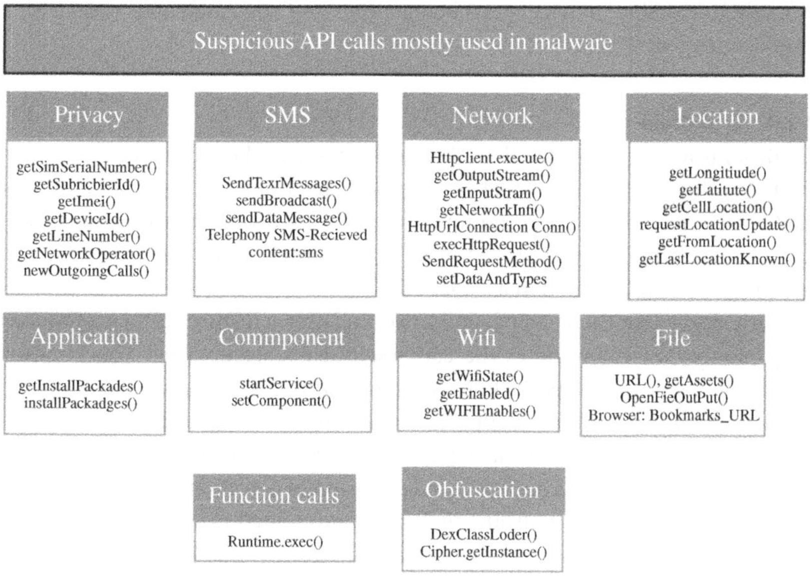

Figure 6.4 Suspicious API calls.

When the duration of system call sequences was varied from 50 to 50000 during testing of the model, the tool was able to attain an accuracy rate of 93.7% and 9.3% false positives [14].

6.2.2.3 System Call Logs

In this method, a dataset of malicious and normal android applications is employed. Prior to recording the system call, the applications are initially run in a regulated setting for a predetermined amount of time [5]. Each application is then given a Boolean vector. This specifies whether each of 18 more pertinent system calls exists along its execution after the less statistically significant system calls are discarded. An algorithm for machine learning is then fed this data. The Random Forest algorithm, the Naive Bayes algorithm, and the stochastic descent gradient algorithm are the three learning techniques used in this method. Finally, the tool classifies an unknown application as dangerous or benign using this dataset [3].

It should be emphasized that if the dangerous behavior does not appear during the training period, a malware could potentially circumvent this detection system. This method automatically picks the system call sequences most likely to be predictive of malware detection from the extremely enormous number of possible system call sequences. It categorizes the execution traces as malware or not based on the repetition of the sequences of the chosen system calls. Using this strategy, this method was able to detect 1000 benign apps and 1000 malicious ones with a rate of accuracy of 97% [11].

6.2.2.4 Crowdroid

Crowdroid is a program created by Iker et al. that uses the advantages of crowdsourcing to find viruses in repackaged apps. Crowdroid employs a tracing tool called Strace, which exists on the majority of Linux distributions. It tracks system calls that running apps make to the Linux kernel on the end-users devices. After that, this data is stored in a server [13].

With the server, for each pair of application and user, a feature vector is produced which counts how many times the 250 system calls are invoked. The k-means algorithm is then used to perform clustering on this data in order to distinguish amongst apps that, despite sharing the same name and identifier, demonstrate diverse behaviors. Naturally, as more people use Crowdroid, more data will be sent to the server, increasing the accuracy and precision of detection. Crowdroid tested well against three types of malware, including one created specifically for this test by the paper's authors. Its detection rates ranged from 85% to 100%.

6.2.3 Monitoring of System-Level Behaviors

In order to identify malware, this group of dynamic techniques emphasizes on system-level data except the system calls. System calls are analyzed by several of these methods as well [15].

EnDroid is a malware detection system that Feng et al. suggested. It is based on several kinds of dynamic behavior at the system level. To remove pointless features and retrieve crucial features from the behavior, EnDroid uses a feature selection method. The learning phase and the detecting phase are the two stages of the EnDroid process. By observing input/output processes, the learning phase entails extracting the dynamic behavioral traits of a certain application. The authors tracked ten different application action categories, including file activities, network operations, and cryptography operations [7].

Each of these features is handled as a separate functionality, with a view to producing a feature vector. EnDroid trains many elementary classifiers using the feature vectors produced by both malicious and benign applications as input. Using these fundamental classifiers' forecast probability, it creates a final categorization model for each application by utilizing an extra classifier. Then, this classification model is forwarded to the phase of detection. EnDroid extracts the dynamic behavioral features of an unidentified application during the subsequent detection phase and creates a feature vector for it. The classification model can determine whether the application is appropriate based on this vector. According to experimental findings, this method successfully identified 97.97% of malware and a false positive rate of 1.85% [2].

6.2.4 Monitoring of User-Space Level Behaviors

This method looks for malicious apps using data acquired at the user-space level. This often includes call data at the API level, as opposed to the system level.

6.2.4.1 RepassDroid

Semantic and syntactic analysis are used by the tool RepassDroid to automatically identify malicious Android applications.

RepassDroid synthesizes the API used in the program as a semantic function and the necessary permissions as a syntactic function to examine the Android application. The next step is to automatically identify whether an application is malicious or benign using learning.

The architecture of RepassDroid is built on two basic building blocks:

- The module for feature extraction. Each application's call graph is created by the feature extraction module from a particular Android application using FlowDroid. The features of the application (APIs and permissions) are then extracted from this graph to create feature vectors.
- The Module for Classifiers. The classification model was created by the authors using the Weka library and the feature vectors.

Applications that were previously unknown, after being categorized as either malicious or benign, are combined into the model [4].

6.2.4.2 Malware Detection Using Dynamically Generated Data and Machine Learning

A malware detection method for Android smartphones was proposed by Wen et al. and is based on the SVM automated learning classifier. Their technology is designed specifically for this use and runs straight on the user's smartphone. There are two main modules in the tool. Every time a new app is downloaded, the client module checks an existing database with known malicious apps (identified using their corresponding MD5 hash). Users are so forewarned if they try to install a malicious app. Otherwise, the server will get the app and process it further [16]. The feature extraction module on the server module uses both static and dynamic analysis to extract the features of the application. Permissions, intentions, and API are among the static features. The software is then run in an isolated environment to collect dynamic features like CPU usage, battery usage, and the number of processes that are active. After that, a feature selection module receives the features and filters out any duplicate features [19] (Figure 6.5).

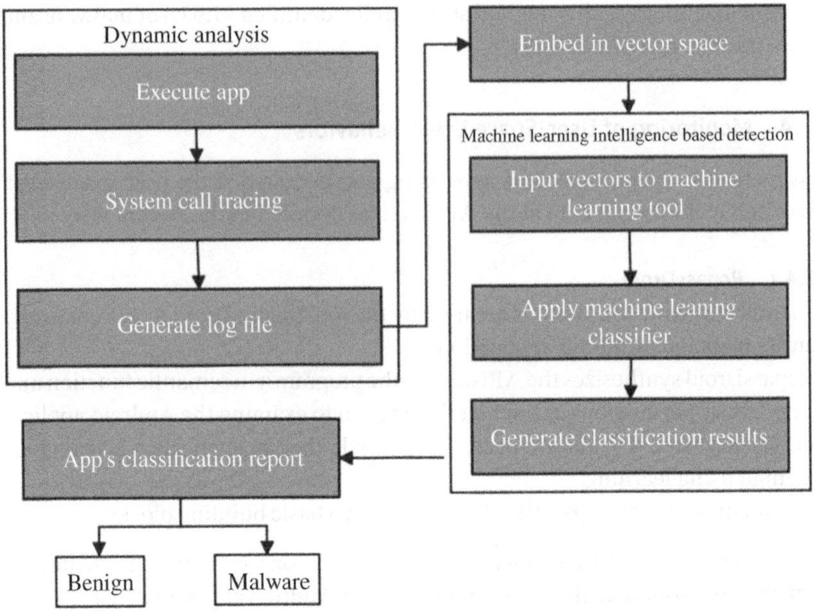

Figure 6.5 Dynamic feature extraction and detection.

6.3 Hybrid Analysis

The development of hybrid analysis makes use of both dynamic and static features and it improves the efficiency of learning algorithms. To achieve high reliability in the hybrid analysis, some studies offered multi-classification strategies. Additionally, Publisher ID, Java package name, API call, class structure, crypto operations, intent receivers, and permission are examples of static aspects. Dynamic features include crypto operations, file operations, and network activity. The APK file extracted functionalities from Androidmanifest.xml and static components from classes.dex files. In hybrid analysis, static and dynamic features are combined and the purpose of these features is to identify malicious programs [18] (Figure 6.6).

6.4 Result

While Static Analysis comprises techniques that make code easy to extract with low computational power required, it is also susceptible to imitation attacks and code obfuscation. These techniques have low accuracy and high false positive rates. On the other hand, dynamic analysis gives high accuracy but at the cost

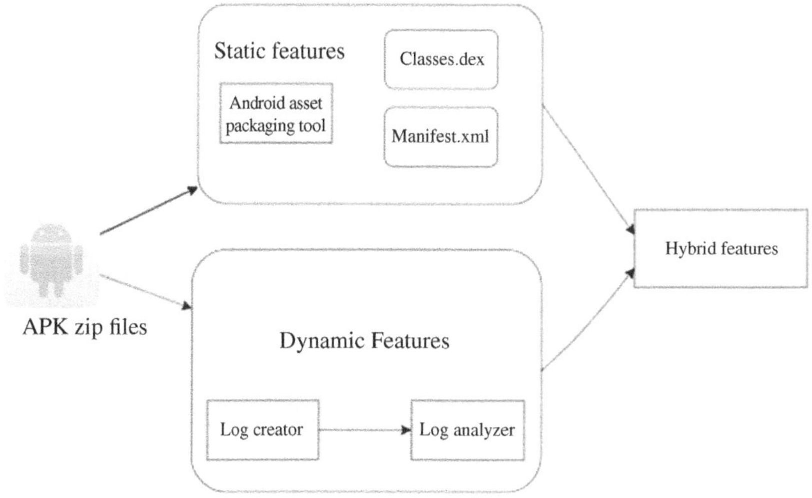

Figure 6.6 Hybrid malware analysis.

of higher computational power and resources. It is difficult to handle multiple features in the case of dynamic analysis along with a higher time complexity. Comparing hybrid analysis to static and dynamic analysis, the primary advantages are that hybrid analysis performs with the highest accuracy. It also poses some challenges that include high time complexity, complicated framework, and high resource utilization.

6.5 Conclusion

Malware detection techniques are classified largely on their nature. Due to changing nature of threats robust detection techniques are highly required. Machine learning methods can also identify unknown malware in related families. Malware are classified into their respective family based on their features. The survey provides insight about risks associated in malicious code along with tools and techniques suitable to deal with respective malware. This chapter examined a wide range of techniques for detecting and analyzing Android malware, revealing commonalities in how these mechanisms are emerging. The ability of Android malware to obstruct research and evade detection, including deep learning and machine learning techniques, was also covered in this chapter. This chapter evaluated the efficacy of current strategies for studying malware and for detection. In contrast to earlier surveys, which typically focused exclusively on mobile attacks, this chapter introduces static, dynamic, and hybrid analytic methodologies as well as suggested algorithms.

References

1 Kumar, R., Zhang, X., Khan, R. et al. (2019). Research on data mining of permission-induced risk for android IoT devices. *Applied Sciences* 9: 277.
2 Li, D., Wang, Z., and Xue, Y. (2018). Fine-grained android malware detection based on deep learning. In: *2018 IEEE Conference on Communications and Network Security (CNS)*, 1–2. IEEE.
3 Venkatraman, S. and Alazab, M. (2018). Use of data visualisation for zero-day malware detection. *Security and Communication Networks* 2018.
4 Raheja, S. and Munjal, G. (2021). Classification of Microsoft office vulnerabilities: a step ahead for secure software development. *Bio-inspired Neurocomputing* 381–402.
5 AV-Comparatives, *Android Test 2019 – 250 Apps*, 2019, https://www.avcomparatives.org/tests/android-test-2019-250-apps/.
6 P. Wang and B. Li, "*Vehicle Re-Identification Based on Coupled Dictionary Learning*," 2018.
7 Raheja, S. and Munjal, G. (2016). Shagun: analysis of linux kernel vulnerabilities. *Indian Journal of Science and Technology* 9: 12–29.
8 Asma Razgallah, Raphaël Khoury, Sylvain Hallé, Kobra Khanmohammadi A survey of malware detection in Android apps: recommendations and perspectives for future research (2021).
9 Hasegawa, C. and Iyatomi, H. (2018). One-dimensional convolutional neural networks for Android malware detection. In: *Proceedings – 2018 IEEE 14th International Colloquium on Signal Processing and its Application, CSPA 2018*.
10 Feng, P., Ma, J., Sun, C. et al. (2018). A novel dynamic Android malware detection system with ensemble learning. *IEEE Access* 6: 30996–31011.
11 Xu, K., Li, Y., Deng, R.H., and Chen, K. (2018). DeepRefiner: multi-layer android malware detection system applying deep neural networks. In: *2018 IEEE European Symposium on Security and Privacy (EuroS&P)*, 473–487. IEEE.
12 Khanmohammadi, K., Khoury, R., and Hamou-Lhadj, A. (2019). On the use of API calls to detect repackaged malware apps: challenges and ideas. In: *The 30th International Symposium on Software Reliability Engineering, ISSRE 2019*.
13 Saracino, A., Sgandurra, D., Dini, G., and Martinelli, F. (2016). MADAM: effective and efficient behavior-based Android malware detection and prevention. *IEEE Transactions on Dependable and Secure Computing* 1–14. https://doi.org/10.1109/TDSC.2016.2536605.

14 Zangief, *Gfan Provides You Free Android Apps and Games*, 2017, http://appcakefans.com/gfan-provides-you-free-android-apps-and-games/.

15 Canfora, G., Medvet, E., Mercaldo, F., and Visaggio, C.A. (2015). Detecting Android malware using sequences of system calls. In: *Proceedings of the 3rd International Workshop on Software Development Lifecycle for Mobile*, 13–20. ACM.

16 Khanmohammadi, K., Ebrahimi, N., Hamou-Lhadj, A., and Khoury, R. (2019). Empirical study of android repackaged applications. *Empirical Software Engineering*. https://doi.org/10.1007/s10664-019-09760-3.

17 Alzahrani, N. and Alghazzawi, D. (2019). A review on Android ransomware detection using deep learning techniques. In: *Proceedings of the 11th International Conference on Management of Digital EcoSystems*, 330–335.

18 Chen, T., Mao, Q., Yang, Y. et al. (2018). TinyDroid: a lightweight and efficient model for Android malware detection and classification. *Mobile Information Systems* 2018: 4157156:1–4157156:9, https://doi.org/10.1155/2018/4157156.

19 Sarma, B.P., Li, N., Gates, C. et al. Android permissions: a perspective combining risks and benefits. In: *Proceedings of the 17th ACM Symposium on Access Control Models and Technologies, SACMAT '12*, 13–22. New York, NY, USA: ACM. https://doi.org/10.1145/2295136.2295141.

20 Liu, P., Wang, W., Luo, X. et al. (2020). NSDroid: efficient multiclassification of android malware using neighborhood signature in local function call graphs. *International Journal of Information Security*. https://doi.org/10.1007/s10207-020-00489-5.

21 Hallé, S., Khoury, R., and Awesso, M. (2018). Streamlining the inclusion of computer experiments in a research paper. *IEEE Computing* 51 (11): 78–89. https://doi.org/10.1109/MC.2018.2876075.

7

Cyber Threat Detection and Mitigation Using Artificial Intelligence – A Cyber-physical Perspective

Dalmo Stutz[1], Joaquim T. de Assis[2], Asif A. Laghari[3], Abdullah A. Khan[4], Anand Deshpande[5], Dhanashree Kulkarni[6], Andrey Terziev[7], Maria A. de Jesus[8], and Edwiges G.H. Grata[8]

[1] *Centro Federal de Educação Tecnológica Celso Suckow da Fonseca (CEFET) at Nova Friburgo, Nova Friburgo, RJ, Brazil*
[2] *Instituto Politecnico do Rio de Janeiro, Nova Friburgo, RJ, Brazil*
[3] *Sindh Madresstul Islam University, Karachi, Sindh, Pakistan*
[4] *Research Lab of Artificial Intelligence and Information Security, Faculty of Computing, Science and Information Technology, Benazir Bhutto Shaheed University, Karachi, Sindh, Pakistan*
[5] *Electronics and Communication Engineering, Angadi Institute of Technology and Management, Belagavi, India*
[6] *Department of Computer Science and Engineering, Angadi Institute of Technology and Management, Belagavi, India*
[7] *TerziA, Sofia, Bulgaria*
[8] *Department of Telecommunications, Federal Fluminense University (UFF), Niterói, RJ, Brazil*

7.1 Introduction

Recent technologies, e.g., "cloud computing" (CC) [1], "cyber-physical systems" (CPSs) [2], "artificial intelligence" (AI) [3], robotics [4, 5], and blockchain [3–6] have been revolutionizing all realms [7, 8], integrating data treatment, connectivity, storage, and physical methods/worlds. The universe and its processes embrace interconnected computational entities that work together as a CPS [1–8]. Albeit CPSs closely relate to the "Internet of Things" (IoT), they differ, but complement each other owing to their unique association with the "real world" (RW), aka physical or material objects [5], encompassing smart entities like self-driving cars, robots, buildings, power grids, manufacturing, and wearables, to cite a few [6]. Even in CPSs, cyberattacks (CAs) can lead to physical/real system failure or collapse [3]. The automatic fault compensation consequences and the system's performance maintenance up to some appropriate standard are conflicting [4].

Applying Artificial Intelligence in Cybersecurity Analytics and Cyber Threat Detection, First Edition.
Edited by Shilpa Mahajan, Mehak Khurana, and Vania Vieira Estrela.

Businesses' infrastructures have morphed owing to these breakthroughs and with substantial triumph worldwide. CPSs offer sensor- and actuator-reliant links with some intelligence, new trade models, opportunities for fostering cutting-edge "information and communication technology" (ICT) ways out, and resources for enhancing computer structures, e.g., intelligent and IoT environments, which are exciting new AI application areas. Reworking AI models and instruments to meet the new CPS prerequisites will be difficult [3–6, 9–19]. "Neural network" (NN) algorithms learn from data akin to how the human mind behaves. Using NNs allows devices to make smart judgments with minimal anthropogenic input since they can learn and predict complex correlations concerning input and output information.

CPSs offer comprehensive computer, storage, and networking capabilities through "ICT" can be tailored to meet the needs of a wide range of businesses and organizations using intrusion prevention security systems (IPSSs). Reduced ICT costs give small and medium-sized enterprises high performance by sanctioning the precise purchase of the amount of software (SW) or hardware (HW) required. "Service-oriented architectures" (SOAs) and intelligent systems tied to CC and fog computing (FC) in manufacturing are grounded on CPSs. So, affording computational power for manufacturing and services is accepted in NN. This way, assets are accessible for current output, and target consumers. Internet suppliers can access items via CPSs and other ubiquitous networks. AI-driven apparatuses experiment exponential growth when interacting with their contexts, viz., driverless vehicles supervising and connecting with their contexts and home automation with optimized power consumption thanks to innovative analytics, AI, and ICTs. These frameworks can embed ever-increasing knowledge to make better and faster decisions in vastly intricate data environments. Control systems can supplement CPSs' information security shields, withstanding attacks. Moreover, they can belong to more extensive intrusion recognition and macroeconomic variables. Even in CPSs, however, CAs can cause physical system breakdowns. AI models and their placement form the virtual producer's device foundation, whether the business employs the edge, FC, or CC resources, and if its tools and structures for regulating mechanisms are unified or scattered. Manufacturing aspects comprise and combine into the overall architecture, establishing the industrialized item basis in a CPS.

Moreover, they can belong to more extensive intrusion recognition and macroeconomic variables [20–32]. Even in CPSs, however, CAs can cause physical system breakdowns. AI models and their placement form the virtual producer's device foundation. The business may employ "edge computing" (EC), FC, or CC resources if its tools and structures for regulating mechanisms are unified or scattered. Manufacturing aspects encompass the overall architecture, establishing the industrialized item basis in a CPS.

Systemic performance must be satisfactory even if faults are automatically or deliberately rewarded. Sensors, actuators, and system processes often target CAs or defects consolidated into a single system of thought. Various vendors initially link SMEs utilizing multiple standards and interaction systems. The overall performance helps detect CPSs' faults and attacks. The different CA types concentrated on CPSs call for new methods to consider environmental diversity and consistently structured advancements. AI CPSs must prevent defects or CTs from being automatically satisfied with system performance maintained satisfactorily. Systemic CTs and flaws often target sensors, decision-making, and associated actuators' procedures. Hence, a unified and coherent framework is necessary. Third-party providers raise trust obstructions to businesses' adoption of these models, notably on communication structures. This chapter's primary aim involves the ensuing.

a) Intelligent control usage for compensating scalar CAs on nonlinear CPSs.
b) List of steps to implement tolerable security controls at many CPS levels through IPSSs and NN.
c) Project description and in-depth investigation of recent CPS security processes utilizing AI.

Section 7.2 depicts the CPS models' contexts. Section 7.3 describes a possible AI-established CPS (CPS-AI) framework. Section 7.4 portrays the SW analysis and assessment. Lastly, Section 7.5 concludes and mentions the new technological revolution's glitches, linking numerous CPSs to autonomous activities in small environments as a future scope.

7.2 Types of Cyber Threats

The most common types of CTs follow [33–44]:

Computer virus (CV): This malware, once executed, reproduces itself by altering other programs and inserting its code. CVs generally necessitate a host program to write its code in it. After the code runs, the written CV is executed first, triggering infection and losses, while a "computer worm" (CW) needs no host program (as it is an autonomous code or program chunk). Consequently, the host program does not restrict it; nevertheless, it can run self-sufficiently and aggressively carry out CAs. Virus writers utilize SE deceptions and exploit detailed cybersecurity (CS) knowledge weaknesses to infect systems and spread the problem initially. CVs employ complex anti-detection/stealth stratagems to elude antivirus SW Motivations for creating CVs include pursuing profit (e.g., ransomware), aspiring to convey a political message, personal joke, demonstrating an SW vulnerability, sabotaging and creating a DoS, or simply exploring CS concerns, evolutionary algorithms and artificial lives. CVs provoke billions of dollars of economic damage per year. In response, an antivirus SW industry has cropped up, marketing or freely dispensing CV protection to various operating systems' users. Certain CVs may be enough to at least flag a suspicious file. A longstanding albeit compact way will be through arithmetic operations (viz, addition, subtraction, and Boolean operations like exclusive-or (XORing)), where each CV byte is a constant. Thus, the XORing operation can only reoccur for decryption. It is suspected for a code to transform itself, so the code for encryption and decryption may be a signature part in many virus definitions. A more straightforward older methodology did not exploit a key (i.e., encryption only has operations with no parameters, e.g., incrementing, decrementing, arithmetic negation, logical NOT, and bitwise rotation). Some CVs, termed polymorphic viruses, will perform encryption inside an executable. The virus is encrypted on certain occasions, e.g., the virus scanner being turned off for updates or the machine being rebooted. Polymorphic CVs were the first modus operandi that seriously threatened virus scanners. A polymorphic virus contaminates files with its encrypted copy, resembling regular encrypted CVs decoded through a decryption building block. However, polymorphic viruses modify this decryption module on each infection. Thus, a well-written polymorphic CV has no identical parts between infections, complicating their direct detection via "signatures." Antivirus SW can catch it by decrypting CVs via an emulator or statistical pattern breakdown of the encrypted CV body. The virus must have a polymorphic engine (aka "mutation engine") in its encrypted body to facilitate polymorphic code. Some viruses utilize polymorphic code that significantly constrains the virus's mutation rate. For illustration, a CV can mutate only slightly as time progresses or cease metamorphosing once it infects a file that already holds the CV's copies. The slow polymorphic code gain hinders antivirus professionals and investigators from obtaining representative virus samples because "bait" files infected in one run normally hold identical or similar virus samples. This tactic will make virus scanner detection more unreliable, and some CV instances can evade detection. Some viruses' codes are rewritten completely after new executables' infection to avoid detection by emulation. CVs utilizing this practice are deemed metamorphic codes, requiring a "metamorphic engine," and are usually vast and complex.

Computer worm: This standalone malware program replicates itself to contaminate other computers. It often spreads via a computer network, relying on CS failures on the target HW to access, utilizing this host to scan and infect other equipment. When these new worm-invaded devices are controlled, they stay watching and infect other computers, perpetuating this behavior. CWs use recursive methods to spread copies (without host programs) and redistribute themselves, hinging on exponential growth's advantages, thus quickly controlling and infecting more computers. CWs almost always trigger at least some network impairment, even if only bandwidth is consumed, whereas CVs almost always corrupt or alter files on a targeted machine. Many CWs only spread without changing systems. Yet, the Morris and Mydoom CWs revealed that even if "payload-free," they could engender significant disruption by snowballing network traffic and other unplanned effects.

Social engineering (SE): It is the psychological exploitation of folks into performing actions or divulging confidential data for fraud or system access. An SE perpetrator differs from a customary "con" because SE often involves many phases in a more multifaceted fraud pattern. It is also described as "any act that influences somebody to do some action that may not be in their best interests." An SE example is an attacker requesting info from a help desk, impersonating someone else, and asking for a forgotten password. If the help desk staff member resets the password, granting the invader full account access. The SE lifecycle comprises the stages below:

a) Information gathering (IG): It is the first and foremost lifecycle step. It calls for much patience and keen inspecting of the victim's habits. This step gathers facts/records concerning the victim's interests and personal information. It defines the overall CA success rate.
b) Engaging with the victim: After gathering the required facts, the invader starts talking to the prey smoothly so the victim believes the interaction is legitimate (without anything inappropriate).
c) Attacking: This step generally follows a lengthy period of engaging with the victim and, during SE, retrieves and exploits the target's material. In phase, the invader gets outcomes/answers from the target.
d) Closing interaction: This last step includes, bit by bit, shutting down the invader's communication without raising any suspicion from the victim. Hence, the purpose is fulfilled, and the victim seldom realizes a CA occurred.

Malware (MW): Malware refers to a malignant SW application purposefully introduced into a system to impair data reliability, confidentiality, or availability. Covertly executed, MW has the potential to impact an individual's data, apps, or operating system. The proliferation of malware has emerged as a prominent external threat to computer systems. The MW presence can provoke extensive harm and disruption, necessitating significant resources and efforts inside most enterprises.

Ransomware (RW): This crypto virology MW threatens significantly by coercing the victim into paying a ransom or facing the consequences (e.g., publishing their data or permanently blocking their access). While rudimentary RW forms may restrict system access without harming files, more sophisticated MW employs cryptoviral extortion techniques. The perpetrator's encryption methodologies make the targeted individual's files inaccessible, compelling the victim to pay a ransom for the decryption key. In a meticulous cryptoviral extortion operation, retrieving files without decryption key access is tricky.

Furthermore, utilizing digital currencies, particularly those that are challenging to hunt down, in the form of ransoms complicates locating and prosecuting accountable individuals. RW assaults commonly involve a Trojan, camouflaged as a genuine file, deceiving the victim into unwittingly downloading or opening it, often through an email attachment. Nevertheless, a prominent example, the WannaCry CW, could propagate autonomously across machines without user intervention.

Phishing attack (PhA): This method uses deceptive emails or bogus websites to steal sensitive data like bank account details. The criminal impersonates an honest company or person. PhAs are fraudulent emails, texts, phone calls, or fake websites that con users into MW downloading, sharing sensitive data (e.g., SE and credit card/bank account numbers, login info), or taking other cybercrime-exposing actions. Successful PhAs cause credit card scams, identity stealing, RW outbreaks, data breaches, and large personal or corporate monetary losses. The most typical SE is a PhA, which deceives, pressures, or manipulates victims into delivering money or information to incorrect people. SE assaults succeed due to human error and pressure. The attacker usually impersonates a coworker, manager, or business the victim trusts, creating an urgency to make the victim act quickly, which is cheaper and easier than hacking into a computer or network. Most CAs spread RW to individuals and organizations via phishing emails. "Spear phishing" is a PhA campaign that targets individuals and encompasses their interests, viz current personal events or finances.

"Distributed Denial-of-Service" (DDoS) attack: The attacker floods a server to prevent Internet handlers from accessing online services and sites, instigating the site's average traffic, known as legitimate packets, to halt. Invaders accomplish this by directing more traffic than the prey can handle, triggering it to fail and unable to cater service to its customary users. Targets might include websites, email, online banking, or other service dependent on a network or machine. A computer or network undergoing "denial of service" (DoS) attacks has problems related to reducing, restricting, or stopping the system's resources' accessibility to authorized consumers. A DDoS attack may compromise multiple systems simultaneously. An attacker can select zombies randomly or topologically. Once impaired, this entity sets up a controller/commands to manipulate zombies. A bot is a hazardous SW installed on damaged machines, giving the attacker control over zombies. A botnet boils down to a network of bots. DoS varieties:

Botnet: This CA infects numerous networked devices with bots and attacks a server, corporation website, other appliances, or individuals. Once infected, a bot can gather and steal user data, read and write system data, monitor user activity, perform DDoS attacks, send spam, start brute force attacks, crypto mine, etc.

Volumetric CA: It consumes the entire bandwidth, so certified users cannot attain resources thanks to flooding network devices (e.g., hubs and switches) with plentiful of ICMP echo request/reply packets. Accordingly, the entire bandwidth is spent. Moreover, other clients cannot join the target network.

SYN flooding: An invader compromises numerous zombies while flooding the prey with manifold SYN packets. SYN requests will inundate the victim. Either its performance drops drastically, or it shuts down.

Fragmentation attacks: This CA compromises the reassembling target's ability. Copious fragmented packets go to the target, hampering its assemblage capacity, thus negating access to authorized clients.

TCP-state exhaustion attack: The invader causes a DoS CA, setting up and extinguishing TCP connections. This overwhelms stable tables.

Application layer attacks: The invader exploits application programming errors to cause a DoS. It is realized by directing multiple target application requests to exhaust resources. Consequently, it cannot cater to any valid customers. A programming mistake (e.g., a buffer overflow outbreak) may engender memory allocation to a variable smaller than the one requested. Then, memory leakage or the whole application crashing may occur. Other application layer CAs include account lockout and request flooding.

Plashing: This CA causes permanent HW damage via fraudulent system updates, making it unusable. The only way out is to reinstall HW Countermeasures include:

- Utilizing the latest antivirus and "intrusion detection structure" (IDS) tools.
- Performing network analysis seeking a DoS attack.
- Shutting down extra target network services.
- Finding and neutralizing handlers to protect secondary victims.
- Performing activity profiling and intelligent filtering to remove unwanted traffic.
- Enforcing in-depth packet analysis.
- Employing a defense-in-depth tactic.
- Adding additional load balancers to attract traffic and control it.
- Correcting program errors.
- Employing robust encryption mechanisms.

Trojan horse (TH): This MW disguises itself as regular software to deceive users. The word stems from the Greek myth of TH's deception that brought Troy down. SE can spread Trojans, e.g., a user is tricked into clicking an email attachment that looks regular or on a false social media ad. Their payload varies, but many function as a backdoor, contacting an unauthorized controller with computer access. RW attacks are common for THs. Trojans cannot reproduce or inoculate themselves into other archives like CVs and CWs.

Man-in-the-middle attack (MITMA): Stalkers insert themselves between two parties that are certain they are communicating directly and secretly, modifying their communications. Active eavesdropping is an MITMA in which the invader creates independent victims' connections and transmits messages to con them into thinking they talk directly via a restricted link when the aggressor controls the conversation. The invader must seize and inject all applicable messages amongst targets. Without encryption, an attacker within the Wi-Fi access point range could perform an MITMA. The attacker must impersonate each endpoint well enough to fulfill their expectations to circumvent mutual authentication in an MITM assault. Most cryptographic protocols are built on endpoint authentication to avoid MITM occurrences. An equally trusted certificate authority can validate one or both sides in a TLS. Corporate security policy may include adding bespoke certificates to workstations' web browsers to scrutinize encrypted traffic. Thus, a green padlock does not guarantee remote server security certification but with the business server/proxy in charge of SSL/TLS inspection. Possible remedies:

a) **HTTP public key pinning (HPKP)**: The server prevents an MITM outbreak on the certificate authority by listing pinned public key hashes throughout the first action. Consequent transactions require server authentication with one or more listed keys. DNSSEC (a DNS extension) utilizes signatures to verify DNS records, preventing MITM attacks from sending clients to malicious IP addresses.
b) **Tamper detection**: A latency check can spot the CA in certain situations, like with long calculations in hash functions. To discover potential CAs, involved parties test response times' discrepancies. Suppose two parties normally take some interval to perform a given operation. If something takes an abnormal time to go to the other party, there is the possibility of having a third party's interference, which adds additional latency.
c) **Quantum cryptography (QC)**: It delivers tamper substantiation for transactions employing the no-cloning theorem. QC protocols authenticate some or all exchanges with a secure authentication strategy, e.g., Wegman-Carter's scheme.
d) **Forensic analysis (FA)**: It captures network traffic from a suspected CA and can be investigated to determine if an attack occurred. This being indeed a CA, FA selects the CA source utilizing substantial evidence to analyze network forensics on a mistrusted outbreak, including:
   i) Server's IP address
   ii) Servers' DNS name
   iii) Servers' X.509 certificate
   iv) Self-signed certificate
   v) Trusted authority's signed certificate
   vi) Revoked certificate
   vii) Recently changed certificate
   viii) Other stakeholders on the Internet with the same certificate.

Spyware: It violates privacy, turning out to be a chief concern to establishments. Though privacy-violating MW has been around for several years, it has gotten much more common, invading systems to follow private activities and run monetary fraud.

SQL injection (SQLi): An SQLi is a widespread web hacking technique responsible for injecting malicious code in SQL statements via web pages that might impair a database. This web security weakness allows an enemy to interfere with users' queries to a data reservoir. It will enable an invader to observe data they cannot normally retrieve. It happens once the application accepts a malevolent operator input as part of an SQL statement to inquire about a backend databank. Attackers can insert SQL commands and control characters to modify the query structure.

IoT attack (IoTA): With IoT gadgets' network access, invaders can redirect information toward the cloud while pressurizing to retain, delete, or expose data lest a ransom is paid. Sometimes, payment is insufficient for a group to regain all its records, and the RW automatically deletes files.

Insider threat (InT): This CS risk originates within a business. It habitually strikes when a present or former worker, contractor, retailer, or collaborator with genuine user credentials can detrimentally access the establishment's networks, systems, and data.

Cryptojacking: It is a machine hijack to mine cryptocurrencies against the handler's will through websites or while the operator is unsuspecting. Coinhive is/was a SW for cryptojacking. The cryptocurrencies mined most often are privacy coins with hidden transaction histories. Even though this harmful CA aims at profit, unlike other CTs, it remains wholly concealed from the customer. Cryptojacking MW can slow down and crash machines by draining computational assets. Blockchain mining by infected devices can be confronted by dedicated HW (e.g., FPGAs and ASICs). This expedient is more effective concerning energy intake and may have inferior costs than stealing computational resources.

Zero-day (0-Day): This severe SW threat demands more vendor mitigation efforts. Hackers can exploit the exposure to adversely affect programs, data, additional machines, or networks until the glitch is alleviated. Initially, the expression "zero-day" denoted the days since a new SW patch was released to the public. Hence, "zero-day SW" meant invading a developer's machine before release. Currently, it means vulnerabilities permitting this hacking and the number of days the vendor had to fix them. Vendors who comprehend vulnerabilities usually create patches or advise how to mitigate them. The faster the vendor becomes aware of the exposure, the repair-patch development need tends to zero. Once a problem is fixed, the exploitation success chance drops as more operators apply the repair. Unless an exposure is mistakably fixed, like by an unrelated update that fixes the weakness, the probability that a consumer had a vendor-supplied patch fixing the trouble tends to zero, so the exploitation is still viable.

Brute-force attack (BFA): It is hacking by trial and error to gather login credentials, passwords, and encryption keys. BFA gains unauthorized access to private accounts and organizations' structures and networks via a simple yet dependable tactic.

Advertising software (Adware): Innumerable pop-up ads on one's computer or mobile device can become malign and harm an appliance by hijacking someone's browser, bloating/slowing it down, and inserting CVs or spyware.

DNS spoofing (DNSS): It is also termed DNS cache poisoning. DNSS harms the domain name system (DNS) data within the DNS resolver's cache, instigating the name server into returning an incorrect record (e.g., an IP address) and redirecting traffic to any hacker-selected computer.

CS hacker: A CA is any intention toward stealing, exposing, modifying, disabling, or destroying data, applications, or other assets employing unauthorized entrance to a network, computer system, or other device. Invaders launch CAs for all sorts of motives. Two-factor verification often keeps hackers from accessing one's personal information. Nevertheless, factual contact information is too dangerous for hackers who prefer ring phones, numerous dummy emails, and correctly encoded messaging services to preserve privacy.

Rootkit: A malicious SW that delivers privileged, root-level (i.e., managerial) right of entry to a machine while camouflaging its machine presence. This nasty MW can severely impact a machine's performance and place personal data at risk. Rootkits can enter computers when handlers open spam emails and inadvertently download malicious SW keyloggers, which can also capture user login information.

Identity theft (IT): It is a severe CS risk when someone steals another individual's information for profit, especially lacking the person's consent. IT is a transgression in which a criminal utilizes fraud or dishonesty to get sensitive information from a target and misuses it to pretend to be the prey. Usually, perpetrators want monetary gain. The four IT types involve medical, criminal, financial, and child/juvenile records.

7.3 Cyber Threat Intelligence (CTI)

Cyber threat intelligence (CTI) amounts to knowledge, skills, and empirical familiarity about incidences and appraisals of cyber and RW threats to help lessen potential CAs and harmful cyberspace events [30–44]. CTI sources embrace open-source intelligence, keen social media, human cognition, technical aptitude, HW log archives, forensically picked-up pieces of evidence or understanding from internet traffic, and deep/dark web information. CTI has become a crucial companies' CS strategy since it makes companies more proactive and determines which dangers pose the largest business risks. Hence, firms on a more assertive front actively try to discover their liabilities and prevent CAs before they happen. This scheme has gained prominence recently since the most common hacking approach is via threat exploitation.

The COVID-19 pandemic drove more people to work from home, making companies' BD more exposed. Due to augmented CTs and CTI complexity, many organizations outsource CTI to a "managed security provider" (MSSP).

7.3.1 CTI Process – Intelligence Cycle

The CTI fivefold developing process or intelligence cycle is circular and continuous:

1) Planning and directing means the intelligent product consumer must know a specific topic or objective.
2) Collection begins by accessing the vital raw information to create the finished intelligence product.
3) Processing (or pre-analytical) phase filters and prepares raw information for analysis via procedures like decryption, translation, dimensionality reduction, and so forth. As data are not intelligence, transformations, treatment, and analysis are required.
4) The analysis step transforms prepared information into knowledge.
5) The dissemination phase sends the found threat intelligence outcomes to the various users.

Some paramount usage issues are:

- Sensitive information requires protection to prevent data losses.
- Since data breaches mean costs, lessening the risk of data breaches saves money.
- Institutions need help to implement CS measures to avoid future CAs.
- The CS community must share knowledge, skills, and experiences.
- Identifying CTs helps to improve delivery tools, indicators of compromise, and forthcoming, specific actors and instigators.
- Detecting CAs during and before the CPS stages.
- Providing indicators of actions taken throughout each attack stage.
- Sending information on threat surfaces, attack vectors, and malicious activities to ICT platforms.
- Serves as an evidence repository of successful and unsuccessful CAs.
- Arranges for indicators for HW emergency response and incident response teams.

7.3.2 CTI Types

The three CTI fundamental levels to appraise threats follow [26–44]:

1) Tactical: They help identify CT actors employing indicators of compromise (e.g., Internet domains, IP addresses, or hashes), albeit the analysis of "tactics, techniques, and procedures" (TTP) utilized by cybercriminals is in its infancy. Insights engendered at this level can help security teams immediately predict and identify upcoming CAs.
2) Operational: This is CTI's most technical level, sharing attacks' intricate and specific minutiae, rationale, CT actor skills, and individual campaigns. CTI expertise at this level encompasses emerging CTs' nature, intent, and timing, being more challenging, and often comes from deep, obscure, inaccessible web forums for internal teams. Security and attack response experts utilize this operational intelligence.
3) Strategic: The goal is to scrutinize the current and projected business risks and the potential CTs' consequences to aid leaders and non-technical audiences in prioritizing their responses.

7.3.3 CTI Benefits

CTI affords several gains, which encompass [26–44]:

- It allows agencies, organizations, or other individuals to develop proactive, robust CS postures to bolster whole risk controlling and CS policies/responses.
- It drives momentum toward an assertive, predictive CS posture instead of simply reacting to a CA.
- It delivers contextual info and insights about active CAs and potential CTs to aid decision-making.
- It prevents data breaches from liberating sensitive information, thus precluding data loss.
- It reduces costs since data breaches are costs, and reducing their risk helps save money.
- It helps and instructs institutions on implementing CS measures to protect against future CAs.
- It enables the CS community to share knowledge, skills, and experience.
- It helps to identify CTs, delivery mechanisms, indicators of compromise across the infrastructure, and potential specific actors and motivators more quickly and better.
- It helps in CA detection during and before these stages.
- It provides indicators of actions taken during each attack phase.
- It communicates threat surfaces, attack vectors, and malicious activities to information and operational technology platforms.

- It is a fact-based repository for evidence of successful and unsuccessful CAs.
- It imparts indicators for emergency and contamination response groups.

7.3.4 Fundamental CTI Elements

Three key elements must be present in CTI [26–44]:

- Evidence-based: Any intelligent validation must first stem from proper evidence-gathering approaches. Other processes, viz MW analysis, can enhance CTI.
- Utility: For CTI to positively remediate CS event consequences, the intelligence must clarify specific behaviors and methods regarding context and data.
- Actionable: Action stems from CTI information to drive CA contention and elimination.

7.4 Materials and Methods

More CPS research is needed to put together CTI ideas and uses. This section contemplates the significant efforts from various viewpoints, comprising application domains, privacy, and weaknesses, among other orthodox approaches.

CPS and Blockchain are progressively more popular. Yet, developing robust and precise "smart contracts" (SCs) for cutting-edge usages is an ongoing struggle [1–6, 9, 10]. The existing schemes indicate that intricate SCs cannot alleviate safety and privacy hindrances. Thus, various "AI tactics for safeguarding SC privacy" (AIT-SSCP) are suggested in this chapter for a better understanding.

"Medical CPSs" (MCPSs) are platforms for acquiring, preprocessing, and CC-based treatment of healthcare material by evolving IoT sensors/actuators [1–6, 9–19, 45]. MCPSs embrace how vital and other signals incite functionalities/actions/outputs or are used by "machine learning (ML) algorithms" types.

There are new prospects thanks to AI. Despite this, AI systems face hefty challenges attributable to the pertinent information and the lack of truthfulness needed. As a substitute, the CPS advent opens up new options for human-AI collaboration, such as a "machine intelligence symbiotically human CPS" (MIS-HCPS) framework. It has been initiated for workplace AI systems, which still tackle significant hindrances due to a shortage of appropriate data and honesty requirements.

Besides crafting a suitable BD analysis, noteworthy data architecture had to be joined with data modeling, infrastructures, and technology catalogs. The information available at the decision time and approaches to assess a large-scale data architecture [OLSDA]. The CC's role, behaviors, and functional components can now be defined with greater clarity and neutrality through a case modeling scheme applied to an abstract BD structure.

Combining IoT and BD resulted in the "cognitive-based IoT BD" (COIBD) model, crafting an industrial IoT device-oriented CPS. The COIBD could not extract the looked-for knowledge from sampling and integrating data to advance management. Experts recommended a five-layered Industry 4.0 data architecture containing sensors, power actuators, networking, clouds, and IoT technology. Likewise, information supervision helped safeguard the long-term data reactions' viability.

In spite of introducing a framework for an (MIS-HCPS), workplace AI systems face substantial impediments due to relevant data absence and an integrity necessity.

With IoT devices and AI SW proliferation, securing CPSs from CAs is increasingly problematic. Here, one can investigate in what manner adversarial CAs affect "deep learning" (DL) strategies for CPS networks' anomaly detection and defense forms against them through reinforcing models utilizing antagonistic data, which models two CPS networks after the Bot-IoT and Modbus IoT benchmark datasets. Experiments show that contentious inputs in FGSM can impact predictive performance and that a constrained model can deflect the attack.

Analytical tactics to current CPS analysis/modeling rely on principles that change contingent on whether or not one considers, for instance, safety or celerity criteria. Plenty of methods, viz stochastic modeling, and contracts, abstract complexity. Reinforcement learning (RL) can be necessary owing to the ambiguity stemming from distributed procedures, AI-based approaches, and the consumer's perspective or unanticipated impacts like accidents or the weather. This study contrasts the AI viewpoint on researching unknown multifaceted systems with that of CPS design and prediction experts.

A CPS encompasses RW electronic elements with general-use smart designs for grids, transportation, manufacturing, etc., and virtual parts. Integral CPSs' parts will be the "digital twin" (DT), a tangible object or entity cyber-clone. This research paradigm creates a taxonomy to inspect many CAs against DT-based CPSs and their effects. DT-based CPSs provide a CA space established on four-layer levels (i.e., subject, complete line, DT, and application server), three CA objects (i.e., integrity, confidentiality, and availability), and CA varieties paired with power and expertise. Conclusively, various enabling methodologies (viz intrusion recognition, Blockchain, modeling, simulation, besides emulation) can secure a DT-centered CPS with a defensive arrangement named "secured DT development life cycle" (SDTDLC).

Blockchain's advantages can be combined with "SW-defined networking" (SDN) to address energy and CS concerns. For the upcoming CPS stage, the "proof-of-work" (PoW) utilizing private and public Blockchains for "Peer-to-Peer" (P2P) communication helps solve CS and energy management difficulties.

Using computational resources (CCs, FC, and ECs) for centralized or decentralized CPSs is possible. Considering AI leads to an individual control topic termed CPS-AI. An AI control describes how it may be realized to manage interdependencies among various CPSs and factories operating under Industry 4.0 outputs.

A model employing the "You Only Look Once" (YOLOv4) procedure affords high-performance real-time fine-grain object recognition to overcome issues through plant disease discovery methods, e.g., irregular shape, density dispersion, multi-scale object categories, and textural similarities.

WilDect-YOLO has introduced an automated high-performance recognition model trained using DL to spot species from extinction in real time. There is a leftover block with the CSPDarknet53's backbone to facilitate discriminative robust extraction of deep high-dimensional feature space objects and combine their info with DenseNet blocks to augment the vital, specific data preservation.

A novel design called a "precise single stage detector" (PSSD) is a refined variant of the "single shot multi-box detector" (SSD) and deals with feature extraction and classification problems. PSSD can produce impressive real-time fallouts. Experimental fallouts show a better speed and accuracy balance.

An intelligent combo of methodologies and perceptions from CA scenarios helped evaluate their danger on smart metered structures. Selected papers' breakdowns lacked progress in developing analytics applications.

CPS-AI framework estimates the request time by paralleling it with the existing options. The present form cannot detect particular CAs, having low predictive performance. The prevailing tactics do not warrant long-term viability. The data analytics and associated architectures with CPS-AI modeling rationales have fewer assessment policies for data acquisition. Safeguarding records' confidentiality may fail in the healthcare industry, which calls for ways to overcome the CPS-AI framework gap in critical fields.

A possibility is to use a conceptual framework for future CPS-AI research that is more effective and entails less time than existing methods. AI-based CS techniques exemplify common CPS dangers and unresolved research snags in constructing intelligent CPS security safeguards when employing intrusion detection and prevention systems.

7.5 Cyber-Physical Systems Relying on AI (CPS-AI)

A cyber-physical systems relying on AI (CPS-AI) concisely overviews various CS threats across varying CPS levels and the technical hindrances preventing people from developing CS measures. CPS-AI thoroughly scrutinizes the static detection and tracking systems and their methodological caveats. The IPSSs' ineffectiveness at detecting, evading, and blocking low-level CTs deserves examination. With a VSC-reliant nonlinear monitoring system, NNs can predict CAs and prevent the CTs' danger in tracking applications.

Safeguarding CPS networks is a more problematic task because of these networks' unique complexities and troubles. The limited CPS devices' computational power illustrates this. CS must work effectively within austere constraints without draining all available assets. Hence, it is imperative to properly inspect CPS design, special applications, and CS challenges concerning customized security solutions development.

Physical domain behavior poses CPS CS risks, leading to applications necessitating physical defense and stability. CS menaces must be organized for effective, preventive remediation measures. Networked actuators, detectors, control elements, and communications HW comprise a more extensive distributed CPS, represented below.

Figure 7.1 shows the CPS's unique structure. Wi-Fi tags, satellites, devices, routers, gateways, and administration methods in CPSs can connect components in a networked arrangement. Different sensor nodes protect the Internet's cyber domain. Gateways and Wi-Fi send satellite data to the user interface. Every sensor node receives data from the router. User interfaces connect to physical domains. Sensor data is processed and actuated in the cyber realm via wired and wireless transmission. Results from the cyber core can be sent to the physical domain to aid system transformation and Internet backbone self-organization. Because of real-time operation, CPSs behave predictably and control AI systems. Due to its capacity to remotely connect RW and virtual systems to a cyber core, CPSs are used more. CPSs underline the importance of good CS measurements. A scalable risk assessment and user interface require a quantification model to quickly detect high-priority CPS security problems in a base station, which requires vulnerability scanning to recognize CPS CS requirements. This model represents CPS privacy issues as directed vulnerability dependency graphs. Risk graphics show which CPS locations are most vulnerable to assault. Acyclic graph problems grow as potential CTs are found until they are unfeasible. This model cannot be used for larger designs because it does not allow methodology changes or excessive expansion. These can be applied to sensors, communication networks, or the entire CPS. Learning algorithms, probabilistic reasoning, and CA detection mechanisms must collaborate to prevent modest attacks in most AI systems.

Providers receive production services like machine tools and robotic systems from this layer. The model depicts security aspects of recognizing and overcoming attacks. Security is crucial to overcome all network layer CTs and CAs. Operative information exchange between consumer HW facilities and CC-based system SW

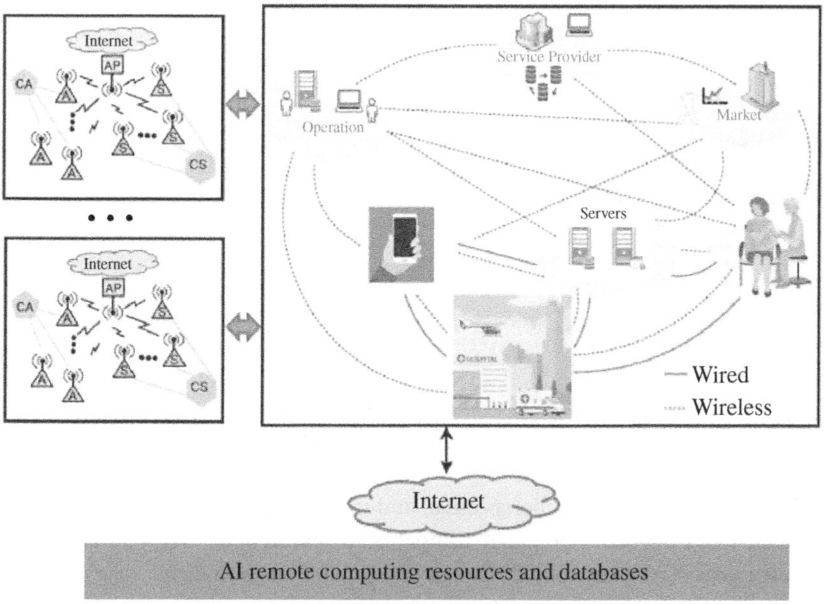

Figure 7.1 Generic CPS structure: real and virtual worlds.

can enable human-machine collaboration. Most AI systems must collaborate to prevent minor attacks, including AI algorithms and probabilistic reasoning, boosting CA detection.

CPS attacks that combine cyber, virtual, and RW processes can exploit many security flaws. The impact of a CPS threat vulnerability risk is assessed using system characteristics as part of comprehensive risk management. The anatomical structures of a cyber-physical network incursion and the security concerns outlined earlier can identify these traits.

Arithmetic, control, and communication are integrated with physical, electrical, and biological engineering sensory processes in CPSs. The suggested approach bases risk scores on the total cost of a severe assault on a CPS-using organization (Figure 7.2). Operational downtime, data restoration time, and financial expenses can be calculated. Examples include employee reimbursements, clean-up costs, and facility abandonment costs in cases of permanent damage. Prices for replacing and renovating broken physical systems are possible. CPSs face security issues that traditional ICT frameworks may not. Attempts at map-based solutions from sensor networks have had mixed results. However, CPSs sometimes fail to meet security requirements since their alternatives were not previously planned.

Current CPS analysis methods rely on safety or liveness: stochastic modeling and contracts abstract complexity. Due to ambiguity from scattered algorithms

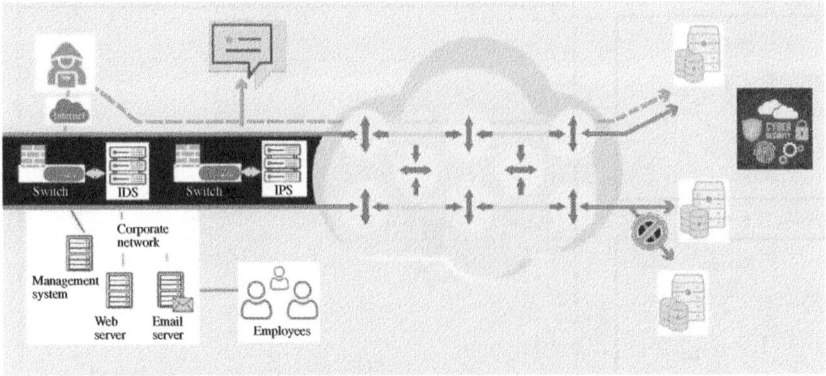

Figure 7.2 Graphic representation of IPSS. First, there is the intrusion detection structure (IDS). Depending on diagnosis, the intrusion prevention security (IPS) takes on.

and AI methods, the user's perspective, and unexpected events like accidents or weather, RL is needed. The paper compares AI researchers' views on unknown complex systems to those of CPS design and prediction specialists.

This guideline promotes system creation from the start. Top-down creation and construction of additional elements are typical. Bottom-up processes involve frameworks and other structures that need to be incorporated. Existing technologies are combined to create complex systems.

Physical assets link digital CC assets and follow a paradigm to deliver cloud data to both. It sends biological process data to service providers via networked IoT devices. There are numerous network CS systems. The IPSS, which searches networks for harmful activity and records it, is the most frequent. The IPSS may close exposed access points or install firewalls. To prevent outbreaks, IPSS answers every policy matter to deter network employees and visitors from violating corporate security policies. Probability functions aid analytics models.

Using a comprehensive network of CA scenario approaches and concepts, researchers can assess the CA hazard on intelligent metering systems. These models enabled sophisticated analytics and architectural design. Complex frameworks and concepts built from various CA scenarios can evaluate CA risk as CPS ecosystems require more data processing. This shows that BD is still young. Since no analytics SW handles probability functions well, architectural concepts that combine advanced analytics with insights are intriguing.

The network must be relentlessly probed for likely infringement and CT indicators since many access points happen, as per Figure 7.2. Even the most all-inclusive CS measures do not surmount all of today's CTs. Defending a network from illicit access is the major IPSS's goal to escape an attack by keeping an eye on logs regarding any unusual activity and responding suitably as they are not projected to stop appropriations. IDSs observe the design and notify network administrators once something suspicious occurs to disrupt the manipulated connection and obstruct any Internet or person's account regarding illegal access to any implementation, wished-for hosts, or other resource provisioning.

Observed events' data on IPSSs notify security administrators of major perceived events and produce reports. Many IPSSs can respond to many CTs by impeding them from being consummated. The IPSS can employ various response praxes, e.g., CA halting, altering the security situation, or modifying the attack's element.

Network monitoring is ever more reliant on artificial NNs. Intrusion detection and offensive prevention investigation heavily count on AI to develop, assimilate, and fortify security. CS breakdowns have exposed that current deployments of outlier recognition crash while giving few false alarms. Pros and cons of DL variants for CPS-AI systems' intrusion detection and shielding in commercial, academic, and public settings [1–8] are related to time, cost, and input dimensionality. NNs can alleviate the dimensionality curse by preprocessing and curbing the DL stage input. An adaptive AI system makes IDS more adaptable to new CTs.

One can appraise the (i) total operational cost from working downtime, (ii) time consumed restoring missing data, and (iii) financial downtime expenses. This model impacts employee paybacks, alleviates costs, and cuts the abandoning facilities' costs due to irreversible impairment. Repairing or replacing faulty HW boosts the CT detection cost.

Figure 7.3 depicts how NNs can be used in CPS-reliant CS. An NN's overall structure comprehends the following layers: (a) input, (b) intermediate, and (c) output.

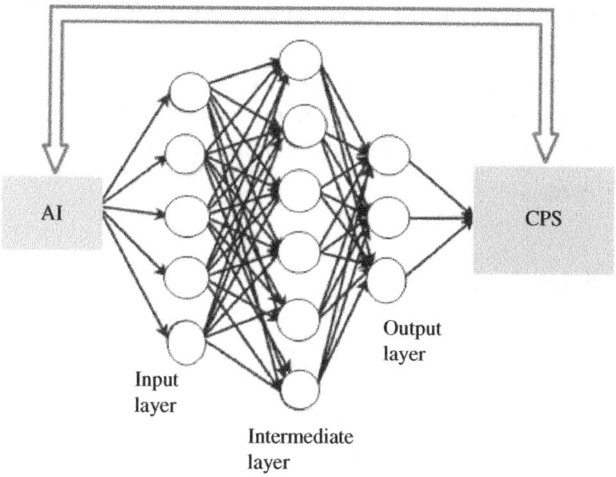

Figure 7.3 Neural network method in a CPS-AI.

Thus, the amounts of neurons per layer and of layers can impact the system's complexity, requiring the determination of the best network architecture to handle a given problem. Three-layer NN architectures are the most customary design picks using an AI gateway.

An NN can model human and HW/SW activities in computer simulation-based CTs by processing inputs and delivering smart outputs for a wide information range. A layer's neurons receive the data from the input layer and send them along through weighted neurons' connections to the topmost layer. Mathematically speaking, the data is saved and conveyed to the subsequent neurons' layer. The last layer's neurons afford the network's output. Changes to weights connecting each node happen during the training procedure and iteratively modify weight values. A criterion or set of criteria works out the weights until training stops, e.g., employing a steepest gradient descent methodology. The information collected from a given layer undergoes equations per model to produce outputs. The hyperbolic tangent function frequently activates a layer.

The NN model is nearly eclipsed in the CBPSAI system [1–15]. Since many hidden learning layers exist, it emphasizes a mechanism's output's critical significance. The unique ICS characteristics require some "variable structure control" (VSC) approach. Model-based methods can introduce bias when a system changes, requiring a dynamic response. Thus, real-time assessment may be ignored. Likewise, CT evaluation methods must be quantifiable. CPS-AI analyzes some parameters to quantify risk conditions. Several strategies, in effect, can approximate quantitative fallouts, like threshold risk costs. Precision in risk assessment is paramount for obtaining a trustworthy defense strategy. This CPS-AI focuses on VCS by coupling Bayesian network models banking on incomplete data to determine risks [1–18]. VCS traits can ameliorate modeling tools critical for augmenting performance by employing moment factors.

A Bayesian network can also help benchmark risk assessment. Developers can gauge risk with online parameterization via the recommended CPS-AI scheme. In such situations, real-time data can be delivered by ICS in CA scenarios with absent values to estimate accuracy.

7.6 Experimental Analysis

The CICIDS2019 database has been used in the simulation to perform a suggested task. Most DoS attack databases contain significant restrictions on essential data (such as erroneous duplication). Since these data are unbalanced, a duplication method is used to bring it into line to assess how well DL is working.

The performance indicators can be used for simulation purposes to conduct assessments of the CPS-AI framework, including analyses of accuracy and loss, and to compare the response times of various request types. For example, the suggested CPS-AI framework's accuracy and dependability are evaluated and compared to industry standards. In the simulation, the section offers and evaluates a CPS-AI architecture. Accuracy, reliability, request time, etc., are only some simulated assessed metrics with the current and planned CPS-AI frameworks and more traditional approaches like AIT-SSCP, MIS-HCPS, OLSDA, and COIBD. Based on the results, the CPS-AI architecture benefits more from using IoT devices and an AI model than before. History's many assaults have all been simulated beforehand. A CPS-AI can be subject to intermittent and continuous pulse attacks, depending on the transmission characteristics or disruption from outside the system. The suggested method employs nonlinear control and an NN. Dynamic programming theory ensures reliability and resilience. The NN estimator's learning capabilities are used to make attack determinations. CPS is capable of significantly more than was previously believed; a new conceptual framework suggests this is happening because of the availability of additional data from IoT devices.

7.6.1 Request Time Analysis Comparison of the CPS-AI

The CPS-AI framework results can be compared to the results of the existing model in terms of the time it takes for the request message to reach the coordinator. Each transaction's request time rises as IoT devices become overwhelmed by the increasing volume of transactions. The CPS-AI framework findings may be compared to those of the current model regarding the time it takes for the request message to reach the coordinator. As the number of requests augments, the processing time for each transaction on IoT devices also increases. The reaction time of the suggested method is faster than that of the other methods [1–15].

7.6.2 Analyzing the Results of a Simulation

The CPS-AI framework analyses, such as accuracy and loss, can be carried out using a simulation tool. AIT-SSCP, MCPSs, MIS-HCPS, OLSDA, and COIBD could be used to compare the new results. The accuracy of the proposed CPS-AI framework depends on the security aspects, reliability, vulnerability to CTs, and loss. The enhanced transaction level increases the transaction request time among IoT devices.

7.6.3 Assessment of the Proposed CPS-AI Framework's Performance

The simulation analysis of the CPS-AI framework is done with a SW tool. The output parameters, such as the accuracy and reliability, can be analyzed and compared with the existing models. The current models fail to utilize IoT devices and ML procedures, resulting in abysmal performance. The CPS-AI framework with six layers with well-defined functions simplifies the operation and ensures higher performance. The CPS-AI framework's accuracy and dependability, among other output metrics, are compared to existing models. The test can appropriately distinguish between sick and healthy instances, determining accuracy. An approximate test's efficacy can be determined by counting the number of positive and negative results across all the cases. Reliability in data analysis is measured total hours of operation to the total failures.

7.6.4 Reliability Breakdown of the CPS-AI Framework

Accuracy and reliability analyses can result from a simulation tool using benchmark datasets. The CPS-AI shows more reliability than current models like AIT-SSCP, MCPSs, and CPS-AI. IoT devices and an ML/DL model in the CPS-AI framework with layered architecture produce better results.

7.6.5 Overall Performance of the CPS-AI

The CPS-AI framework may achieve excellent effectiveness depending on the number of nodes used. Future work can be implemented with more nodes to achieve more system effectiveness. Different dynamic functions and disturbances from external sources can affect the CPS system in two different ways: a continuous and a non-continuous pulse attack. Nonlinear regulation and an NN are employed in the proposed strategy. Reliability and robustness are ensured by using nonlinear control theory. Attack determination is based on the NN estimator's ability to learn. CPS is skillful at far more than previously thought; according to a new conceptual framework, CPS is becoming more computer-controlled due to the availability of new data from IoT devices.

The simulation results for the generic CPS-AI framework can be compared to other conventional methods (e.g., AIT-SSCP, MCPSs, MIS-HCPS, OLSDA, and COIBD) on the basis of metrics akin to accuracy, reliability, request time analysis, loss, effectiveness, etc. Incorporating IoT devices and an AI model can lead to better outcomes for the CPS-AI framework.

Manipulation of data channels, equipment details, and virtualization SW are just a few of the vulnerabilities arising from the increasing interconnectedness of the IoT and CPSs. Connecting several CPSs to carry out independent duties in a confined space is a potential future scope for this new technology advancement. The CPS-AI employs AI as a key tool to boost the integration of CPSs in a smart system that requires little manual effort.

7.7 Conclusion

This manuscript goes through various layers of "CPSs," correlating CPS models briefly to highlight developing secure CPS research problems. NNs examined here are to overcome the current limitations of the most cutting-edge static and adaptable detection and protection techniques and the technologies' current state of development. This chapter proposes a conceptual framework for further investigations. Several typical CPS layer threats and outstanding research issues in developing intelligent CPS security precautions are demonstrated by AI-based security approaches [46–55], in the end, using IPSSs. Aside from that, the proposed work provides a glimpse into CPS safety research's future and relevance, motivating evaluations of research issues. An approach to estimating and compensating attacks launched by a forward link of nonlinear CPSs can be developed using intelligent nonlinear system control. NNs are combined with nonlinear control in the proposed method. It is evident from this review that CPSs are on the verge of a complex program because all the necessary technology is already in place. This new technological revolution's challenges include connecting multiple CPSs to perform autonomous tasks in a compact environment, which is a future scope. AI is highlighted as a critical tool to increase the incorporation of CPSs in an intelligent system that requires little human effort. A CPS-AI can evaluate its performance via effectiveness, accuracy, and loss through security analysis and confidentiality. Future work can be implemented with more nodes to achieve more system effectiveness in detecting the threats and attacks related to security and confidentiality issues.

References

1 Laghari, A.A., Zhang, X., Shaikh, Z.A. et al. (2023). A review on quality of experience (QoE) in cloud computing. *Journal of Reliable Intelligent Environments* https://doi.org/10.1007/s40860-023-00210-y.

2 Estrela, V.V., Saotome, O., Loschi, H.J. et al. (2018). Emergency response cyber-physical framework for landslide avoidance with sustainable electronics. *Technologies* 6: 42.

3 Deshpande, A., Estrela, V.V., and Razmjooy, N. (2021). *Computational Intelligence Methods for Super-Resolution in Image Processing Applications*. Zurich, Switzerland: Springer Nature https://doi.org/10.1007/978-3-030-67921-7.

4 Estrela, V.V., Hemanth, J., Loschi, H.J. et al. (2020). Computer vision and data storage in UAVs. In: *Imaging and Sensing for Unmanned Aircraft Systems*, vols. 1 and 2 (ed. V.V. Estrela, J. Hemanth, O. Saotome, et al.), 23–46. London, UK: IET https://doi.org/10.1049/PBCE120F_ch2.

5 Monteiro, A.C.B., Franca, R.P., Estrela, V.V. et al. (2020). UAV-CPSs as a test bed for new technologies and a primer to Industry 5.0. In: *Imaging and Sensing for Unmanned Aircraft Systems*, vol. 1 and 2 (ed. V.V. Estrela, J. Hemanth, O. Saotome, et al.), 1–22. London, UK: IET https://doi.org/10.1049/PBCE120G_ch1.

6 Khan, A.A., Laghari, A.A., Shaikh, A. et al. (2021). A blockchain security module for brain-computer interface (BCI) with multimedia life cycle framework (MLCF). *Neuroscience Informatics* 100030. https://doi.org/10.1016/j.neuri.2021.100030.

7 Alowaidi, M.A., Sharma, S., Alenizi, A., and Bhardwaj, S. (2023). Integrating artificial intelligence in cyber security for cyber-physical systems. *Electronic Research Archive (ERA)* 131 (4): 1876–1896. https://doi.org/10.3934/era.2023097.

8 Yaacoub, J., Salman, O., Noura, H. et al. (2020). Cyber-physical systems security: limitations, issues and future trends. *Microprocessors and Microsystems* 77: 103201.

9 Keshk, M., Sitnikova, E., Moustafa, N. et al. (2020). An integrated framework for privacy preserving based anomaly detection for cyber-physical systems. *IEEE Transactions on Sustainable Computing* 6: 66–79.

10 Guzman, N., Wied, M., Kozine, I., and Lundteigen, M. (2020). Conceptualizing the critical features of cyberphysical systems in a multi-layered representation for safety and security analysis. *Systems Engineering* 23: 189–210. https://doi.org/10.1002/sys.21509.

11 Wang, T., Liang, Y., Yang, Y. et al. (2020). An intelligent edge-computing-based method to counter coupling problems in cyber-physical systems. *IEEE Network* 34: 16–22.

12 Chaudhry, S., Shon, T., Al-Turjman, F., and Alsharif, M. (2020). Correcting design flaws: an improved and cloud-assisted key agreement scheme in cyber-physical systems. *Computer Communications* 153: 527–537.

13 Lv, Z., Chen, D., Lou, R., and Alazab, A. (2021). Artificial intelligence for securing industrial-based cyber-physical systems. *Future Generation Computing Systems* 117: 291–298.

14 Alippi, C. and Ozawa, S. (2019). Computational intelligence in the time of cyber-physical systems and the Internet of Things. *Artificial Intelligence in the Age of Neural Networks and Brain Computing* 245–263.

15 Nazerdeylami, A., Majidi, B., and Movaghar, A. (2021). Autonomous litter surveying and human activity monitoring for governance intelligence in coastal eco-cyber-physical systems. *Ocean and Coastal Management* 200: 105478.

16 Radanliev, P., Roure, D., Nicolescu, R. et al. (2022). Digital twins: artificial intelligence and the IoT cyber-physical systems in Industry 4.0. *International Journal of Intelligent Robotics and Applications* 6: 171–185.

17 Shaw, S., Rowland, Z., and Machova, V. (2021). Internet of Things smart devices, sustainable industrial big data, and artificial intelligence-based decision-making algorithms in cyber-physical system-based manufacturing. *Economics, Management, and Financial Markets* 16: 106–116.

18 Mihalache, S., Pricop, E., and Fattahi, J. (2019). Resilience enhancement of cyber-physical systems: a review. *Power System Resilience* 269–287.

19 Verma, R. (2022). Smart city healthcare cyber-physical system: characteristics, technologies and challenges. *Wireless Personal Communications* 122: 1413–1433.

20 Fitzgerald, J., Larsen, P., and Pierce, K. Multi-modelling and co-simulation in the engineering of cyberphysical systems: towards the digital twin. In: *From Software Engineering to Formal Methods and Tools, and Back. Lecture Notes in Computer Science* (ed. M. ter Beek, A. Fantechi, and L. Semini).

21 Popescu, G., Petreanu, S., Alexandru, B., and Corpodean, H. (2021). Internet of Things-based real-time production logistics, cyber-physical process monitoring systems, and industrial artificial intelligence in sustainable smart manufacturing. *Journal of Self-Governance and Management Economics* 9: 52–62.

22 Agarwal, T., Niknejad, P., Rahimnejad, A. et al. (2019). Cyber-physical microgrid components fault prognosis using electromagnetic sensors. *IET Cyber-Physical Systems: Theory & Applications* 4: 173–178.

23 AlZubi, A., Al-Maitah, M., and Alarifi, A. (2021). Cyber-attack detection in healthcare using cyber-physical systems and machine learning techniques. *Soft Computing* 25: 12319–12332.

24 Durana, P., Perkins, N., and Valaskova, K. (2021). Artificial intelligence data-driven internet of things systems, real-time advanced analytics, and cyber-physical production networks in sustainable smart manufacturing. *Economics, Management, and Financial Markets* 16: 20–30.

25 Jadidi, Z., Pal, S., Nayak, N. et al. (2022). Security of machine learning-based anomaly detection in cyber physical systems. In: *2022 International Conf. Computer Communications and Networks (ICCCN)*, 1–7.

26 E. Veith, L. Fischer, M. Tröschel, A. Niebe, Analyzing cyber-physical systems from the perspective of artificial intelligence, in Proc. 2019 Int'l Conf. Artificial Intelligence, (2019), 85–95.

27 Hussaini, A., Qian, C., Liao, W., and Yu, W. (2022). A taxonomy of security and defense mechanisms in digital twins-based cyber-physical systems. In: *2022 IEEE International Conferences on Internet of Things (iThings) and IEEE Green Computing & Communications (GreenCom) and IEEE Cyber, Physical & Social Computing (CPSCom) and IEEE Smart Data (SmartData) and IEEE Congress on Cybermatics (Cybermatics)*, 597–604.

28 Latif, S., Wen, F., Iwendi, C. et al. (2022). AI-empowered, blockchain and SDN integrated security architecture for IoT network of cyber physical systems. *Computer Communications* 181: 274–283.

29 Gurjanov, A., Babenkov, V., Zharinov, I., and Zharinov, O. (2022). Cyber-physical systems control principles and congregation of resources for a centralized and decentralized artificial intelligence. *Journal of Physics: Conference Series* 2373: 062017.

30 Roy, A., Bose, R., and Bhaduri, J. (2022). A fast accurate fine-grain object detection model based on YOLOv4 deep neural network. *Neural Computing and Applications* 34: 3895–3921.

31 Roy, A., Bhaduri, J., Kumar, T., and Raj, K. (2022). WilDect-YOLO: an efficient and robust computer vision-based accurate object localization model for automated endangered wildlife detection. *Ecological Informatics* 101919.

32 A. Chandio, G. Gui, T. Kumar, I. Ullah, R. Ranjbarzadeh, A. M. Roy, et al., Precise single-stage detector, preprint, arXiv:2210.04252.

33 Yu, S., Gu, G., Barnawi, A. et al. (2015 Jan). Malware propagation in large-scale networks. *IEEE Transactions on Knowledge and Data Engineering* 27 (1): 170–179.

34 Estrada, E., Kalala-Mutombo, F., and Valverde-Colmeiro, A. (2011). Epidemic spreading in networks with nonrandom long-range interactions. *Physical Review E* 84 (3): 036110.

35 Yu, W., Zhang, N., Fu, X., and Zhao, W. (2010). Self-disciplinary worms and countermeasures: modeling and analysis. *IEEE Transactions on Parallel and Distributed Systems* 21 (10): 1501–1514.

36 Wang, Z., Zhu, H., and Sun, L. (2021). Social engineering in cybersecurity: effect mechanisms, human vulnerabilities and attack methods. *IEEE Access* 9: 11895–11910.

37 Wang, Z., Zhu, H., Liu, P., and Sun, L. (2021). Social engineering in cybersecurity: a domain ontology and knowledge graph application examples. *Cybersecurity* 4: 1–21.

38 Savant, V.B. and Kasar, R.D. (2021). Computer virus attack and their preventive mechanisms: a review. *International Journal of Technology* 11 (2): 78–72.

39 Kizza, J.M. (2020). *Guide to Computer Network Security*, Computer Communications and Networks, 4ee. Springer.

40 Szor, P. (2005). *The Art of Computer Virus Research and Defense.*

41 Eilam, E. (2011). *Reversing: Secrets of Reverse Engineering*. John Wiley & Sons.

42 Erbschloe, M. (2004). *Trojans, Worms, and Spyware: A Computer Security Professional's Guide to Malicious Code.*

43 Sulieman, S.M. and Fadlalla, Y.A. (2018). Detecting zero-day polymorphic worm: a review. In: *2018 21st Saudi Computer Society National Computer Conference (NCC)*, 1–7.

44 Gupta, C., Singh, L., and Tiwari, R. (2022). Wormhole attack detection techniques in ad-hoc network: a systematic review. *Open Computer Science* 12: 260–288.

45 Davidson, R. (2020). Cyber-physical production networks, artificial intelligence-based decision-making algorithms, and big data-driven innovation in Industry 4.0-based manufacturing systems. *Economics, Management, and Financial Markets* 15: 16–22.

46 Yildirim, M. (2021). Artificial intelligence-based solutions for cyber security problems. In: *Artificial Intelligence Paradigms for Smart Cyber-Physical System*, 68–86.

47 Naik, N. and Nuzzo, P. (2020). Robustness contracts for scalable verification of neural network-enabled cyberphysical systems. In: *2020 18th ACM-IEEE International Conf. Formal Methods and Models for System Design (MEMOCODE)*, 1–12.

48 Lavaei, A., Zhong, B., Caccamo, M., and Zamani, M. (2021). Towards trustworthy AI: safe-visor architecture for uncertified controllers in stochastic cyber-physical systems. In: *Proc. 2021 Workshop on Computation-Aware Algorithmic Design for Cyber-Physical Systems*, 7–8.

49 Mazumder, S., Enslin, J., and Blaabjerg, F. (2021). Guest Editorial: special issue on sustainable energy through power-electronic innovations in cyber-physical systems. *IEEE Journal of Emerging and Selected Topics in Power* 9: 5142–5145.

50 Khalid, A., Kirisci, P., Khan, Z. et al. (2018). Security framework for industrial collaborative robotic cyber-physical systems. *Computers in Industry* 97: 132–145.

51 Li, B., Wu, Y., Song, J. et al. (2020). DeepFed: federated deep learning for intrusion detection in industrial cyber-physical systems. *IEEE Transactions on Industrial Informatics* 17: 5615–5624.

52 Ye, D., Zhang, T., and Guo, G. (2019). Stochastic coding detection scheme in cyber-physical systems against replay attack. *Information Sciences* 481: 432–444.

53 Kholidy, H. (2021). Autonomous mitigation of cyber risks in the cyber-physical systems. *Future Generation Computer Systems* 115: 171–187. https://doi.org/10.1016/j.future.2020.09.002.

54 Radanliev, P., Roure, D.D., Kleek, M.V. et al. (2021). Artificial intelligence in cyber-physical systems. *AI & Society* 36: 783–796.

55 Mahmoud, M., Hamdan, M., and Baroudi, U. (2019). Modeling and control of cyber-physical systems subject to cyberattacks: a survey of recent advances and challenges. *Neurocomputing* 338: 101–115.

8

Performance Analysis of Intrusion Detection System Using ML Techniques

Paridhi Pasrija, Utkarsh Singh, and Mehak Khurana

The NorthCap University, Gurugram, India

8.1 Introduction

In today's speedily growing technological landscape, guaranteeing the safety of documents and systems has turned into a vital task. With the ever-growing complexity of cyber threats and the escalating number of attackers, the development of robust defense mechanisms has become a top priority. This has led to the growth of Intrusion Detection Systems (IDS), which play an important role in safeguarding these digital environments. An IDS functions as a surveillance mechanism, identifying potentially malicious actions, and producing notifications upon their discovery. These notifications enable a Security Operations Center (SOC) analyst to examine the situation and implement necessary measures to address the identified risk [1]. There are three major types of IDS- Host-based Intrusion Detection Systems (HIDS), Network-based Intrusion Detection Systems (NIDS), and a hybrid of the two. HIDS focuses its attention on individual host machines within a network [2]. It monitors system logs, file activities, and host-specific events to identify potential security breaches, such as unauthorized modifications to critical files or suspicious user behaviors. On the other hand, NIDS functions at the network level, analyzing the incoming and outgoing traffic flows. By analyzing network packets and assessing communication patterns, NIDS can detect anomalous activities, such as unauthorized access attempts, denial-of-service attacks, and other suspicious behaviors. The hybrid IDS amalgamates the capabilities of NIDS and HIDS, offering a comprehensive approach that leverages network-wide and host-specific insights to enhance threat detection and response. A pivotal advancement in the field of cybersecurity lies in the infusion of Machine Learning (ML) techniques into IDS. ML algorithms bring

Applying Artificial Intelligence in Cybersecurity Analytics and Cyber Threat Detection, First Edition.
Edited by Shilpa Mahajan, Mehak Khurana, and Vania Vieira Estrela.

their distinctive capability to absorb from previous data and adapt to emerging patterns, presenting a dynamic and efficient avenue for identifying both familiar and unfamiliar threats. ML-empowered IDS can effectively process massive datasets, uncover subtle irregularities, and analyze previously unseen attack patterns, thereby involving precision and speed in detecting security breaches [3]. The adaptability of ML-driven IDS equips them to address the complexities introduced by a wide range of cyberattacks, as they autonomously refine and evolve their detection strategies in response to ever-evolving threat landscapes.

In this context, this research embarks on a comprehensive exploration of the performance analysis of numerous ML procedures in IDSs. The study delves into the evaluation of some popular ML algorithms, including Random Forest, k-Nearest Neighbors (kNN), Support Vector Machines (SVM), Gradient Boosting, and Density-Based Spatial Clustering of Applications with Noise (DBSCAN). A meticulous examination of these algorithms encompasses their accuracy, precision, recall, and adaptability across different feature subsets. Employing the Jupyter Notebook software for coding implementations, the proposed approach combines supervised and unsupervised techniques, leveraging the strengths of each to gain deeper insights into the performance analysis of IDSs. By shedding light on the behavior and efficiency of these advanced techniques, this research contributes to the advancement of cybersecurity by informing the development of more effective and reliable defense mechanisms against a diverse array of threats.

8.2 Literature Survey

Various studies have been done on the performance analysis of IDS using ML procedures. Work is being done on enhancing the efficiency and accuracy of these systems, which play a significant part in safekeeping computer networks and systems from evolving cyber threats. In a detailed study by Zhang et al. [1], an approach for intrusion detection was proposed, using a hybrid model that combines ML algorithms to improve detection rates. The study accentuates the effectiveness of various techniques in enhancing IDS performance. In the work of Jain et al. [2], a detailed study was conducted on the application of ML techniques to IDSs. The researchers investigated the performance of kNN, SVM, and Random Forest algorithms on large datasets. Their findings depicted the significance of feature selection and algorithm choice in achieving optimal IDS outcomes. Further research by Kumar et al. [3] delved into the study of the NSL-KDD (https://www.unb.ca/cic/datasets/nsl.html) dataset using numerous ML techniques. The study matched the performance of decision tree-based classifiers, SVM, and kNN algorithms. The authors emphasized the role of feature selection and preprocessing in influencing the accuracy and efficiency of IDS. An exploration of intrusion detection through ML techniques was presented by Nain et al. [4], where the authors evaluated the performance of several algorithms, including Naïve Bayes, Decision Tree, and SVM, on real-world network datasets. The study focused on the potential of ML in differentiating between normal and anomalous network activities. The work of Bhatt and Trivedi [5] focused on enhancing the performance of IDS using deep learning (DL) approaches. The researchers used a convolutional neural network (CNN) model for intrusion detection, achieving likely results in accurately identifying network intrusions. Building upon these investigations, Sharma and Gupta [6] conducted a study on enhancing IDSs using ML techniques. The authors highlighted the role of feature engineering and algorithm selection in achieving robust IDS performance.

These studies collectively emphasize the significance of feature selection, algorithm choice, and hybrid approaches in effectively detecting and mitigating cybersecurity threats.

8.3 ML Techniques

One of the main aims of ML is to build systems that can inevitably learn patterns and insights from data, allowing computers to make predictions, classifications, decisions, or perform tasks without being explicitly programmed for each specific instance [7]. It consists of a wide range of methods, including supervised learning, unsupervised learning, reinforcement learning, and more, which are applied across many domains like natural language processing (NLP), image recognition, recommendation systems, and many more. Some of the algorithms used in the paper are explained as follows.

8.3.1 Random Forest

This technique is a popular method that comes under supervised learning. One of its biggest strengths is its ability to manage complex datasets thus it is a very important method for many predictive tasks in Machine Learning. It is based on the concept of a forest consisting of multiple trees, the more the number of trees, the more robust the forest. It employs the principle of ensemble learning by joining multiple classifiers to address complex problems and improve model performance. By combining various decision trees, it is able to achieve precise predictions. Each tree is trained on a subset of the data, and the final prediction is determined through a majority vote or averaging [8]. It is used for classification which contains continuous variables and regression tasks consisting of categorical variables and handles overfitting as well. It also captures complex relationships within data and is

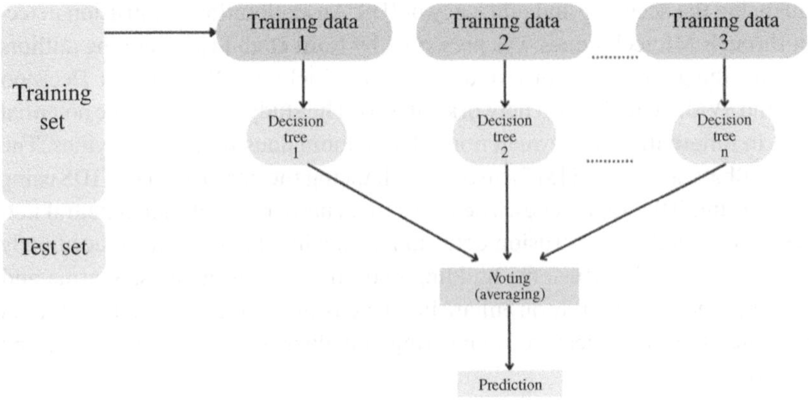

Figure 8.1 Working of random forest algorithm.

resilient to noisy features. The following Figure 8.1 summarizes the working of this algorithm.

8.3.2 Gradient Boosting

Gradient boosting is an additional form of ensemble technique that builds a predictive model through the combination of feeble predictive models like decision trees. This approach diminishes errors inherited from preceding models by concentrating on rectifying the inaccuracies they generated, thereby enhancing the precision [9]. It is a versatile technique widely used for various tasks, offering high accuracy, and robustness against overfitting as shown in Figure 8.2.

8.3.3 Support Vector Machine (SVM)

It is a strong classification procedure designed to find the best line or decision boundary that separates an n-dimensional space into different classes, precisely assigning new data points to their respective categories. This boundary is known as a hyperplane [10]. The procedure detects crucial points or vectors, referred to as support vectors that aid in defining the hyperplane. This concept is demonstrated in Figure 8.3.

8.3.4 k-Nearest Neighbors (kNN)

It categorizes data points by assessing their similarity and reallocates new instances to the category that most closely resembles the existing ones [11]. Figure 8.4a,b show the classification of new data that are assigned to what

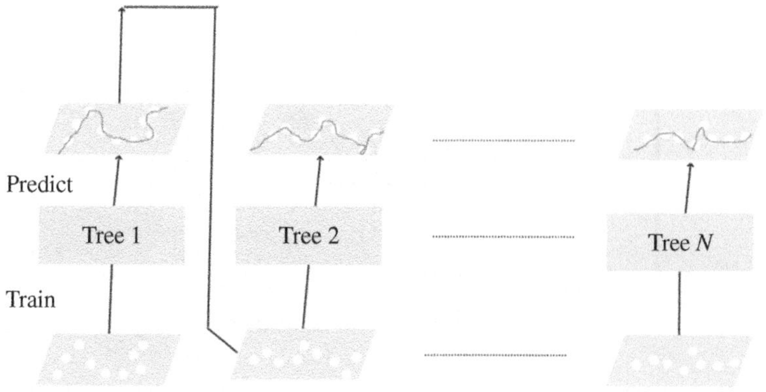

Figure 8.2 Working of gradient boosting algorithm.

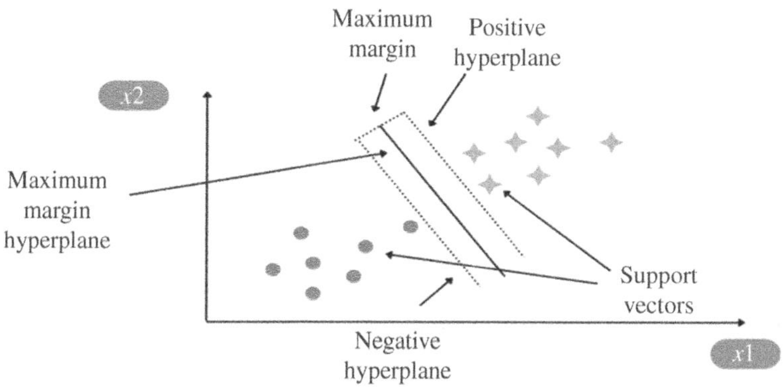

Figure 8.3 Working of support vector machine algorithm.

category after applying kNN. This helps whenever any new data appears; it can be easily shifted to a category which suits it more. kNN is adaptable to different kinds of data, making it suitable for various classification tasks. However, the disadvantage of this is its sensitivity to noisy data and careful tuning of the 'k' parameter.

8.3.5 Density-Based Spatial Clustering of Applications with Noise (DBSCAN)

This is unsupervised clustering that algorithm organizes similar data points together by considering the density distribution across the feature space. Its capability includes recognizing clusters of different sizes and shapes within

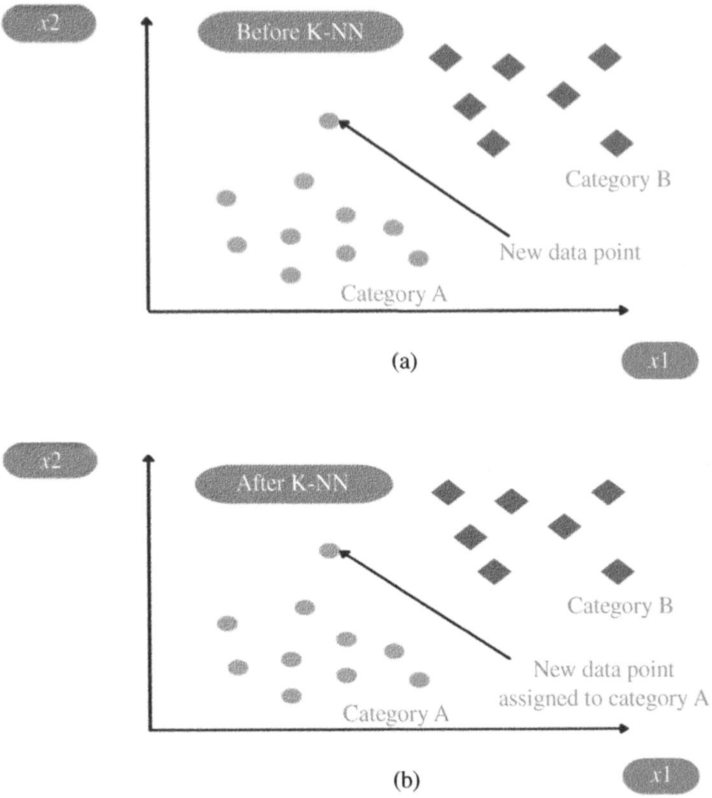

Figure 8.4 (a) Before applying K-NN. (b) After applying K-NN.

extensive datasets, encompassing even noisy data points and outliers [12]. The number of clusters doesn't have to be identified in advance in DBSCAN, making it suitable for various clustering tasks, especially when the data has irregular structures. Figure 8.5a,b present results of clusters before and after applying DBSCAN respectively.

In the forthcoming sections, the study delves deeper into how the ML techniques were employed and their respective impacts on intrusion detection.

8.4 Overview of Dataset

The analysis utilizes the NSL-KDD dataset to assess the effectiveness of the IDS. This dataset is constructed to simulate real-world situations, encompassing both normal and attack instances. As compared to its earlier version, the original KDD

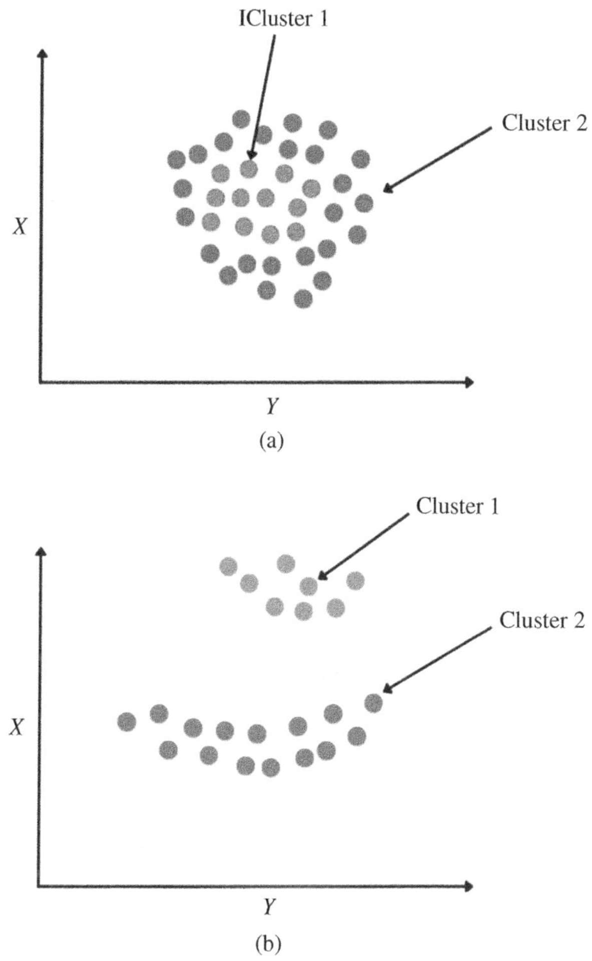

Figure 8.5 (a) Before applying DBSCAN algorithm. (b) After applying DBSCAN algorithm.

Cup 1999 dataset, the NSL-KDD dataset has undergone preprocessing to remove duplications and irrelevant attributes, making it more refined and representative. The NSL-KDD dataset features two main classes: "normal" and "attack," further categorized into subtypes like "DoS," "R2L," "U2R," and "Probe" [13]. While challenges from the original dataset persist, including class imbalance and feature selection complexities, the NSL-KDD dataset has gained widespread adoption in research and industry. By providing a controlled environment for testing and advancing intrusion detection techniques, the NSL-KDD dataset contributes significantly to the ongoing improvement of network security strategies. The

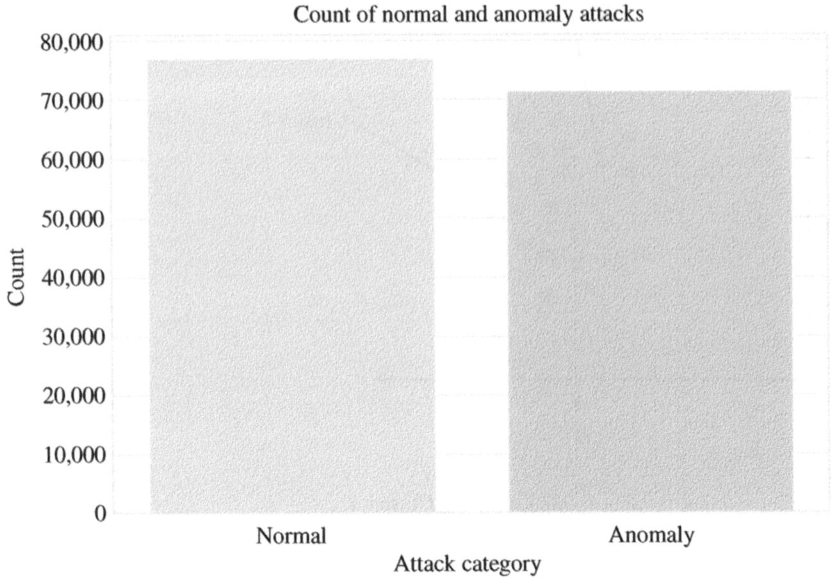

Figure 8.6 Count of normal and anomaly attack.

count of normal and anomaly attacks from the dataset was calculated, which can be shown visually as follows in Figure 8.6.

8.5 Proposed Approach

The research methodology involved a detailed examination of the performance of IDS utilizing the mentioned ML algorithms. The execution of this methodology was conducted using the Jupyter Notebook software. The stages encompassed in this process are outlined as follows:

- The preprocessing commenced with the NSL-KDD dataset, which involved employing the Min–Max scaling technique. The normalization technique facilitates the scaling of data within a predefined range by utilizing the minimum and maximum values of each feature.
- Subsequently, a chi-square test was conducted on the pre-processed data to perform feature selection. This step leads to the identification of the top 10 features from the original set of 41 features.
- To assess performance, the study selected Random Forest, SVM, gradient boosting, kNN, and DBSCAN algorithms. The accuracy of each algorithm was evaluated initially using all available features and then with the top 10 selected features.

Table 8.1 Selected features from the NSL-KDD dataset.

S. No	Feature	Description
1	Service	Refers to the category of network service linked with the network connection
2	Flag	The status of the network connection (e.g., SYN, ACK, RST)
3	Logged_in	Indicates whether a user is presently authenticated and logged into the system
4	serror_rate	Characterizes the proportion of connections experiencing SYN errors
5	srv_serror_rate	Signifies the percentage of connections to the same service encountering SYN errors
6	same_srv_rate	Illustrates the percentage of connections directed toward the identical service
7	dst_host_srv_count	Quantifies the number of connections to the same service on the target host
8	dst_host_same_srv_rate	Depicts the percentage of connections to the same service on the destination host
9	dst_host_serror_rate	Communicates the percentage of connections to the destination host encountering SYN errors
10	dst_host_srv_serror_rate	Characterizes the percentage of connections to the same service on the destination host that experience SYN errors

- In addition to accuracy, precision and recall values were also computed for the aforementioned algorithms. The resulting precision and recall metrics were then compared.

The analysis of these outcomes gave insights into the efficacy and appropriateness of various ML methods for bolstering intrusion detection capabilities.

Description of the selected features is summarized as follows in Table 8.1.

8.6 Simulation Results

In this paper section, an extensive evaluation of the chosen ML algorithms is conducted for the IDS task using the NSL-KDD dataset. This consists of assessing the efficiency of the mentioned algorithms, initially utilizing all features within the dataset, and subsequently employing only the top 10 features identified through

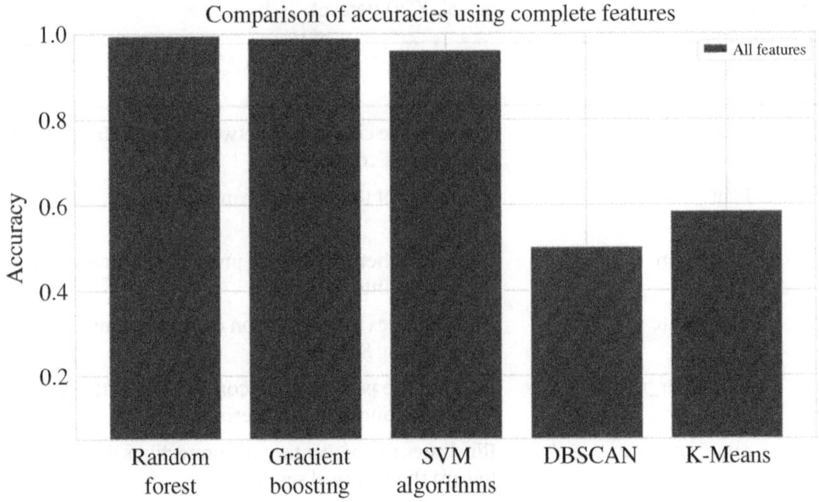

Figure 8.7 Accuracy analysis using all features.

the Chi-square test. The analysis consists of finding the accuracy, precision, recall, and silhouette scores.

8.6.1 Accuracy Comparison

Accuracy stands as an important metric for analyzing classification models. In simpler terms, it represents the proportion of accurate predictions made by the model [14, 15]. Mathematically, accuracy is expressed by the formula presented in Eqs. (8.1) and (8.2).

$$\text{Accuracy} = \frac{\text{Number of correct predictions}}{\text{Total number of predictions}} \tag{8.1}$$

In case of binary classification, it can also be calculated on the basis of positives and negatives

$$\text{Accuracy} = \frac{\text{TP} + \text{TN}}{\text{TP} + \text{TN} + \text{FP} + \text{FN}} \tag{8.2}$$

where TP = True positives, TN = True negatives, FP = False positives, and FN = False negatives.

In context of this research, the accuracy results are summarized in Figure 8.7. These depict the separate comparison of accuracies first considering all the features, using only the selected features, and then a combination of both. This depicts for which algorithms using all the features are better or using some selected features as shown in Figures 8.8 and 8.9.

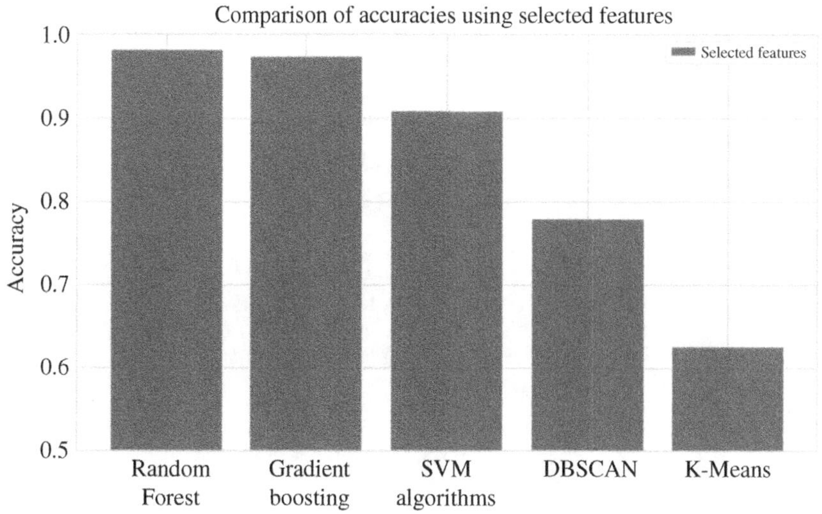

Figure 8.8 Accuracy analysis using selected features.

From the above graphs, it can be analyzed that Random Forest and gradient boosting demonstrate remarkable accuracy, achieving the highest accuracy rates of 99.75% and 99.13%, respectively when considering all features. This performance is further evident with the best features, yielding accuracies of 98.24% and 97.43%, respectively. However, its accuracy slightly declines to 90.88% with the best features, accentuating the significance of prudent feature selection in practical implementations. For unsupervised clustering techniques, the silhouette score of DBSCAN is computed. This metric quantifies the resemblance of an object to its assigned cluster (cohesion) relative to other clusters (separation) [15–17]. The silhouette score of 0.53 for all features and the elevated score of 0.78 for the best features imply that the latter leads to more well-defined clusters, potentially enhancing intrusion detection capabilities. The kNN Classifier consistently impresses with accuracy rates of 99.50% and 98.44% for all features and the best features, respectively, signifying its dependability for network anomaly detection. To conclude, in terms of accuracy, Random Forest and Gradient Boosting classifiers emerge as the top performers, particularly when all the features are considered.

8.6.2 Precision and Recall Analysis

Precision quantifies how correct were the predictions made by the model, while recall assesses the percentage of relevant data points correctly recognized by the model [18–20]. The formulas for precision and recall are mathematically expressed

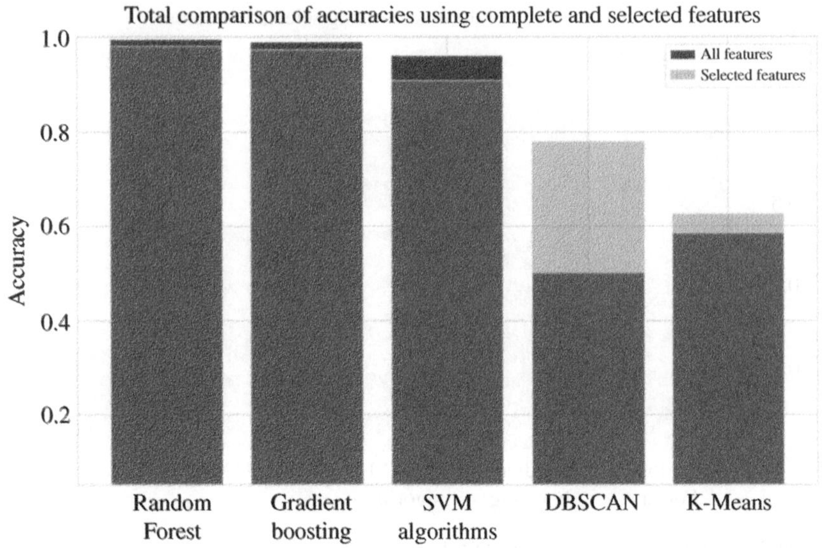

Figure 8.9 Accuracy analysis comparison using complete and selected features.

in Eqs. (8.3) and (8.4)

$$\text{Precision} = \frac{\text{True positives}}{\text{True positives} + \text{False positives}} \tag{8.3}$$

$$\text{Recall} = \frac{\text{True positives}}{\text{True positives} + \text{False negatives}} \tag{8.4}$$

In context of this research, the precision and recall results are summarized in following Figures 8.10 and 8.11.

As it can be seen from Figures 8.10 and 8.11, in the case of Random Forest, precision and recall for all features and best features are consistently high, indicating well-balanced performance in detecting both normal and anomalous instances. For gradient boosting, similar to the Random Forest Classifier, precision and recall values are consistently high for both feature sets, demonstrating robust performance. While the SVM Classifier shows competitive accuracy, its precision and recall values vary between feature sets. Notably, the precision and recall values for the "Best Features" scenario are inferior, suggesting a potential trade-off between feature selection and classification performance. The DBSCAN silhouette scores provide information regarding the quality of cluster assignments. Higher silhouette scores indicate well-defined clusters. The scores obtained for both feature sets (All and Best Features) are 0.53 and 0.78, respectively. This suggests that the Best Features lead to more distinct clusters. The kNN Classifier shows impressive precision and recall values for both feature sets, emphasizing its

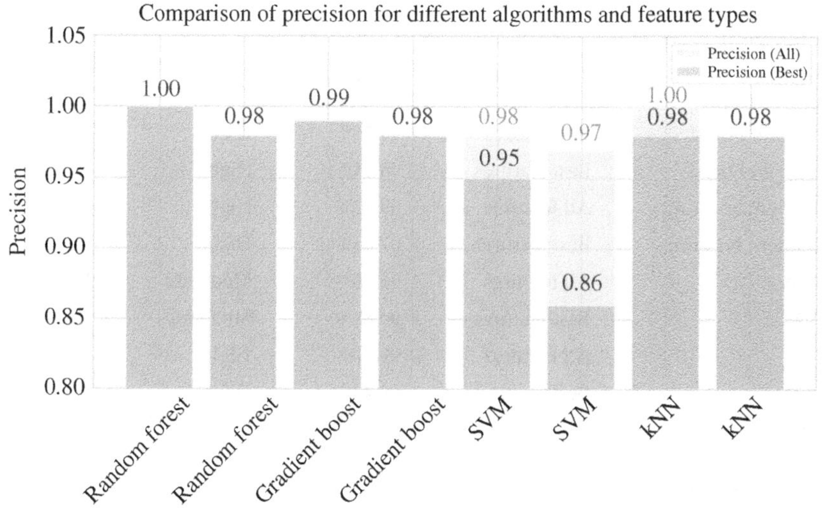

Figure 8.10 Precision analysis for different algorithms and feature types.

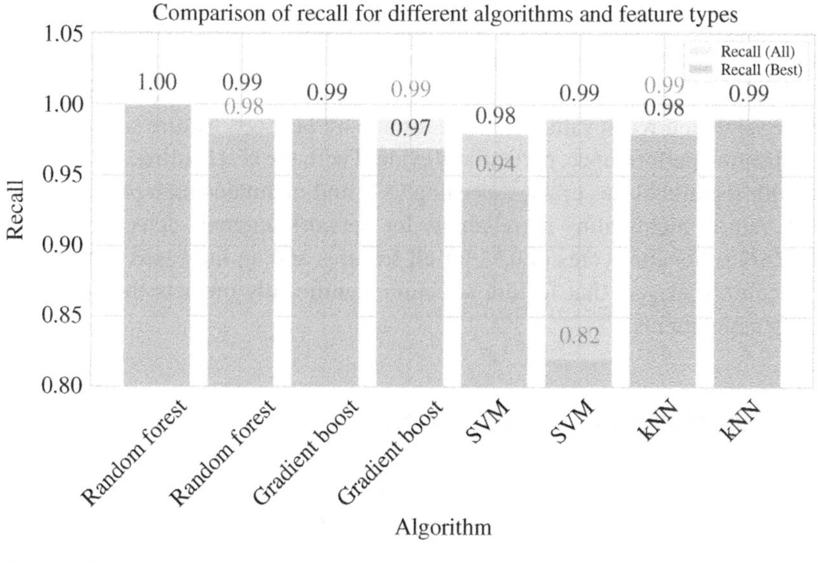

Figure 8.11 Recall analysis for different algorithms and feature types.

effectiveness in detecting network anomalies. The supervised learning algorithms provide better precision and recall with feature selection as compared to the clustering algorithms.

Table 8.2 Comparative analysis of the various algorithms based on different parameters.

Algorithm	Feature set	Accuracy	Precision	Recall
Random Forest	All features	99.75%	High	High
Random Forest	Best features	98.24%	High	High
Gradient boosting	All features	99.13%	High	High
Gradient boosting	Best features	97.43%	High	High
SVM	All features	96.33%	Moderate	Moderate
SVM	Best features	90.88%	Moderate	High
kNN	All features	99.50%	High	High
kNN	Best features	98.44%	High	High

8.6.3 Comparative Analysis

The overall analysis of all algorithms based on the accuracy, precision, and recall applied on the dataset including both the feature sets, with all features and only with the best features is presented in Table 8.2.

Random Forest and Gradient Boosting classifiers exhibit consistently high accuracy levels, exceeding 99%, and demonstrate robust precision and recall rates across both feature sets. Furthermore, SVM achieves competitive accuracy, but its precision and recall values indicate a trade-off between feature selection and classification performance, particularly evident with the best features. kNN stands out with remarkable accuracy, exceeding 98%, and maintains high precision and recall values, highlighting its reliability for network anomaly detection. Lastly, DBSCAN silhouette scores of 0.53 for all features and an increased 0.78 for the best features suggest that feature selection significantly impacts the quality of cluster assignments.

8.7 Conclusion and Future Work

To conclude, this research delved into the performance analysis of IDS using a range of ML techniques. The study explored the efficacy of Random Forest, SVM, gradient boosting, kNN, and DBSCAN algorithms in detecting network anomalies and intrusions. The results showcased the effectiveness of these algorithms in accurately discerning both familiar and unfamiliar security threats. Notably, Random Forest and Gradient Boosting classifiers exhibited remarkable accuracy levels, showcasing their potential for accurate intrusion detection. The precision and recall metrics further accentuated the reliability and robustness of these techniques in distinguishing normal and anomalous activities. The integration of ML into IDS has demonstrated its significance in developing the accuracy, speed, and flexibility of intrusion detection mechanisms. This contribution plays an important role in advancing the realm of cybersecurity. In the future, the integration of DL models and neural networks could offer greater insight into complex attack patterns and contribute to more accurate identification of advanced threats. Continued research in this area holds the potential to refine and advance the field of intrusion detection, ultimately contributing to the overarching goal of safeguarding digital platforms against evolving cyber threats.

References

1 Zhang, X., Huang, C., Lin, Y., and Lai, H. (2020). Performance analysis of intrusion detection systems using machine learning techniques. *Journal of Big Data* 7 (1): 1–17.

2 Jain, P., Bhavsar, A., and Thakkar, P. (2020). A detailed analysis on NSL-KDD dataset using various machine learning techniques for intrusion detection. *International Journal of Engineering Research & Technology (IJERT)* ISSN: 2278-0181 2 (12).

3 Kumar, S.R., Sivakumar, A.I., and Raju, K.S. (2020). Analysis on intrusion detection system using machine learning techniques. *International Journal of Engineering Research and Technology* 9 (3): 168–176.

4 Nain, R.S., Karuppiah, M., and Mahapatra, R. (2020). Enhancement of intrusion detection systems using machine learning. *International Journal of Engineering Research and Technology* 12 (1): 315–321.

5 Saranya, T., Sridevi, S., Deisy, C. et al. (2020). Performance analysis of machine learning algorithms in intrusion detection system. *Procedia Computer Science* 171: 1251–1260.

6 Sharma, N. and Gupta, S. (2021). Enhancement of intrusion detection system using machine learning techniques. *International Journal of Advanced Science and Technology* 36 (3): 1466–1475.

7 Meliboev, A., Alikhanov, J., and Kim, W. (2022). Performance evaluation of deep learning based network intrusion detection system across multiple balanced and imbalanced datasets. *Electronics* 11: 515.

8 Hadi, A.A. (2018). Performance analysis of Big Data intrusion detection system over random forest algorithm. *International Journal of Applied Engineering Research*, ISSN 0973-4562 13 (2): 1520–1527. Research India Publications.

9 Zhang, H., Ge, L., Zhang, G. et al. (2023). A two-stage intrusion detection method based on light gradient boosting machine and autoencoder.

Mathematical Biosciences and Engineering 20 (4): 6966–6992. https://doi.org/10.3934/mbe.2023301.

10 Jha, J. and Ragha, L. (2013). Intrusion detection system using support vector machine. *International Journal of Applied Information Systems (IJAIS)* ISSN: 2249-0868.

11 Liao, Y. and Vemuri, R. (2002). Use of K-nearest neighbor classifier for intrusion detection. *Computers & Security* 21: 439–448. https://doi.org/10.1016/S0167-4048(02)00514-X.

12 Ingre, Bhupendra & Yadav, Anamika. (2015). "*Performance Analysis of NSL-KDD Dataset Using ANN*. 92-96". https://doi.org/10.1109/SPACES.2015.7058223.

13 Sabha, A. and Sharma, L.S. (2020). Performance analysis of different machine learning techniques for anomaly-based intrusion detection. *International Research Journal of Engineering and Technology (IRJET)* 07 (09): e-ISSN: 2395-0056 p-ISSN: 2395-0072.

14 Kok, S.H., Abdullah, A., Jhanjhi, N.Z., and Supramaniam, M. (2019). A review of intrusion detection system using machine learning approach. *International Journal of Engineering Research and Technology*, ISSN 0974-3154 12 (1): 8–15. International Research Publication House.

15 Khurana, M. and Singh, H. (2018). Asymmetric optical image triple masking encryption based on gyrator and Fresnel tranforms to remove Silhouette problem. *Periodical* 9 (3): ISSN:2092-6731.

16 Abedin, M.Z., Siddiquee, K.N.-e.-A., Bhuyan, M.S. et al. (2018). Performance analysis of anomaly based network intrusion detection systems. In: *IEEE 43rd Conference on Local Computer Networks Workshops (LCN Workshops), Chicago, IL, USA, 2018*, 1–7. https://doi.org/10.1109/LCNW.2018.8628599.

17 Jadhav, A.D. and Pellakuri, V. (2019). Performance analysis of machine learning techniques for intrusion detection system. In: *5th International Conference On Computing, Communication, Control And Automation (ICCUBEA), Pune, India, 2019*, 1–9. https://doi.org/10.1109/ICCUBEA47591.2019.9128917.

18 Bingu, R. and Jothilakshmi, S. (2023). Design of intrusion detection system using ensemble learning technique in cloud computing environment. *International Journal of Advanced Computer Science and Applications (IJACSA)* 14 (5).

19 Kumar, E.A., Kaur, J., and Kaur, I. (2016). Intrusion detection system by machine learning review. *International Journal of Advanced Research, Ideas, and Innovations in Technology* https://doi.org/10.1007/978-81-322-2529-4_51, page-1.

20 Shyla, Kumar, K., and Bhatnagar, V. Machine learning algorithms performance evaluation for intrusion detection. *Journal of Information Technology Management* 13 (1): 42–61.

9

Spectral Pattern Learning Approach-based Student Sentiment Analysis Using Dense-net Multi Perception Neural Network in E-learning Environment

Laishram Kirtibas Singh[1] *and R. Renuga Devi*[2]

[1]*Department of Computer Science, Vels Institute of Science, Technology and Advanced Studies (VISTAS), Chennai, India*
[2]*Department of Computer Science and Applications (MCA), SRM Institute of Science and Technology, Ramapuram, Chennai, India*

9.1 Introduction

E-learning has emerged as one of the most effective training methods. In particular, collaborative learning is considered a great way to support and understand students and their learning problems. Using the e-learning platform and its collaborative tools, students can interact with other students and share questions on specific topics.

Learning plays an important role. Lifelong learning aims to enhance people's sense of achievement throughout life and on a personal and social level. In a learning community, time sustaining is an essential need for survival and sustaining change. By integrating into the process of creating new technological tools, an impressive tool for lifelong learning is provided: e-learning. For nearly 20 years, the phenomenon of "e-learning" has pervaded the distance learning landscape. The Internet and its services allow you to easily integrate user support and monitoring programs into the educational and technical aspects of dynamic learning.

Sentiment analysis in particular, also known as sentiment classification or sentiment mining, helps humans make decisions by analyzing large amounts of opinion data to effectively understand and interpret opinions and sentiments. It is a computational method by design. For example, in business, sentiment analysis helps companies analyze customer feedback to improve their products, provide better customer service, and discover new business opportunities. In the governmental land, sentiment analysis can predict changes in public perception of election candidates. In daily life, people can get more information in choosing electronic products, watching movies, reading books, etc., thus making

Applying Artificial Intelligence in Cybersecurity Analytics and Cyber Threat Detection, First Edition.
Edited by Shilpa Mahajan, Mehak Khurana, and Vania Vieira Estrela.

better purchasing decisions. For online learning, sentiment analysis employs an automated text analysis process with the aim of extracting opinions and various expressions expressed in online learning blogs and forums where learners discuss and explain their personal opinions. The goal is to recognize emotions and evaluate of services provided. In fact, early detection of learning student complaints and service deficiencies can reduce the risk of widespread dissemination of improving learning capabilities and improve promotional strategies. In this way, sentiment analysis plays an important role in improving the quality of services provided by developers, e-learning systems, and enhancing their identification of opportunities for new users (learners and tutors).

9.2 Related Work

E-learning has become less attractive, and as the level of online courses increases, move to more personalized and varied learning to work with students for better learning outcomes [1]. The school focuses on the placement of examinations, concentration, and skills to inspire innovation in our vision and educational programs. E-Learning questions are standard test questions for all of us. E-learning and Open Online Courses are more popular with today's generation of learners. E-learning systems have proven to be an important pillar of education [2]. This may shed light on what many previous studies have done. Complete traditional classroom tasks and create a platform to maximize the effectiveness of your learning outcomes [3]. To achieve such a platform, the study considers the gambling and personalization of educational resources to transform the education system by targeting learners through intensive learning analysis [4].

Attempts to close the educational gap with the rapid growth of the growing economy, the scope of e-learning is stronger than ever. Due to its low cost, convenience, and availability, e-learning is rapidly emerging as the primary driving force in the educational landscape of the 21st century. "Lack of monitoring" is a particularly difficult problem in e-learning or distance learning environments [5]. Extensive research efforts and techniques have been sought to mitigate the effects of student involvement such as mood and learning behavior. However, current research does not yet have multi-dimensional computational tools to analyze learner involvement from interactions that occur in digital learning environments [6].

It integrates different data sources of learning pathways and provides an opportunity to gain broad insights into the learner's behavior and the complexity of the learning process [7]. In developing countries with limited resources such as India, e-learning tools and sites provide the opportunity to provide education to low- and middle-income families. In such an environment, students can be monitored, habits analyzed and personal data retrieved, as well as new privacy concerns raised in the virtual learning framework [8]. This is a new information technology paradigm that is making e-learning systems more user-friendly. As a result, e-learning application is expanding rapidly and is far superior to traditional educational processes [9]. This revolutionary change is due to the advancement that has taken place in digital technology.

Online learning allows people the freedom to control their own learning process and to follow their own learning style [10]. However, research shows that most e-learning sites do not have human-like interactions, so e-learning users may feel isolated or disconnected. These emotions reduce the motivation to learn. Some companies choose e-learning in the workplace because it offers the benefit of a new way of improving employees [11]. However, implementing e-learning in the workplace is a challenge because there are many barriers to controlling its success [12]. The choice of a particular website directly affects the performance of the end user, while e-learning goals and expected outcomes depend on the quality of the educational process and the effectiveness of online access.

However, due to the large amount of data, it is difficult to manually analyze the impression, so we need to enable automation to make it easier [13]. It explores machine learning techniques for categorizing the emotions of film critics. In academic assessment, sentiment analysis helps educators to identify students' true feelings about subjects in a timely manner, to adjust curricula in a timely and accurate manner, and to improve the quality of education. Addressing the challenges related to low efficiency and high workload in the university course evaluation method [14]. Sentiment analysis of numerous user comments about the e-commerce platform can effectively improve user satisfaction. The existing emotion embedding method embeds the emotion dictionary directly into traditional word expressions [15]. This emotional expression method can only distinguish emotional information of different words, but it cannot distinguish the same word in different contexts, so it cannot provide accurate emotional information of words in different contexts.

9.3 Proposed Implementation

Toward the development of E-learning Environment, the student learning capabilities are analyzed through feedback evaluation through microblog short-term content analysis. This proposed system works on Spectral Pattern Learning Approach (SPLA) based student sentiment analysis using Dense-net Multi Perception Neural Network (DMPNN) in E-learning Environment. This finds the optimal solution in sentiment analysis-based student performance analysis by evolution content from feedback analysis system.

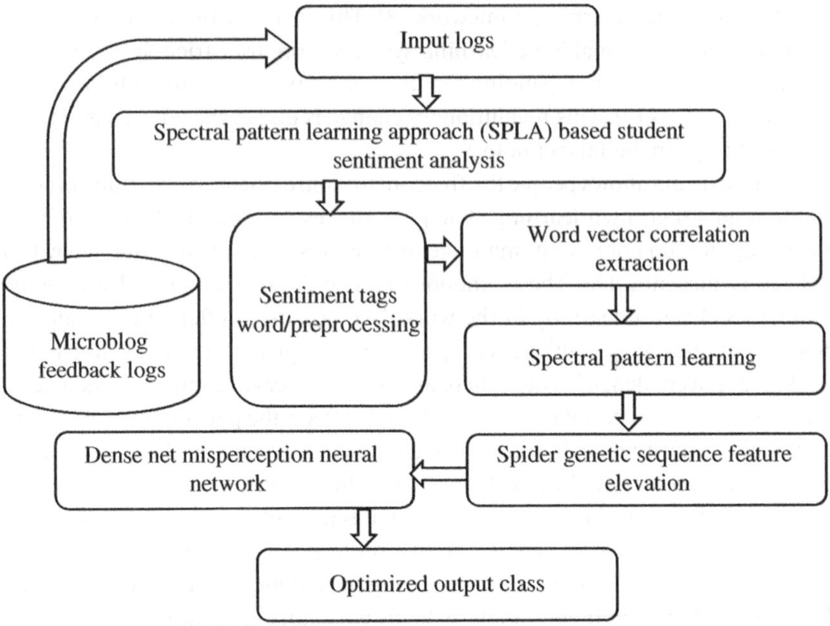

Figure 9.1 Proposed architecture diagram-SPLA-DMPNN.

The sentiment evaluation, word vector, and intensive features are evaluated to select the features. These get iterative spider layer optimization to form genetic patterns. Figure 9.1 proposed architecture diagram- SPLA-DMPNN. The attention of successive feature selection is carried out based on the sentiment terms of evolution and classified with DMPNN. The preprocessing was carried out to reduce noise based on filtering key terms, cleansing, stemming, word count, etc. to formalize the content evaluation through sentiment package to extract labeled features.

9.3.1 Word Vector Correlation Extraction

Microblogs are analyzed to extract the sequence of word correlation to define under the predefined sentiment from word vector to transformation of contents specifics. Sentiment 5 is used to process the sentiment terms in type of extraction. To get the optimal word vector ranking of neighboring neighbors, you need a pre-trained word vectors and an emotion dictionary with emotion scores. First, the semantic similarity between each target word and other words in the emotional vocabulary is calculated based on the cosine similarity of the pre-trained vector and then elevated to the closest word. It rearranges those who are semantically similar in close proximity, according to the emotional score provided by the emotional vocabulary. Neighbors with similar emotional poles are ranked higher, and neighbors with different emotions are ranked lower.

First, we need to determine the word encoder method and exercise function. The coding used in this paper is genuine coding, and the coding process is simple and not subject to local extremism. Fitness is an important foundation of population evolution, which is expressed and defined as,

$$fun = \sum_{j=1}^{k+1} \frac{w_j}{dist(v_i, v_j)} \tag{9.1}$$

where k means the amount of nearest nationals, $dist(v_i, v_j)$ denotes the detachment among separate $v(i)$, and nearest neighbor v_j. To ease the control, $dist(v_i, v_j)$ in above reckonings is unhurried by the shaped Euclidean distance, clear as:

$$dist(v_i, v_j) = \sum_{d=1}^{D} \left(v_i^d, v_j^d\right)^2 \tag{9.2}$$

9.3.2 Spectral Pattern Learning

In this stage, the sentiment word count pattern was generated to marginalize the word impact rate to extract the sentiment pointiness of perspective words. Group relevant features by searching for measurement values based on limit weights. The mutual relevance sentiments terms are built-in clustering system that predicts data at each iteration. Next to form semantic relationships to create successive mid average means weight. It measures the closeness of semantic similarity of interconnected cluster groups.

Algorithm

```
Input: feedback short text process dataset 'PD'
Output: sequence pattern
Step 1: input R-Fds  as PDs data initialization.
Step 2: perfect logs PDs for each Class Cl→Ts
          Identify search term attribute initialization A(i) for
          frequent query F_vi
                    Attribute For each Cl→A_i of Fv_i class cl
                         Pattern compute data
                         PCl = ∫_{i=1}^{N} Σ (A_i (F_vi) − A_i (F_v))²
               End
               Ds(i) = ΣDsi + Cl
          End
 End
Step 3: identify each class Cl of data request set Ts
          A_i→for each case attribute Standard access rate STh.
               Compute the Relational feature count
               FC = ∫_{i=1}^{N} Σ Dsi (A_i) ≥ STh
          End
          Measure relative pattern case Dm = Fc / size(Cli) × 100
 End
Step 4: read end
```

The average weight measures are categorized into class variables and domain values as data points. The data points with high confidence and low support in the weightage will be ignored. The method selects a single cluster based on the measure estimated to which the data point has to be indexed.

9.3.3 Spider Genetic Sequence Feature Elevation

By the chance of extracting sentiment terms of pattern formation, the word dependencies refer to various scores for evaluating the features. So, the feature depending under different categories are evaluated based on the sentiment term fitness evaluation. This was evaluated through spider optimization intent with genetic sequence pattern mining algorithm. These evaluate the best-case sentence analyzer with sequence form of content learning formation in best-case evaluation.

With excellent universal optimization and strength, through the generic feature evaluation was carried out to predict the rem sequence. Among them, GEN is the sequence formation, M is the generate seize pattern keyword, and e is the expected one to form sentiment sequence.

$$\begin{cases} y_{mi} = \gamma\left(x_{mi} - x_{ni}\right) + \alpha x_{mi} + \beta x_{ni} \\ y_{ni} = \gamma\left(x_{mi} - x_{ni}\right) + \alpha x_{ni} + \beta x_{mi} \end{cases} \tag{9.3}$$

The y_{mi} and y_{ni} is offspring genetic sequence representation of

$$\alpha x_{ni} + \beta x_{mi} \tag{9.4}$$

$$x_{max} = \begin{cases} x_{mm} + \left(x_{mn} - x_{max}\right) \cdot f(g), r > 0.5 \\ x_{mm} + \left(x_{min} - x_{mn}\right) \cdot f(g), r \leq 0.5 \end{cases} \tag{9.5}$$

Based on the genetic formation, the equalized successive factor be at forming pattern sequence,

$$f(g) = r_2\left(1 - g/G_{max}\right) \tag{9.6}$$

The maximum representation of sequential terms x_{max} be presented as maximum support sentiment term with relative sequence the category of class representation. This max class sequence tail pattern with x_{mn} with interactive genetic class; G_{max} $in_i'r$ number of random variables.′ will be selected based on your personal fitness value. The fitness values are individually selected to form fitness values.

Algorithm:

```
Step 1: Process the intensive word vectors feature form
relative class
            Compute correlation 'c'Cif→(Lr∩Br)
Step 2: Embrace spider decision Tree → Strengthening class forma-
tion (Cif);
```

```
            Maximum successive rate (Mir→Nodes (spider))
Step 3: calculate constraint cif(Mir) weight to form cluster index Ci
            For each cluster ci→Fas feature weight relative term 'i'
          Analyses decision process Rn→F(i) to make successive mar-
gin
                Form genetic sequence Gs→attain Mean rate Cif→Mir
                         Sum maximum count terms F(i)
                         Relative sentence Cfs→ closest F(i)
                      Return Cfs
            End if
        End for
Step 4: Compute he sequence generator for word count Cfs← fre-
quent sentiment term (Frc)
         Check relative margin each 'C'←Frs class to each cluster
class
             Retain the index to feature list count as sentiment
terms
                        Frc←C-ids
                        Return Frc-Ids
                End
               Return Frc
             End for
Stop
```

To maintain an improved separation and minimize the arbitrariness of the exam, we continue as obscurities. After gaining each one's correlation strength, sort the ones with the highest semantic level to the relative feature weight, and divide them into the best, the middle, and the lowest, and select from the three according to probability. The determination of this procedure is sects the individual's patterns as sequent to optimize the sentiment terms weight.

9.3.4 Dense Net Multi-perception Neural Network (DMPNN)

In this stage, the observed sentence features weights are marginalized into dense net and crates multi perception neural network to classify the categories to sentiment weight into different class. This proves the student's capability and observation into different classes by marginalizing them into classes. This system generates neurons from each set of each group. The generated neurons are initiated with the ensemble feature. The high-density net multiplier performs the convolution at the operational level by selecting the desired function. Neurons eliminate unwanted functions. This is done by using a convolution function with the selection function, and the remaining functions feed to the activation function. Neurons are fed by two different metrics, the first of which generates functional activity over a normal chronological order for sentiment and relative terms analysis. The network consists of seven layers, including the input layer and the output layer. The convolution layer uses the convolution function for features, and the pooling layer evaluates weight measurements for various features.

Algorithm:

Step 1: Input features class ‘F’ ←(Frc)

Step 2: Training samples; choosing the optimal classifier for each challenge takes time and effort. As a result, a technique can simultaneously model features and classify them as required

$$Z(\theta) = \sum_{h,y}^{n-1} - (E(v,h)) \tag{9.7}$$

$Z(\theta)$ is the training samples, and $E(v, h)$ is the number of nodes.

The data Transformation to a regression function may be smoothed out in the training procedure. The prognostic prototypical laboring may be linear. Based on that, below algorithm steps are used in training samples. Multi perception is to find the limits as to whether it is low or high. If high or low, the output stops the data analysis process which indicates the alert to the concerned person. The output of the calculating prescient method uses significant mathematical modeling to process data in complicated ways.

$$Z(v,h;\theta) = -\sum_{i}^{i=1} w_{i,j} - \sum_{i=1}^{n-2} \left(P_{s-1}\right) \tag{9.8}$$

where $Z(v, h; \theta)$ is the Partitioning value, n is the number of data, and $w_{i,j}$ is calculating sampling data.

Step 3: Testing Data: The test set is setting the address of initializing the sentiment term as word vector features.

$$Z_{rw} = \left(r_{s0} + P_s\right) = -P_{s-1} \tag{9.9}$$

Here Z_{rw} is the source of the getting, P_{s-1} is calculating the limit of data.

To evaluate performance, the “test” or “validation” dataset is required for training sentiment. Traditionally, the dataset cast-off to measure the concluding representation’s presentation has been mentioned as the testing and training validation. The dense net is a better error analyzer that gets the expected output. The distributions at each node are multiplied and then renormalized. Use the data for another prototype as the values of the factor loadings are calculated from the instinctive rate to fix the margin as dense layers.

Step 4: Offset Vector: Calculate the sentiment word fervency relative margins on each feedback

$$Z_{rw} = I_{s0}, P_c = 0, P_{c-} = P_{s-1} \tag{9.10}$$

Step 5: Hidden Layer; a similar mean value indicates the $\sigma(c_i + W_i\, V)$ which is an average classification accuracy with cross-validation and classification error.

$$Z\ \left(h_i = 1 \mid v\right) = \frac{e^{c_i} w_i\, V}{1 + e^{C_i}} = \sigma\ \left(c_i + W_i\, V\right) \tag{9.11}$$

where $P(h_i = 1 \mid v)$ Creates frequent semantic relation sentiment of length 1 with $k = 1$.

Repeat until a new group of W_i items with a high frequency of occurrence are formed.

Step 6: Offset Vector; the $Z(\theta)$ iteration ends data when the specified number of iterations or success criterion is achieved.

$$Z(\theta) = \sum_{i=1}^{n} \log\left(1 + e^{C_i + W_j h}\right) \tag{9.12}$$

Step 7: Constant Diversion: The output data is based on or without error.

Step 8: Error calculating: Each node is calculating the different dataset, where I_{s0} is of inputs.

This classification produces high performance to predict the phishing strategies. This attains the feature levels by forming the feature selection and classification to find the sentiment score from the feedback resolution from students by class by category.

9.4 Result and Discussion

This section describes the proposed implementation result analysis parameters are sensitivity, specificity, classification accuracy performance, false rate analysis, and time complexity.

The proposed algorithm Simulation parameters settings are present in Table 9.1. The proposed Wisconsin High Order Neural Network (WHONN) algorithm is compared to Recurrent Neural Network (RNN) and Perceptual Neural Boltzmann Machine (PNBM).

The above Table 9.2 and Figure 9.2 define the classification of accuracy performance. The proposed SPLA-DMPNN produces 93%, WHONN algorithm provides

Table 9.1 Simulation parameters settings.

Parameters	Values
Language	Python
Tool	Anaconda
Dataset name	E-learning student reactions
Number of data	4000
Training dataset	3500
Testing dataset	500

Table 9.2 Analysis of classification accuracy performance.

No of data	RNN in %	PNBM in %	WHONN in %	SPLA-DMPNN
400	32	44	48	52
800	48	59	64	71
1200	59	69	75	83
1600	64	87	92	93

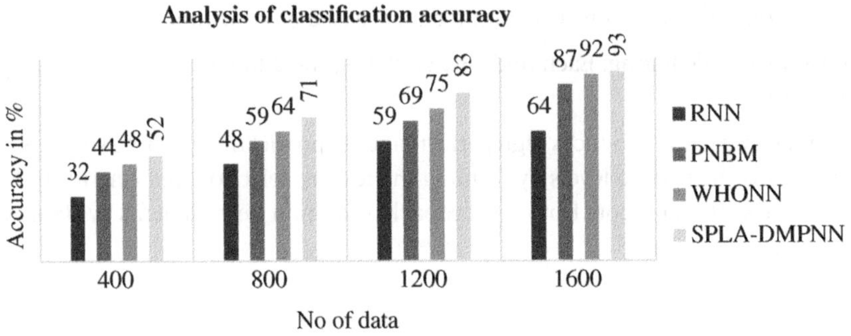

Figure 9.2 Analysis of classification accuracy performance.

92% for 1600 data, similarly, the existing study RNN algorithm has 64% and PNBM has 64 for 1600 data [16].

The above Figure 9.3 and Table 9.3 define the sensitivity performance graph comparison results. The proposed **SPLA-DMPNN** algorithm 91%, WHONN has 89% for 1600 data, similarly the exiting algorithm PNBM algorithm has 85%, and RNN algorithm has 66%.

Figure 9.4 and Table 9.4 represent the analysis of specificity performance graph comparison results. The proposed, SPLA-DMPNN produces 91%, WHONN

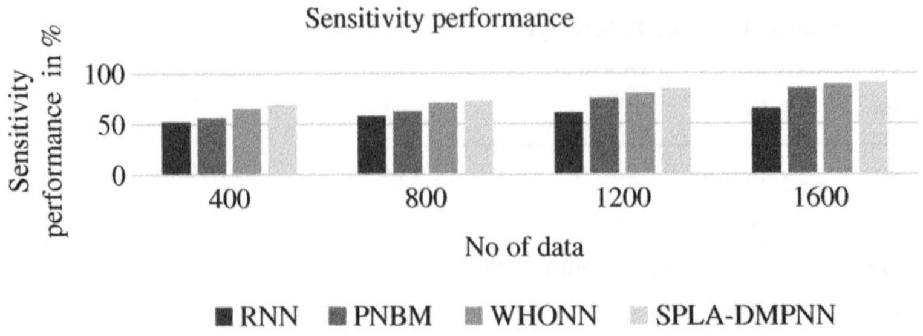

Figure 9.3 Analysis of sensitivity performance.

Table 9.3 Analysis of sensitivity performance.

No of data	RNN in %	PNBM in %	WHONN in %	SPLA-DMPNN
400	52	56	65	69
800	58	62	71	73
1200	61	75	80	85
1600	65	85	89	91

Table 9.4 Analysis of specificity performance.

No of data	RNN in %	PNBM in %	WHONN in %	SPLA-DMPNN
400	54	60	66	70
800	62	66	72	74
1200	70	74	78	85
1600	74	83	88	91

algorithm has 89% for 1600 data, similarly, the existing algorithm PNBM algorithm has 86%, and RNN algorithm has 74%.

The above Figure 9.5 and Table 9.5 false rate performance comparison results. The proposed **SPLA-DMPNN** algorithm provides 5% for 1600 data likewise the existing algorithm PNBM algorithm has 13%, and RNN algorithm has 36% for 1600 data.

Figure 9.6 defines the analysis of time complexity performance of the proposed and existing algorithm comparison results. The proposed algorithm WHONN time

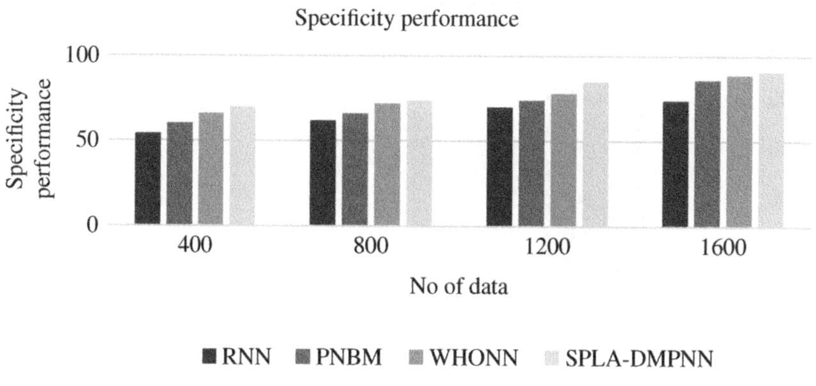

Figure 9.4 Analysis of specificity performance.

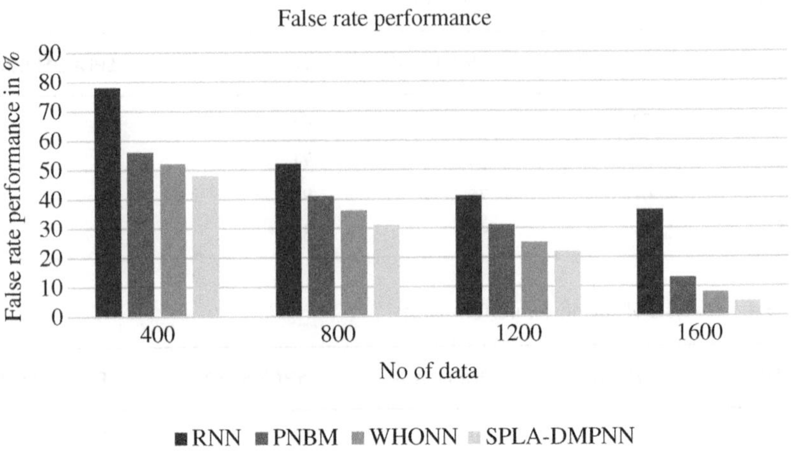

Figure 9.5 Analysis of false rate performance.

Table 9.5 Analysis of false rate performance.

No of data	RNN in %	PNBM in %	WHONN in %	SPLA-DMPNN
400	78	56	52	48
800	52	41	36	31
1200	41	31	25	22
1600	36	13	8	5

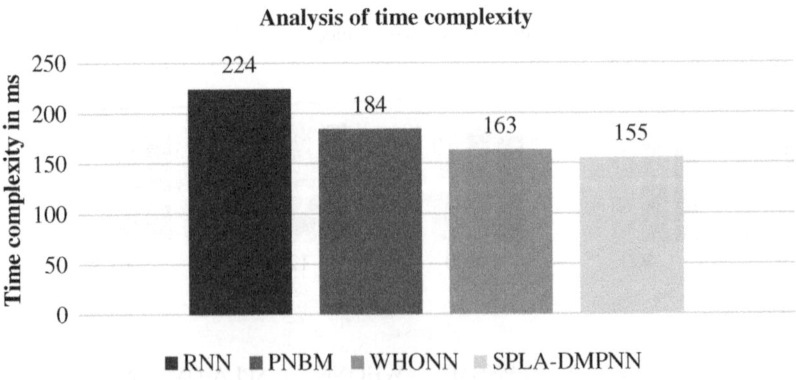

Figure 9.6 Analysis of time complexity.

complexity has 163 ms, similarly, the exiting algorithm PNBM has 184 ms, and RNN algorithm has 224 ms.

9.5 Conclusion

In this research, we propose a new term SPLA based student sentiment analysis using DMPNN in E-learning Environment. This model can be applied directly to pre-trained word vectors. The set of neighbors with similar meanings to the target word is derived through the emotional vocabulary and gives different weights based on the emotional score. Adjacent words, along with the original pre-trained word vectors, are optimized by an enhanced genetic algorithm to obtain a word vector with emotional information. The proposed system produces high performance compared to the other system as well in Classification accuracy performance is 94%, sensitivity performance is 92%, specificity performance is 91%, false rate performance is 6%, and time complexity is 125 ms.

References

1 Aslam, S.M., Jilani, A.K., Sultana, J., and Almutairi, L. (2021). Feature evaluation of emerging E-learning systems using machine learning: an extensive survey. *IEEE Access* 9: 69573–69587. https://doi.org/10.1109/ACCESS.2021.3077663.

2 Rajkumar, R. and Ganapathy, V. (2020). Bio-inspiring learning style chatbot inventory using brain computing interface to increase the efficiency of E-learning. *IEEE Access* 8: 67377–67395. https://doi.org/10.1109/ACCESS.2020.2984591.

3 Maher, Y., Moussa, S.M., and Khalifa, M.E. (2020). Learners on focus: visualizing analytics through an integrated model for learning analytics in adaptive gamified E-learning. *IEEE Access* 8: 197597–197616. https://doi.org/10.1109/ACCESS.2020.3034284.

4 Alojaiman, B. (2021). Toward selection of trustworthy and efficient E-learning platform. *IEEE Access* 9: 133889–133901. https://doi.org/10.1109/ACCESS.2021.3114150.

5 Yue, J. et al. (2019). Recognizing multidimensional engagement of E-learners based on multi-channel data in E-learning environment. *IEEE Access* 7: 149554–149567. https://doi.org/10.1109/ACCESS.2019.2947091.

6 Mangaroska, K., Vesin, B., Kostakos, V. et al. (2021). Architecting analytics across multiple E-learning systems to enhance learning design. *IEEE Transactions on Learning Technologies* 14 (2): 173–188. https://doi.org/10.1109/TLT.2021.3072159.

7 Agarwal, S., Sharma, V.K., and Kaur, M. (2021). Effect of E-learning on public health and environment during COVID-19 lockdown. *Big Data Mining and Analytics* 4 (2): 104–115. https://doi.org/10.26599/BDMA.2020.9020014.

8 De Kiennert, N., Vos, M.K., and Garcia-Alfaro, J. (2019). The influence of conception paradigms on data protection in E-learning platforms: a case study. *IEEE Access* 7: 64110–64119. https://doi.org/10.1109/ACCESS.2019.2915275.

9 Naveed, Q.N., Mohamed Qureshi, M.R.N., Shaikh, A. et al. (2019). Evaluating and ranking cloud-based E-learning critical success factors (CSFs) using combinatorial approach. *IEEE Access* 7: 157145–157157. https://doi.org/10.1109/ACCESS.2019.2949044.

10 Wu, E.H.-K., Lin, C.-H., Ou, Y.-Y. et al. (2020). Advantages and constraints of a hybrid model K-12 E-learning assistant chatbot. *IEEE Access* 8: 77788–77801. https://doi.org/10.1109/ACCESS.2020.2988252.

11 López, V., Fragoso Díaz, O.G., Santaolaya Salgado, R. et al. (2019). Learning web services for E-learning in the workplace. *IEEE Latin America Transactions* 17 (11): 1894–1901. https://doi.org/10.1109/TLA.2019.8986429.

12 Garg, R., Kumar, R., and Garg, S. (2019). MADM-based parametric selection and ranking of E-learning websites using fuzzy COPRAS. *IEEE Transactions on Education* 62 (1): 11–18. https://doi.org/10.1109/TE.2018.2814611.

13 Gifari, M.K., Lhaksmana, K.M., and Mahendra Dwifebri, P. (2021). Sentiment analysis on movie review using ensemble stacking model. In: *2021 International Conference Advancement in Data Science, E-learning and Information Systems (ICADEIS)*, 1–5. https://doi.org/10.1109/ICADEIS52521.2021.9702088.

14 Zhai, G., Yang, Y., Wang, H., and Du, S. (2020). Multi-attention fusion modeling for sentiment analysis of educational big data. *Big Data Mining and Analytics* 3 (4): 311–319. https://doi.org/10.26599/BDMA.2020.9020024.

15 Yang, L., Li, Y., Wang, J., and Sherratt, R.S. (2020). Sentiment analysis for E-commerce product reviews in Chinese based on sentiment lexicon and deep learning. *IEEE Access* 8: 23522–23530. https://doi.org/10.1109/ACCESS.2020.2969854.

16 Singh, L.K. and Renuga Devi, R. (2022). Analysis of student sentiment level using perceptual neural Boltzmann machine learning approach for E-learning applications. In: *2022 International Conference on Inventive Computation Technologies (ICICT), Nepal*, 1270–1276. https://doi.org/10.1109/ICICT54344.2022.9850860.

10

Big Data and Deep Learning-based Tourism Industry Sentiment Analysis Using Deep Spectral Recurrent Neural Network

Chingakham Nirma Devi[1] *and R. Renuga Devi*[2]

[1] *Department of Computer Science, Vels Institute of Science, Technology and Advanced Studies (VISTAS), Chennai, India*
[2] *Department of Computer Science and Applications (MCA), SRM Institute of Science and Technology, Ramapuram, Chennai, India*

10.1 Introduction

Big data has attracted the attention of many researchers due to its great potential and ability to solve problems associated with large amounts of data. The tourism industry is one of the industries that seeks to improve business processes using the concept of big data. How tourism researchers use this data, and this new type of data may be part of a new research paradigm that requires new methods that improve the theoretical understanding of tourism. It's time to find out. So far, online data sources are mainly used for application research. It provides (often free) data that provides insights into the travel/tourism industry and its customer activities. It is not surprising that previous research has focused on business strategy development, innovation and product development, and marketing activities.

The concept of tourism satisfaction is important in the context of the tourism industry, as it is a service-oriented industry that relies on positive emotions and feedback from the customer. Satisfaction as a theoretical structure has long been explored and discussed, and there are many tools to manipulate and measure it.

Online review data is an important part of Tourism Big Data, which directly reflects the true feelings of tourists, so it has been widely researched. The role of big data in tourism is reflected in two key aspects. On the other hand, the big data of the tourism sector is optimistic for the transformation of the tourism sector and has a major impact on the healthy and rapid growth of the tourism sector. On the other hand, the tourism industry has big data on the potential to contribute to the innovation of tourism management tools. "Sentiment Analysis" automatically determines the emotional trajectory of ideas by targeting textual ideas.

Applying Artificial Intelligence in Cybersecurity Analytics and Cyber Threat Detection, First Edition.
Edited by Shilpa Mahajan, Mehak Khurana, and Vania Vieira Estrela.

There are two main branches of emotion analysis methods: machine learning-based emotion analysis and semantic method-based emotion analysis. There are several text classification methods, such as text classification using neural network methods. It has been pointed out that online reviews of tourist sites affect the confidence of tourists and stimulate their purchase demand. Text emotion polarity classification based on semantic features and binary models for Weibo conceptual data analysis. In addition, applications for data processing and emotion analysis are gradually being developed in the tourism industry.

Established the shortcomings of machine learning-based emotion analysis methods in travel review analysis, and established a semantic dictionary-based emotion analysis model. Effectively improving the management performance of travel appraisal reports. A sentimental analysis model to help improve service quality and image marketing in tourist areas.

Deep Learning (DL) methods have the advantage of automatically extracting features from data. Current tourism studies based on in-depth learning techniques have explored the travel experience of budget hotels, target image identification, and review classification. Although the DL method is used for the tourism sector. Therefore, this study reviews feature-level perception analysis performed by in-depth learning techniques, compares the performance of in-depth learning models, and explores the model training process.

10.2 Related Work

With the advancement of the Internet, innovation and correspondence frameworks, the making of movement information at all levels (lodgings, cafés, transportation, legacy, the travel industry occasions, exercises, and so on) will increment, particularly with the development of Online Travel Agencies (OTA) [1]. Notwithstanding, the rundown of potential outcomes that these web search tools (or concentrated travel destinations) propose to guests is gigantic, and the related outcomes are frequently submerged in the "commotion" of the data, ruining or if nothing else dialing back the choice cycle [2].

Breaking down paper texts through huge information examination, contrasts in provincial media reactions to the travel industry all in all give new exploration viewpoints to researchers in the fields of worldwide data, large information, and the travel industry. Making an organization of traveler locales utilizing this retagged information will provide you with a superior comprehension of the travel industry exercises [3].

With the quick development and fame of web-based entertainment destinations, the travel industry specialists and chiefs have given an enlightening channel that gathers a lot of text-based surveys or remarks and photographs connected with clients' past movement encounters [4]. In the field of the travel industry, many examinations utilize connected open information to coordinate information with other incorporated open datasets to improve information and the travel industry content to address the issues of explorers. Tackle an essential proposal issue [5].

Carried out brilliant the travel industry administrations, presented the Internet of Things (IoT) in parks and executed different shrewd data administrations [6]. Contrasted with conventional travel industry arranging plans, this model improves the general travel industry experience and working productivity of the district overall as far as ensuring the vacationer experience of sightseers and the interests of those working the arranging focuses [7].

Organized factors, for example, informal communication information, climate, and occasions are utilized to drive a travel industry interest conjecture model in view of the slant-expanding relapse tree. At long last, taking for instance, we will utilize truly measurable information from traveler stations and person-to-person communication information to play out an experiential examination to foresee the travel industry interest in Huangshan [8]. A top-to-bottom learning model in view of the Dense Feature Pyramid Network (DFPN), which considers the uniqueness and intricacy of street signs. DFSN coordinates shallow component channels with shallow element channels to make shallow element maps accessible for profound elements with a high goal and phenomenal detail [9].

Taking into account the impact of this virtual entertainment site, the examination of Twitter content has turned into a piece of exploration as it gives helpful bits of knowledge on the subject. Travel surveys are an extraordinary way for vacationers to find out about movement locations. Sadly, a few remarks are improper and the information is clear. Highlight-based feeling grouping strategies have been demonstrated to be promising in clamor concealment. Close-to-home investigation is acquiring and more consideration as a significant field of normal language handling [10]. In scholarly evaluation, opinion examination assists teachers with distinguishing understudies' actual sentiments about courses as soon as possible, to change educational plans in an opportune and exact way, and to work on the nature of training [11].

Various posts on these virtual entertainments are distributed every day and seen by general society [12]. Obviously, long-range interpersonal communication media can straightforwardly impact individuals' perspectives on a specific subject. This information can be utilized for significant data, which can assist organizations with understanding what patterns or opinions [13]. The quantity of these day-to-day produced signs have developed dramatically and thus there is a colossal measure of data addressing a huge piece of the new world called Big Data [14]. This huge information is utilized by an assortment of undertakings to pursue showcasing choices, track explicit ways of behaving, or remove important data to recognize [15]. Sentiment Analysis (SA) is perhaps the most dynamic area of exploration.

10.3 Materials and Method

The availability of large data related to tourism enhances the ability to improve the accuracy of tourism demand forecasting but presents significant challenges to forecasting such as the curse of dimension and the high model complexity. Fixed results in several schemes show that the proposed Deep Spectral Recurrent Neural Network (DSRNN) system is superior to the basic model in terms of horizontal accuracy, directional accuracy and statistical significance. Effectively analysis the tourism for Big Data and improve the predictive performance of the model. The group in-depth learning model contributes to the tourism forecasting literature and benefits relevant officials and tourism sentiment reviews.

Figure 10.1 describes a proposed block diagram for tourism SA based on hospitalized data. In the first step, initialize the tourism review data and next preprocessing the data using Individual value Decomposition Analysis (IVDA) then extracting the particular data from feature extraction for analysis, and evaluating the features weights using spider optimization method, and analyzing the features based on the sentiment reviews. In the trained features, calculating the Softmax logical function. Finally, classifications using DSRNN give better accuracy compared to the previous methods.

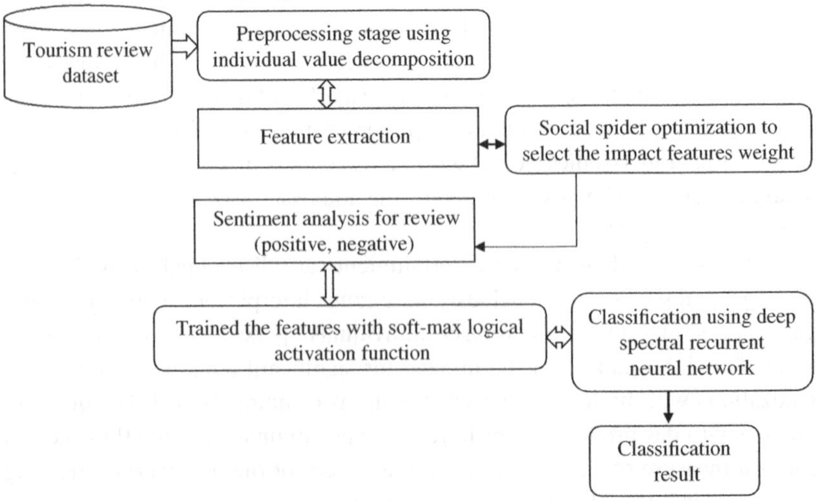

Figure 10.1 Proposed block diagram.

10.3.1 Individual Value Decomposition Analysis (IVDA) for Pre-processing Stage

This is the initial stage of the system. Data pre-processing IVDA to transform source data into an easy-to-use and efficient format for processing practices. In the early stages, use the min–max method to arrange the data. Normalization of training time can be improved because all the data used during training are the same (e.g., in the range 0 to 1).

$$P_{norm} = \frac{P - P_{min}}{P_{max} - P_{min}} \tag{10.1}$$

Steps for Preprocessing

Begin

Input: Each values of the dataset
Maximum values of data
Minimum values of data

Output: removed unwanted data
Step 1: Set maximum and minimum ranges of data $(a,b)//a$ and b is data variable
Step 2: Identify the values $(P_{max}\ P_{min})$
Step 3: For each (data item) do

$$P_a = \frac{P - P_{min}}{P_{max} - P_{min}} * (a - b) + a \tag{10.2}$$

where P_{norm} the effect of normalization and P is the initial value before normalization. Where P_{max} and P_{min} represent the maximum and minimum values of each aspect, respectively. Data preprocessing is defined as the process of converting the value of a continuous data attribute into an array of finite intervals by minimizing the loss of information in the data.

10.3.2 Extracting Features Using Spider Optimization to Select the Effective Features Weight (SO-EFW)

The purpose of analyzing feature selection and feature extraction techniques is to understand how these techniques can be effectively used to implement high-performance learning algorithms that ultimately improve the predictive accuracy of classifiers. The Spider Optimization to select the Effective Features Weight (SO-EFW) algorithm based on the learning and decision-making activities of minimum and maximum weights in locating data resources. After launch, enable the minimum and maximum weights are improving their data review in the SA phase. Finally, minimum weights and maximum weights of data determine optimization.

Steps for Feature Extraction

Stage 1: Initialization of parameters: maximum features weights, minimum features weights

Estimating the weights of each features
Choose features (maximum and Minimum)

Stage 2: While meeting the nearest values do

Update the individual *n* minimum weights of features
An Effective selection for all features based on the weights
Evaluate the Probability ($prob_s$) of selecting for each values

Stage 3: In the best and worst value of weight features S_r

$$\text{Determined the Features weights } FWs = \frac{F(S_r) - worst_i}{good_{i\_}worst_i} \quad (10.3)$$

if_w = feature weight
im_w = maximum weights
$[i_0 ff_{sso}]$ = Calculating (if_w, i_{mw})
$[i_{mw}, i_{fw}]$ = Interchange worst $(im_w if_{sso},)$
S

Until $S < itern$

R = Feature subset of i_{best}

where, i_{mw} – maximum weights, i_{fw} – initialize feature weights, if_{sso} – Feature using Social spider optimization, S_r – feature weights, $S+1$, S-variables. The SSO-IFW algorithm has the best accuracy in achieving the optimal solution, but it also has the highest integration. Impact features to change movement and weight parameters Effective spider optimization for selecting weight (SO-EFW). Spider ratings are defined and assigned weights to each spider. Feature selection to exclude inappropriate features from the original database.

10.3.3 Sentiment Analysis for Review of Positive and Negative Score

SentiwordNet is used to calculate the sum of the positive and negative points of a sentence or concept. In this study, using the SentiwordNet, the words in each positive and negative sentence are counted, and the positive and negative scores

Table 10.1 Sentiment analysis score.

Wordcount	Pos_score	Neg_score
The	0.67	0.60
Bus	0.56	0.52
Hospitalized	0.78	0.78
Food	0.4	0.43
Options	0.56	0.45

of all words are added to calculate the overall positive and negative scores of the sentence. The positive and negative marks are calculated as follows:

$$\text{Positive\_score\_sentence} = \frac{\text{Sum of the positive score}}{\text{Total number of words in reviews}} \tag{10.4}$$

$$\text{Negative\_score\_sentence} = \frac{\text{Sum of the negative score}}{\text{Total number of words in reviews}} \tag{10.5}$$

In the example, tourism sentiments review is used to generate the following positive and negative scores:

Table 10.1 shows the overall positive score of the sentence is 0.57 and the negative score is 0.45. Point of Score (POS) number, POS probability, positive and negative scores, after detecting the feature vector.

10.3.4 Trained the Features with Softmax Logical Activation Function

The activation function is very important because it helps to learn and understand nonlinear and complex mapping between input and related output. Softmax functionality is a combination of several sigmoid functions. Know that the values given by the sigmoid function are in the range 0 to 1, so we can assume that these are the probabilities of the data points for a given class. The sigmoid function used for binary classification, the Softmax function can be applied to a variety of classification problems. This function returns the probability of each data point in each class. It can be expressed as below.

$$\sigma(z)_j = \frac{e^{zj}}{\sum_{s=1}^{S} e^{zj}} \text{For } j = 1 \ldots S \tag{10.6}$$

When creating a network or model for many classes, there are as many neurons as there are target classes in the output layer of the network.

10.3.5 Classification Using Deep Spectral Recurrent Neural Network (DSRNN)

SA is the process of extracting a sense of tourism about a destination from an online travel review text. The results of SA are an important basis for tourism decision-making. So far, there has been no focus on how sentimental analysis techniques can be effectively used to improve the effectiveness of sentimental analysis. The main reason for the popularity of tourism is to provide a multi-layered experience to tourists, and this information can be obtained through a strategically driven data big data classification. Classifiers such as the window size of the DSRNN model and the long-distance bias problem of the straight-forward and DSRNN model mechanism, DSRNN recommend using Long Short-Term Memory (LSTM) as a pooling layer to facilitate emotional classification. Since the context is similar to the expression of emotional words such as "good" and "bad" as opposed to the emotional course of the word, they propose to introduce sentiment information into the word vector.

Steps for Deep Spectral Recurrent Neural Network (DSRNN)
Step 1: Initialize the dataset features

For $(F) = 1$ to $F//F$ is the number of base classifiers

Step 2: Evaluating the (F) number of instance features from Whole training set
Step 3: Select the variable from the dataset for classification
Step 4: DSRNN → training individual Classifier and train the feature (F)
Step 5: Making a prediction

For the input and predict the output with the weights score (F)
End

Step 6: Compute the overall prediction for accuracy

The Input of DSRNN is F_i. Then the output of hidden layer (H), the current stage H_i is calculated as,

$$\vec{H}(F) = F^H(A), \tag{10.7}$$

$$\vec{H} = \frac{1}{f}\sum_{F=0}^{F}\vec{H}(F) \tag{10.8}$$

The DSRNN classifiers show a set of basic classifications trained with Feature (F). For input A, the f-DSRNN classifier provides a separate prediction score. Each DSRNN classifier makes predictions using the fractional values of a subset of related variables. DSRNN classifiers use different variations to generate multiple forecast scores. The final prediction is obtained by averaging all the scores.

10.4 Result and Discussion

The implementation of the tourist review-based SA is done using the simulation tool Anaconda with the programming language Python. Python is a dynamic, interpreted, and general-purpose programming language and it provides lots of high-level data structures.

Table 10.2 illustrates details of simulation parameters for tourist review-based SA using the proposed method. The proposed method DSRNN comparison techniques are DFPN, Superior Expectation-Maximization Vector Neural Network (SEMVNN), and Probabilistic Adversarial Neural Network (PANN). Also refer [16] for more details.

Table 10.3 explores a classification performance for tourist sentiment analysis the proposed method produces better performance results.

Exploration of classification performance:
The proposed performance provides better result as shown in Figure 10.2. The proposed DSRNN gives 93% for 400 data likewise the previous method result is DFPN is 80%, SEMVNN result is 85%, PANN result is 89%, and DFPN algorithm result is 80%.

Table 10.2 Details of simulation parameters.

Parameter	Value
Tool	Anaconda
Programming language	Python
Data set name	Trip advisor
Total number of data	1300
Number of trained data	1000
Number of test data	300

Table 10.3 Exploration of classification performance.

No of data	DFPN in %	SEMVNN in %	PANN in %	DSRNN in %
100	50	57	60	70
200	61	65	71	78
300	72	78	80	86
400	80	85	89	93

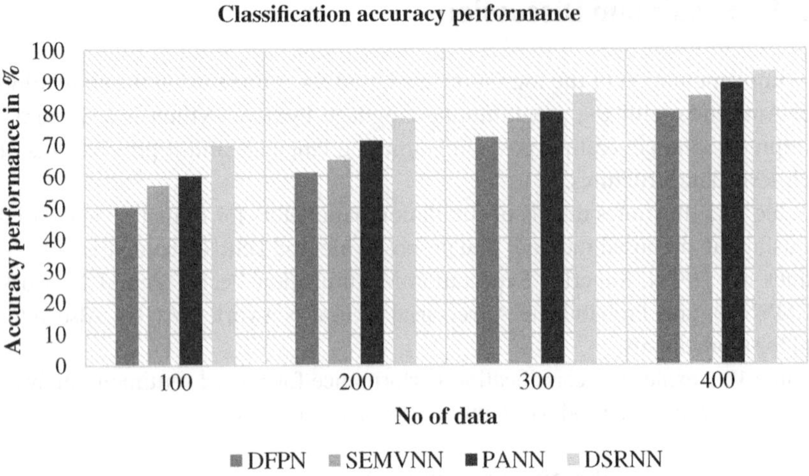

Figure 10.2 Exploration of classification performance.

Table 10.4 Exploration of precision and recall performance.

Comparison methods	Precision in %	Recall in %
DFPN	72	74
SEMVNN	74	76
PANN	84	85
DSRNN	89	91

The proposed and existing comparison results of precision and recall performance are shown in Table 10.4.

Figure 10.3 defines a detailed description of precision and recall performance in the graph. The proposed method DSRNN precision has 89% and recall has 91% for 400 tourist data; similarly, the existing method result is SEMVNN precision has 74% and recall has 76%, PANN algorithm recall has 91% and precision has 89% and DFPN algorithm precision has 72% and recall has 74%.

Table 10.5 expresses an F-measure performance for tourist review-based sentiment analysis performance results.

Exploration of F-measure performance: The proposed and existing results are shown in Figure 10.4. The proposed method provides higher F-measure performance than previous methods.

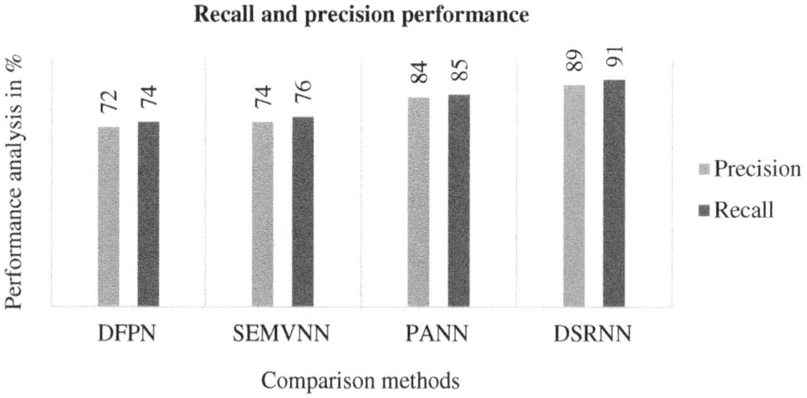

Figure 10.3 Exploration of precision and recall performance.

Table 10.5 Exploration of *F*-measure performance.

No of data	DFPN in %	SEMVNN in %	PANN in %	DSRNN in %
100	52	58	62	75
200	64	66	71	80
300	70	72	80	86
400	76	78	84	92

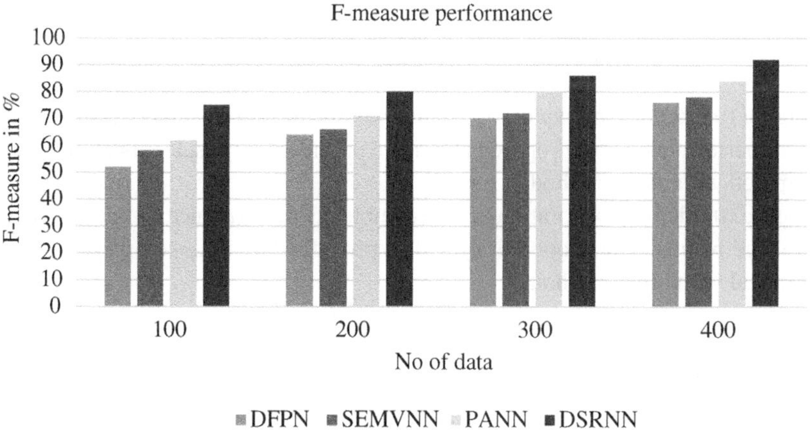

Figure 10.4 Exploration of *F*-measure performance.

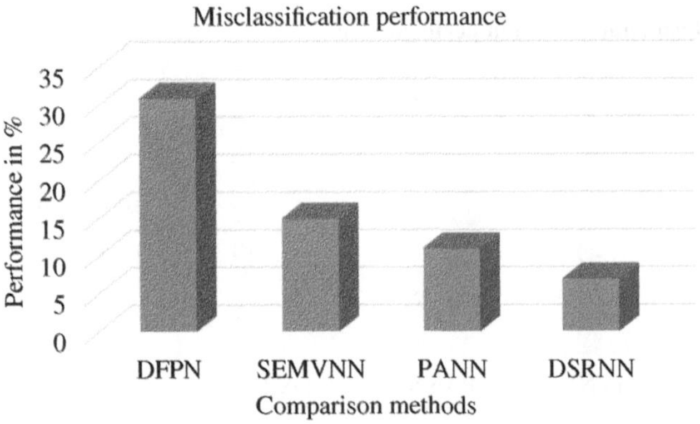

Figure 10.5 Exploration of misclassification performance.

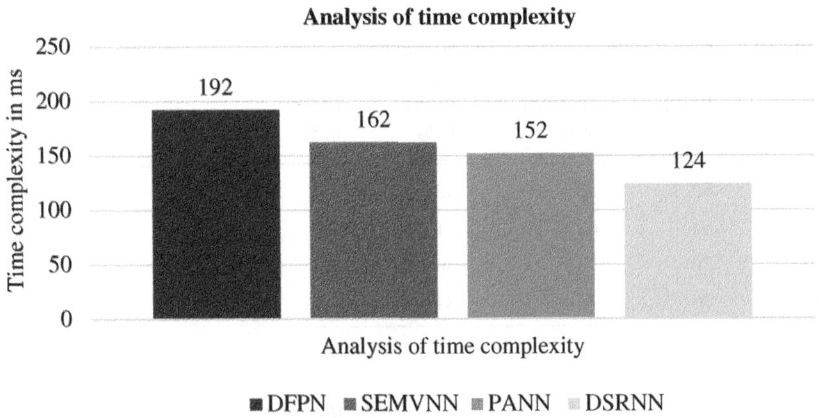

Figure 10.6 Exploration of time complexity performance.

Figure 10.5 defines the exploration of misclassification performance comparison results performance. The proposed algorithm provides low misclassification result compared with other methods.

Figure 10.6 defines exploration of time complexity performance comparison performance results. The proposed algorithm provides low time complexity result compared with other methods.

10.5 Conclusion

Tourism sector is a steadily growing economic sector; research and analysis of the data generated is very important for its management. The proposed DSRNN method is used to efficiently identify the sentiment terms. In the proposed first step, initialize the tourism review data and next preprocessing the data using IVDA then extracting the particular data from feature extraction for analysis, and evaluating the features weights using spider optimization method, and analysis of the features based on the sentiment reviews. In the trained features, calculating the Softmax logical function. The proposed DSRNN algorithm provides results as classification accuracy performance is 93%, precision has 89%, recall has 91%, F-measure performance 91%, misclassification is 7%, and time complexity is 124 ms. The proposed DSRNN algorithm gives better accuracy compared to the previous methods.

References

1 K. A. Fararni, F. Nafis, B. Aghoutane, A. Yahyaouy, J. Riffi and A. Sabri, "Hybrid recommender system for tourism based on big data and AI: a conceptual framework," in *Big Data Mining and Analytics*, vol. 4, no. 1, pp. 47–55, 2021, doi: https://doi.org/10.26599/BDMA.2020.9020015.

2 C. Wang, N. Guo, M. Lian and X. Xiao, "Differences in regional media responses to China's Holistic Tourism: big data analysis based on newspaper text," in *IEEE Access*, vol. 8, pp. 135050–135058, 2020, doi: https://doi.org/10.1109/ACCESS.2020.3011229.

3 X. Wu, Z. Huang, X. Peng, Y. Chen and Y. Liu, "Building a spatially-embedded network of tourism hotspots from geotagged social media data," in *IEEE Access*, vol. 6, pp. 21945–21955, 2018, doi: https://doi.org/10.1109/ACCESS.2018.2828032.

4 L. Zhong, L. Yang, J. Rong and H. Kong, "A big data framework to identify tourist interests based on geotagged travel photos," in *IEEE Access*, vol. 8, pp. 85294–85308, 2020, doi: https://doi.org/10.1109/ACCESS.2020.2990949.

5 P. Yochum, L. Chang, T. Gu and M. Zhu, "Linked open data in location-based recommendation system on tourism domain: a survey," in *IEEE Access*, vol. 8, pp. 16409–16439, 2020, doi: https://doi.org/10.1109/ACCESS.2020.2967120.

6 C. -C. Lin, W. -Y. Liu and Y. -W. Lu, "Three-dimensional Internet-of-things deployment with optimal management service benefits for smart tourism services in forest recreation parks," in *IEEE Access*, vol. 7, pp. 182366–182380, 2019, doi: https://doi.org/10.1109/ACCESS.2019.2960212.

7 F. Su, C. Duan and R. Wang, "Optimization model and algorithm design for rural leisure tourism passenger flow scheduling," in *IEEE Access*, vol. 8, pp. 125295–125305, 2020, doi: https://doi.org/10.1109/ACCESS.2020.3007180.

8 T. Peng, J. Chen, C. Wang and Y. Cao, "A forecast model of tourism demand driven by social network data," in *IEEE Access*, vol. 9, pp. 109488–109496, 2021, doi: https://doi.org/10.1109/ACCESS.2021.3102616.

9 S. Chen, Z. Zhang, R. Zhong, L. Zhang, H. Ma and L. Liu, "A dense feature Pyramid network-based deep learning model for road marking instance segmentation using MLS point clouds," in *IEEE Transactions on Geoscience and Remote Sensing*, vol. 59, no. 1, pp. 784–800, 2021, doi: https://doi.org/10.1109/TGRS.2020.2996617.

10 A Feizollah, S. Ainin, N. B. Anuar, N. A. B. Abdullah and M. Hazim, Halal products on Twitter: data extraction and sentiment analysis using stack of deep learning algorithms," in *IEEE Access*, vol. 7, pp. 83354–83362, 2019, doi: https://doi.org/10.1109/ACCESS.2019.2923275.

11 M. Afzaal, M. Usman and A. Fong, "Tourism mobile app with aspect-based sentiment classification framework for tourist reviews," in *IEEE Transactions on Consumer Electronics*, vol. 65, no. 2, pp. 233–242, 2019, doi: https://doi.org/10.1109/TCE.2019.2908944.

12 G. Zhai, Y. Yang, H. Wang and S. Du, "Multi-attention fusion modeling for sentiment analysis of educational big data," in *Big Data Mining and Analytics*, vol. 3, no. 4, pp. 311–319, 2020, doi: https://doi.org/10.26599/BDMA.2020.9020024.

13 Z. Sun, D. C. -T. Lo and Y. Shi, "Big data analysis on social networking," *2019 IEEE International Conference on Big Data (Big Data)*, 2019, pp. 6220–6222, doi: https://doi.org/10.1109/BigData47090.2019.9006153.

14 M. Ngaboyamahina and S. Yi, "The impact of sentiment analysis on social media to assess customer satisfaction: case of Rwanda," *2019 IEEE 4th International Conference on Big Data Analytics (ICBDA)*, 2019, pp. 356–359, doi: https://doi.org/10.1109/ICBDA.2019.8713212.

15 I. E. Alaoui, Y. Gahi and R. Messoussi, "Full consideration of big data characteristics in sentiment analysis context," *2019 IEEE 4th International Conference on Cloud Computing and Big Data Analysis (ICCCBDA)*, 2019, pp. 126–130, doi: https://doi.org/10.1109/ICCCBDA.2019.8725728.

16 C. N. Devi and R. Renuga Devi, 2022. "Big data analytics based sentiment analysis using superior expectation-maximization vector neural network in tourism," *2022 6th International Conference on Computing Methodologies and Communication (ICCMC), Erode, India*, pp. 1708–1716, doi: https://doi.org/10.1109/ICCMC53470.2022.9753738.

Part III

Applied Artificial Intelligence Approaches in Emerging Cybersecurity Domains

11

Enhancing Security in Cloud Computing Using Artificial Intelligence (AI)

Dalmo Stutz[1], Joaquim T. de Assis[2], Asif A. Laghari[3], Abdullah A. Khan[4], Nikolaos Andreopoulos[5], Andrey Terziev[6], Anand Deshpande[7], Dhanashree Kulkarni[8], and Edwiges G.H. Grata[9]

[1]*Centro Federal de Educação Tecnológica Celso Suckow da Fonseca (CEFET) at Nova Friburgo, Nova Friburgo, RJ, Brazil*
[2]*Instituto Politecnico do Rio de Janeiro, Nova Friburgo, RJ, Brazil*
[3]*Sindh Madresstul Islam University, Karachi, Sindh, Pakistan*
[4]*Research Lab of Artificial Intelligence and Information Security, Faculty of Computing, Science and Information Technology, Benazir Bhutto Shaheed University, Karachi, Sindh, Pakistan*
[5]*Computer Science Department, Technological Institute of Iceland, Reykjavík, Iceland*
[6]*TerziA, Sofia, Bulgaria*
[7]*Electronics and Communication Engineering, Angadi Institute of Technology and Management, Belagavi, India*
[8]*Department of Computer Science and Engineering, Angadi Institute of Technology and Management, Belagavi, India*
[9]*Department of Telecommunications, Federal Fluminense University (UFF), Niterói, RJ, Brazil*

11.1 Introduction

Cybersecurity (CS) comprises practices, technologies, and processes. These entities protect and defend networks, devices, software (SW), and data from CA, damage, or illicit access. The exponential augmentation of interconnected gadgets, systems, and networks urges complex CS. Digital economy and infrastructure advances worsen this by causing a significant CA increase, which has serious repercussions. Nation-state-affiliated and criminal antagonists and the mounting CAs' intricacy prompt new and intrusive ways to target menaces, thus requiring constant updating via "artificial intelligence" (AI). This CAs' snowballing happens in number, scale, impact, and calls or AI-driven CS (AICS) for dynamic defenses against CAs. AICS can also tackle "big data" (BD). Advisory organizations, viz. the "National Institute of Standards and Technologies"

Applying Artificial Intelligence in Cybersecurity Analytics and Cyber Threat Detection, First Edition.
Edited by Shilpa Mahajan, Mehak Khurana, and Vania Vieira Estrela.

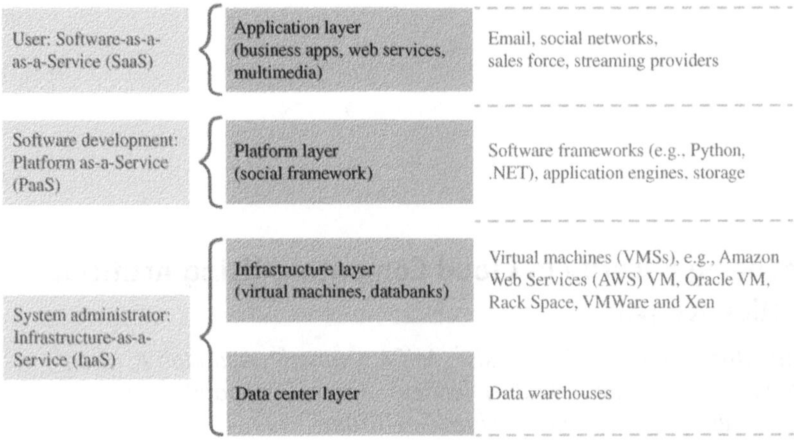

Figure 11.1 Multi-layer cloud computing framework.

(NIST) [1], have and encourage proactive and adaptive strategies by shifting towards real-time (RT) appraisals, continuous scrutiny, and data-driven analysis to pick up, protect against, and respond to. Catalog CAs prevent future "cyber threat" (CT) incidents (CTinc) [1]. AI affords intelligent analytics to shield against ever-evolving CAs by swiftly scrutinizing many events and tracking various CTs to anticipate and act before the problem. Therefore, AI increasingly integrates into the CS fabric in multiple "use cases" (UCs) that automate safekeeping tasks or sustain human security teams. Before returning to (AI) in CS, alias AICS, cloud computing (CC) models must be defined (Figure 11.1):

Software-as-a-Service (SaaS): It lets clients connect to and run cloud apps throughout the Internet, where email, electronic agendas, spreadsheets, and desktop tools (like Microsoft Office software (SW)) are some instances. SaaS delivers a complete SW-purchased solution from a cloud service supplier through buying licenses (aka subscriptions), which allow SW access employing external servers, enabling each user to reach and execute programs via the Internet rather than installing the SW on the user's machine. SaaS services offer small businesses an opportunity to better handle existing markets with fair pricing and accessibility via an Internet browser from any device uninterruptedly.

Platform-as-a-Service (PaaS): PaaS or "platform-based service" is a CC service type that permits clients to generate, instantiate, execute, and manage modules encompassing a computing platform with at least an application without the infrastructural complexity necessary to build and maintain assets typically associated with applications' development, launching and patching, while permitting developers to plan, develop, and release SW bundles.

Infrastructure-as-a-Service (IaaS): This CC service model supplies computing resources from a cloud vendor, e.g., servers, storage space, network, and virtualization to emulate hardware. IaaS frees users from maintaining data centers (DCs) and affords them to host these assets in the public cloud (by sharing the same hardware, memory, and network structure with other users), private cloud (resources are not shared), or hybrid cloud (a public/private combination). It offers high-level APIs for customers to dereference several low-level particulars of network arrangements like data partitioning, backup, scaling, physical computing resources, security, etc. A hypervisor organizes the virtual machines like guests. The cloud operational system contains hypervisors' pools that sustain many virtual machines and can upscale and downscale services consistently with customers' fluctuating necessities.

In CC use cases, BD can be organized in clouds whose nature can be threefold: private, public, or hybrid. Backup-as-a-service (Baas). IaaS revolves around DCs, all their usages, and data handling. DCs have specific consulting services. When redesigning DCs for CC, one must implement services like storage arrays or incorporate offsite storage into a current network.

AI's and CS's growing research enthusiasm fostered numerous studies to solve CAs' identification, protection, detection, response, and recovery caveats. This chapter mentions how AICS or CS intelligence (CTI) assists UCs, discussing ways to foster future developments. Looking at the above picture, one can conclude that CC can apply AI to any of its layers. AICS focuses on practical applications, as per NIST [1, 2]. Key issues are (i) adequate taxonomical AICS representations, (ii) some specific AICS UCs, (iii) current AICS, and (iv) AICS trending themes and future directions. These points led to the following:

- An AICS taxonomy with CS functions, solution categories, and specific UCs.
- Specific AICS UCs can reveal potential areas to harness AI capabilities.
- An acute analysis to identify CS gaps.

Section 11.2 clarifies some different AICS concepts and lists the main five AICS taxonomic aspects that will be detailed subsequently. Section 11.3 discusses the "identification function" (IF). Section 11.4 is about the "protection function" (PF). The "detection function" (DF) is considered in Section 11.5. Section 11.6 vividly analyzes the "response function" (RF) with some possibilities. The "recovery function" (RcF) appears in Section 11.7. Section 11.8 presents "supply-chain" (SC) "risk management" (RM) (alias SCRM) alternatives. Finally, a terse description of the main subjects and research implications can be found in the conclusion.

11.2 Background

11.2.1 Cybersecurity

CS situates policies, procedures, and technical tools to protect, defend, detect, and correct damage or unauthorized usage, handling, or adjustment of "information and communication technology" (ICT) structures. The rapid ICT pace of change and innovation and the rapidly evolving CT nature further obscure situations. AICS tools help security teams by alleviating risks and bettering security response in case unprecedented drawbacks strike. AICS's heterogeneity calls for a uniformly embraced and consolidated taxonomy that aids in utilizing AICS. Structured taxonomies will help understand and improve technical procedures and services.

A well-known NIST CS framework helps realize solutions to safeguard, detect, act in response, and defend against CAs [1, 2]. The NIST framework's core is fourfold: (i) functions, (ii) categories, (iii) subcategories, and (iv) informative references. The first two levels have 5 CS functions and 23 solutions to catalog the identified AI UCs. The functions provide a comprehensive lifecycle view for managing CS over time. The solution classes itemized under each function offer a good initial point for AI UC recognition to expand CS. The primary purpose of levels' selection is to facilitate intuitive tagging of the dominant AICS systems. The taxonomy can accommodate a third level by specifying AI-founded UCs for each CS framework level [2].

11.2.2 Artificial Intelligence

AI systems relate to (a) target applications and (b) their lifecycle states, like research, design, development, deployment, and usage, exhibiting intelligent behavior by analyzing their environment and achieving specific goals with some autonomy. AI denotes different, multiple technologies and applications. AICS describes the desirable and undesirable environmental situations and assigns actions to sequences. The AI taxonomy from defines its (i) core (i.e., learning, planning, reasoning, communications, and data/result perception) and (ii) transversal domains and subdomains. Knowledge representation and different perceptions comprise reasoning. Planning also covers searching and optimization. Learning includes "machine learning" (ML). Communication leads to "natural language processing" (NLP). Perception entails "computer vision" (CV) and audio processing. AI domains embrace but are not circumscribed to "artificial neural network" (ANN), "deep learning" (DL) (alias "deep neural networks" (DNN)), "fuzzy logic" (FL), NLP, "genetic algorithms" (GAs), "evolutionary algorithms" (EAs), "Bayesian optimization" (BO), "support vector machines" (SVMs), metaheuristics, "planning graphs," "text mining" (TM), "case-based reasoning" (CBR), "sentiment analysis" (SA), planning graph, CC, intelligent image processing, Internet of Things (IoT), sensor/actuator networks, object recognition, and speech processing [3–15].

AI is large, and multidisciplinary (translational). So, an ample literary corpus addresses various perspectives, e.g., philosophical, technical, operational, and practical. This chapter discusses AICS implications and scenarios. It details how AI methods can identify, safeguard, sense, respond to, and recuperate CS. AICS describes which ecological situations are looked for and unwanted to assign actions to sequences. The core AI domains encompass the main scientific AI areas. Reasoning apportions knowledge representation and distinctive ways of "thinking," while planning also covers searching and optimization. Communication is related to NLP. Perception is about CV and audio handling [1, 4].

After primary studies, data mining began to feed the up-to-date, descriptive analysis phase. Data extraction (i) breaks down each report into its essential parts, (ii) describes the overall relationships and connections, and (iii) amasses qualitative and circumstantial data parameters. The collected qualitative data summarize each preliminary revision to present the contribution and demographic information. Contextual data include details about the CS function, solution type, UCs, and core AI dominion. Both data types are further examined to identify possible connections between the studies.

A taxonomy classifies existing frameworks to identify and evaluate the prospective AICS applications, accounting for the first two CS NIST levels. The core IaaS functions are fivefold:

(1) Identification (IF),
(2) Protection (PF),
(3) Detection (DF),
(4) Response (RF), and
(5) Recovery (RcF).

These functions cover AI tasks, e.g., preventing security attacks, mechanisms to actively look for new CTs and counterattack maneuvers. IaaS controls different CAs' lifecycle traits for effective defense.

11.3 Identification Function (IF)

The IF stage subsidizes other functions by pinpointing decisive tasks and CTs for systems, public, assets, and data, helping comprehend CS, recognizing gaps, and creating proper risk supervision strategies for the organization's necessities, CTs, and costs. The various IF solutions appear below.

11.3.1 CS Asset Management (CAM)

It identifies and keeps track of the organization's information, people, equipment, systems, and buildings to accomplish its goals with minimum risks. It encompasses assets' discovery, inventories, supervision, and tracking to protect them. CAM's complexity grows as organizations have more platforms than ever, from IoT operational technology systems to on-premises and CC services. Assets' proliferation and remote work have created highly distributed resources that are difficult to manage and inventory. An AI-centered CAM system can solve many challenges by feeding new intelligence levels to the human team across the following UCs.

Asset inventory management (AIM) is critical to warrant total visibility and control over all extended network assets. AI can foster continuous and automatic discovery of all devices, applications, and customers besides their critical operation classification. With accurate and up-to-date inventories, resources can be tracked and analyzed for an RA against known CA vectors. Compliance monitors can spot rogue resources and unauthorized use. Different approaches classify assets through ML algorithms. K-means clustering can classify the assets according to nuclear power plant requirements concerning safety, functionality, and integrity [3]. A "random forest" (RFor)-based ML classifier can categorize operating systems and identifies vulnerable network devices [2]. Several studies [4–6] focus on identifying and classifying IoT devices centered on network traffic features. Correspondingly, multiple and multi-stage ML methods can be used for single-device identification and classification and are only proper for small IoT networks [5, 6]. A classification problem solution in rapidly evolving, mixed, and dynamic environments can exploit a supervised ML method to allot IoT modules to predefined classes centered on their traffic flow values. There is work on identifying and blocking malware-infected assets, determining asset criticality, and the RA of individual resources to manage and ensure their security [8].

Automated configuration management (ACM) is a governance process that defines and maintains preferred system states and delivers timely misconfiguration alerts. The ACM system will consistently define the system settings and keep the system, thus only tolerating deviations in a controlled and authorized environment. Tailoring the system's configuration guarantees the mandatory performance, and its security reduces human error owing to manual or sub-optimal configuration setups. Dynamic configuration systems exist for online file-sharing and distributed CC storage established on system features and operating environments using multi-objective reinforcement learning (RL) and GAs [11]. A fully automated framework for adapting security controls works by observing the user's behavior and refining high-level security requirements expressed in human-friendly language [14]. ACM allows the compliance team to continuously review and test configurations to identify momentarily vulnerable structures to reduce or avoid CT incurrences (CTincs). A SW product line tactic can analyze systemic vulnerabilities automatically [16]. Alternatively, an RFor model application predicts CTincs based on the DNS and BGP protocol misconfiguration and externally discernible malicious activities commencing from the network [17].

Automated security control validation will monitor security RT in changing environments and CT landscapes, e.g., AI for a definitive CS system's appraisal through a network's telescope data, a CS framework, or by correlating the CTs, weaknesses, and security measures [2, 4].

11.3.2 Business Environment

A "business environment" (BE) identifies precarious processes and applications that guarantee business continuity amid adversity. BE is vital to business sustainability, responding effectively, and engendering recovery strategies. AI can automate this process via the following UC. Business impact analysis is crucial to determine critical BE functions and applications by evaluating CTincs' impacts on the business. AI can automate business impact analysis by economic RA based on a known attack vector or by calculating the CT feasibility and the probability of high-impact security events in critical businesses. Researchers gauge the financial CT risks in different BEs using other known attack profiles' modeling, rare-event simulation, or linking the corporation's intent to attackers' aptitudes to guide a scenario breakdown to find its impact on assets [18].

11.3.3 Governance

Governance embroils procedures, processes, and policies for understanding environmental and operational requisites, perceiving the organization's regulatory necessities, helping know an organization's responsibilities, and affording CT information to the management. AI can administer policies or automate the retrieval of strategic "vulnerability risk indicators" (VRIs). So, a future goal is an early-warning system to detect and indicate risk development vs. time attributable to red flags, policy disruptions, or other symptoms. The automatic VRI retrieval embraces the mean time between failures, unpatched systems' occurrences, risk appetite, or the total attempted breaches. These caveats can turn into knowledge that will assist in preventing CT breaches by rapidly remediating the risk.

Automated policy enforcement (APE) is vital for organizations to ensure compliance with suitable "risk management" (RM) and regulations. AI-driven policy enforcement in conventional non-SDN networks that utilize a controller with policy proxies [19]. The controller is a centralized management server that manages SW-defined middleboxes for regular routers and policy proxies to identify the traffic subject to rules and assist it in policy enforcement.

11.3.4 Risk Assessment

The "risk assessment" (RA) identifies, estimates, and prioritizes CS risks associated with operations, operational resources, and individuals currently or soon. It requires a careful CT analysis, susceptibility, and attack information to determine the extent to which CAs' could adversely impact the organization and the likelihood of such events. The manual RA process is complex, expensive, and time-consuming due to countless risk factors, and it requires active human involvement at every stage. The AI-based RA addresses these challenges by supporting the RM team in the following UCs.

Automated vulnerability identification and assessment (AVIA) modules systematically review structures' security weaknesses with automated susceptibility identification tools, classification, probing, and prioritization. These automated tools rely on frailty repositories, vendor susceptibility identification announcements, asset management systems, and CTI feeds to identify, classify, and gauge CAincs' severity while advising remediation.

Automated vulnerability detection is a vital bug isolation step in an organization's applications, servers, or other structures and assets. SW susceptibility discovery can occur by probing the source code using DL and transfer learning [20], employing text-mining practices to feed the ML-based error recognition models as per a "recommendation (alias recommender) system" (RS) that aids programmers in writing secure code. Frailty repositories or social networks aid in detecting emergent SW and cybernetic infrastructural glitches [21]. An exposure identification scheme across the system and network levels models the behavior of cyber-physical systems (CPS)/IoT under system and network levels' outbreaks. Then it exploits ML to discover potential attack spaces [22]. FL can find SW and hardware (HW) vulnerabilities in interfaces and applications by injecting unexpected, incorrect, or arbitrary data into a program or interface. Then, it monitors crashes, failed code assertions, undocumented jumps or debug routines, and potential memory leaks. AICS empowers by (i) spotting potential CAs, input initiation, and probable test case generation and (ii) analyzing crashes (Fig. 4). Reasoning and NLP can spawn seeds to enlarge code coverage with more exclusive execution paths as a basic smart fuzzing system step [23]. Test case generation is a studied FL field for web browsers, compilers, CPSs, SW libraries, and simple programs [4, 24–26]. Computerized penetration tests attempt to intrude attack surfaces via known or zero-day flaws to identify what the attacker can profit from current environments. Devising autonomous RL penetration testing for large networks and microgrid control algorithms undergoes studies [27].

Automated vulnerability classification expedites a deeper data security grasp to accelerate evaluation, automatic classification, and description labeling in reports. A frailty summarization that labels them within an industrial taxonomy model exists [28]. TM to classify weaknesses employs the "**Common Vulnerabilities and Exposures" (CVE) list** [29].

Vulnerability exploration pinpoints the potential CAs' vectors that can exploit weaknesses to appraise and achieve them effectively. A model-driven practice to automatically map adversarial stratagems and shared knowledge to the given system emerges in [2, 4]. A probabilistic model can appraise and manage systemic flaws by rapidly adjusting to the fluid network and attack features [30–33].

Vulnerability assessment and prioritization aim to prioritize weaknesses and provide a valuation report of systems' frailty exposure and severity. AICS assigns a severity score to each CPS frailty (e.g., equipment, data, business risk, etc.) along with a consequential CA's ease, severity, and prospective damage. Frailties' automatic assessment and severity from conflicting weakness reports through the ML pipeline based on the frailty severity and threat profile metrics [30–33]. Vulnerabilities and risk scores help every IoT gadget in the attack graph and are conceived by the network administrator to organize network topologies [33–35].

Automated threat-hunting searches for security across networks, datasets, and endpoints proactively, seeking potentially malicious, distrustful, or risky organizational activities. It identifies and categorizes eventual CTs ahead through fresh CTI on gathered data. CT hunting is a somewhat new paramount area for early detection. Yet, existing methodologies still work on anomaly-centered CT detection and oversee abounding external CT knowledge provided by "open-source (OS) CTI" (OSCTI) [2, 4, 34–37].

Attack path modeling proactively lessens risks, supporting security teams by mapping vulnerable network routes to judge risk, catch vulnerabilities, and take countermeasures to safeguard critical assets, e.g., intrusion alerts or weakness descriptions. All cyber data, including attention alerts, frailties, logs, and network traffic, may matter to simulate attacker/defender deeds and prevent them in RT [2, 4, 37, 38].

Automated risk analysis and impact assessment strengthen the RM team by ingeniously using internal and external risk records to gauge danger and related RT metrics. AI can hurry the RM progress by automating the risk score calculation [39, 40], the inference of the probability of CTincs [41], paramount VRIs' identification [42], and RA and decision analysis [43, 44] using log data and CTI within and outside the organization.

Predictive intelligence is lawful and relevant and can anticipate CAs, helping deliver an active defense by predicting an intrusion's type, intensity, and target. DL [45, 46] helps forecast alerts from malicious sources or on a given target using the sequence of previous warnings, historic spam emails, and network traffic data. Malware forecast involves predicting and blocking deleterious files before finishing their payload to prevent CAs rather than remedy them. Malware prediction models with "recurrent neural networks" (RNNs) forecast malicious behavior through machine activity data [47]. CT prediction can advance "cyber resilience" (CR) proactively. Attack prediction schemes may utilize different data types retrieved from news sites and websites, "dark web" (DW) forums, national frailty databanks, CT event reports, and public databases' flaws/exposure [48].

11.3.5 Risk Management Strategy

RM strategies assist operational risk decisions by forming priorities, risk tolerance, and constraints. It must warrant acceptable risk levels are established and documented along with reasonable resolution times and investment. AI can automate the following activities.

Decision support for risk planning involves implementing a sought-after countermeasures portfolio within a fixed budget. Formal decision support systems [28, 49, 50] and CA graph modeling [28] can help security designers contrast cost-effectively with countermeasures and ongoing risk budgets. The CS decision-making in risk planning matters due to the risk plan's sensitivity to the decision maker's attitude towards risk vs. the funding available. Thus, a decision support system implementation is vital for estimating uncertain CA risks affecting an organization, factoring uncertain CT rates, countermeasure expenditures, and assets' impacts. The GA in Ref. [49] combines countermeasures to block or mitigate CAs, letting users determine the ideal trade-off between investment costs and resulting risks. Robust optimization supports optimal balance studies between the anticipation, detection, and repression defenses while handling CS uncertainty [50]. An attack graph model can identify a portfolio of security controls to diminish risk [28]. Their model chooses the best possible rules to ascertain that the whole budget does not exceed the organizational budget.

"Supply chain" (SC) "risk management" (RM), aka SCRM, supports menace-related decisions for identifying, weighing, and managing SC risks. Successful SCRMs necessitate a broad CTs' view and weaknesses, cost-effective SC risk planning strategies, and a CR assessment to warrant CS. AI can automate CT analysis and prediction [29], optimal CS risk investment [51], and the SC CR [52].

SCs require a secure, integrated network between the incoming and outgoing chain subsystems. Hence, it is indispensable to understand and predict CTs using internal and CTI resources to limit business disruption. CTI data has been incorporated and used ML to predict CA patterns on cyber SC systems [29]. Optimizing CS risk investments is crucial for SCs to speedily detect, alleviate, and balance security breaches' impact with the available budget. There are different models for optimal CS investment with a limited budget and a security control portfolio to balance CS [51]. An SC CR appraisal is crucial to protect the SC from cyber intrusions and secure a competitive business advantage. An integrated, ample Dempster-Shafer (D-S) approach can build a framework for CR evaluation of an additive manufacturing SC [52].

11.4 Protection Function (PF)

PF assists in the planning and execution of appropriate controls to restrict or contain a potential CS event impact, including technical and procedural guidelines to shield against internal and external CTs proactively. AI can ameliorate the CPS's resilience through authenticating devices, clients, and other assets, checking customer behavior, automated access control, adaptive training, data leakage prevention and integrity monitoring, automated information defense processes, and protective solutions' provision to secure the system proactively.

11.4.1 Controlling, Identity, Authentication, and Access

Identity management, authentication, and access (IMAA) control limits admission to accompanying facilities and assets to accredited users, processes, apparatuses, and authorized activities. AI can manage and protect physical and remote access by (a) intelligent client and server authentication, (b) automated access regulation through authorizations, and (c) permissions to prevent unapproved access and its consequences.

AI-supported user authentication (AISUA) can improve user authentication with physical biometrics, behavioral biometrics, or multi-factor authentication instead of usernames, passwords, and even one-time text tokens. Biometrics employs inborn users' physical traits for identification like iris, blood vessels, fingerprints, and other bio-signals [53, 54] "Behavioral biometrics" (BB) are inimitably discernible and measurable human activity patterns that can deliver user-friendly and continuous CS. There are several BBs, including usage behavior and gait [52–54]. The user's comportment patterns related to a user's interaction with their own devices is the main basis of the continuous authentication systems via mobile functions and usage data, e.g., accelerometer, pacemakers, intelligent watches, and statistics from different applications' interactions, to conclude whether the present user remains the same as the individual authenticated beforehand [53]. A continuous authentication scheme can rely on the users' BBs' profiles according to their interaction with different office devices for smart offices using CC and an RFor algorithm. Still, these solutions are gradually entering the realm of federated identity management elucidations, raising interest in them [54]. A transparent, non-intrusive, and continuous authentication scheme that can assist mobile devices' gait authentication is the required information to corroborate the user's authenticity as the person walks. Multi-factor authentication entails a layered methodology to safeguard data and applications requiring two or more credentials for user identity verification or login.

Intelligent HW authentication endorses devices by their credentials or behavior in the network to warrant M2M communication security. Researchers are actively working on sensor/actuator identification and authentication to warrant CPSs' security. Channel [55], sensor [56], and actuator flaws catch transient and steady-state parameters as input to the ML model for sensor identification.

"**Automated access control**" **(ACC)** restricts systems' right of entry to authorized users per situations or their organizational roles/regulations. AI techniques help maintain the access control state [57], role mining [58], and situation-aware decision-making [59] to prevent unauthorized access and its consequences.

"**Role-based access control**" **(RBAC)** bestows entrance to different customers consistent with their organizational roles. AICS can update and maintain the access control state when exceptions or violations are reported [57] by providing an optimized action plan to reconfigure the RBAC state to facilitate maintenance. An optimal role-mining, scalable tactic to unearth user-role and role-permission associations obtain cues from existing access control lists [58]. Attribute-based access control considers various pre-configured attributes related to the user, environment, and access resource. AICS situation-aware decision-making performance for attribute-reliant access control has been tested in fisheries and manufacturing systems [59].

11.4.2 Awareness and Training

This response category covers CS awareness and training for personnel and partners to accomplish their information security responsibilities in compliance with procedures and policies. AI can be used for adaptive and personalized CS training, awareness, or recommendations by automatically selecting content via NLP algorithms [60] or providing an ML-enabled coach for solution-guiding hints [61]. Adaptive security awareness and training help overcome training challenges of outdated content, material selection, and acceptable approaches. An adaptive web-established learning CPS getting up-to-date DBpedia training content and giving automated content selection based on a learner's prior knowledge of information security appears in [60]. On the other hand, programmers were helped by topic modeling or exploiting serious games to recommend/raise secure coding practices awareness [60, 61].

11.4.3 Data Security

Data security administrates information management as per risk strategy for defending sensitive records by (i) shielding information at rest and in transit and (ii) managing the assets' lifecycle, comprising their decommissioning or disposal. AI can actively prevent data leakage, protect email, block/report malicious domains, and monitor agent-based integrity for data confidentiality, integrity, and availability.

Data leakage prevention (DLP) encompasses detecting and protecting data breaches, exfiltration, or unwanted data destruction. AICS can surveil data access, information movement, users' activities [62, 63], automated data sensitivity exposure [64], and APTs' detection [65] to prevent data leakage. Identifying authorized individuals and how they use sensitive information affords accurate comprehension for data leakage preclusion by observing their behaviors or activities. AI helps monitor user activity to identify abnormal behavior regarding a spike in unusual activities by correlating multiple sources' data [62, 63]. These needs led researchers to employ an insider CT test dataset from CERT to get data leakage prevention insights for using different temporal representations of user activity or daily activity summaries, email contents, and email networks [62]. A model that only identifies data leakage events during the sensitive period before a staff member leaves an organization appears in [63]. Automated data sensitivity detection identifies and classifies data by analyzing, labeling, and organizing them into relevant groups (viz, confidential, individual, and public) employing shared traits [63], hampering data leakage prevention techniques to monitor users' actions towards only particular relevant sensitive data portions rather than always pursuing all data. An automated classification practice relying on security similarity to mitigate the sensitive data leakage threat from insiders is in Ref. [64]. Sensitive facts inherent to unstructured data make involuntary data leakage easier [64], which can be mitigated by a content and context-based information identification scheme using BiLSTM and an attention mechanism.

APTs are targeted CA types that last long and overlook the target network's defenses. The main purpose of this attack type is to steal data rather than trigger any damage. Researchers are working on efficiently capturing telemetry from endpoints, networks, and clouds to integrate and analyze diverse telemetry to extract "indicators of compromise" (IoCs), anomalies, and other relatable behaviors [65].

Intelligent protection means SW solutions to avert sophisticated email CAs. A spam email tactic traditionally seeks goods and services via unsolicited emails from/to bulk lists. Today, however, it is actively spreading malware, stealing authentication credentials, or committing financial fraud. AI can automate harmful spam protection. Supervised classification and DL-based [66] techniques can identify RT spam utilizing dynamic inward email data, including general, subject, visual, imagery, and attachment, among other content traits [67].

"Malicious domain blocking and reporting" (MDBR) offers a better security level for email protection by catching up with any evil network traffic from opening spam emails or attachments. AI helps identify suspicious websites for each DNS lookup and block malicious websites that may contain malware, phishing, ransomware, and other CTs. Detecting malicious websites works by training ML algorithms with an opulent collection of harmful and healthy website features. These features can be fourfold [68–72]: website design, domain, URL, and hybrid. A new website categorization method can pinpoint malware or crack websites employing the automated scraping and treatment of too many visual and non-visual design are trendy from detection results from malicious websites. Supervised ML [68] and DL [69] models can catch evil domain names employing classical domain-name structures. URL strings' parts containing linguistic, lexical, contextual, and statistical information can reveal malicious websites. Malicious websites with URL features have been analyzed as input to the ensemble ML and DL models [70]. Hybrid attributes for malevolent website identification help figure out botnets [73] or phishing website detections [71, 72] by combining features related to domain name structure and DNS response, viz resolution source, daily resolution amount, etc.

11.4.4 Information Protection, Processes, and Procedures

Information sources and assets consistent with security strategies, processes, and procedures must be safe. It includes protecting information and establishing, managing, and implementing response, retrieval, and vulnerability supervision plans: AI-powered backup and an AI-enhanced frailty management plan sustain processes and procedures for information protection.

AI-powered backup (AIPB) aims to back up critical data and SW components according to priorities and requirements for efficient backup. AI techniques can perform dynamic backup scheduling and optimized backup scheduling. A dynamic backup system with clever scheduling algorithms improves the stability and predictability of the backup environment that schedules the backup efficiently by determining which backup commences first and which storage goes to that backup to expand efficiency [74]. A 2-D Markov chain can model data backups and study their scheduling optimization by examining a probabilistic backup policy to initiate at each time slot, regardless of the backup size [75].

AI-enhanced vulnerability management plans are frameworks designed to proactively shrink risk exposure, which can disrupt and impact the whole system. Aligning the weakness management plan with systemic prerequisites and critical success factors becomes paramount, given the recently reported defenselessness rise. AICS techniques can determine context-based weakness risk scores and fragility exploitation trends in RT to protect assets and information systems. Context-based vulnerability risk scoring will help analysts (i) prioritize some particular assets' or information systems' risks and (ii) enable them to undertake protective action. An exciting risk prioritization scheme for vulnerability RA consists of an attacker's model integration to apprehend the invader's preference for exploiting weaknesses [76]. The risk score corresponds to the criticality and likelihood of the exploitation through a logic-reasoning engine. A frailty exploitation trend will help the analyst prioritize patching and remediation by envisaging the most probable exploited instabilities. Novel AICS approaches can estimate exploitability and unravel the class imbalance problem to improve ML algorithms' performance, focusing on (a) liability exploitation prediction using transfer learning to help experts prioritize patch applications [77] or (b) via sequential batch-learning, i.e., RT, dynamic adaptive learning, which tackles abnormalities and dynamic class imbalance within exploitability prediction [78].

11.4.5 Protective Technologies

Security and resilience for CPSs and assets utilize tamper-evident features to identify and deter attempts to breach, change, infiltrate, and get the organization's assets' knowledge. AI can engender protective ways through "intrusion prevention systems" (IPSs), anti-virus/anti-malware solutions, log analysis tools, and protection by deception.

Log analysis appraises computer-generated event logs to proactively isolate bugs, security concerns, or other risks. AICS log analysis can automate routine tasks to handle large amounts of distributed log data well. Performance tests of assorted supervised ML tactics for detecting malicious "remote desktop protocol" (RDP) in Windows sessions utilizing RDP event logs emerge in [77–79]. Other data presentation arrangements exploited a storytelling scheme to yield a natural language report for recognizing CT information according to users' knowledge levels [79]. Solutions for a variety of interoperability concerns in log management have emerged. The AI variety issue has been addressed to extract and treat textual records from different sources for satisfactory log feature representation via information retrieval [80]. Likewise, the work in [81] handled security analytics of the heterogeneous log data from different network sensors by employing automated feature extraction and selection techniques.

IPSs monitor the network traffic for apt action to thwart CAs by reporting, obstructing, dropping, or resetting connections through (i) unsupervised isolation forest [82] and (ii) self-organizing incremental ANNs and SVM-based IPSs [82–84] for embedded automotive systems and IoT networks, respectively.

Anti-virus/anti-malware solutions can scrutinize thousands of files and extract advantageous features to label them as nonthreatening or malware. Anti-virus programs can detect malware using executables' retrieved features [83] or dynamic data analysis [84] as an input to ANNs or RNN models.

Protection by deception is a technique to protect critical documents after attackers penetrate the network. AI can generate credible fake text documents to mislead CAs. Decoy files can divert the adversary from the factual target when the invader has already taken the system [85]. This decoy GA-centered text-creation handles actual documents' directness to hard-to-comprehend, albeit credible, fake documents.

11.5 Detection Function (DF)

DF enables timely CT event discovery by designing and implementing applicable activities to identify their occurrence. DF is crucial for security as prompt detection will minimize the disruption, comprising (i) actions for the suitable detection of invasions and glitches, (ii) impact assessment, (iii) implementation of a continuous monitoring security framework to verify the defensive measures' effectiveness, and (iv) appropriate detection processes' maintenance to ensure the cyber events' awareness. AI can speed detection by monitoring internal and external sources and expeditiously correlating this information to detect unusual activities to minimize aftermaths. AI solution categories appear below.

11.5.1 Anomalies and Events

Solutions discern and classify abnormal activities by establishing and managing baselines for multiple sources' operations and data flows. These baselines detect and analyze events to understand CA targets and approaches. "Intrusion detection systems" (IDSs) monitor CPS and network traffic to analyze anomalous and suspicious activities to detect possible system intrusions. IDS was realized as three classification types: binary, multi-category, or both. Binary classification assumes two labels: normal and attack. Conversely, multi-category schemes can classify three or more classes. Multi-category IDS classification discerns between different CA types, displaying users more information for CA remediation. Operational development and assessment metrics for binary and multi-category IDSs involve benchmark datasets. Datasets examples follow [86–97]:

1. SAA for system call-based IDS [98].
2. Aegean Wi-Fi (AWID) for wireless networks [99].
3. BGP RIPE for routing information services [100].

4. Canadian Institute of Cybersecurity's databanks [86].
5. CIFAR-10 with imageries.
6. CTU-13 for several botnet scenarios.
7. Ethereum Classic depicts CAs on an OS, a blockchain-reliant distributed computing framework via smart contracts.
8. ICS CA gas-pipeline dataset.
9. KDD99 and NSL-KDD partake in network traffic records.
10. "Coburg intrusion detection datasets" (CIDDS) with labeled flow from abnormality detection.
11. UNSW-NB15 comprises raw traffic collections for different attack types.
12. BOT-IoT dataset of normal and botnet traffic in an IoT network [4].
13. Hadoop logs for log-built anomaly detection benchmarking.
14. SEA to verify behavioral logs of Unix clients.
15. "Secure water-treatment dataset" (SWaT) with different sensors' and actuators' network data from a water-treatment plant.
16. UGR'16 has well-labeled traffic evidence from tier-3 internet service suppliers.
17. DARPA'99 has online and offline real/synthetic samples from an experimental environment.
18. UCM 2011 contains actual traffic traces.
19. TON_IoT for new Industry 4.0/IoT needs.

Intrusion detection relies heavily on binary (or basic) classification, exploiting different ML classifiers [86–97]. Still, some utilize other techniques like grouping through hyperparameter optimization, dataset class imbalance conundrum, and databank feature extraction [73, 101–125].

In multi-category grouping, the databank comprehends multiple disconnected classes. Data items belonging to a similar category receive the same label. Besides the normal tag, other traffic classes exist, e.g., denial-of-service (DoS), distributed DoS (DDoS), and user-to-root (aka, remote-to-local) attacks. Multi-category IDS sorting also applies different classifiers, advanced feature extraction tools [73, 101–125], hyperparameter classifiers' tuning, and tactics to handle class imbalance [73, 101–125]. Classification can be binary and multi-category for the intrusion detection problem. Multi-category ones can address class imbalance, 3-D or high-dimensional data visualization, and feature extraction [104] problems for the datasets.

11.5.2 Secure and Continuous Monitoring

RT, secure continuous surveillance of systems and assets, helps understand their environment and perceive security events. AI can automate observations by delivering CTI via a dynamic, heterogeneous information network to manage data logs from perceiving physical environments, networks, customers, service suppliers, and sensitive information systems.

Security monitoring encompasses amassing, analyzing, and presenting data from various sources to develop an almost universal answer revealing the wrongdoer's modus operandi and intents. This scenario actively requires efforts to process and correlate heterogeneous sources' records [105] and situational awareness [73, 105–130] to understand security information. An essential problem is processing colossal, dynamic, and assorted security information from evolving and growing sources and algorithms. Thus, AI can offer meticulous analyses to chase coupled security events in a reliable, fine-grained way. A system for event management with security information custom-made for intelligent grids to detect, normalize, and correlate CAs and anomalies against a range of smart-grid application layer protocols can be found in [105].

Similarly, physical and cyber domains' logs can be combined and undergo data correlations to detect prospective critical infrastructure anomalies. RT situational awareness affords a holistic, particular view of large-scale networks, enabling security analysts and investigators to recognize, process, and comprehend data. For this, a platform can process and visualize RT, large-scale network data to monitor and study network flow data and develop novel analytics [73, 105–130]. An automated situational awareness platform can use RT awareness features via the "SW-defined network" (SDN) to judge network-enabled entities' fragility, allocation to a connectivity-appropriate slice, and the underlying infrastructure's continuous surveillance. Maintaining an all-inclusive CPSs situational awareness is desirable due to the bound cyber and physical systems' combination in mission-critical applications [73, 105–130].

11.5.3 Detection Processes

It involves activities to maintain detection readiness procedures to provide CTI and CS events awareness reliably while continuously refining and testing the detection processes for efficient working. AI can offer proactive online vigilance by automatic CTI extraction from innumerable web and internal resources. The resources embrace the DW, CTI sharing platforms, and honeypots. The following UCs detail AI practices for the maintenance of detection processes.

"DW investigation" (DWI) continuously monitors cybercrime resources, like criminal forums and the black market, to spot illicit activities and act to minimize risk. DW investigations occur by exploiting textual data SA from DW scenes [73, 105–130]. CTI utilizing DW data, besides identifying key attackers, their assets, and expertise levels can automate exploration tools to isolate potential CTs by analyzing hackers' vocabulary and intentions without inspecting by hand the bulky DW posts' volume. SA may automate textual opinions, views, and emotions mining via NLP. In this, a bilingual lexical resource (BiSAL) achieves the emotional analysis of English and Arabic texts linked to CTs, radicalness, and conflicts. An approach for predicting malign cyber events exploits malign actors' behavior via SA of posts on hacker forums from the surface web and DWs to insert some predictive power usable outside the network to predict attacks using direction and time-series models. Proactive CTI identifies and addresses security risks before CAs occur by collecting evidence from hacker forums and marketplaces offering products and services focusing on malicious attacks. An ML scheme can pursue attacks and the growth of infected devices via a DW traffic study appears. Their breakdown explores the underlying correlation between network services under attack, as designated by the target port amounts of scanning packets. Expert DW information retrieval techniques can support CT textual mining with business intelligence. Exploring DW forums is paramount to extracting key ideas and uncovering popular topics, emerging CTs, and key actors in the attacker community, benefiting CS professionals. Topic modeling may remove topics, track the evolution of matters, identify dangerous hackers with their fortes, and uncover their underground market role.

Automated assessment of diverse CTI sources assists in extracting handy information from plentiful sources like vulnerability databases, X (former Twitter), news sites, and incident reports to take timely actions to ensure overall system security. This involves processing knowledge from multiple sources about CTs and actors to improve safety and the decision-making process and solve the problem of the quantity and heterogeneity of CTI sources and their formats to provide actionable intelligence. Security mavens face a fundamental challenge when exploring CS reports since immeasurable cyber information amounts emerge daily, imposing automated information mining technologies to simplify data retrieval and query. In this direction, there are innovative ways to extract evidence from CTI reports via named-entity recognition to aid security analysts in gaining accurate threat specifics as quickly as possible. Well-timed and relevant "OS intelligence" (OSINT) evidence mining posted daily by consumers, security organizations, and investigators is critical for maintaining a high-security level. Twitter is a crucial OSINT platform and a CTI hub due to its natural aggregation capability, timeliness, centers for public and secretive opinions, and chiefest CS feeds (e.g., NVD, ExploitDB, CVE, Security Focus). So, social media processing pipelines and mining can extract sources' CS relevance scores and concerns for clever verification.

Vulnerability intelligence extracts information about SW and system vulnerabilities from public vulnerability datasets (e.g., CVE and NVD) to help identify vulnerabilities and CA vectors to prioritize CS efforts and mending schedules. An automated system can diagnose and detect potential IoT vulnerabilities in a specific content-based extraction ontology provoked by evidence fluctuations fostered by the CVE databank and IoT system circumstances.

CS data explosive growths on platforms [73, 105–130], the DW, and social sites require automated tools for CT evolution identification, structured CTI records' generation, CT warning, and CTI appraisals from local CTI sources. A dynamic topic modeling can show the key topics' evolution in a time-stamped CS document collection to identify the threat evolution. The growing unstructured data nature shared on "OS threat intelligence publishing platforms" (OSTIPs) deters automatic CTI records gatherings. Automatic structured CTI data generation from OSTIPs combines ML and NLP to accomplish accurate, structured, and detailed data that can readily empower security tools and specialists regarding CT alleviation. The early CT warning systems helped defend against CAs by sending timely outbreaks and security alerts through information feeds. Security experts' Tweets and related blogs/social media can be mined to issue a CT warning. CTI tools targeting specific languages can help CTI professionals gain better CT insights in their local language. An automated Chinese analyzing structure to increase CTI visibility can operate in cooperation with preparing an automatic classification framework containing RS and CT-labeling tactics.

CS data explosive growths on platforms, the DW, and social sites require automated tools for CT evolution identification, structured CTI records generation, CT warning, and CTI appraisals from local CTI sources.

Multilingual CTI needs stem from Internet demands for translating CTI sources to draw trustworthy conclusions. Third-party translation engines are unsuitable due to their lack of CS terminology and inadequate privacy and confidentiality policies, where the importance of developing CTI tools for non-English languages must be highlighted [73, 105–130].

AI-powered honeypots study CAs' tactics and behaviors to expand and prepare CS systems for attacks [73, 105–130]. For a case in point, honeypots can rely on ML to predict the CA probability, utilizing numerous honeypots' DW or data sites to preclude far-reaching security events at the earliest. Mixing ML and honeynet-reliant detection can flag a potential botnet camouflaged as an IoT device. An early-warning IDS can apply a distributed network with honeypots and darknets for data collection.

11.6 Response Function (RF)

RF creates a roadmap for managing and restraining potential CS events' impacts. RF is critical as it epitomizes the first defense line in incident management and develops mitigation tactics for the future. This function includes planning to create effective processes to address the caveat, analyzing incidents to define their cause, scope, impact, incident containment, and communication orchestration throughout and, subsequently, to an attack. AI-reliant response activities can resolve incidents faster and with less labor and time from security analysts. Various AICS and UC solutions follow.

11.6.1 Response Planning

Planning a well-maintained reaction course of actions to pursue during and after an incident to limit its scope and impact includes defining a contingency plan that captures various CA scenarios with the apt response action and incorporating experiences gathered from other incidents' responses to revise plans. AI can automate response planning by launching a dynamic case supervision tool to record, perform, and modernize the contingency plan.

Dynamic case management utilizes technologies that tackle prior security breaches to record various attack scenarios and suggest relevant reaction measures before an event occurs [73, 105–130]. This helps with knowledge management for recording when an event is closed and organizing the response activities for particular breach types. Most studies have been on automated response recommendations that employ CBR to match the most comparable incident from a knowledge manager and then update the knowledge manager after the occurrence. Domain experts outline the precedent model in a case-based CTincs resolution system for preserving and retrieving knowledge base precedents. Researchers actively apply a hierarchical structure, ML, and an ontological approach to formalize the precedent base. A hierarchical structure with the qualities of the "recency, frequency, and monetary" (RFM) method can quickly respond to a security breach. Their scheme contemplates the security event's circumstances by observing its frequency and various attribute values. The target organization, information on the intruders, disturbed resources, and potential effects on the target are just attributes from prospective assault scenarios that can be accumulated in a hierarchical structure. Maintaining, reusing, and sharing the problem-solving knowledge of CTincs resolution is possible by mingling CBR with the incident-object description exchange format. The K-nearest neighbor procedure can handle case similarity. An RS can map CTincs into embeddings with ANNs and find the nearest incident embedding to sanction a similar resolution measure.

11.6.2 Communications

This activity helps coordinate stakeholders' communication during and after a CTinc, including collaboration support between security analysts throughout an attack and cross-sector CTI partaking to enrich the protection team's responses in emergencies and warrant contingency tasks and responsibilities' allocation when responding [73, 105–130]. AI can assist with this activity via these two UCs.

"Automated responsibility allocation" (ARA) can serve as intelligent and adaptive decision sustenance for "security operation center" (SOC) managers in incident response duties substantiated by the occurrence traits, staff expertise, and ease of use. The best resources (like time or extra labor) are directed toward maintaining a cyber-SOC optimal operational effectiveness in the face of multiple factors' interference, viz new alert categories, augmenting alert-generation rate, and expert absenteeism. Nonetheless, stochastic, dynamic programming-based, adaptive, and dynamic decision-making model via RL exists.

"Collaboration support systems" (CSSs) facilitate the efficient data and knowledge allotment amongst various actors participating in incident response, for example, teams and employees inside or outside the organization [4, 73, 105–130]. AI can help with cyber-defense, analytical CSS support for cross-sector CTI partaking, and community data distribution between security analysts. CSSs are twofold: asynchronous and synchronous. Asynchronous CSSs do not provide RT communication; team members can examine information when convenient, i.e., engage in a conversation or leave according to a present necessity. A CSS type employing a message board and utilizing a cross-sector CTI sharing with a multi-agent monitoring mechanism may solve the concurrency problems of CTI sharing and improve tasks' execution efficiency. Synchronous CSSs provide RT communication to support an RT response by yielding security analysts to quickly exchange findings and introduce effective task divisions. The last concept with visualization, RT communication, and the efficient conversion of BD can be handled by plentiful analysts to broadly comprehend CTs and corresponding responses.

11.6.3 Analysis

The analysis module evaluates CTincs and response activities to ensure the correct incident mitigation process, gathering and evaluating received data to support event categorization and notify investigators to assess incident severity and impact. Forensic analysis helps retrieve and preserve evidence for litigation. AI can analyze these use case procedures.

Automatic incident characterization (AIC) addresses the incident identification processes per the response plan, including identifying incident criticality and relationships with other incidents to automatically prioritize incidents for further investigation. Different CS events [73, 105–130] dictate the adequate AI model type or action per occurrence's severity.

Alert processing and triage (APTr) investigate intrusion alerts efficiently and accurately to prioritize and analyze their relationship and decide on incident response. AICS can enable an effective alert triage established on automated knowledge inference, alert classification, and alert prioritizing tools [2, 4, 33] to identify and escalate CT alerts for further investigation. Knowledge inference explores the knowledge base with logical rules for new information evaluations and interpretations. A sequential rule mining scheme that extracts knowledge from shared intrusion detection alerts can create predictive and customized blocklists. Aggregating or key triaging warns from enormous CT alert records can reduce CT alert fatigue. Security warnings related to the same attack scenario could be grouped using "self-organizing maps" (SOMs) and unsupervised clustering techniques. Each evaluated event characteristic had an anomaly score to determine security event priority and identify anomalies.

Post-mortem forensic analysis (FA) starts a CA timeline [2, 4, 73, 105–130]. It illuminates the breach's scope and cause. Next, remove and prevent the threat via tools and approaches. The invader's data pieces are also examined to establish a footprint that can be utilized in court or for prosecution. Incident response teams can use AI for intelligent attribution, anomaly identification in a forensic chronology, evidence correlation from different devices, and forensic investigation optimization. Smart attribution finds entity-event links to determine security event causes. Contextual learning can indicate source attribution and status. A forensic chronology covers pre-, mid-, and post-CTincs events. Identify anomalies in the forensic timeline, such as security incidents. A deep autoencoder can establish a baseline model for log file normal occurrences and an anomaly threshold for reconstructed values using the baseline to identify anomalies. Fraud detection and analysis are forensic investigators' key goals for court case reports. Various forensic tools can analyze devices.

Nonetheless, their data formats complicate studies. Thus, a novel semantic strategy helps forensic investigators analyze evidence by linking it with other knowledge. New adversarial tools make it difficult for forensic analysis teams to examine occurrences quickly and efficiently within scarce resources' scenarios. A unique decision support system model uses CTI data from adversarial scheme repositories to aid inspections, optimizing forensic breakdowns by resolving these issues. The likelihood relationship and proximity values between potential attack actions, present investigation findings, and investigation budget are considered in this model.

11.6.4 Mitigation

Mitigation involves preventing the expansion outbreaks and remediating their effects to dispel any long-term security breach consequences. This critical step contains the incident facts and remediates or documents new frailties concerning risks.

"Automated isolation" (AuI) excludes devices after detecting an indicator of compromise. AuI disconnects devices or gadgets' groups after infection or identifies high-risk infected clients for extra care. NFV and SW-defined networking lets AuI locate CAs on the physical network and isolate or replace compromised devices or clients. CS professionals can reduce CA consequences in networks by tying CAs to specific physical system attributes or metrics. A CA classification and localization model for the smart grid physical layer uses ensemble and representational learning for CA classification and a Chi-squared algorithm to correlate the CA scenario with specific features and localize the attack to precise measurements or a system location [73, 105–130]. RT mitigation is essential for fast vulnerability processing in integrated clinical environments. ML/DL can detect and categorize ransomware threats and leverages NFV and SDN out to isolate and replace affected devices.

"Automated remediation" (AuR) is a guided problem-solving method that automates corrective measures with simple scripts or powerful context-aware RSs [73, 105–130]. AI can choose the best countermeasures for CT removal in RSs to help security analysts configure and orchestrate security tools and track the attacker's lateral movement. A defensive CS key pillar is developing speedy and effective responses to disruptive CAs, and picking the appropriate countermeasures to reply to CTs is crucial for a fully automatic response. CS reaction based on artificial immune systems can select and apply the optimal atomic countermeasures for risky protected structure assets. Decision support systems and intelligent RSs for security analysts to swiftly and effectively defend resources and services from CAs are also important. An RS suggests the most resilient critical infrastructure setup with network orchestration and security technologies for fast mitigation and to quickly stop malware spread or track the attacker's lateral movement.

11.6.5 Improvements

Improvements ensure lessons are absorbed from incident detections and response activities, including response update plans and strategies consistent with the lessons learned by employing AI for automated knowledge extraction [2, 4, 73, 105–130] centered on incident reports.

"Long-term improvements" (LTIs) entail knowledge extraction from incidents, and CTI reports arrange for dependable corroboration so that security analysts detect or find CA indicative patterns. A framework can mine knowledge from after-action reports, aggregate it by grouping similar items, and display retrieved facts in CS knowledge graphs. This arrangement helps security analysts to find matches between different CAs [73, 105–130].

11.7 Recovery Function (RcF)

RcFs primarily warrant CS resilient designs with well-timed restitution of abilities or services, fostering a prompt return to regular operations to lessen the CS event impact and distill important information as lessons learned. RcF can assist in returning to normal with the help of these CS solutions.

Recovery planning involves processes and procedures for maintenance, testing, and execution to restore systems or assets compromised by CT incidents, timely recuperating lost data, and impaired capacities to ensure that everything functions aptly. AI-based recovery planning can automate data and system recovery and delete malware or tainted data during a CT event.

Security incident reviews improve recovery by understanding security breaches. It involves updating recovery methods based on lessons learned and reviewing efforts to meet security goals. AI may automatically identify advanced breach prospects for future response planning by reviewing policies, incident reports, and audit logs. Analyzing and combining security incident data and reports can furnish insights and suggestions to improve CS. Unfortunately, incident data management and analyses are strenuous and slow. AI can simplify data collection, aggregation, information extraction, visualization, and prediction of heterogeneous incident material for post-mortem vulnerability assessments with NLP [61].

Communication restores inner-outer synchronization. A platform for communicating recent security breaches or CTs promises to ensure critical infrastructure CS.

The "recovery function" (RcF) primary goal is to maintain resilience planning and the timely restoration of abilities or services impaired due to a CS incident, encouraging a prompt return to normal operations to lessen the CS event impact and distill important information as lessons learned. RcF can serve as a roadmap for returning to normal with the help of the next CS solutions.

11.8 Analysis, Discussion and Research Gaps

AI Smartly stated algorithms, data, structures, and knowledge formalisms are AI. The key AI fields for analysis encompass thinking, development, learning, communication, and perspicacity. Primary reasoning domain studies examine how machines infer from data. Planning automates strategy design and execution using cautiously optimized solutions. Automatic learning, prediction, adaptation, and change response are addressed in the learning domain. Communication domain studies focus on machines' ability to understand, interpret, and produce spoken or written human dialogues. Perception domain studies examine visual and auditory environmental sensing.

AICS research requires developing application areas, adequate resources (e.g., data sources, records management, computing infrastructure), and advanced AI approaches for AICS adoption. Emerging CS applications, data representation, enhanced AICS methodologies, and new infrastructure research and development are promising research fields.

11.8.1 Emerging CS Areas

Advancing AICS obliges a solid foundation for multiple application domains. Likewise, the future necessitates new CS activities' automation and existing CS continuing amelioration. The emergent applications are described below:

Automated retrieval of key VRIs encourages future research about early-warning structures to signpost risk happenings over time due to policy abuses, red flags, or other indicators. Automatically retrieving key risk indicators, like the manifestation of unpatched modules, attempted breaches' totals, average in-between failure times, etc., and transforming them into beneficial knowledge to prevent a CS breach by timely remediation of the risk.

Zero-day CA defense is one of modern CS's most intriguing challenges. CAs targeting fresh SW vulnerabilities are called zero-day attacks. Naturally, guarding against something you don't know exists is difficult. This requires full ICT visibility across endpoints, networks, and CC.

Predictive intelligence simplifies common CS decisions like vulnerability categorization, attack route prediction, malware forecast, data triage, spam filtering, security estimation, and mission mapping. Despite being widely used and well-defined, many methods are manual or have significant false positive rates. Advanced, sophisticated predictive analytics can address some of these challenges. Time-centered neural graph networks, deep Bayesian forecasting, burst recognition, deep generative prototypes with temporal constrictions, and other predictive methods appear promising. Industrial policies, information, tasks, and needs can be included in each plan. Superior operational and tactical business projections can benefit SOC analysts and CTI experts.

The Internet's linguistic character requires CS to creatively mine social media, blogs, and DW markets. CAs mainly target non-English-speaking nations [73, 105–130]. Thus, non-English content datasets should gauge TM in other languages. Lots of pre-processing tools and libraries solely support English. For private security, new technologies targeting other idioms or translators are needed.

AI-powered cyber protection and resilience use analytics to automatically deploy security rules. Threat modeling, patching, remediation, network segmentation, and reorganization are automated. Intelligent work automation benefits SOC analysts and operators greatly. Modern AI capabilities include enhanced AI agents, RL, actor critical networks, chosen defensive, adversarial learning schemes, and Bayesian networks. Future research can determine how each strategy protects scientific cyberinfrastructure, enterprise IT, sensor- and actuator-based settings, etc.

Data breach prevention and discovery require significant investigators' attention because most research focuses on insider behavior or endpoint telemetry to detect insider CTs and "advanced persistent threats" (APTs). However, sensitive data identification studies to prevent unintentional exposure are inadequate. ML and NLP can find, monitor, and govern sensitive data flow between endpoints in big-data environments to avoid or analyze data leakages. DW's search for inadvertent exposures is essential to regaining control and reputation.

Fake document generation protects critical assets like intellectual property and national security records, contributing to the utmost cyber warfare impact. AI synthetic document generation means safeguarding sensitive material by information falsification to produce several counterfeit documents [4].

Security teams necessitate skilled CTI professionals to process and triage thousands of warnings and events methodically collected for daily threat analysis. Current research uses high-level management to correlate security alerts, analyze their logical relationship, and prioritize them before sending them to consumers. They avoid distinct network event settings. Other language models can learn event context representations and construct adaptive methods for dynamic network contexts. Additional data visualization and online updating capacity are needed for alerts and efficient triage mechanism design.

Due to the shorter time it takes an attacker to take over an enterprise's infrastructure, AI-powered incident response must be rapid. Also important is automating assault mitigation, containment, and outsmarting. Incident response automation requires knowledge documentation from prior CTincs, events caused by a solution, and new CT patterns and attributes throughout time. This knowledge can enable automated incident response playbooks to recommend, allocate resources, and assign tasks based on expertise, availability, and case history. These automated security playbooks will reinforce proactive protection and prevent hardening CTs. Future CTI platforms will allow enterprises to consume these standardized security playbooks to respond to incidents in real-time.

11.8.2 Data Representation

Effective AI needs good data. The major issues are choosing training datasets and managing data diversity and velocity. Data representation and quality, mining the latest facts, and context awareness are crucial for AICS model training and modeling.

AI needs "**refined data representations**" to perform. Flattened feature vectors are most commonly used to describe CS. Despite its popularity, this technique ignores essential data links like sequences. Thus, in production, this representation can yield worse results. Future AICS researchers could carefully assess how CS data exist in the CPS or parts of it and find proper replacements best portraying the studied phenomena to alleviate this problem. Trees or graphs showing data dependencies can characterize virtual machines' hierarchical file schemes and applications. Sequences, grids, and non-Euclidean depictions (e.g., tensors, cubes) also require adequate representations that consider essential data features, organizational needs, and relevant social and behavioral economics theories.

CS data possess a variety of low-level properties due to context awareness. Data mining and ML can find a meaningful pattern for datasets. However, temporal and spatial relationships/dependencies between occurrences or connections can explain if an action is suspicious. For example, security professionals may not consider linkages evil, but other strategies may consider them DoS assaults. The inability to predict threats or attacks by contextual knowledge weakens CS. AI research includes context-aware adaptive CS solutions.

"**Incremental Learning and Regency Mining**" refer to how ML-based security models make data-driven choices using static data. However, consumers' and malignant opponents' behavior may change over time. Thus, contemporary behavioral patterns and ML rules promise more regarding predictive analytics in typical CS jobs like data triage, spam filtering, vulnerability categorization, and mission mapping. Effectively exploiting analysis outcomes to craft solutions is another AICS research problem.

11.8.3 Advanced AICS

More advanced AI may maximize the data sources, application regions, and representations. Multiple data source analysis, "explainable AI" (XAI), and "automated human-AI" interactions are nascent tactics affecting practical and usable AICS. Understanding how and why an algorithm concludes is vital for XAI applications in CS. Unfortunately, existing AI decision-making is opaque. They are known for their "black box" character despite their superior performance in high-impact CS applications like DW investigations, vulnerability assessments, and others. Future AICS research can decipher interpretable and explicable AI to improve an algorithm's performance and reveal its black-box nature to reduce these constraints, enhancing stakeholder trust.

"**Multiple Data Source Analysis**" can fix AICS's biggest problem, i.e., isolated datasets, which means lacking access to multiple datasets or failing to compare and interpret them. Future AICS research should use other data sources' properties more to address this issue. Entity matching, short-text matching algorithms (like deep structured semantic models), multi-view approaches (e.g., multi-source), and multi-task learning promise many data source analysis solutions. Fusion of information can yield additional attributes, improved risk management (e.g., vulnerability assessments), and a complete picture of an organization's CS posture.

"**Human-AI Interfaces**" improve decision-making by integrating AI with human action (e.g., having a security expert run an analysis). AI-human interfaces can surpass algorithms and humans. Although needed, human-AI interaction's range, breadth, and depth in critical and fundamental tasks have not yet been fully explored. Psychology, cognitive science, human-computer interaction, and other domains might inform such transdisciplinary research.

11.8.4 Exploring and Developing Innovative Infrastructures

AI is becoming a key CS component for enterprises of all sizes and industries to improve CS productivity. Developing new RT infrastructures to assist AI requires dealing with internal BD and external security research feeds to give CS for global and internal security incidents. Key research gaps for successful AICS designs follow.

Cyber reality is complicated by the lack of national/international CTI platforms and their dynamic character, albeit new CTs and CAs can evade it. Proprietary platforms must debate and share CT data with peers. CTI platforms must be flexible, adaptable, and networked to share CT information, relying mainly on selected national and international information-sharing hubs currently lacking. The government, owners, and operators of critical infrastructure and others will profit from efficiently distributing accurate, functional, timely, and relevant CT information shared by CTI platforms. Sharing improves situational awareness and risk-informed decision-making, boosting critical infrastructure security and dependability.

Lack of fresh, RT, or larger datasets: AICS datasets are the most important. Most are old and may not explain CA behavior today. Many detection investigations used AI approaches on the same dataset (e.g., DARPA98, KDD99, NSLKDD, and CICIDS2017); nevertheless, their methods have not been evaluated on newer datasets. Validating context research across several datasets allows scenario analysis.

11.9 Conclusion

CS includes methods, tools, and processes that aid companies in safeguarding networks, devices, SW, and data from CA, damage, and unauthorized access. Complex CS is needed as devices, systems, and networks proliferate exponentially.

A taxonomy defines existing frameworks at the first bottom two CS NIST levels to identify and gauge possible AICS applications. IaaS has five main functions: identification (IF), protection (PF), detection (DF), response (RF), and recovery (RcF). Preventing security threats, actively searching for new CTs, and counter-attack maneuvers are AI functions. To defend CAs, IaaS regulates their lifecycle particular characteristics.

Numerous activities stemming from different AICS techniques regarding taxonomy are examined: contribution type and the AI model targeting the IaaS layer. An in-depth assessment of specific user cases and theoretical investigations further enriches these issues. This chapter inspects the AICS evolution by analyzing and identifying research gaps about functions, solution sets, specific UCs, and the elected AI technique. Still, practical AICS implementations require more attention to acquiring and representing chronological data related to different CS functions [131-135].

References

1 Barrett, M. (2018). *Technical Report*. Gaithersburg, MD, USA: National Institute of Standards and Technology.

2 Kanna, K., Estrela, V.V., and Rodrigues, J.J.P.C. (2021). *Cyber Security and Digital Forensics – Proc. ICCSDF 2021*. Zurich, Switzerland: Springer Nature https://doi.org/10.1007/978-981-16-3961-6.

3 Promyslov, V.G., Semenkov, K.V., and Shumov, A.S. (2019). A clustering method of asset cybersecurity classification. *IFAC-Papers OnLine* 52 (13): 928–933.

4 Kaur, R., Gabrijelcic, D., and Klobučar, T. (2023). Artificial intelligence for cybersecurity: literature review and future research directions. *Information Fusion* 97: 101804.

5 Estrela, V.V., Deshpande, A., Lopes, R.T. et al. (2023). The building blocks of health 4.0–Internet of Things, big data with cloud and fog computing. In: *Intelligent Healthcare Systems* (ed. V.V. Estrela), 24–44. London, UK: CRC Press Chapter 2.

6 Sivanathan, A., Gharakheili, H.H., Loi, F. et al. (2018). Classifying IoT devices in smart environments using network traffic characteristics. *IEEE Transactions on Mobile Computing* 18 (8): 1745–1759.

7 Deshpande, A., Estrela, V.V., and Razmjooy, N. (2021). *Computational Intelligence Methods for Super-Resolution in Image Processing Applications*. Zurich, Switzerland: Springer Nature https://doi.org/10.1007/978-3-030-67921-7.

8 Cam, H. (2017). Online detection and control of malware infected assets. In: *IEEE Military Communications Conference (MILCOM)*, 701–706.

9 Estrela, V.V., Grata, E.G.H., Deshpande, A. et al. (2023). In-body devices and sensors communication – how implantables, ingestibles, and injectables interact with the Internet. In: *Intelligent Healthcare Systems* (ed. V.V. Estrela), 236–258. London, UK: CRC Press Chapter 12.

10 Deshpande, A., Estrela, V.V., Patavardhan, P., and Kallimani, G. (2023). Super-resolution in a world of scarce resources for medical imaging applications. In: *Edge-AI in Healthcare: Trends and Future Perspectives* (ed. S. Vyas et al.). London, UK: CRC Press Chapter 13.

11 Tozer, B., Mazzuchi, T., and Sarkani, S. (2015). Optimizing attack surface and configuration diversity using multi-objective reinforcement learning. In: *Proc. 14th Int'l Conf. Machine Learning and Applications*, 144–149. IEEE.

12 Laghari, A.A., Zhang, X., Shaikh, Z.A. et al. (2023). A review on quality of experience (QoE) in cloud computing. *Journal of Reliable Intelligent Environments* https://doi.org/10.1007/s40860-023-00210-y.

13 Estrela, V.V., Intorne, A.C., Batista, K.K.S. et al. (2023). Metaheuristics applied to pathology image analysis. In: *Intelligent Healthcare Systems* (ed. V.V. Estrela), 322–340. London, UK: CRC Press Chapter 16.

14 Bringhenti, D., Marchetto, G., Sisto, R. et al. (2019). Towards a fully automated and optimized network security functions orchestration. In: *Proc. 4th Int'l Conf. Comp., Comm. and Sec. (ICCCS)*, 1–7.

15 Estrela, V.V., Deshpande, A., Sroufer, R. et al. (2023). Digital twin framework for intelligent healthcare facilities through ISO/IEEE 11073. In: *Intelligent Healthcare Systems* (ed. V.V. Estrela), 279–297. London, UK: CRC Press Chapter 14.

16 Varela-Vaca, A.J., Gasca, R.M., Ceballos, R. et al. (2019). CyberSPL: a framework for the verification of cybersecurity policy compliance of system configurations using software product lines. *Applied Sciences* 9 (24): 5364.

17 Liu, Y., Sarabi, A., Zhang, J. et al. (2015). Cloudy with a chance of breach: forecasting cyber security incidents. In: *Proc. 24th USENIX Security Symp. (USENIX Security 15)*, 1009–1024.

18 Narasimhan, V.L. (2021). Using deep learning for assessing cybersecurity economic risks in virtual power plants. In: *2021 7th International Conference on Electrical Energy Systems (ICEES)*, 530–537.

19 Odegbile, O., Chen, S., and Wang, Y. (2019). Dependable policy enforcement in traditional non-SDN networks. In: *2019 IEEE 39th International Conference on Distributed Computing Systems (ICDCS)*, 545–554.

20 Jeon, S. and Kim, H.K. (2021). AutoVAS: an automated vulnerability analysis system with a deep learning approach. *Computers & Security* 106: 102308.

21 Huff, P., McClanahan, K., Le, T., and Li, Q. (2021). A recommender system for tracking vulnerabilities. In: *The 16th International Conference on Availability, Reliability and Security*, 1–7.

22 Saha, T., Aaraj, N., Ajjarapu, N., and Jha, N.K. (2021). SHARKS: smart hacking approaches for RisK scanning in internet-of-things and cyber-physical systems based on machine learning. *IEEE Transactions on Emerging* 10 (2): 870–885.

23 Wang, Y., Wu, Z., Wei, Q., and Wang, Q. NeuFuzz: efficient fuzzing with deep neural network. *IEEE Access* 7: 36340–36352.

24 Chen, Y., Poskitt, C.M., Sun, J. et al. (2019). Learning-guided network fuzzing for testing cyber-physical system defences. In: *34th IEEE/ACM International Conf. Automated Software Eng. (ASE)*, 962–973.

25 Estrela, V.V., Khan, A.A., Shaikh, A.A. et al. (2023). Some issues regarding content-based image retrieval (CBIR) for remote healthcare theradiagnosis. In: *Intelligent Healthcare Systems* (ed. V.V. Estrela), 110–134. London, UK: CRC Press Chapter 6.

26 Liu, X., Li, X., Prajapati, R., and Wu, D. (2019). DeepFuzz: automatic generation of syntax valid C programs for fuzzy testing. In: *Proc. AAAI Conference on Artificial Intelligence 33*, 1044–1051.

27 Zhou, S., Liu, J., Hou, D. et al. (2021). Autonomous penetration testing based on improved deep Q-network. *Applied Sciences* 11: 8823.

28 Zheng, K., Albert, L.A., Luedtke, J.R., and Towle, E. (2019). A budgeted maximum multiple coverage model for cybersecurity planning and management. *IISE Transactions* 51 (12): 1303–1317.

29 Yeboah-Ofori, A., Islam, S., Lee, S.W. et al. (2021). Cyber threat predictive analytics for improving cyber supply chain security. *IEEE Access* 9: 94318–94337.

30 Russo, E.R., Di Sorbo, A., Visaggio, C.A., and Canfora, G. (2019). Summarizing vulnerabilities' descriptions to support experts during vulnerability assessment activities. *Journal of Systems and Software* 156: 84–99.

31 Aota, M., Kanehara, H., Kubo, M. et al. (2020). Automation of vulnerability classification from its description using machine learning. In: *IEEE Symp. Computers and Communications (ISCC)*, 1–7.

32 Chatterjee, S. and Thekdi, S. (2020). An iterative learning and inference approach to managing dynamic cyber vulnerabilities of complex systems. *Reliability Engineering & System* 193: 106664.

33 Jiang, Y. and Atif, Y. (2021). A selective ensemble model for cognitive cybersecurity analysis. *Journal of Network and Computer Applications* 193: 103210.

34 Deshpande, A., Patavardhan, P., and Estrela, V.V. (2020). Super resolution and recognition of unconstrained ear image. *International Journal of Biometrics, Inderscience* 12 (4): 396–410. https://doi.org/10.1504/IJBM.2020.110813.

35 Brown, J., Saha, T., and Jha, N.K. (2022). GRAVITAS: graphical reticulated attack vectors for internet-of-things aggregate security. *IEEE Transactions on Emerging* 10 (3): 1331–1348.

36 Gao, P., Shao, F., Liu, X. et al. (2021). Enabling efficient cyber threat hunting with cyber threat intelligence. In: *IEEE 37th Int'l Conf. Data Engineering (ICDE)*, 193–204.

37 Falco, G., Viswanatha, A., Caldera, C., and Shrobe, H. (2018). A master attack methodology for an AI-based automated attack planner for smart cities. *IEEE Access* 6: 48360–48373.

38 Estrela, V.V., Razmjooy, N., Monteiro, A.C.B. et al. (2021). A computational intelligence perspective on multimodal image registration for unmanned aerial vehicles (UAVs). In: *Metaheuristics and Optimization in Computer and Electrical Engineering*, Lecture Notes in Electrical Engineering, vol. 696 (ed. N. Razmjooy, M. Ashourian, and Z. Foroozandeh). Cham: Springer https://doi.org/10.1007/978-3-030-56689-0_13.

39 Sancho, J.C., Caro, A., Avila, M., and Bravo, A. (2020). New approach for threat classification and security risk estimations based on security event management. *Future Generation Computer Systems* 113: 488–505.

40 Tubis, A.A., Werbinska-Wojciechowsk, S., Goralczyk, M. et al. (2020). Cyber-attacks risk analysis method for different levels of automation of mining processes in mines based on fuzzy theory use. *Sensors* 20 (24): 7210.

41 Qin, Y., Peng, Y., Huang, K. et al. (2020). Association analysis-based cybersecurity risk assessment for industrial control systems. *IEEE Systems Journal* 15 (1): 1423–1432.

42 Falco, G., Caldera, C., and Shrobe, H. (2018). IIoT cybersecurity risk modeling for SCADA systems. *IEEE Internet of Things Journal* 5 (6): 4486–4495.

43 Kalinin, M., Krundyshev, V., and Zegzhda, P. (2021). Cybersecurity risk assessment in smart city infrastructures. *Machines* 9 (4): 78.

44 Biswas, B., Mukhopadhyay, A., Bhattacharjee, S. et al. (2022). A text-mining based cyber-risk assessment and mitigation framework for critical analysis of online hacker forums. *Decision Support Systems* 152: 113651.

45 Ansari, M.S., Bartos, V., and Lee, B. (2022). GRU-based deep learning approach for network intrusion alert prediction. *Future Generation Computer Systems* 128: 35–47.

46 Al Najada, H., Mahgoub, I., and Mohammed, I. (2018). Cyber intrusion prediction and taxonomy system using deep learning and distributed big data processing. In: *IEEE Symp. Series on Computational Intelligence (SSCI)*, 631–638.

47 Rhode, M., Burnap, P., and Jones, K. (2018). Early-stage malware prediction using recurrent neural networks. *Computers & Security* 77: 578–594.

48 Polatidis, N., Pimenidis, E., Pavlidis, M. et al. (2020). From product recommendation to cyber-attack prediction: generating attack graphs and predicting future attacks. *Evolving Systems* 11 (3): 479–490.

49 Rees, L.P., Deane, J.K., Rakes, T.R., and Baker, W.H. (2011). Decision support for cybersecurity risk planning. *Decision Support Systems* 51 (3): 493–505.

50 Paul, J.A. and Zhang, M. (2021). Decision support model for cybersecurity risk planning: a two-stage stochastic programming framework featuring firms, government, and attacker. *European Journal of Operational Research* 291 (1): 349–364.

51 Sawik, T. and Sawik, B. (2022). A rough cut cybersecurity investment using portfolio of security controls with maximum cybersecurity value. *International Journal of Production Research* 60 (21): 6556–6572.

52 Rahman, S., Hossain, N.U., Govindan, K. et al. (2021). Assessing cyber resilience of additive manufacturing supply chain leveraging data fusion technique: a model to generate cyber resilience index of a supply chain. *CIRP Journal of Manufacturing Science and Technology* 35: 911–928.

53 Jorquera Valero, J.M., Sanchez Sanchez, P.M., Fernandez Maimo, L. et al. (2018). Improving the security and QoE in mobile devices through an intelligent and adaptive continuous authentication system. *Sensors* 18 (11): 3769.

54 Martín, A.G., Beltran, M., Fernandez-Isabel, A., and de Diego, I.M. (2021). An approach to detect user behaviour anomalies within identity federations. *Computers & Security* 108: 102356.

55 Hafeez, A., Topolovec, K., and Awad, S. (2019). ECU fingerprinting through parametric signal modeling and artificial neural networks for in-vehicle security against spoofing attacks. In: *15th Int'l Comp. Eng. Conf. (ICENCO)*, 29–38.

56 Baldini, G., Giuliani, R., Gemo, M., and Dimc, F. (2021). On the application of sensor authentication with intrinsic physical features to vehicle security. *Computers and Electrical Engineering* 91: 107053.

57 Benedetti, M. and Mori, M. (2019). On the use of Max-SAT and PDDL in RBAC maintenance. *Cybersecurity* 2 (1): 1–25.

58 Abolfathi, M., Raghebi, Z., Jafarian, H., and Banaei-Kashani, F. (2021). A scalable role mining approach for large organizations. In: *Proceedings of the 2021 ACM Workshop on Security and Privacy Analytics*, 45–54.

59 Chukkapalli, S.S., Aziz, S.B., Alotaibi, N. et al. (2021). Ontology driven AI and access control systems for smart fisheries. In: *Proceedings 2021 ACM Workshop on Secure and Trustworthy Cyber-Physical Systems*, 59–68.

60 Tan, Z., Beuran, R., Hasegawa, S. et al. Adaptive security awareness training using linked open data datasets. *Education and Information Technologies* 25 (6): 5235–5259.

61 Espinha Gasiba, T., Lechner, U., and Pinto-Albuquerque, M. (2020). Sifu-A cybersecurity awareness platform with challenge assessment and intelligent coach. *Cybersecurity* 3 (1): 1–23.

62 Le, D.C. and Zincir-Heywood, N. (2021). Anomaly detection for insider threats using unsupervised ensembles. *IEEE Transactions on Network and Service Management* 18 (2): 1152–1164.

63 Al-Shehari, T. and Alsowail, R.A. (2021). An insider data leakage detection using one-hot encoding, synthetic minority oversampling and machine learning techniques. *Entropy* 23 (10): 1258.

64 Guo, Y., Liu, J., Tang, W., and Huang, C. (2021). Exsense: extract sensitive information from unstructured data. *Computers & Security* 102: 102156.

65 Li, H., Wu, J., Xu, H. et al. (2022). Explainable intelligence-driven defense mechanism against advanced persistent threats: a joint edge game and AI approach. *IEEE Transactions on Dependable and Secure Computing* 19 (2): 757–775.

66 Wu, D., Shi, W., and Ma, X. (2021). A novel real-time anti-spam framework. *ACM Transactions on Internet Technology (TOIT)* 21 (4): 1–27.

67 Gualberto, E.S., De Sousa, R.T., Vieira, T.P. et al. (2020). The answer is in the text: multi-stage methods for phishing detection based on feature engineering. *IEEE Access* 8: 223529–223547.

68 Marques, C., Malta, S., and Magalhaes, J.P. (2021). DNS dataset for malicious domains detection. *Data Brief* 38: 107342.

69 Yu, B., Pan, J., Gray, D. et al. (2019). Weakly supervised deep learning for the detection of domain generation algorithms. *IEEE Access* 7: 51542–51556.

70 Indrasiri, P.L., Halgamuge, M.N., and Mohammad, A. (2021). Robust ensemble machine learning model for filtering phishing URLs: expandable random gradient stacked voting classifier (ERG-SVC). *IEEE Access* 9: 150142–150161.

71 Li, W., Jin, J., and Lee, J.H. (2019). Analysis of botnet domain names for IoT cybersecurity. *IEEE Access* 7: 94658–94665.

72 Alotaibi, B. and Alotaibi, M. (2021). Consensus and majority vote feature selection methods and a detection technique for web phishing. *Journal of Ambient Intelligence and Humanized Computing* 12 (1): 717–727.

73 Kraeva, I. and Yakhyaeva, G. (2021). Application of the metric learning for security incident playbook recommendation. In: *IEEE 22nd Int'l Conf. Young Professionals in Electron Devices and Materials (EDM)*, 475–479.

74 Qin, Y., Hoffmann, B., and Lilja, D.J. (2018). Hyperprotect: enhancing the performance of a dynamic backup system using intelligent scheduling. In: *IEEE 37th International Performance Computing and Communications Conference (IPCCC)*, 1–8.

75 Van de Ven, P.M., Zhang, B., and Schorgendorfer, A. (2014). Distributed backup scheduling: modeling and optimization. In: *IEEE INFOCOM 2014-IEEE Conference on Computer Communications*, 1644–1652.

76 Zeng, Z., Yang, Z., Huang, D., and Chung, C.J. (2021). LICALITY-Likelihood and criticality: vulnerability risk prioritization through logical reasoning and deep learning. *IEEE Transactions on Network and Service Management* 19 (2): 1746–1760.

77 Yin, J., Tang, M., Cao, J., and Wang, H. (2020). Apply transfer learning to cybersecurity: predicting exploitability of vulnerabilities by description. *Knowledge-Based Systems* 210: 106529.

78 Yin, J., Tang, M., Cao, J. et al. (2022). A real-time dynamic concept adaptive learning algorithm for exploitability prediction. *Neurocomputing* 472: 252–265.

79 Estrela, V.V., Andreopoulos, N., Sroufer, R. et al. (2021). Transmedia ecosystems, quality of experience and quality of service in fog computing for comfortable learning. *IEEE Global Engineering Education Conference (EDUCON)* 2021: 1003–1009.

80 De la Torre-Abaitua, G., Lago-Fernandez, L.F., and Arroyo, D. (2021). A compression-based method for detecting anomalies in textual data. *Entropy* 23 (5): 618.

81 Sisiaridis, D. and Markowitch, O. (2018). Reducing data complexity in feature extraction and feature selection for big data security analytics. In: *1st International Conference on Data Intelligence and Security (ICDIS)*, 43–48.

82 De Araujo-Filho, P.F., Pinheiro, A.J., Kaddoum, G. et al. (2021). An efficient intrusion prevention system for CAN: hindering cyber-attacks with a low-cost platform. *IEEE Access* 9: 166855–166869.

83 de Lima, S.M., Silva, H.K., Luz, J.H. et al. (2021). Artificial intelligence-based antivirus in order to detect malware preventively. *Progress in Artificial Intelligence* 10 (1): 1–22.

84 Marques, P., Rhode, M., and Gashi, I. (2021). Waste not: using diverse neural networks from hyperparameter search for improved malware detection. *Computers & Security* 108: 102339.

85 Karuna, P., Purohit, H., Jajodia, S. et al. (2020). Fake document generation for cyber deception by manipulating text comprehensibility. *IEEE Systems Journal* 15 (1): 835–845.

86 Saveetha, D. and Maragatham, G. (2022). Design of Blockchain enabled intrusion detection model for detecting security attacks using deep learning. *Pattern Recognition Letters* 153: 24–28.

87 Nguyen, G.N., Le, N.H., Viet, M. et al. (2021). Secure blockchain enabled cyber–physical systems in healthcare using deep belief network with ResNet model. *Journal of Parallel and Distributed Computing* 153: 150–160.

88 Alhowaide, A., Alsmadi, I., and Tang, J. (2021). Ensemble detection model for IoT IDS. *Internet of Things* 16: 100435.

89 Rashid, M., Kamruzzaman, J., Imam, T. et al. (2022). A tree-based stacking ensemble technique with feature selection for network intrusion detection. *Applied Intelligence* 52: 9768–9781.

90 Perez, S.I., Moral-Rubio, S., and Criado, R. (2021). A new approach to combine multiplex networks and time series attributes: building intrusion detection systems (IDS) in cybersecurity. *Chaos, Solitons & Fractals* 150: 111143.

91 Catillo, M., Pecchia, A., and Villano, U. (2022). AutoLog: anomaly detection by deep autoencoding of system logs. *Expert Systems with Applications* 191: 116263.

92 Zhao, R., Yin, Y., Shi, Y., and Xue, Z. (2020). Intelligent intrusion detection based on federated learning aided long short-term memory. *Physical Communication* 42: 101157.

93 Nedeljkovic, D. and Jakovljevic, Z. (2022). CNN based method for the development of cyber-attacks detection algorithms in industrial control systems. *Computers & Security* 114: 102585.

94 Vidal, J.M., Monge, M.A., and Monterrubio, S.M. (2020). EsPADA: enhanced payload analyzer for malware detection robust against adversarial threats. *Future Generation Computer Systems* 104: 159–173.

95 Latif, S., Huma, Z.E., Jamal, S.S. et al. (2021). Intrusion detection framework for the Internet of Things using a dense random neural network. *IEEE Transactions on Industrial Informatics* 18 (9): 6435–6444.

96 Huang, S. and Lei, K. (2020). IGAN-IDS: an imbalanced generative adversarial network towards intrusion detection system in ad-hoc networks. *Ad Hoc Networks* 105: 102177.

97 Gupta, N., Jindal, V., and Bedi, P. (2022). CSE-IDS: using cost-sensitive deep learning and ensemble algorithms to handle class imbalance in network-based intrusion detection systems. *Computers & Security* 112: 102499.

98 Ajayi, O. and Gangopadhyay, A. (2021). DAHID: Domain adaptive host-based intrusion detection. In: *IEEE International Conference on Cyber Security and Resilience (CSR)*, 467–472.

99 Granato, G., Martino, A., Baldini, L., and Rizzi, A. (2020). Intrusion detection in Wi-Fi networks by modular and optimized ensemble of classifiers. *IJCCI* 412–422.

100 Li, Z., Rios, A.L., and Trajkovic, L. (2021). Machine learning for detecting anomalies and intrusions in communication networks. *IEEE Journal on Selected Areas in Communications* 39 (7): 2254–2264.

101 Shafiq, M., Tian, Z., Bashir, A.K. et al. (2020). IoT malicious traffic identification using wrapper-based feature selection mechanisms. *Computers & Security* 94: 101863.

102 Li, G., Shen, Y., Zhao, P. et al. (2019). Detecting cyberattacks in industrial control systems using online learning algorithms. *Neurocomputing* 364: 338–348.

103 Liu, Q., Wang, D., Jia, Y. et al. (2022). A multi-task based deep learning approach for intrusion detection. *Knowledge-Based Systems* 238: 107852.

104 Radoglou-Grammatikis, P., Sarigiannidis, P., Iturbe, E. et al. (2021). Spear siem: a security information and event management system for the smart grid. *Computer Networks* 193: 108008.

105 Kodituwakku, H.A., Keller, A., and Gregor, J. (2020). InSight2: a modular visual analysis platform for network situational awareness in large-scale networks. *Electronics (Basel)* 9 (10): 1747.

106 Marino, D.L., Wickramasinghe, C.S., Tsouvalas, B. et al. (2021). Data-driven correlation of cyber and physical anomalies for holistic system health monitoring. *IEEE Access* 9: 163138–163150.

107 Al-Rowaily, K., Abulaish, M., Haldar, N.A., and Al-Rubaian, M. (2015). BiSAL – a bilingual sentiment analysis lexicon to analyze dark web forums for cyber security. *Digital Investigation* 14: 53–62.

108 Deb, A., Lerman, K., and Ferrara, E. (2018). Predicting cyber-events by leveraging hacker sentiment. *Information* 9 (11): 280.

109 Ishikawa, S., Ozawa, S., and Ban, T. (2020). Port-piece embedding for darknet traffic features and clustering of scan attacks. In: *International Conference on Neural Information Processing*, 593–603.

110 Sarhan, I. and Spruit, M. (2021). Open-cykg: an open cyber threat intelligence knowledge graph. *Knowledge-Based Systems* 233: 107524.

111 Dionísio, N., Alves, F., Ferreira, P.M., and Bessani, A. (2019). Cyberthreat detection from Twitter using deep neural networks. In: *International Joint Conference on Neural Networks (IJCNN)*, 1–8.

112 Georgescu, T.M., Iancu, B., and Zurini, M. (2019). Named-entity-recognition-based automated system for diagnosing cybersecurity situations in IoT networks. *Sensors* 19 (15): 3380.

113 Sun, T., Yang, P., Li, M., and Liao, S. (2021). An automatic generation approach of the cyber threat intelligence records based on multi-source information fusion. *Future Internet* 13 (2): 40.

114 Sapienza, A., Ernala, S.K., Bessi, A. et al. (2018). Discover: mining online chatter for emerging cyber threats. In: *Companion Proceedings of the The Web Conference*, 983–990.

115 Tsai, C.E., Yang, C.L., Chen, C.K., and CTI, A.N.T. (2020). Hunting for Chinese threat intelligence. In: *IEEE International Conference on Big Data (Big Data)*, 1847–1852.

116 Ranade, P., Mittal, S., Joshi, A., and Joshi, K. (2018). Using deep neural networks to translate multi-lingual threat intelligence. In: *IEEE International Conference on Intelligence and Security Informatics (ISI)*, 238–243.

117 Memos, V.A. and Psannis, K.E. (2020). AI-powered honeypots for enhanced IoT botnet detection. In: *3rd World Symposium on Communication Engineering (WSCE)*, 64–68.

118 Kim, H.K., Im, K.H., and Park, S.C. (2010). DSS for computer security incident response applying CBR and collaborative response. *Expert Systems with Applications* 37 (1): 852–870.

119 Nunes, R.C., Colome, M., Barcelos, F.A. et al. (2019). A case-based reasoning approach for the cybersecurity incident recording and resolution. *International Journal of Software Engineering and Knowledge Engineering* 11 (12): 1607–1627.

120 Shah, A., Ganesan, R., Jajodia, S., and Cam, H. (2018). Dynamic optimization of the level of operational effectiveness of a CSOC under adverse conditions. *ACM Transactions on Intelligent Systems and Technology* 9 (5): 1–20.

121 Thomas, L., Vaughan, A., Courtney, Z. et al. (2018). Supporting collaboration among cyber security analysts through visualizing their analytical reasoning processes. In: *IEEE Int'l Conf. Multimedia & Expo Workshops (ICMEW)*, 1–6.

122 DeCastro-García, N., Munoz Castaneda, A.L., and Fernandez-Rodríguez, M. (2020). Machine learning for automatic assignment of the severity of cybersecurity events. *Computational and Mathematical Methods in Medicine* 2 (1): e1072.

123 Dey, A., Totel, E., and Navers, S. (2020). Heterogeneous security events prioritization using auto-encoders. In: *International Conference on Risks and Security of Internet and Systems*, 164–180.

124 Nisioti, A., Loukas, G., Laszka, A., and Panaousis, E. (2021). Data-driven decision support for optimizing cyber forensic investigations. *IEEE Transactions on Information Forensics and Security* 16: 2397–2412.

125 Sakhnini, J., Karimipour, H., Dehghantanha, A., and Parizi, R.M. (2021). Physical layer attack identification and localization in cyber–physical grid: an ensemble deep learning based approach. *Physical Communication* 47: 101394.

126 Nespoli, P., Marmol, F.G., and Vidal, J.M. (2021). A bio-inspired reaction against cyberattacks: ais-powered optimal countermeasures selection. *IEEE Access* 9: 60971–60996.

127 Husak, M., Sadlek, L., Spacek, S. et al. (2022). CRUSOE: a toolset for cyber situational awareness and decision support in incident handling. *Computers & Security* 115: 102609.

128 Piplai, A., Mittal, S., Joshi, A. et al. (2020). Creating cybersecurity knowledge graphs from malware after action reports. *IEEE Access* 8: 211691–211703.

129 Meyers, B.S. and Meneely, A. (2021). An automated post-mortem analysis of vulnerability relationships using natural language word embeddings. *Procedia Computer Science* 953–958.

130 Carriegos, M.V., Castaneda, A.L., Trobajo, M.T., and De Zaballa, D.A. (2021). On aggregation and prediction of cybersecurity incident reports. *IEEE Access* 9: 102636–102648.

131 Deshpande, A., Estrela, V.V., and Patavardhan, P. (2021). The DCT-CNN-ResNet50 architecture to classify brain tumours with super-resolution, convolutional neural network, and the ResNet50. *Neuroscience Informatics* 1 (4): 100013. ISSN 2772-5286.

132 Almiani, M., AbuGhazleh, A., Jararweh, Y., and Razaque, A. (2021). DDoS detection in 5G-enabled IoT networks using deep Kalman backpropagation neural network. *International Journal of Machine Learning and Cybernetics* 12 (11): 3337–3349.

133 Corsini, A., Yang, S.J., and Apruzzese, G. (2021). On the evaluation of sequential machine learning for network intrusion detection. In: *16th International Conference on Availability, Reliability and Security*, 1–10.

134 Kumar, K.S., Nair, S.A., Roy, D.G. et al. (2021). Security and privacy-aware artificial intrusion detection system using federated machine learning. *Computers and Electrical Engineering* 96: 107440.

135 Le, D.C., Zincir-Heywood, A.N., and Heywood, M.I. (2016). Data analytics on network traffic flows for botnet behaviour detection. In: *IEEE Symposium Series on Computational Intelligence (SSCI)*, 1–7.

12

Utilization of Deep Learning Models for Safe Human-Friendly Computing in Cloud, Fog, and Mobile Edge Networks

Diego M.R. Tudesco[1], Anand Deshpande[2], Asif A. Laghari[3], Abdullah A. Khan[4], Ricardo T. Lopes[5], R. Jenice Aroma[6], Kumudha Raimond[7], Lin Teng[8], and Asiya Khan[9]

[1]*Department of Telecommunications, Federal Fluminense University (UFF), Niterói, RJ, Brazil*
[2]*Electronics and Communication Engineering, Angadi Institute of Technology and Management, Belagavi, India*
[3]*Sindh Madresstul Islam University, Karachi, Sindh, Pakistan*
[4]*Research Lab of Artificial Intelligence and Information Security, Faculty of Computing, Science and Information Technology, Benazir Bhutto Shaheed University, Karachi, Sindh, Pakistan*
[5]*Federal University of Rio de Janeiro (COPPE/UFRJ), Nuclear Engineering Laboratory (LIN), Rio de Janeiro, RJ, Brazil*
[6]*Department of CSE, Karunya Institute of Technology and Sciences, Karunya University, Coimbatore, India*
[7]*Department of Computer Science and Engineering, Karunya Institute of Technology and Sciences, Coimbatore, India*
[8]*Software College, Shenyang Normal University, Shenyang, China*
[9]*School of Engineering, Computing and Mathematics (Faculty of Science and Engineering), University of Plymouth, Plymouth, UK*

12.1 Introduction

Significant usage of "artificial intelligence" (AI) (e.g., "machine learning" [ML]) cybersecurity (CS) [1, 2] is over "intrusion detection and prevention systems" (IDPSs) to constantly examine networks [3–6]. IDPSs [7] can spot likely incidents and their logging information, impeding incidents and conveying them to security administrators. The IDPS family hinges on ML examining network traffic and isolating anomalies to signpost potential intrusions. A paramount CS issue is that "human-centered (HC) computing" (HCC) caters to the design, development, and setting out of mixed-initiative HC systems. HCC usually deals with hardware (HW) and practices hinging on technology. Altogether, "human-computer interaction" (HCI) relies more on usability and computing ergonomics than issues on studying and designing how people interrelate with "information and

Applying Artificial Intelligence in Cybersecurity Analytics and Cyber Threat Detection, First Edition.
Edited by Shilpa Mahajan, Mehak Khurana, and Vania Vieira Estrela.

communication technologies" (ICT) like "cyber-physical systems" (CPSs) [6]. ICT focuses on practices surrounding data collection, manipulation, and usage. The three computing "layers" are described below [3, 8–10].

Could Computing (CC): It handles business logic, "big data" (BD), analytical databases, and data "warehousing." CC does not need to over-provide assets up front to control business activity peak levels soon. Alternatively, one provisions the assets that one needs. One can scale these assets up or down to grow or shrink capacity as a business changes. CC delivers services over the Internet, e.g., storage, processing, and analytics. HCI positively impacts centralized data controlling with suitable data protection and BD workloads. This latter reason explains why it now has augmented popularity among companies. CC helps avail data centers to multiple customers with accredited access throughout the Internet.

Fog Computing (FC): It runs local network means, and micro-data centers, amid other things. All the storage, computation, data, and applications stay between CC and the physical host in FC. All these functionalities work more toward the host with faster processing since it occurs almost where data are created. Popular FC usages embrace intelligent cities, smart grids, innovative constructions, vehicular networks, and "software (SW)-defined networks" (SDNs). FC delivers low latency, while CC has high latency. CC collapses without the Internet. FC utilizes various protocols and standards to lessen failure risks. FC is more secure than CC owing to its distributed design. FC's eight columns are scalability, security, hierarchy, openness, "reliability, availability, and serviceability" (RAS), autonomy, agility, and programmability. FC does not replace CC but supplements it by becoming more conceivable to the information source. An additional data processing design similar to FC, "mobile edge computing," processes data straight on the devices without extra nodes or data centers, e.g., intermediary processing.

Multi-access Edge Computing (Mobile Edge Computing or MEC, also Edge Computing [EC]): MEC engages in real-time data processing on computers, mobile devices, wearables, info from sensors and actuators, process-specific usages, and autonomous HW. MEC is near local customers and HW, extending CC to the network edge. MEC is the near-real-time BD processing produced via applications and edge devices closest to where evidence is captured – in other words, lengthening the edge of one's network infrastructure. The two technologies differ as in MEC. The data processing occurs locally, while "Internet of Things" (IoT) devices refer data to the CC for analysis, being one of the most substantial differences between IoT Internet-enabled gadgets for proper operation and edge devices that can be taken as part of the IoT once the item has plenty of storage and computing to make low-latency decisions and process data fast enough.

"Deep learning" (DL) [11], ordinarily referred to as "deep neural networks" (DNNs), models a CPS with a structure having multiple layers that exploit the primary output as input from the uppermost level. From bottom to top, it remains an unsupervised learning process that autonomously discovers beneficial traits and expresses low-level features as complex structures. Starting from top to bottom, this supervising learning process optimizes and adjusts the network as the whole's parameters to boost its learning ability via labeled data to the complete network. DL has advanced swiftly because of both reasons below.

1) The application of tagged BD alleviates training issues. In DL, data serves as an "engine," and Imagenet contains millions of annotated data; and
2) Rapid HW advancement lets the training of huge-scale "neural networks" (NNs) with colossal computing potential, e.g., a high-performance "graphical processor unit" (GPU) that can mingle thousands of cores [12–14].

DL is efficient for the most complex engineering tests. At the same time, HCC in FCs and MECs is a serious apprehension nowadays. Thus, developing DL-based solutions is expected to be essential in cloud, fog, plus mobile edge networks (MENs) employing HCC [15–17], summarizing and sharing hi-tech research and technological answers worldwide. This chapter sketches DL topics but is not circumscribed to Refs. [18–22]:

- Evidence disclosure and privacy in HCC in FCs and MECs.
- Industrial systems in FCs and MECs.
- HCC security protocols in FCs and MECs.
- FCs' and MECs' modeling and security issues.
- Security, confidentiality, and multimedia records supervision in FCs and MECs.
- Gain novel insights into HCC FCs and MECs.
- HCC and DL conceptions and applications.
- Algorithms learn the HCC behavior analysis in FCs and MECs.
- HCC dynamic practices in FCs and MECs.
- DL for FC multimedia data management.

This chapter's DL models for HCC processing rely on CC, FC, and MEC networks and other interrelated areas [23–25], designated after a laborious review. HCC is described in Section 12.2. Section 12.3 handles improving cybersecurity via DL models, while case studies appear in Section 12.4. Section 12.5 brings in some discussions. Conclusions end this chapter.

12.2 Human-Centered Computing (HCC)

HCC delves into the design, development, and accomplishment phases of mixed-initiative human-computer systems. It began with the convergence of

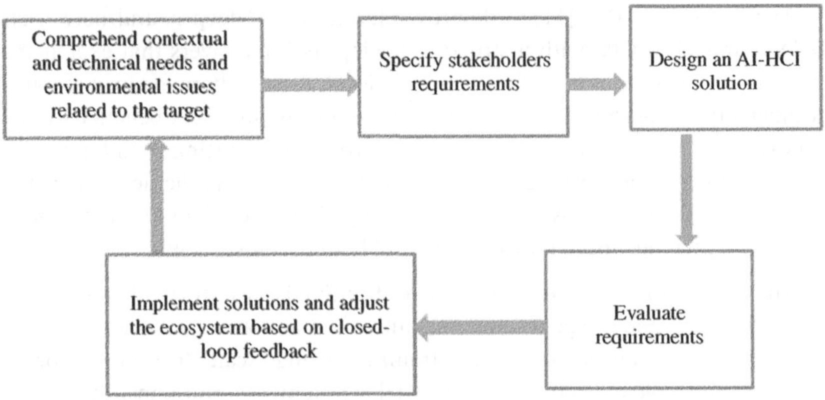

Figure 12.1 Convergence between human-centered computing and AI-HCI within a process cycle.

multiple disciplines concerned with comprehending human beings and designing computational artifacts [26], as in Figure 12.1. HCC is close to HCI and information science, being commonly involved with systems and practices utilizing technology, while HCI is more focused on ICT ergonomics and its usability. Information science aims at practices enclosing the collection, manipulation, and information usage.

HCC investigators and other staff frequently comprise folks from disciplines, e.g., engineering, computer science, anthropology, humanities, psychology, cognitive science, sociology, communication studies, graphic projects, and industrial design. They may emphasize comprehending humans as beings and in social cliques by looking at the forms they embrace and organizing their existences around ICT. Others concentrate on planning and developing new ICT.

HCC aims to bridge the gaps between the countless disciplines involved with CPSs' designs and implementations that maintain and strengthen human activities [27, 28]. In the interim, it covers a methodology set for any field employing computers in which individuals directly interact with devices or CPSs via ICTs. HCC takes into account particular, social, and cultural facets and addresses matters like information design, human knowledge interaction, HCI, human-human collaboration, and relationships between ICT, art, social, and cultural subjects [27, 28].

The "National Science Foundation" deems HCC developments the same as "a 3-D space incorporating humans, computing machines, and environments" [29]. Consistent with the NSF, anthropology embraces research that attends to individual needs, goal-oriented teams, and the social order as an unstructured pool of connected persons. The computer dimension brings immovable computing equipment pieces, mobile devices, and computational systems of visual/audio gadgets into the real world. The environmental dimension involves discrete computational apparatuses, mixed reality, and immersive virtual environments [29]. Some HCC themes are listed.

1) Problem-solving in distributed environments across Internet-established systems, grids, and information networks relying on sensors, actuators, mobile gadgets, and wearable information appliances.
2) Multimedia and multimodal interfaces employ combinations of audio, written text, illustrations, gesture, motion, touch, etc., by folks and equipment to interconnect. Intelligent interfaces, consumer modeling, data visualization, and content adaptation must accommodate different display traits, modalities, bandwidth, and latency.
3) Multi-agent systems control and orchestrate actions to solve complex shortcomings in distributed environments from multiple domains, like disaster response teams, education, e-commerce, and healthy aging.
4) Models for efficient computer-intermediated human-human interaction under multiple constrictions (e.g., cooperation between high- and low-bandwidth networks, video conferencing, etc.).
5) Designation of multimedia semantic structures to sustain cross-modal input and output.
6) Specialized solutions to tackle the unique prerequisites of particular communities.
7) Collaborative systems that assist knowledge-demanding and dynamic exchanges for innovation and smartness generation through organizational frontiers, national borders, and specialized fields.
8) Novel tactics to assist and enhance social interaction, including innovative ideas like social orthotics, affective computing, and experience capture.
9) More studies of how social organizations are necessary, as is in the case of governmental agencies or corporations. Elaborating better responses to and shaping new information technologies' insertion significantly advances scientific understanding and technical design.
10) Knowledge-driven HCI exploiting ontologies to address semantic vagueness and mutual behaviors between humans and computers. Both sides understand things differently.
11) HC semantic relatedness measures employ human power to estimate the semantic connection between perceptions.

HC systems, often called HCSs, are specifically developed to cater to HCC [9]. The HCI arena primarily concerns itself with the interactive systems' conceptualization and development in relation to human activities. The "Committee on Computing, Information, and Communication" (CCIC) [30] under the "National

Science and Technology Council" [31, 32] has recognized human-centered systems (HCS) as a constituent of a "high-performance computing program" [33, 34]. Human-centered automation can be employed as a word to refer to HCSs. HCSs are planned grounded on the analysis of human tasks. These arrangements are envisioned to assist and monitor human performance, concentrating on maximizing anthropological benefits [9].

Moreover, HCSs are constructed to consider human talents and can adjust readily to evolving human demands [31, 32]. Still, when labeling a system's parts, reflecting on four human-centeredness components becomes paramount: (a) the analysis of structures necessitates an examination of the tricky nature of the targeted social clique, as well as (b) the diverse social units encompassing work and information. Hence, one should accentuate that human-centeredness is not an intrinsic systemic constituent but a paramount process in which stakeholders associated with a specific system aid in gauging and supplying feedback on the "quality of experience" (QoE) and expected vs. obtained benefits [16, 35, 36]. The fundamental system architecture should accurately reflect the realistic bond between beings and machines. The motive and intended viewership of the CPS are carefully planned to explicitly demonstrate the design, appraisal, and use case components [37] as in Figure 12.2.

"HC activities in multimedia" (HCM) can be deemed as follows [33, 38]: (i) media production, (ii) annotation, (iii) organization, (iv) archival, (v) retrieval, (vi) sharing, analysis, and (vii) communication, which can be further clustered into three major groups: production, analysis, and interaction.

Multimedia production entails anthropological creative media tasks [39] for illustration, photographing, generating audio, remixing, etc. All media production aspects implicated must directly encompass humans in HCM. Multimedia creation has two main dimensions:

1) The first entails cultural and social dynamics. HCM production should ponder cultural differences and be planned consistent with the target culture of a given deployment.
2) The second is to mull over human abilities. HCM production participants should be able to finalize their activities throughout production.

Multimedia analysis is an HCM activity type that automatically scrutinizes general human deeds and social behavior. There is a wide-ranging area of potentially relevant usages, from simplifying and enhancing human communications to refining data access and recovery in business, entertainment, and individual domains.

Multimedia interaction is the dialog activity portion of HCM, whose behavior comprehension is crucial. For this reason, professionals can employ technologies

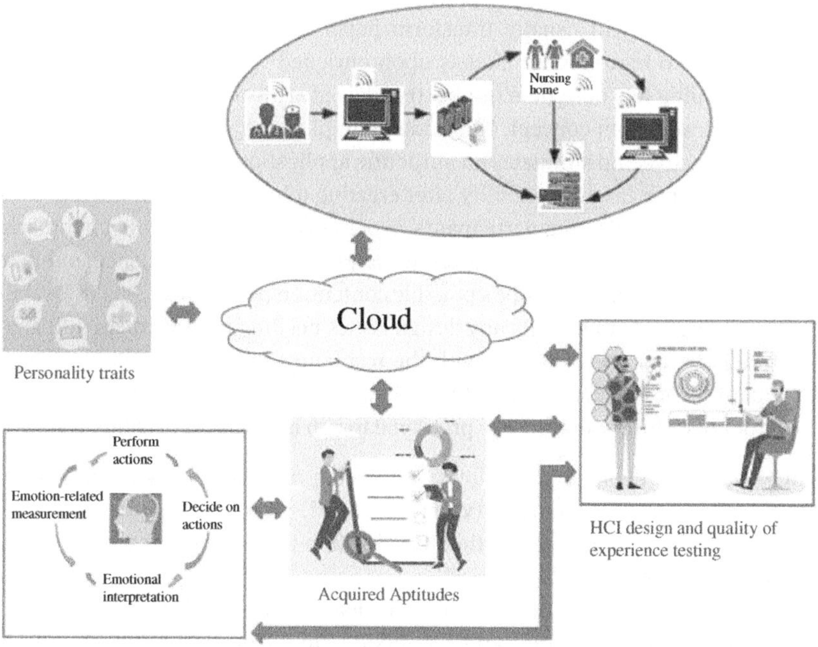

Figure 12.2 Intelligent cyber-physical system involving sub-systems that rely on AI.

to assist such communication so that humans can connect with computers organically. Cultural differences and social environment are essential facets for creating natural contact owing to the probable various cultural origins. Some varieties encompass (a) face-to-face communications wherever the interaction is physically located and real time, (b) live-computer-mediated communications with physically remote interaction but remains real time, and (c) non-real-time computer-mediated communications, for instance, instant SMS, email, etc.

The "HC Design Process" (HCDP) first involves how the user learns about the product's target audience and understand clients' needs. Empathizing will lead to research and asking the target audience precise questions about their growth goals. Competitor analysis may be used to uncover extra product market design opportunities during this research stage. After gathering user and product demand data, the designer will utilize sketches and wireframes to brainstorm design alternatives. A user interface's information architecture, space allocation, and content functionality are outlined in wireframing. Consequently, a wireframe usually lacks colors and visuals and focuses on interface functionality [40]. HCDP has two final phases:

(a) The designer will usually transform paper sketches or low-fidelity wireframes into high-fidelity models upon enriched wireframing or sketching. Prototyping lets designers' probe, try their ideas further, and take notice of the overall design concept. High-fidelity implies the prototype is "clickable" or interactive and simulates an authentic application.
(b) The designer can test usability after creating a high-fidelity prototype. This test involves collecting participants' experiences for the sake of benchmarking. These partakers must represent the product's target audience and take them through the prototype's possible contention points as if using it. Usability testing aims to identify any design issues needing improvement and analyze how real users interact with the resultant product. It is vital to follow up on the users' comportment and choices besides asking them about their thoughts while operating the prototype to run a hands-on usability test.

HCM can be deemed as follows: (i) media production, (ii) annotation, (iii) organization, (iv) archival, (v) retrieval, (vi) sharing, analysis, and (vii) communication, which can be further bundled into three key groups: production, analysis, and interaction.

Multimedia production entails anthropological creative media tasks for illustration, photographing, generating audio, remixing, etc. All media production aspects implicated must directly encompass humans in HCM. Multimedia creation has two main dimensions:

1) The first entails cultural and social dynamics. HCM production should ponder cultural differences and be planned consistent with the target culture of a given deployment.
2) The second is to mull over human abilities. HCM production participants should be able to finalize their activities throughout production.

Multimedia analysis is an HCM activity type that automatically scrutinizes general human deeds and social behavior. There is a wide-ranging area of potentially relevant usages, from simplifying and augmenting anthropological communications to refining data access and recovery in business, entertainment, and individual domains.

Multimedia interaction is the dialog activity portion of HCM. For this reason, professionals can connect with computers organically. Cultural differences and social environments are essential facets for creating natural contact. Some communication varieties encompass (a) face-to-face wherever the interaction happens indoors, physically, and in real time, (b) live-computer mediated with remote interaction that remains real time, and (c) non-real-time , for instance, SMS, and email.

The HCDP helps the operator to learn about the product's target audience and understand needs to direct research and inquire the audience about their goals.

Competitor analysis may uncover extra product market design opportunities during this research stage. After gathering user and product demand data, the designer will utilize sketches and wireframes to brainstorm alternatives. A user interface's information structural design, space apportionment, and content functionality are outlined in wireframing. Consequently, a wireframe usually lacks colors and visuals, focusing on interface functionality. HCDP has two final phases:

(a) The designer usually transforms low-fidelity wireframes or sketches into high-fidelity models. Prototyping lets designers probe, further their ideas, and take notice of the whole project concept. High-fidelity implies the prototype is "clickable" or interactive, simulating an authentic application.
(b) The designer can test usability after crafting a high-fidelity prototype. This test involves collecting participants' experiences for the sake of benchmarking. These partakers must represent the product's target audience and examine the prototype's possible contention points as if using it. Usability testing aims to identify any design issues needing improvement and to analyze the way real users interact with the resultant product. It is vital to follow up on the users' comportment and choices besides asking them about their thoughts while operating the prototype during a hands-on usability test.

12.3 Improving Cybersecurity Through Deep Learning (DL) Models: AI-HCC Systems

This section adds another feature to DL/ML methodologies that expedites gaining network knowledge from unsupervised facts and clarifies complex problems. AI and CS can be extensively used to protect companies from phishing, spear-phishing, drive-by attacks, password attacks, denial of service, etc.

12.3.1 Inserting DL in Cloud, Fog, and Edge Computing

First, with three key paradigms (CC, FC, and EC), it is imperative to distinguish the target user from other stakeholders [41]. In Figure 12.2, the most important participants are part of a nursing home. Users interact with a product or service (e.g., outpatients, common sense smartphone handlers, students, etc.). In contrast, stakeholders care about something or participate in a company's action/service delivery. Design must take into account user needs and stakeholder aspirations. Some stakeholders are end users, but not all. The data management initiative affects executives, managers, sponsors, clients, and regulators. Since users are the people using the software or service and stakeholders are business members or someone helping the user in loco (e.g., caretaker, maintenance person, etc.) responsible for planning and preparing features, (i) stakeholders' focus is on the business, and the features are how they create value, and (ii) the user's "quality of experience" (QoE) and associated "quality of service" (QoS) are gateways to the product's features. Overlooking or overemphasizing insights from the stakeholder's perspective can harm the user and the product. Remote resources should preserve strong defenses and records of activities via a blockchain setting that ensures fair play from all sides and viewpoints of a transaction to minimize stakeholder disasters.

Due to a lack of anthropocentric approaches, HCC designs must prevent faults and disasters in CPS elements, including HW and software (SW).

IoT devices connect EC resources to users or applications outside the data center, near the activity it supports. Data center physical, access, and network security are lost due to deployment changes, ill-design, or human error. Edge apps are a massive step toward M2M without human control, which is risky for most businesses. "Edge security" (ES) threats are serious. Understanding these issues and their solutions for seamless business operations. EC security enhances data center security and compliance. This requires protecting edge device access physically and through a user interface as well as data center technologies but is suitable for outside deployment. ES can protect consumers and sensitive data at a company's "edge" by protecting data that lives or travels through devices outside centralized data centers. Data leaks are one of the most prominent ES dangers because hackers can easily access data stored locally on devices rather than centrally. Hackers can access sensitive data on individual or networked devices.

CC provides Internet-based servers, storage, networks, software, and analytics. Data leakage from poor cloud security across cloud networks causes IP theft, contract breaches, and virus assaults. Hackers can control how organizations provide clients. CC cybersecurity (C3) cannot prevent all threats since customers do not control CC. However, a good C3 approach significantly decreases risks. CC is often safer than on-premise computing despite these hazards. Virtualization is crucial to cloud deployment. Multi-tenant ecosystems' customers may not share data [42–49]. Cloud storage is kept, managed, backed up remotely, and accessible to clients via a network. Virtualization relies on the hypervisor, which runs several VMs on a single HW host. Hypervisors manage many operating systems on a shared physical system. NIST again divides into four implementation strategies depending on consumer cloud suitability and intent. Organizations can use public or private cloud services [42–49] and selecting services is problematic for stakeholders (including users) and business decision-makers, leading to user-centered evaluation. Due to the abundance of cloud service providers offering similar cloud services, choosing the best one is tough. Many articles have been proposed in recent years. To detect and prevent unwanted transfer or deletion of valuable data, "data loss prevention" (DLP) software is essential. Cloud infrastructure developers must offer safe APIs for clients, but stakeholders should not worry. Illogical CS exhausts people operating throughout cyberspace and makes them prone to blunders and incorrect decisions. Employee education and conscientization, safe data backup strategies, regulated data access, encryption, strong password protection, repeated tests, and extensive cloud governance policies are needed to prevent cloud security concerns in enterprises. It's crucial to balance automated and human decision-making. Again, combining HCC and blockchain can provide good cybersecurity and privacy without keeping data.

FC receives encrypted data, making data retrieval difficult. Unlike CC, owners must develop a safe index for data search when uploading data to fog nodes. Data will be searched using different keywords after fog node processing. FC makes time-sensitive data storage and analysis easier locally. FC minimizes cloud data volume and distance, lowering security, and privacy risks. FC can be vulnerable to IP address spoofing and MitM attacks. FC uses edge and cloud resources, requiring HW. FC inherits EC, CC vulnerabilities, and distributed infrastructure. New security and privacy issues increase the need to secure communication channels, ensure data integrity, prevent illegal access, and address crucial privacy concerns. Some main DL cybersecurity applications follow [42–49].

Trace of Intrusion Detection: "Artificial NNs" (ANNs), "convolutional neural networks" (CNNs), and "recurrent neural networks" (RNNs) are DL variants that can deliver more competent ID/IP schemes by scrutinizing the Internet traffic with superior accuracy, lessening the false alerts' number, and aiding security teams in differentiating bad from suitable network activities. Some example solutions comprise "user entity and behavior analytics" (UEBA), "web application firewall" (WAF), and "next-generation firewall" (NGFW).

Malware Detection: Traditional malware solutions, e.g., common firewalls, detect malware via a signature-based detection system. If a company keeps a database of notorious threats, it updates the stored data frequently to integrate the latest threats. While this practice is effective against vulnerabilities, it struggles to cope with more innovative threats. DNNs can distinguish more unconventional threats and are not contingent on recalling known signatures and standard attack patterns. As an alternative, they "understand" the system and can identify suspicious doings that might signpost the existence of corrupt actors or malware.

Spam and Social Engineering (SE) Recognition: "Natural language processing" (NLP) can aid one in quickly detecting and dealing with spam and other SE forms. NLP learns everyday communication and language pattern conditions and uses statistical models to spot and block spam, employing TensorFlow to augment email spam detection capabilities.

Network Traffic Analysis (NTA): DL and combinations of ANNs and ML or metaheuristics have shown promising outcomes in investigating HTTPS network traffic to hunt for malicious activities, which is advantageous in dealing with many weaknesses similar to SQL injections and DoS outbreaks.

Behavior Analytics (BA): Analyzing and tracking front-end client activities and comportments is a crucial DL-established security practice in any organization. These tasks are much more defying than recognizing customary malicious doings against networks because they bypass security protection mechanisms and habitually do not raise flags and alarms. User BA (UBA) and User/Entity BA (UEBA) are great tools against such occurrences. After an educative period, it can grasp standard employee behavioral forms and identify suspicious activities, e.g., accessing the system at uncommon hours, possibly indicating an insider attack, and raising alerts.

Monitoring Emails: Watching employees' official email accounts is vital to prevent cyber outbreaks. To exemplify, phishing attacks are commonly instigated through emails to personnel and questioning them for sensitive data. Cybersecurity SW with DNN can evade these kinds of vulnerabilities. NLP can also scan emails for any distrustful behavior.

Analyzing Mobile Endpoints: DL is already reaching mainstream on mobile equipment and driving voice-based experiences through mobile assistants. So, DNN can identify and analyze threats against portable endpoints when the enterprise has to inhibit the growing number of mobile devices' malware.

Enhancing Human Analysis: DL in CS can help humans detect malicious outbreaks, endpoint protection, analyze the network, and perform vulnerability evaluations. Through this, humans can decide on things better by discerning ways and means to solve problems.

Task Automation: The main DL benefit is automating repetitive tasks that enable staff to emphasize more critical work. There exist a few CS tasks that can be automated with ML. Organizations can undertake tasks faster and better by incorporating DL into their functions.

WebShell: A piece of code that can be malevolently loaded into a website to offer access to modify the server's Webroot, allowing attackers to access the database. DL can help perceive normal shopping behavior. The AI model can be trained to discern normal and malign behavior.

Network Risk Scoring (NRS): DL can analyze previous cyberattack datasets and regulate what network's areas were impaired by a particular attack, thus helping prevent the attack concerning a given network area.

12.3.2 DL and HCI

HCI mainly scrutinizes the information exchange between humans and computers, encompassing cognitive psychology, multimedia, ergonomics, "virtual reality" (VR), and "augmented reality" (AR) [50]. The HCI exchange relies on interactive human-handled devices (e.g., keyboard, mouse, joysticks, wearables, and position trackers) and computer-human cooperative devices (viz printers, plotters, monitors, and helmet-mounted monitors) [51–53]. The HCI progression process involves voice interaction, image recognition, AR, VR, and somatosensory interfaces [54–56]. Voice has maximum input effectiveness and the most relaxed interaction, where the products' adoption scenarios can quickly broaden options. Image recognition can help automation of driving and security for traffic situation identification and human features recognition. AR and VR aid in immersion for interaction, visualization, and movement [57, 58]. People's body movements can ease interacting with nearby devices or real/remote environments through motion sensing without any complex controller.

DL has proven relatively hopeful in language processing, speech/image recognition, and information retrieval [59–61] (Figure 12.3). Other tactics embrace context-aware systems, behavioral information synthesis from modeling user investigations, embedded dialog agents, or natural speech treatment, all utilizing DL to support human exchanges with smart designs. DL adoptions hinge on building models mimicking the human neural connections, which process and extract meaning from sound, images, and writings. Data features are labeled hierarchically through several transformation phases, leading to data interpretations. This enables ML and deep NNs designs to improve decision-making by

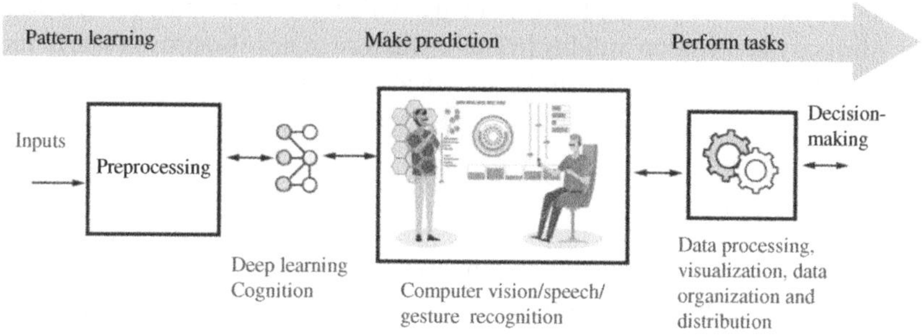

Figure 12.3 An HCC stage with DL.

imitating the human brain and neurons' interconnections [62–65]. DL adoption in HCI can expand speech and image recognition accuracy while enhancing interaction realism. Language understanding explores the language caveats of HCIs. Contrasting to speech recognition, which transforms speech into text or matching commands, language comprehension comprises creating machines that grasp human language. Sensors can gradually ameliorate HCI because of the environmental digitization tendency brought by the IoT. Media content, real/virtual environments, objects, and individuals are all experiencing a digitalized process. Interface design is essential, and how to craft and deploy a natural HCI will turn into a critical proposition. Intelligent devices that comprehend scenes in the environment will become more realistic, stress-free, and humanized HCI, which happens once the user has a suitable help guide and, thus, the user does not need too much knowledge about memory function or instantaneous operation understanding.

Incorporating audio, imagery information, touch screens, and video is vital to HCI, making its design, data output, and user interaction more flexible. Media has transformed people's intercommunication. HCI requirements related to self-service machines, transportation information displays, and shopping mall displays require similar HW solutions. A text mining scheme named two-level conceptual link analysis surpasses the traditional HCI, where the keyboard is obligatory, causing certain adoption limitations. Embedded hardware is paramount for HCI scenes' rendering and aid in many other possibilities. Intelligent HCI combined with DL works intensively in gesture, speech, emotion, and NLP recognition. Various recognition approaches are projected and verified through testing to attain high recognition accuracy. Consequently, applying DL in HCI design can widen the application expectations.

12.4 Case Studies

A rational, shielded two-party protocol model with a hybrid architecture provides new adversary verification/validity [65–67]. This design has also proven safe in the occurrence of new adversaries under the ideal/real paradigm [68] (Figures 12.2 and 12.3).

12.4.1 HCI Use Cases

HCI refers to the information exchange between people and HW with a computer informing folks through any output, like display devices, people entering relevant data through input devices. The concrete virtual realization of a multimodal simulation interface shows the real environment and coexisting agents. The most noticeable content is represented by behavior and dialog. VoxWorld is a simulation platform for making HCIs [69, 70] that follows a multimodal dialog structure that converses through language, gesticulation, facial expressions, actions, and gaze locating in a task-oriented interactive setting. The 3D image acquisition cost is falling with continuous sensor developments. Gesture recognition under depth and red–green–blue (RGB) imageries gradually led to pattern recognition developments.

Nonetheless, most deep gesture image processing methodologies are reasonably simple, ignoring the relationship and impact between both modes and failing to fully use different modes' interrelated factors. Depth image information [71] assists in solving the above problems, assuming the independent and associated multimodal data features and constructing an adaptive weight procedure to fuse different features. Simulation outcomes excelled the customary DL gesture image processing schemes, and the recognition rate was more elevated, with superior recognition accuracy that surpasses other advanced methods. Testes gauge the method's viability and robustness and often point out that multimodal image acquisition through DL can augment gesture recognition accuracy in HCI systems.

The same application consequences are also mirrored in the context-aware framework. Data-driven tools for continuous human motion scrutiny and human–machine cooperation necessitate prediction in future intelligent businesses to ameliorate robots' planning and control besides ending shared tasks [72]. Numerical examples can verify the engine's feasibility, and fallouts should meet the prerequisites. Likewise, a context-aware citation recommender can model an end-to-end memory network [73] utilizing "bidirectional long short-term memory" (Bi-LSTM) to assimilate papers and citation contexts. Still, tryouts on different datasets confirmed the model's superior performance.

Moreover, context-aware intelligent HCI systems, as client modeling research advises, DL also widely applies to user modeling grounded on past interaction matrices and recommender systems under equivalent function learning arrangements. Existing DL-founded recommendation schemes usually employ the user's interaction history to accomplish static user preference modeling. A time-aware DL framework modeling dynamic user predilections through an attention mechanism and estimate matching scores constructed on DL [74]. It considerably and consistently beats current time-aware and DL-reliant recommendation methodologies.

The literature has abundant multidisciplinary content since HCI embraces a wide range, with restricted studies exhibiting the vast picture. Such analyses afford a superior understanding, revealing current issues, obstacles, and potential exploration gaps. HCI research trends revealed topics beyond glimpses, bearing in mind their development stage, number of applications, and acceleration to offer a panoramic outlook presenting trends augmenting and deteriorating over time [75]. The HCI investigations' shift from machine-oriented structures to human-oriented systems signposts its future path toward up-context, intuiting adaptive systems. Combining emotion analysis with humane knowledge absorption research helped construct a forward-thinking, simple, safe, and effective HCI for emotion inspection [76], relating facial expressions and audio signals to discover macro expressions and produce an emotion index that explains users' mental health. Collected users' records are observed to analyze the person's mental health and arrange for counseling solutions for a worthy treatment effect in humans. AI, HCI, and intelligent robot collaboration (cobots) technologies are crucial and thought-provoking content. Regarding SW and HW, the previous techniques investigate and try to craft a natural HCI atmosphere, providing collaborations between HCI and robots [77] through present reading, technologies for writing, listening, speaking, and catering to other senses can be improved to solve some of the noteworthy HCI challenges. Hence, DL performance in other HCI intelligent systems can be better.

12.4.2 Cybersecurity and HCI Use Cases

Adversarial learning (AL) and ML can help address network security concerns at the frontier [78, 79]. The adversarial issue may arise when learning algorithms do not effectively exploit the input feature set, allowing invaders to center on a narrow feature collection to deceive the model. Two crucial classifiers can fix this. A "random forest" (RF) model called "weighted RF" (WRF) can support input feature recognition evenly. Selecting a clustering subset of trees throughout runtime augments performance. NNs can rely on extra soft restrictions that relate the objective function with weight variances to base classification decisions on better-distributed feature groupings. These methods have amended the learned model's robustness compared to baseline systems.

A hybrid "convolution neural network" (CNN) model has emerged in Ref. [80], in which a dilated-based CNN furthers the recognition accuracy. A numerical NN speeds up the identification process. In dilated-based DL designs, the convolution and pooling layers have been substituted by dilated convolution, which shrinks computation costs. Weight parameters are quantized by the quantitative NN-built scheme to an integer power of two, transforming multiplications into shift operations, thus significantly dropping the time.

Employing the IoT in CPSs, like autonomous driving, big data analysis is required with high precision and negligible latency. DL supports robust analytic skills at the cloud and edge layers with low latency for effectual big data exploration. However, existing research failed to address particular obstacles, viz. security, centralized control, adversarial incidents, and privacy. The work in

Ref. [81] proposes DeepBlockIoTNet, a secure DL aimed at an IoT network with blockchain. The DL occurs among edge nodes in a decentralized, safe manner at the edge layer. The blockchain DL module eradicates centralized authority control while strengthening security. The experimental evaluation supported higher accuracy.

Rapid information handling and Internet technology growth has led to "electronic health records" (EHR). The research in Ref. [82] has innovated EHR cybersecurity prevention regarding feature selection and classification through DL methodologies. At this time, input EHR data are processed to eliminate null values and noise. This treated data is selected according to their features, exploiting a kernel-based, gradient-boosting NN with classification via a stochastic CNN. A cryptographic cloud-established CPS blockchain model has enhanced the network's data security.

As the Internet matures, so do security weaknesses. There are numerous ways to secure a cyber-environment, and the best choice must always be elected. AI has given technology a new perspective by making life easier for ordinary users with its unique ideas. In this AI-type of architecture, the computer works with hidden layers to emulate the human mind and produce output. DNA-centered security hinging on DL that behaves like cryptography and secures cyber data transit is being studied [83]. Recent studies confirm that this combination ameliorates data security. The DNA via DL has strengthened security systems by inhibiting significant cyberattacks. Suppose one focuses on the health sector [84, 85], which handles patient health data records. According to Ref. [83], integrating DNA sequence and DL methods improves data confidentiality, integrity, authorization, and authentication for genuine users. Medical practitioners need this. DNA security mechanisms improve the health privacy of information through DL techniques.

Due to wireless mediums' shortcomings, ad hoc networks are vulnerable to several threats and attacks [86, 87]. Due to this, intrusion detection, security, privacy, and validation in ad-hoc networks are currently of great interest. This research identifies wireless ad-hoc network assaults and offers solutions. The work in Refs. [88, 89] covers black holes, wormholes, selective forwarding, Sybil, and denial-of-service attacks. This research presents a trust-based safe routing strategy for mobile ad-hoc networks to reduce black hole node interference. When black hole nodes are in the routing path, network performance suffers. Thus, a routing technique is introduced to minimize black hole node-related packet loss. This routing system has been experimentally tested to determine the best secure path for packet delivery between sources and destinations. A wireless network is segmented and routed poorly when wormholes invade. One may locate wormholes by employing ordinal multi-dimensional scaling and round-trip duration in wireless ad hoc nets with sparse or dense topologies.

The approach described can find wormholes with short routes and long path links. This stratagem is experimentally investigated to ensure that this ad hoc network has no hidden wormholes. Three methods to defend wireless ad-hoc networks from selective forwarding attacks are devised. The first solution exploits a reward-punishment mechanism to stimulate three nodes to forward messages in busy ad-hoc networks [90–93]. A novel adversarial model (with three node kinds and their behaviors) employs the incentive-based technique to prevent nodes from acting separately, warranting packet-forwarding collaboration. The second authenticates intermediary nodes in resource-constrained ad-hoc networks to safely transport packets using non-cooperative game theory. This model leverages game theory. This game finds a desired equilibrium that makes multihop communication physically viable, which is discovered. The third procedure accomplishes binary searches and control packets. It can catch malicious nodes in multihop, hierarchical ad-hoc networks. The cluster head can accurately identify the malign node by analyzing packet sequences dropped from a source node. A lightweight symmetric encryption via binary playfair protects data transmission. Experiments suggested that the encryption approach is energy-, time-, and memory-efficient. This lightweight encryption method reduces Sybil attacks in clustered wireless ad-hoc networks.

12.5 Discussion

HCC-AI systems can identify shadow data, monitor data access irregularities, and inform security personnel about potentially harmful conduct by data users, reducing time in finding and fixing issues. Cybersecurity for CPSs relying on DL can make (i) existing things more usable for people, (ii) something esthetically pleasing, (iii) a product out of an abstract algorithm or idea, and (iv) businesses grow by leveraging technology into a product-market fit; this diversity is why people will say their field is different. Hence, these structures allow the convivence of these entities:

Human: Someone needs to understand people;

Computers: They intercede between humans and CPSs, albeit they also need to talk to other machines;

Interaction: All CPS parts need to work together well. This part comprises networking, sensors, actuators, and controllers.

DL algorithms can detect information-sensitive patterns and monitor access and transmission to avoid unauthorized data leaking. These models can appraise network data flow, reveal shortcomings, and establish security policies to safeguard sensitive data.

Security issues are more likely when large amounts of data are transferred through networks. FC reduces the amount of data being transferred back and forth to the cloud, reducing latency due to local computation while minimizing security risks.

12.5.1 HCC-AI Advantages

HCI is the larger field of understanding how humans and computers interact. HCC only comes up when HCI developers are discovered to be making bad designs that work, allowing companies to make technological products accessible to individuals with disabilities. It helps "user experience" (UX) designers and others understand each user's needs relating to technology. It shows that not all users interact with technology in the same way.

HCC is a reaction to the early emphasis in HCI on figuring out how to make it possible for humans to adapt to computers. HCC suggested that understanding what humans want and need is most important, putting the focus of adaptation on the shoulders of the computer rather than the human. Human error can be reduced with the same HCI technology, and all these losses can be avoided.

AI-HCC design lets one better understand oneself's and people's needs, motivations, and concerns, but it also makes for a more efficient, more flexible design process.

The reliability and scalability of an HCC-AI take people's abilities as human thinkers and allow these ideas to scale to serve much larger data needs. AI aims to help humans, but without human input and understanding, it can only help so much.

12.5.2 HCC-AI Caveats

HCC-AI systems work faster and necessitate fewer hands. This advanced technology has benefits, albeit it does create some dangers. The most upsetting risks are the misapplication of technology and a negative effect on human experiences [94–99]. HCC-AI can impact several realms: human-technology synergy, human-environment collaborations, cause loss of jobs, ethics, moral values, privacy, security, criminality, well-being, health, happiness, general accessibility, universal access, healthy learning without emotional disruption, creativity, social organization, and democracy.

12.6 Conclusion

Human-centered design relies on fostering empathy through being alert to and aware to all implicated human stakeholders and is attentive on identifying resolutions through an open, non-judgmental approach. It is rooted in a conviction that a new participant's mindset will impel one to better, more inventive solutions.

Cloud computing has transformed how devices connect over the Internet, resulting in the IoT, a multitude of linked gadgets that can perceive and answer back to human needs, and a vast data volume. The FC and EC layers pose several HCC problems, too.

In DL, a multi-layer model employs sequential layers. One layer's output turns out to be the subsequent layer's input. Unsupervised learning learns valuable features and advanced structures from low-level qualities. Supervised learning optimizes network parameters with improved learning using labeled data. DL development relies on high-performance computers to train wide-ranging neural networks whose input can benefit from swiftly applying an enormous amount of neural network-labeled data to alleviate training drawbacks. DL models can unravel the most complex problems. HCC in fog and MENs is a major issue. Thus, DL-grounded development solutions are expected to aid fog, and MEN's HCC, sharing means to mitigate the already growing number of cybersecurity glitches besides their aftermaths in a planet that is implementing AI indiscriminately, without considering HCC issues.

References

1 Ho, J. and Wang, C. (2021). Human-centered AI using ethical causality and learning representation for multi-agent deep reinforcement learning. In: *Proc. 2nd Int'l Conference on Human-Machine Systems (ICHMS)*, 1–6. IEEE.

2 Khanna, K., Estrela, V.V., and Rodrigues, J.J.P.C. (ed.) (2021). *Cyber Security and Digital Forensics – Proc. ICCSDF 2021*, Lecture Notes on Data Engineering and Communications Technologies. Singapore: Springer. https://doi.org/10.1007/978-981-16-3961-6.

3 Gupta, B.B., Agrawal, D.P., and Yamaguchi, S. (2019). Deep learning models for human centered computing in fog and mobile edge networks. *Journal of Ambient Intelligence and Humanized Computing* 10: 2907–2911. https://doi.org/10.1007/s12652-018-0919-8.

4 Jaimes, A., Gatica-Perez, D., Sebe, N., and Huang, T.S. (2007). Human-centered computing: toward a human revolution. *Computer* 40 (5): 30–34. https://doi.org/10.1109/MC.2007.169. S2CID 2180344.

5 Zhang, L., Zhu, T., Hussain, F.K. et al. (2023). A game-theoretic method for defending against advanced persistent threats in cyber systems. *IEEE Transactions on Information Forensics and Security* 18: 1349–1364.

6 Estrela, V.V., Saotome, O., Loschi, H.J. et al. (2018). Emergency response cyber-physical framework for landslide avoidance with sustainable electronics. *Technologies* 6: 42. https://doi.org/10.3390/technologies6020042.

7 Sureda Riera, T., Bermejo Higuera, J., Bermejo Higuera, J. et al. (2020). Prevention and fighting against web attacks through anomaly detection technology. A systematic review. *Sustainability* 12 (12): 4945. https://doi.org/10.3390/su12124945.

8 Dong, H., Hussain, F., and Chang, E. (2010). A human-centered semantic service platform for the digital ecosystems environment. *World Wide Web* 13 (1–2): 75–103. https://doi.org/10.1007/s11280-009-0081-5. hdl:20.500.11937/29660. S2CID 10746264.

9 Dong, H., Hussain, F., and Chang, E. (2013). UCOSAIS: a framework for user-centered online service advertising information search. In: *Proc. Web Information Systems Engineering – WISE 2013*, Lecture Notes in Computer Science, vol. 8180, 267–276. Berlin Heidelberg: Springer-Verlag. https://doi.org/10.1007/978-3-642-41230-1_23.

10 Panchanathan, S., Chakraborty, S., McDaniel, T., and Tadayon, R. (2016). Person-centered multimedia computing: a new paradigm inspired by assistive and rehabilitative applications. *IEEE Multimedia* 23 (3): 12–19. https://doi.org/10.1109/MMUL.2016.51.

11 Deshpande, A., Estrela, V.V., and Razmjooy, N. (2021). *Computational Intelligence Methods for Super-Resolution in Image Processing Applications*. Zurich, Switzerland: Springer Nature. https://doi.org/10.1007/978-3-030-67921-7.

12 Jiang, F., Fu, Y., Gupta, B.B. et al. (2018). Deep learning based multi-channel intelligent attack detection for data security. *IEEE Transactions on Sustainable Computing*. https://doi.org/10.1109/TSUSC.2018.2793284.

13 Deng, L. and Yu, D. (2014). Deep learning: methods and applications. *Foundations and Trends in Signal Processing* 7 (3–4): 197–387.

14 Elmisery, A.M., Sertovic, M. et al. (2018). Cognitive privacy middleware for deep learning mashup in environmental IoT. *IEEE Access* 6: 8029–8041.

15 Diro, A.A. and Chilamkurti, N.K. (2018). Deep learning: the frontier for distributed attack detection in fog-to-things computing. *IEEE Communications Magazine* 56: 169–175.

16 Laghari, A.A., Zhang, X., Shaikh, Z.A. et al. (2023). A review on quality of experience (QoE) in cloud computing. *Journal of Reliable Intelligent Environments*. https://doi.org/10.1007/s40860-023-00210-y.

17 Khan, A.A., Laghari, A., Gadekallu, T.R. et al. (2022). A drone-based data management and optimization using metaheuristic algorithms and blockchain smart contracts in a secure fog environment. *Computers and Electrical Engineering* 102: 108234.

18 Li, T., Li, J., Liu, Z. et al. (2018). Differentially private naive Bayes learning over multiple data sources. *Information Sciences* 444: 89–104.

19 Li, Y., Wang, G., Nie, L., and Wang, Q. (2018). Distance metric optimization driven convolutional neural network for age invariant face recognition. *Pattern Recognition* 75: 51–62.

20 Li, J., Sun, L., Yan, Q. et al. (2018). Significant permission identification for machine learning based android malware detection. *IEEE Transactions on Industrial Informatics*. https://doi.org/10.1109/TII.2017.2789219.

21 Gao, C.-Z., Cheng, Q., He, P. et al. (2018). Privacy-preserving naive Bayes classifiers secure against the substitution-then-comparison attack. *Information Sciences*. https://doi.org/10.1016/j.ins.2018.02.058.

22 Gupta, B.B., Agrawal, D.P., and Yamaguchi, S. (2016). *Handbook of Research on Modern Cryptographic Solutions for Computer and Cyber Security*. Hershey: IGI Global Publisher.

23 Jararweh, Y. et al. (2017). Software-defined system support for enabling ubiquitous mobile edge computing. *The Computer Journal* 60 (10): 1443–1457.

24 Stergiou, C. et al. (2018). Secure integration of IoT and cloud computing. *Future Generation Computer Systems* 78: 964–975.

25 Gupta, B.B., Yamaguchi, S., and Agrawal, D.P. (2018). Advances in security and privacy of multimedia big data in mobile and cloud computing. *Multimedia Tools and Applications* 77 (7): 9203–9208.

26 Zhang, Z. et al. (2016). Social media security and trustworthiness: overview and new direction. *Future Generation Computer Systems*, 86: 914–925. https://doi.org/10.1016/j.future.2016.10.007.

27 Wang, B., Zheng, P., Yin, Y. et al. (2022). Toward human-centric smart manufacturing: a human-cyber-physical systems (HCPS) perspective. *Journal of Manufacturing Systems* 63: 471–490.

28 Fang, X., Zeng, Q., and Yang, G. (2020). Local differential privacy for human-centered computing. *EURASIP Journal on Wireless Communications and Networking* 2020, 65: 1–12.

29 Müller-Birn, C., Glinka, K., Sörries, P., Tebbe, M., & Michl, S. (2021). *Situated Case Studies for a Human-Centered Design of Explanation User Interfaces*. ArXiv, abs/2103.15462.

30 Earth, D.O. (2020). *A Vision for NSF Earth Sciences 2020–2030: Earth in Time. Washington, DC: The National Academies Press.*

31 González-Meneses, Y.N., Guerrero-García, J., Reyes-García, C.A. et al. (2019). Formal protocol for the creation of a database of physiological and behavioral signals for the automatic recognition of emotions. In: *Human-Computer Interaction. HCI-COLLAB 2019. Communications in Computer and Information Science*, vol. 1114: 211–226 (ed. P. Ruiz and V. Agredo-Delgado). Cham: Springer. https://doi.org/10.1007/978-3-030-37386-3_16.

32 Alavizadeh, H., Jang-Jaccard, J., Enoch, S.Y., Al-Sahaf, H., Welch, I., Çamtepe, S.A., & Kim, D.D. (2022). A survey on cyber situation-awareness systems: framework, techniques, and insights. *ACM Computing Surveys*, 55, pp. 1–37. https://doi.org/10.1145/3530809

33 Jaimes, A. (2006). Human-centered multimedia: culture, deployment, and access. *IEEE Multimedia* 13 (1): 12–19. https://doi.org/10.1109/MMUL.2006.8

34 Lee, L., Braud, T., Hosio, S.J., and Hui, P. (2020). Towards augmented reality driven human-city interaction: current research on mobile headsets and future challenges. *ACM Computing Surveys (CSUR)* 54: 1–38.

35 Agustianto, K., Utomo, A.H., Ayuninghemi, R. et al. (2022). Eye tracking usability testing using user-centered design analysis method. In: *Proc. 2nd International Conference on Social Science, Humanity and Public Health (ICO-SHIP 2021)*, 265–269. Atlantis Press.

36 Laghari AA, Khan A, He H, Estrela VV, Razmjooy N, Hemanth J, Loschi HJ. (2020). Quality of experience (QoE) and quality of service (QoS) in UAV systems. In: Estrela V.V., Hemanth J., Saotome O., Nikolakopoulos G., Sabatini R. (eds), *Imaging and Sensing for Unmanned Aircraft Systems*, Vol. 2, 10, 213–242, IET, London. https://doi.org/10.1049/PBCE120G_ch10

37 Wiehr, F., Hirsch, A., Daiber, F., Kruger, A., Kovtunova, A., Borgwardt, S., Chang, E., Demberg, V., Steinmetz, M., Jorg, H. (2020). *Safe Handover in Mixed-Initiative Control for Cyber-Physical Systems.* ArXiv, abs/2010.10967

38 Venkateswara, H., McDaniel, T.L., Tadayon, R., and Panchanathan, S. (2018). Person-centered technologies for individuals with disabilities: mpowerment through assistive and rehabilitative solutions. *Technology and Innovation* 20 (1): 117–132.

39 Gupta, B. B., Gupta, D. (Eds.). (2020). *Handbook of Research on Multimedia Cyber Security*. IGI Global. https://doi.org/10.4018/978-1-7998-2701-6

40 Paul, G., Abele, N.D., and Kluth, K. (2021). A review and qualitative meta-analysis of digital human modeling and cyber-physical-systems in Ergonomics 4.0. *IISE Transactions on Occupational Ergonomics and Human Factors* 9: 111–123.

41 Ahmad, S., Shakeel, I., Mehfuz, S., and Ahmad, J. (2023). Deep learning models for cloud, edge, fog, and IoT computing paradigms: survey, recent advances, and future directions. *Computer Science Review* 49: 100568. ISSN 1574-0137, https://doi.org/10.1016/j.cosrev.2023.100568.

42 Odegbile, O., Chen, S., and Wang, Y. (2019). Dependable policy enforcement in traditional non-SDN networks. In: *2019 IEEE 39th International Conference on Distributed Computing Systems (ICDCS)*, 545–554.

43 Liu, S., Lin, G., Han, Q.L. et al. (2019). DeepBalance: deep-learning and fuzzy oversampling for vulnerability detection. *IEEE Transactions on Fuzzy Systems* 28 (7): 1329–1343.

44 Jeon, S. and Kim, H.K. (2021). AutoVAS: an automated vulnerability analysis system with a deep learning approach. *Computers & Security* 106: 102308.

45 Huff, P., McClanahan, K., Le, T., and Li, Q. (2021). A recommender system for tracking vulnerabilities. In: *The 16th International Conference on Availability, Reliability and Security*, 1–7.

46 Iorga, D., Corlatescu, D.G., Grigoresc, O. et al. (2021). Yggdrasil – early detection of cybernetic vulnerabilities from Twitter. In: *23rd International Conference on Control Systems and Computer Science (CSCS)*, 463–468.

47 Saha, T., Aaraj, N., Ajjarapu, N., and Jha, N.K. (2021). SHARKS: smart hacking approaches for RisK scanning in internet-of-things and cyber-physical systems based on machine learning. *IEEE Transactions on Emerging Topics in Computing* 10 (2): 870–885.

48 Chen, Y., Poskitt, C.M., Sun, J. et al. (2019). Learning-guided network fuzzing for testing cyber-physical system defences. In: *34th IEEE/ACM International Conference on Automated Software Engineering (ASE)*, 962–973.

49 She, D., Pei, K., Epstein, D. et al. (2019). NEUZZ: efficient fuzzing with neural program smoothing. In: *IEEE Symposium on Security and Privacy (SP)*, 803–817.

50 Shu, Y., Xiong, C., and Fan, S. (2020). Interactive design of intelligent machine vision based on human–computer interaction mode. *Microprocessors and Microsystems* 75: 103059.

51 Luria, M., Sheriff, O., Boo, M. et al. (2020). Destruction, catharsis, and emotional release in human-robot interaction. *ACM Transactions on Human-Robot Interaction* 9: 22.

52 Demir, M., McNeese, N.J., and Cooke, N.J. (2020). Understanding human-robot teams in light of all-human teams: aspects of team interaction and shared cognition. *International Journal of Human Computer Studies* 140: 102436.

53 Johal, W. (2020). Research trends in social robots for learning. *Current Robotics Reports* 1: 75–83.

54 Jyoti, V. and Lahiri, U. (2020). Human-computer interaction based joint attention cues: implications on functional and physiological measures for children with autism spectrum disorder. *Computers in Human Behavior* 104: 106163.

55 Suwa, S., Tsujimura, M., Ide, H. et al. (2020). Home-care professionals' ethical perceptions of the development and use of home-care robots for older adults in Japan. *International Journal of Human-Computer Interaction* 36: 1295–1303.

56 Gervasi, R., Mastrogiacomo, L., and Franceschini, F. (2020). A conceptual framework to evaluate human-robot collaboration. *International Journal of Advanced Manufacturing Technology* 108: 841–865.

57 Pretto, N. and Poiesi, F. (2017). Towards gesture-based multi-user interactions in collaborative virtual environments. In: *Proceedings of the 5th International*

Workshop Low-cost 3D-Sensors, Algorithms, Applications, Hamburg, Germany, 28–29 November, 203–208.

58 Pani, M. and Poiesi, F. (2018). Distributed data exchange with leap motion. In: *Proceedings of the 2018 International Conference on Augmented Reality, Virtual Reality and Computer Graphics*, 655–667. Cham: Springer.

59 Cao, Y., Geddes, T.A., Yang, J.Y.H., and Yang, P. (2020). Ensemble deep learning in bioinformatics. *Nature Machine Intelligence* 2: 500–508.

60 Wang, G., Ye, J.C., and De Man, B. (2020). Deep learning for tomographic image reconstruction. *Nature Machine Intelligence* 2: 737–748.

61 Minaee, S., Kalchbrenner, N., Cambria, E. et al. (2021). Deep learning–based text classification: a comprehensive review. *ACM Computing Surveys* 54: 1–40.

62 Yuan, Q., Shen, H., Li, T. et al. (2020). Deep learning in environmental remote sensing: achievements and challenges. *Remote Sensing of Environment* 241: 111716.

63 Calvo, I., Tropea, P., Viganò, M. et al. (2021). Evaluation of an automatic speech recognition platform for dysarthric speech. *Folia Phoniatrica et Logopaedica* 73: 432–441.

64 Tao, F. and Busso, C. (2020). End-to-end audiovisual speech recognition system with multitask learning. *IEEE Transactions on Multimedia* 23: 1–11.

65 Shen, C.-W., Luong, T.-H., Ho, J.-T., and Djailani, I. (2019). Social media marketing of IT service companies: analysis using a concept-linking mining approach. *Industrial Marketing Management* 90: 593–604.

66 Wang, Y., Zhang, S., Tang, Y. et al. (2019). Rational adversary with flexible utility in secure two-party computation. *Journal of Ambient Intelligence and Humanized Computing* 10: 2913–2927. https://doi.org/10.1007/s12652-017-0669-z.

67 Ma, J., Chen, Y., Wang, Z. et al. (2021). A rational delegating computation protocol based on reputation and smart contract. *Journal of Cloud Computing* 10: 1–12.

68 Johnson, D.S., Feige, U. (2007). *In Proceedings of the Thirty-Ninth Annual ACM Symposium on Theory of Computing. Symposium on the Theory of Computing.*

69 Kaur, R., Gabrijelcic, D., and Klobučar, T. (2023). Artificial intelligence for cybersecurity: literature review and future research directions. *Information Fusion* 97: 101804.

70 Pustejovsky, J. and Krishnaswamy, N. (2021). Embodied human computer interaction. *KI - Künstliche Intelligenz* 35: 307–327.

71 Duan, H., Sun, Y., Cheng, W. et al. (2021). Gesture recognition based on multimodal feature weight. *Concurrency and Computation: Practice and Experience* 33: e5991.

72 Wang, P., Liu, H., Wang, L., and Gao, R.X. (2018). Deep learning-based human motion recognition for predictive context-aware human-robot collaboration. *CIRP Annals* 67: 17–20.

73 Wang, J., Zhu, L., Dai, T., and Wang, Y. (2020). Deep memory network with bi-LSTM for personalized context-aware citation recommendation. *Neurocomputing* 410: 103–113.

74 Wang, R., Wu, Z., Lou, J., and Jiang, Y. (2022). Attention-based dynamic user modeling and deep collaborative filtering recommendation. *Expert Systems with Applications* 188: 116036.

75 Gurcan, F., Cagiltay, N.E., and Cagiltay, K. (2021). Mapping human–computer interaction research themes and trends from its existence to today: a topic modeling-based review of past 60 years. *International Journal of Human-Computer Interaction* 37: 267–280.

76 Chhikara, P., Singh, P., Tekchandani, R. et al. (2020). Federated learning meets human emotions: a decentralized framework for human–computer interaction for IoT applications. *IEEE Internet of Things Journal* 8: 6949–6962.

77 Ren, F. and Bao, Y. (2020). A review on human-computer interaction and intelligent robots. *International Journal of Information Technology and Decision Making* 19: 5–47.

78 Krishnan, D. and Singh, S. (2021). Cost-sensitive bootstrapped weighted random forest for DoS attack detection in wireless sensor networks. In: *Proceedings of the2021 TENCON IEEE Region 10 Conference (TENCON)*, 375–380.

79 Wang, Y., Sun, T., Li, S., Yuan, X., Ni, W., Hossain, E., Poor, H.V. (2023). *Adversarial Attacks and Defenses in Machine Learning-Powered Networks: A Contemporary Survey*. ArXiv, abs/2303.06302.

80 Zhou, J., Wang, F., Xu, J. et al. (2019). A novel character segmentation method for serial number on banknotes with complex background. *Journal of Ambient Intelligence and Humanized Computing* 1–15.

81 Rathore, S. and Park, J.H. (2021). A blockchain-based deep learning approach for cyber security in next generation industrial cyber-physical systems. *IEEE Transactions on Industrial Informatics* 17: 5522–5532.

82 Qamar, S. (2022). Healthcare data analysis by feature extraction and classification using deep learning with cloud based cyber security. *Computers and Electrical Engineering* 104: 108406.

83 Aqeel, S., Shahid Khan, A., Ahmad, Z., and Abdullah, J.B. (2021). A comprehensive study on DNA based security scheme using deep learning in healthcare. *EDPACS* 66: 1–17.

84 Khan, A.A., Laghari, A.A., Shaikh, A. et al. (2021). A blockchain security module for brain-computer interface (BCI) with multimedia life cycle framework (MLCF). *Neuroscience Informatics* 100030. https://doi.org/10.1016/j.neuri.2021.100030.

85 Estrela, V.V., de Jesus, M.A., Intorne, A.C. et al. (2023). Blockchain technology enabling better services in the healthcare domain. In: *Intelligent Healthcare Systems* (ed. V.V. Estrela) chap. 7, 135–158. London: CRC Press.

86 Nyre-Yu, M. and Caldwell, B.S. (2018). Supporting advances in human-systems coordination through simulation of diverse, distributed expertise. *Systems* 6: 39. https://doi.org/10.3390/systems6040039.

87 Estrela, V.V., Andreopoulos, N., Sroufer, R. et al. (2021). Transmedia ecosystems, quality of experience and quality of service in fog computing for comfortable learning. In: *Proc. 2021 IEEE Global Engineering Education Conference (EDUCON)*, 1003–1009.

88 Pareek, C.C.P., Costa de Albuquerque, V.H., Khanna, A., and Gupta, D. (2022). Deep learning technique based intrusion detection in cyber-security networks. In: *Proc. 2022 IEEE 2nd Mysore Sub Section International Conference (MysuruCon)*, 1–7.

89 Neerugatti, V. and Rama Mohan Reddy, A. (2020). Artificial intelligence-based technique for detection of selective forwarding attack in RPL-based internet of things networks. In: *Emerging Research in Data Engineering Systems and Computer Communications. Advances in Intelligent Systems and Computing*, vol. 1054 (ed. P. Venkata Krishna and M. Obaidat). Singapore: Springer. https://doi.org/10.1007/978-981-15-0135-7_7.

90 Loschi, H.J., Estrela, V.V., Hemanth, D.J. et al. (2020). Communications requirements, video streaming, communications links and networked UAVs. In: *Imaging and Sensing for Unmanned Aircraft Systems*, vol. 2, 6 (ed. V.V. Estrela, J. Hemanth, O. Saotome, et al.), 113–132. London: IET. https://doi.org/10.1049/PBCE120G_ch6.

91 Farooq, S.M., Hussain, S.M., and Ustun, T.S. (2021). A survey of authentication techniques in vehicular ad-hoc networks. *IEEE Intelligent Transportation Systems Magazine* 13: 39–52.

92 Tulaib, L.F., Salman, A.O., and Mohammed, M.A. (2021). Innovative techniques for attack detection in wireless ad-hoc networks. *International Journal of Wireless and Ad Hoc Communication* 3 (1): 49–58. https://doi.org/10.54216/IJWAC.030105.

93 Banerjee, H. and Yadav, S. (2023). Energy-efficient Security technique implementation for selective forwarding attack in WSN. In: *Proc. 11th International Conference on Internet of Everything, Microwave Engineering, Communication and Networks (IEMECON)*, 1–10.

94 Fuentes, C., Herskovic, V., Rodríguez, I. et al. (2017). A systematic literature review about technologies for self-reporting emotional information. *Journal of Ambient Intelligence and Humanized Computing* 8: 593–606. https://doi.org/10.1007/s12652-016-0430-z.

95 Lottridge, D. and Chignell, M. (2009b). Emotrace: tracing emotions through human-system interaction. *Proceedings of the Human Factors and Ergonomics Society Annual Meeting* 53: 1541–1545. https://doi.org/10.1177/154193120905301916.

96 Maña, A. and Koshutanski, H. (2019). Special issue on recent advances in ambient intelligence towards a smart and human-centered internet of things. *Journal of Ambient Intelligence and Humanized Computing* 10: 727–729. https://doi.org/10.1007/s12652-019-01200-w.

97 Estrela, V.V., Grata, E.G.H., Deshpande, A. et al. (2023). In-body devices and sensors communication – how implantables, ingestibles, and injectables interact with the internet. In: *Intelligent Healthcare Systems* (ed. V.V. Estrela) (Ed.), chap. 12, 236–258. London: CRC Press.

98 Estrela, V.V., Khan, A.A., Shaikh, A.A. et al. (2023). Some issues regarding content-based image retrieval (CBIR) for remote healthcare theradiagnosis. In: *Intelligent Healthcare Systems* (ed. V.V. Estrela) chap. 6, 110–134. London: CRC Press.

99 Kure, H.I., Islam, S., Ghazanfar, M.A. et al. (2021). Asset criticality and risk prediction for an effective cybersecurity risk management of cyber-physical system. *Neural Computing and Applications* 34: 493–514.

13

Artificial Intelligence for Threat Anomaly Detection Using Graph Databases – A Semantic Outlook

Edwiges G.H. Grata[1], Anand Deshpande[2], Ricardo T. Lopes[3], Asif A. Laghari[4], Abdullah A. Khan[5], R. Jenice Aroma[6], Kumudha Raimond[7], Shoulin Yin[8], and Awais Khan Jumani[9]

[1] *Department of Telecommunications, Federal Fluminense University (UFF), Niterói, RJ, Brazil*
[2] *Electronics and Communication Engineering, Angadi Institute of Technology and Management, Belagavi, India*
[3] *Federal University of Rio de Janeiro (COPPE/UFRJ), Nuclear Engineering Laboratory (LIN), Rio de Janeiro, RJ, Brazil*
[4] *Sindh Madresstul Islam University, Karachi, Sindh, Pakistan*
[5] *Research Lab of Artificial Intelligence and Information Security, Faculty of Computing, Science and Information Technology, Benazir Bhutto Shaheed University, Karachi, Sindh, Pakistan*
[6] *Department of CSE, Karunya Institute of Technology and Sciences, Karunya University, Coimbatore, India*
[7] *Department of Computer Science and Engineering, Karunya Institute of Technology and Sciences, Coimbatore, India*
[8] *Shenyang Normal University, Shenyang, Liaoning Province, China*
[9] *Department of Computer Science, Sindh Madressa-tul-Islam University, Karachi, Sindh, Pakistan*

13.1 Introduction

A comprehensive cybersecurity (CS) framework must help implement "cyber-physical systems" (CPSs) effectively while managing potential security risks to accommodate the Internet of Things (IoT) hardware (HW) diversity [1–3]. Both factors are becoming increasingly crucial in infrastructure, administration, and daily existence. Under this context, every system incorporates advanced networked structures with computing devices, embedded controllers, sensors, and actuators [4, 5]. These systems' components enable gathering and interacting with the physical world's data while designed for real-time operations and warrant reliable performance, particularly in applications that involve essential safety considerations. The IoT experiences ongoing growth and development due to falling costs and the convergence of sensors, actuators,

Applying Artificial Intelligence in Cybersecurity Analytics and Cyber Threat Detection, First Edition.
Edited by Shilpa Mahajan, Mehak Khurana, and Vania Vieira Estrela.

platforms, controllers, networks, etc. The latest IoT innovation comprises significant assets in the ongoing innovation-driven economy with substantial and inexpensive advantages and presents extensive development and growth forecasts. Simultaneously, integrating CPS and IoT amplifies the vulnerabilities and potential targets for CAs. The "attack surface" (AS) refers to the comprehensive set of possible entry points, commonly known as attack vectors, by which an unauthorized user might enter a system and retrieve data [5]. The easiness of protecting a system tends to be inversely proportional to the surface of attack size.

The unpremeditated faults or malicious CAs could severely impact humans and the planet's natural environment. Hands-on and coordinated efforts are paramount to designing, deploying, and strengthening CPS and IoT's dependability and security [4, 5]. Progresses in networking, computing, detecting, and control systems have aided a multitude of new devices, albeit security is often absent and left for later. Functional prerequisites and fast-moving markets drive the industry. Design paradigms evolve continuously and speedily, whereas standards undergo debates. Many devices whose design lifespans are quantified in decades undergo deployment. Project choices will impact transportation, healthcare, building automation, emergency response, energy production, and other sectors. Modern means of transport can automatically stop to avoid accidents. Healthcare apparatuses can observe conditions in real-time adaptations to changes. Several innovative services can boost the energy grid and intelligent buildings. If CS is overlooked, one risks unintentional faults or malevolent CAs altering the ways vehicles stop, health devices self-adjust, and buildings/smart grids respond to events. CS becomes more puzzling as the number of gadgets with security vulnerabilities escalates. Addressing CS by enforcing models/designs onto extensively deployed systems is unrealistic. Security concerns must be analyzed, assimilated, and managed promptly in the project and deployment phases.

CPSs and IoT interact with cyberspace across numerous sectors. To ensure realistic CS building blocks for particular systems, employing a layered scheme, CPSs must be robust to CS difficulties (e.g., safety, financial side, trustworthiness, interoperability, "social engineering," [SE] and privacy).

CA's success and mission impacts depend on several aspects in complex dynamic contexts. Besides introducing or eliminating machines, programs might change network conditions, which poses a major challenge. The information gap between cyberspace's offensive and defensive sides grows. When faced with a continually updated exposure or attack pattern, defenders typically fail to understand the latest attacking strategies, vulnerability information, and appropriate defense plans to confront the attacker. The endurance and concealment of new attack features like "advanced persistent threat" (APT) CAs [6] limit standard security technologies centered around "machine learning" (ML), metaheuristics,

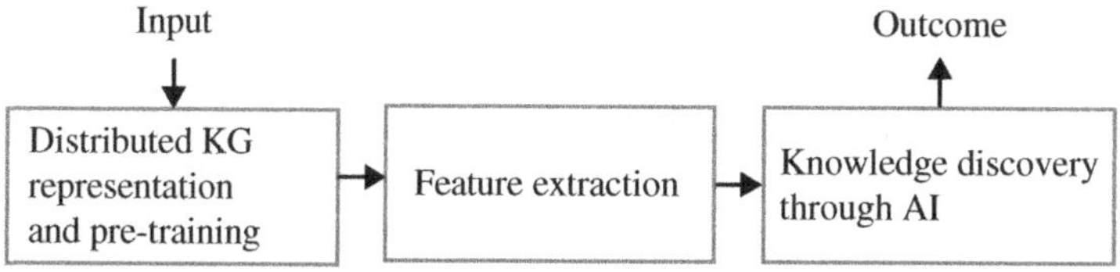

Figure 13.1 Deep learning NER flowchart.

and deep learning (DL) as in Figure 13.1 [7–9]. Simple tasks like feature extraction [10], anomaly detection [11, 12], and data classification [12] cannot reconstruct a full CA behavior depiction. Expert knowledge buried in CS data is still essential to solve the above difficulties.

Nevertheless, CS-related data underwent widespread growth. These diverse, heterogeneous, and fragmented data make it difficult for CS managers to quickly discover vital information. Therefore, the current CS problem is not obtainable data shortage but how to assemble multiple sources' heterogeneous information into one model to better comprehend CS with supplementary decision assistance. The current CS analysis focuses on obtaining correlations and potential CAs from CTI data. Technologies viz. correlation analysis [13], causal inference [14], and semantic reasoning [15] that rely on knowledge modeling helped create new strategies under "big data" (BD) conditions.

The "CS knowledge graph" (CSKG) is a security-specific "knowledge graph" (KG) with nodes and edges that form a large-scale CS semantic network and provide an intelligible modeling structure for numerous CAs and defense setups in the real world. Nodes signify entities or abstract rationales (e.g., weakness designation, CA pattern, product name, business, etc.), and edges denote entities' attributes or relationships. Nodes and edges form a KG whose advantages can be threefold:

(1) KG creation and refinement, ontology [16], "information extraction" (IE) [17], and entity disambiguation [18] help disclose and blend multisource diverse data-driven knowledge.
(2) CS knowledge can be expressed structurally and relationally, and graphically visualizing knowledge is intuitive and efficient.
(3) Semantic modeling, query practices, and inferring technologies can imitate security specialists' thinking processes to get new understanding (aka new relations) or examine data consistency using logic procedures and existent details (i.e., triples, quadruples, etc.) [19].

While several CSKGs apply different CS views, most have focused on KG development. It remains unclear in what way KGs solve real burdens in CA and defense scenarios. Many organizations' CS managers speculate if existing CSKGs can be reused and how they match their "information and communication technology" (ICT) infrastructure. Furthermore, it is worth contemplating what fresh facts a team requires for new relationship inferences. KG design evaluation needs "cyber-situational awareness" (CSA), safety analysis, security assessment, and association studies, restricting the hyperspace security assessment region and temporal and spatial dimensions. The chronological aspect entails the prevention, recognition, or reaction security phases. Spatially, it offers a probability to incorporate various operational modules (i.e., CTs, network infrastructure, security outlook, task dependencies, and so on) into a cohesive "knowledge base" (KB) for many CS undertakings. Other CSKG characteristics, including ontology, construction tools, data sources, and reasoning procedures [20–22], address their usability effort to solve hands-on problems. The main contributions in this chapter are

- Comprehensive CSKG setting analysis, i.e., a CSKG scenario categorization framework, requires background and creation technology research.
- Relevant datasets are curated datasets' analyses and open-source (OO) libraries facilitate future CSKG construction and IE tasks.
- Future directions summarize each category and highlight promising trends.

This chapter's next Section introduces the basics of KGs in CS. Section 13.3 lists CSKG construction methodologies, with definitions, the development flow, ontological aspects, named entity detection schemes, and relation extraction approaches. The usual datasets, their fortes, and inadequacies are in Section 13.4 to assist in applying CSKG and extracting information. Section 13.5 overviews CSKG application settings. Section 13.6 tackles existing research benefits, shortcomings, and prospects. Conclusions surface in Section 13.7.

13.2 KGs in Cybersecurity

While modeling CPSs with knowledge organization arrangements or communication networks, there are four main KG scenarios:

(i) **Type I** characterizes a network infrastructure, hinging on the granularity where nodes may embody either:
   - Simulated or real-life network infrastructures, device entities with their properties; arcs indicating physical and logical relations concerning them,
   - Autonomous systems and their properties, and the arcs illustrate their relations,
   - Network data stream and arcs typify routing, or
   - A CA graph comprehends arcs that epitomize outbreak paths.

(ii) **Type II** characterizes CTI, enfolding system information/parameters, CT data, and user/malware behavioral data.
(iii) **Type III** uses nodes to represent a prearranged vocabulary or an ontology as
- CS properties and concepts plus the arcs relating them;
- Network devices and their properties interconnect through arcs;
- Vulnerabilities where arcs define properties, viz. vulnerability scoring, types of faults, and platforms.

(iv) **Type IV** encompasses multiple, uniquely identified connected graphs, each capturing data from a distinctive source for information fusion and dimensionality cutback.

Utilizing concepts and properties for independently created knowledge domains like CS, CSA, and CTI, OWL32 ontologies can partially automate operations that would otherwise be done manually or with SW instruments under human supervision. For timeline development and event reconstruction, digital forensic investigations can be automated if knowledge and semantics are kept. In a fused CSKG, which collects every detail and organically integrates seemingly unrelated CKGs, `owl:sameAs` can match and define identical entities (such as specific malware) from several sources, such as after-action attack reports. Structured, semantic KGs symbolize real-world concepts and interactions [23–25]. Simple KG entities represent collections, categories, object kinds, and classes (production, vendor, vulnerability, and invader). Entity relationships build a graph; attributes contain traits and parameters.

Formal, semantical knowledge representation is an AI branch that aids in (i) defining CS concepts, properties, and relationships formally, (ii) allowing software (SW) agents to catalog vulnerabilities, CTs, and CAs, (iii) resolving entities, (iv) detecting anomalies, and (v) matching CAs' patterns. KGs might disclose data correlations even experts would ignore. CSKGs call for storage when dealing with CSKGs (habitually directed, labeled graphs). Numerous data security and network processes' features exist that perceive CS semantics changes impressively depending on the graph model [20–22], one of the following:

(A) **"Resource Description Framework" (RDF)[b0]:** It engenders a graph Q_R, amounting to a group of RDF triples or statements $(s, p, o) \in (\mathrm{I} \cup \mathrm{B}) \times \mathrm{I} \times (\mathrm{I} \cup \mathrm{L} \cup \mathrm{B})$. I, L, and B are pairwise disconnected infinite sets clarified below:

- I pertains to the "International Resource Identifiers" (IRIs) set, comprising sets of Unicode characters' strings below

```
scheme:[//[user:pwd@]host[:port][/]path[?query]
[#fragment]
```

or a legitimate subset of them (viz URLs).

- L and L_P represent, respectively, RDF and self-denoting plain literals like"<string>"(@<lang>. The notation obeys the ensuing definitions:
  <string> is a string, and
  <lang> is an elective language tag (or typed literals) L_T behaving as <string>""^^, <datatype> denotes a data type as per a schema (e.g., the XML), and
  <string> stands for a lexical space element consistent with the data type.
- B is a blank nodes' set, i.e., unique albeit anonymous assets that disobey IRIs and RDF literals.

(B) **Labeled Property Graph:** It is a graph Q_{LP} = (V, E, α, β, γ), with a finite set of vertices (aka nodes) ***V***. **E** is a graph edges' finite set disjoint from **V**. The incidence function that maps each edge in ***E*** into a vertices' pair in V, α: **E** → (***N*** × ***N***), is an β: (***V***∪***E***) → L_S maps every single edge from ***E*** and its set of labels from L, and γ: (***N***∪***E***) × ***P*** → V_S is a function that assigns properties to a collection of values from ***V***, with the second and third properties being partial functions.

(C) **Hypergraph:** It assumes the form QH = (***V***, ***E***), where ***E*** is a set of hyper-edges among the vertices so that or a given a set of vertices ***V***, ***E***{***u***, ***v***,...} $\in 2^V$.

(D) **Multigraph:** In this case, Q_M = (***V***, ***E***). ***E*** denotes a bag of edges. A growing number of graph databases are assisting multiple graph data models [22].

Different graph-based implementations possess distinct advantages and disadvantages. In fact, not all support n-ary relations, despite their usefulness in modeling networked communication. CS provenance deals with the chronology of the origin, advance, ownership, locality, and alterations to a system or sub-system and associated data. It may also embrace employees and processes intermingling with or modifying the arrangement, element, or related data. CSA, CS decision support, anomaly detection, network forensics, etc. can benefit from data provenance [20], which some KGs enable, but hybrid solutions exist. The RDF data model does not catch provenance. However, the Semantic Web research community developed sophisticated formalisms. These numerous approaches have been introduced over time, highlighting the need to explain a graph data model.

13.3 CSKG Construction Methodologies

Knowledge depiction benefits a lot from logic and AI "Web ontology language" (OWL), and RDF is helping modern KGs gain tremendous popularity [23, 24] to boost the search engines and the users' search quality. The CSKG creation process embraces these aspects: (i) there is a CSKG building framework with the security ontology design denoting the security domain knowledge, and (ii) named entity recognition (NER) tasks are reviewed. Finally, relation extraction and investigations regarding similar mechanisms in this domain are called.

13.3.1 CSKG Building Flow

Akin to broad-spectrum KG construction procedures, the CSKG employs the same methodology and framework. Due to the relative maturity and completeness of the CS knowledge data, CSKGs can be crafted utilizing a top-down approach [25]. Fragmented domain data could be joined under the direction of a particular framework or a pre-designed CS ontology from domain experts. Then, expertise in IE and entity alignment can split entities and relationships starting from the earliest CS data. Knowledge reasoning tools can return new CS comprehension evidence from KGs in effect to aid in prediction and inference, as in Figure 13.2.

13.3.2 CS Ontology

CS ontologies designate concepts and relationships using a standard, unambiguous, and unique definition, permitting humans and machines to communicate (Figure 13.3). Unified ontologies, similar to STUCCO and "unified CS ontology" (UCO) [9, 26], combine heterogeneous data and schemas from various CS systems with the most commonly employed CS standards for evidence sharing and exchange. For different specific scenarios, other established ontologies exist, for instance, intrusion detection, malware classification and behavior modeling, CTI analysis, CA analysis [27–30], CT and security evaluation, vulnerability

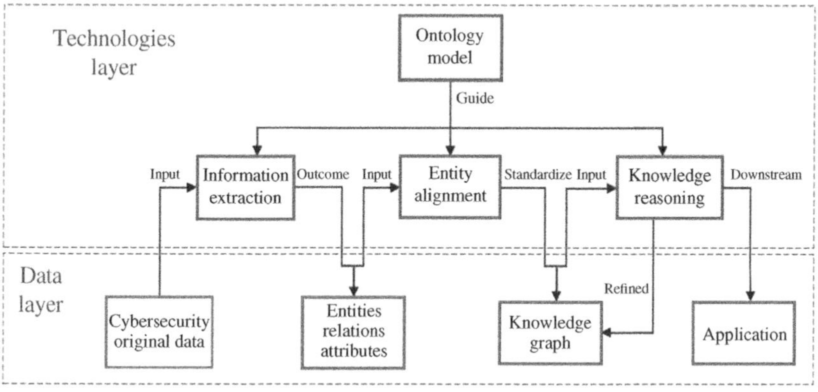

Figure 13.2 A CSKG construction framework.

analysis, and CT actor analysis [9]. Creating a generic network security ontology in today's multifaceted cyber environment is demanding, time-consuming, and heavily hinges on network security experts' domain and ICT knowledge. So, appliance scenarios should steer the proper security ontology project while simultaneously demanding dynamic and automatic amelioration of the information security ontology [30–32].

13.3.3 CS Entities Extraction

IE has drawn incremental attention with two main tasks: "relation extraction" (RE) and NER. Traditional NER has three broadly built forms: by rule, unsupervised, and feature-established supervised learning. Rule-centered approaches, e.g., regular expression, bootstrapping methods, etc., work fine when the exhaustive lexicon cannot reach other domains. Comparatively, traditional statistical-based extraction methods, embracing "hidden Markov models" (HMMs), decision trees, "maximum entropy model" (MEM), "support vector machines" (SVMs), and "conditional random fields" (CRFs), achieve good results albeit relying heavily on "feature engineering" (FE), which poses some constraints [33]. DL represents learning and endows semantic composition through vector representation and "neural network" (NN) processing. Figure 13.3 contains the three essential

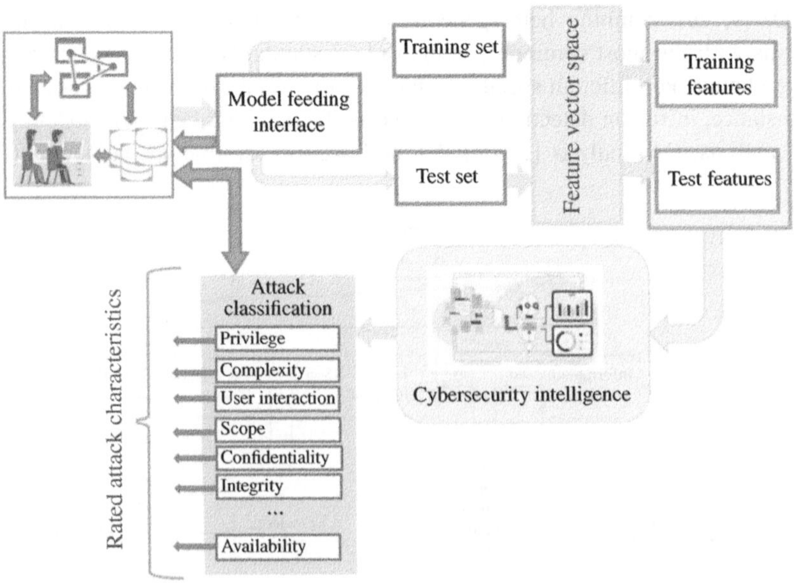

Figure 13.3 Intelligent cybersecurity ontologies.

components (i.e., distributed models, feature extractors, and decoders) and some DL NER instances.

A machine can be fed raw data, automatically finding latent representations and processing for categorization or detection. Many methods [34] have been tried, including multi-task DL, deep transfer learning, deep active learning, deep reinforcement learning, attention mechanism, deep adversarial learning, etc.

13.3.4 Relations Extraction of CS Entities

Fruitful entities' inter-relationships are an indispensable KG part of combining independent entities into a KG Unstructured, text-relationship extraction is a core KG construction task. An end-to-end CNN-based method that could automatically capture relevant lexical and sentence-level features to overcome traditional practices' limitations enormously count on the quality of hand-engineered features [11]. "Recurrent neural network" (RNN) besides "long short-term memory" (LSTM) schemes have arisen [35], but most supervised relation-extraction approaches require extensive labeled training information, which is costly to build. "Distant supervision" (DS) allows building datasets automatically [36].

Relation extraction used sentence-level attention and multi-instance learning [37] to reduce DS noise. IE tasks are usually solved via extract-then-classify or unified labeling. However, these methods have duplicate entity pairs or overlook the essential underlying structure in extracting entities and relations. A joint extraction of entities and associations method outperformed the pipelined approach to address these restrictions [38]. Some ignore label data scarcity and extract CS entity-relation triples employing a joint extraction technique from unpublished datasets [39].

However, collecting information from unstructured CS language has three key obstacles. First, most IE research has focused on daily life events, e.g., the TAC KB Population [40] or ACE [41]. Domain-relevant expertise distinguishes extracting life's understanding from CS knowledge. Insufficient labeled training data plagues the IE task. Another distinction between pulling natural life and CS knowledge is its intricacy. CA events can be CA patterns with several attempted or accomplished actions. These actions can be described as discrete CS events, increasing the number of event references. Thirdly, unstructured data contains implicit information that cannot be stated.

KG quality requires knowledge analysis, verification, and redundancy to resolve contradictions and prevent reasoning errors. KGs can benefit from entity disambiguation and named entity linkage [42]. The KG, developed with IE, largely shows sentence associations. It must leverage implicit knowledge and reasoning to enrich the CSKG [43]. Knowledge reasoning can use association queries, rule-based reasoning, distributed representation learning-built reasoning, and NN rationale [44] to complete tasks.

13.4 Datasets

Security analysts use known and emerging vulnerabilities, flaws, CTs, and CA patterns. Research institutes, government agencies, and industry professionals like MITRE and "computer emergency response teams" (CERTs) collect, publish, and arrange such knowledge [45]. The "National Vulnerability Database" (CVE, CWE, CPE, CVSS, etc.) is often utilized [46] in addition to "Common Attack Pattern Enumeration and Classification" (CAPEC) [47]. Significant datasets for constructing CSKGs can use OO, IE in CS, and other datasets to find novel solutions.

(A) **Open-source datasets**

Some CSKG datasets are

SEPSES CKB details the CSKG dataset/work in Ref. [48].

CWE-KG [49, 50] helps discover potential CTs from CWE, CAPEC, and X (former Twitter) data.

Vulnerability KGs [50, 51] only show visualization outcomes on a webpage without describing their structure or experiment performance.

Open-CyKG [52] presents a CTI-KG framework constructed on an attention-based NN. Open IE model to mine valuable "cyber threat" (CT) facts from unstructured APT depictions.

MalKG [53] adds information on malware intelligence.

These open-source CSKGs address different purposes that need various datasets with apparent drawbacks.

(B) **Information Extraction (IE) Datasets**

IE is essential for CSKGs. Providing quality-assurance annotated datasets to train robust IE models is crucial and cannot be bypassed. Data annotation is the labeling process of assigning relevant tags to data from queries, imageries, text, audio, video, etc., to simplify understanding and interpretation. These records can be labeled by data annotators as accurately as possible. Thus, datasets should be divided for NER and RE tasks. However, most datasets are for NER tasks. NER and RE studies can only rely on the malware dataset in Ref. [53]. The entities and relationships are generally specified in an unambiguous security ontology, which curbs the potential for usage outside the designated domain. Although collected and annotated from various data sources, the majority comes from English corpora. Instead, much security knowledge emerges in multiple languages. This often intermingled scenario forces multi-language dataset creation.

(C) **Other CSKG Datasets**
Mastering the environment, understanding dangerous actors, mixing external intelligence, and amassing basic information to apply theory. Environmental (assets and weaknesses), behavioral (network warnings, terminal alerts, and logs), in-house/external CTI, and knowledge-related (ATT&CK and CAPEC) data classification [54]. Current research targets CTI and knowledge data when building a CSKG and overlooks environmental and behavioral ICT data. These data possess no developed, consistent specification.

13.5 Application Scenarios

Google's introduction of KG technology has sparked attention. KG research in CS can focus on (i) construction techniques centered on the IE, representation, fusion, and deduction of knowledge in graphs [55], like correctly connecting entities and their interactions to KG after removing them from unstructured writing and inferring new specifics from such KG, and (ii) applications to solve down-to-earth glitches in different network environments through CSKGs.

Most literature hinges on KGs to assess the network situation, discover potential CTs, and investigate the ongoing or ending CA, presenting several specific applications to orientate operators and managers with operation, vulnerability management, decision-making, malware designation, analysis along the physical environment, and other CSKG application possibilities, like SE.

13.5.1 CSA and Security Assessment

Administrators must assess and understand an enterprise network's security. These issues include multifaceted enterprise network HW and services. Security corporate network administrators must fight multi-stage and multi-host attacks. CSA and security assessment can benefit from CSKG. MITRE's CyGraph [56, 57] CSA system focused on network combat task analyses, visual breakdowns, and knowledge management. CyGraph, a four-layer KG, analyzes CA paths, predicts critical vulnerabilities, examines intrusion alarm correlation, and provides interactive visual queries by integrating isolated data and events. CyGraph provides query-driven efficacy cases but no datasets.

A security assessment novel ontology can be constructed for individual networks to standardize security knowledge, e.g., assets, exposures, and CAs [58]. The ontology presents an efficient system for creating attack graphs, identifying vulnerability-caused attacks, and assessing network security utilizing ontological model inference. Their method produces the CA graph and property set descriptions. Flow diagrams show how hackers hit and dismantle several test network objectives through multiple hosts and stages, allowing enterprise administrators to perform security risk assessments and respond to new CTs. CS ontologies include STUCCO, UCO, and CTI [9, 26, 59]. An ontology will query whether data assets may be wide open in the local model, exploiting organization-specific asset information with recurrently known, updated opennesses to assess the aftermath of a newly revealed vulnerability. KGs with three dimensions – counting terminal assets, fault-detection intelligence, and CT alarm – can assess IoT terminal security based on application scenarios and CT characteristics [60]. The approach correlates independent power IoT terminal security monitoring data to build the terminal threat index, which indicates terminal security.

13.5.2 CTs' Discovery

In advanced surveillance, sophisticated assailants spend a long time in a system before detection [61]. Many factors, ranging from flooding alerts to slow response time, render existing practices ineffective and incapable of lessening these CAs' impairments. The CSKG could meet this void with knowledge representation and reasoning power. CSKG application research findings can aim at CA prediction, CT hunting, and intrusion detection so that security analysts predict outbreak signs prematurely via CT hunting before cyberattacks. During CAs, security administrators can discover suspicious undertakings with intrusion detection tools.

CA Prediction: A cognitive detection system perceives CS events early by mingling sensors' measurements, dynamic online sources, and KGs has extended UCO to infer the inputs from numerous network devices resembling Snort, "intrusion detection systems" (IDSs), etc., and the cyber-kill chain information [62]. "Semantic Web Rule Language" (SWRL) specified rules that orientate entities. The aggregator segment combines alerts with a reasoning model to identify newer CAs by testing and evaluating custom-built ransomware resembling WannaCry and showing the performed CA timeline and the system's actions. A prediction method that utilizes cyber defense KG to solve the 0-day CA vulnerability emerges in Ref. [40]. CTs, assets, and exposures engender the KG, transforming the outbreak prediction task into a KG link prediction. Accordingly, a path ranking algorithm could mine the potential 0-day attack in the target system and build the 0-day CA graph. The experiments showed that the KG could improve the proposed method's accuracy of 0-day CA prediction. Moreover, the path ranking procedure can also aid in backtracking reasons for appraising results to strengthen the explaining estimation ability.

CT Hunting: This trait [41, 63, 64] expedites log-founded CT pursuit by leveraging the vast external OSCTI knowledge [42]. It employs two sub-systems: a knowledge annexation pipeline for fashioning a CT behavioral KG and a query built upon system auditing to amass logging data crossway hosts. A "threat behavior query language" (TBQL), along with query synthesis mechanisms, automatically gets a TBQL query, with sequential event information, from the CT behavioral part of the CSKG to encounter the matched auditing records. Still, a system's limitation is not considering attacks not caught by auditing. Likewise, existing methods often exhibit essential restrictions regarding created alerts' quantity, interpretability, and relevance.

Intrusion Detection: The CSKG could also aid in detecting intrusion [65]. A query-based case that illustrates how the SEPSES CSKG can receive warnings starting the "network intrusion detection system" (NIDS) to better understand potential CTs and ongoing CAs is in Ref. [48]. A DDoS CA recognition scheme employing KG, mainly for the DDoS CA on TCP traffic, is in Ref. [66]. KGs convey the TCP traffic communication among two CPS hosts. After estimating the one-way broadcast metrics, thresholds help select the source host that commences a DDoS outbreak. A twofold distributed KB described DDoS outbreaks and malicious behavior detection [66] comprises (i) a traffic database to detect and classify malign DDoS traffic CA s and (ii) the core network security KB part to partakes in a DDoS harmful behavioral KB with graphs for network topologies, malevolent traceability, dangerous features, and traffic acquaintance. The network security KB responds to data structure treating, destructive behavior KG creation, behavior perception, and feedback. ML can make KGs detect unexpected activity in automation systems [67]. The readily available ontology from Ref. [47] builds a KG integrating three primary knowledge sources: automation system evidence, network observations (like connections between hosts), and application-stage observations (akin to data access events). KG completion methods inspired this framework, adopting a graph-embedding procedure for the likelihood ranking of observed events' triple statements. Experimentally, the suggested process yields well-calibrated, plausible alarms in various contexts, potentially benefiting relational ML modules on KGs for intrusion detection. Though these outcomes occurred on a small-scale prototype lacking CTI, it synergistically blended KG and industrial control systems.

13.5.3 Attack Probing

CSKGs are becoming key instruments for CA analysis very fast. Recent evolvements in employing KGs to CA investigation will be treated from the following four aspects: path analysis, attribution, consequence prediction, and analysis.

Attack Path Analysis: The CyGraph could query potential outbreak paths by comprehending the network environment. A CyGraph-type graph-centered strategy with a CA graph model unifies intricate network data with exposures, topology, firewall stratagems, CA patterns, and invasion alerts via CS data standardized languages [68]. This work's model predicts outbreak paths utilizing network events (as with intrusion warnings, sensor logs, etc.). Correlating identified CA s with prospective attack paths is best, principally for critical assets' defense, and improves CSA, e.g., inferring missed CA steps and eradicating false positives. The Neo4j database [48, 69] houses the output attack graph for query and visualization. Despite its efficiency in query and visualization for potential CA paths, this KG still faces several shortcomings: (i) it does not demonstrate how to infer new knowledge using KG, (ii) datasets with input data alert format with unclear firewall rules, and (iii) its designs misrepresent OSCTI (METRE knowledge). A KG to treat CAs has four entity types: SW, HW, vulnerabilities, and CA entity, to extend the CA path information [49, 70]. With these CA entities' attributions (i.e., success rate, conditions, approaches, and earnings), this design used KG to build an attack path and augment the vulnerability assessment before trusting on the CVSS score [71]. The CA path could renovate local information through multiple sources thanks to KG's depiction and information management. A graph strategy to obtain the ideal penetration path can increase efficiency further for insider and unknown attacks. A "two-layer CT penetration graph" (TLTPG) defines the upper layer as a network environment penetration graph, and the lower one is any host's pair penetration graph linking any host's pair [29]. The KG describes each host's CA-related resources (e.g., SW, defenselessness, ports in usage, and privilege corresponding to a successful CA). This rationale greatly benefits the penetration path relating to hosts and integrating acquired information of 0-day threats for unknown attack prediction. A KG could also represent and generate 0-day CA paths with a link prediction and path ranking procedure [40]. KGs can comprehensively consider the CA existence, availability, impacts, knowledge deterioration intents, and asset types.

Attack Attribution: For a cyber warfare advantage, a defense must answer who attacked, where the occurrence point is, and to identify the attack vector. This step is assault attribution. Attack attribution solutions can identify the CA source, intermediate medium, and attack vector, enabling more targeted prevention and active defense. Attack attribution is essential to passive to an active effective defense. An automatic CA attribution framework was built using a six-dimensional CSKG ontology that mixes a space-ground with network information having multiple unique qualities and data sources [72]. Security people can probe the CSKG utilizing the host resource dimension to find the host asset in danger and assumed under attack, related vulnerabilities, and attribution tactic in sequence. After isolating CA evidence and locations, the attribution methodology can find the affected host resource. Causation-based provenance graph creation technology from NSFOCUS's blog appears in Ref. [73], introducing terminal, Syslog's perspective, application log correlation, and network/terminal association. The terminal perspective ignored the second dimension's application log and focused on files, filenames, and processes in one insulated host. The third level scheme prolonged the provenance graph from one host to a multi-host network that might ameliorate causal analysis for a complete CA process. Still, it disregarded OSCTI and CSKG's semantic context.

Consequence Prediction: Poor input validations and integer overflows can cause denial-of-service (DoS) and unauthorized code execution. Understanding weakness's effects help assess system risk and respond quickly. A "common weakness enumeration" (CWE) KG [74, 75] includes textual descriptions, predicted repercussions, and SW weakness relationships. Present CWE data do not enable sophisticated reasoning tasks on SW frailties, such as forecasting missing concerns and CWE results. This study embedded KG weaknesses and their linkages in a semantic vector space relying on translation, description, and knowledge representation learning. Extensive studies developed vector embeddings to measure KG performance in CSA acquisition and inference tasks: CWE link prediction, triple classification, and end-result prediction. Security tools can help stakeholders without CS skills understand a CA's effects. Researchers can reduce cognitive effort by automatically forecasting CA repercussions for novel attacks.

Attack Analysis: The CSKG core graph shows vulnerabilities' knowledge, CAs, assets, and interconnections. It is updated from different CA analysis websites. Scene KGs use outbreak-specific node and network connectivity to extend graphs. All analytical input data comes from data collection and detection systems. Exploiting CSKGs, attack rule KBs, and spatiotemporal restrictions aids in elaborating composite attack chains of numerous CAs. Cyber professionals typically ignore alerts and miss actual CAs due to exhaustion from probing several alarms. Despite exploited vulnerabilities and payloads, CAs may deploy comparable abstract approaches. A causal graph-based ATLAS system creates an end-to-end CA story from off-the-shelf audit logs [76]. Besides developing a sequential model, ATLAS utilizes NLP, causality analysis, and ML to identify critical CA patterns and non-attack actions from a causal network. A causal graph CA symptom node is acknowledged for a CT warning event at inference time. ATLAS then creates a collection of candidate sequences for the symptom node, utilizes the sequence-based model to find attack-related nodes, and unifies the CA nodes to craft an attack history. The intelligence of 6G CPSs must support inner and exterior network knowledge. CA technique to generate KGs used CAPEC [47] and CWE in Neo4j [69], a graph database. This study only presented two query-based application scenarios for identifying and responding to DDoS flood

CAs and multi-stage CAs using Neo4j's query and display function rather than the KG reasoning function.

13.5.4 Clever Security Operation

Intelligent Operation: OT-AI security can support security data dynamic queries and aggregation analysis, augmenting the reliability of security data operation studies [54]. KGs have a unified data view, realizing multi-level technical experiences like risk perception, causal awareness, and robust decision-making. Intelligent processing challenges emanate from models, data, and semantic perspectives [77]. KG application scenarios in security operation can be threefold as per CA [78]: (i) profiling, (ii) path pursuit and response strategy recommendation, and (iii) challenges of intelligent operation. It sorts out directional content viz. stipulated scenarios, application resolutions, and prospects, albeit not involving technical details.

Security Alert (SA) or Event Correlation Analysis (ECA): The "security operation center" (SOC) security researchers are often overwhelmed by security issues and trying to stay up with the latest CTs in the wild due to the ever-changing CT landscape. Effectively correlating vast volumes of various alert or event data might prevent CAs by identifying concerns before they become problems. Traditional techniques store security evidence aspects in separate KBs, preventing synergy. A semantic mismatch between a KG using abstract CA knowledge like STIX 2.0 and system network logs containing behavior information hinders CSKG's use [79]. Complex CAs make it difficult to efficiently incorporate context information for real-time, correct analysis. Traditional relationship analysis with rules requires specialists' CA scene construction knowledge without automatic reasoning. By unifying the network setup KG, vulnerability KG, CT-KG, and intrusion warnings' KG with the CSKG and describing each dimension's data source, an integrated security ECA system may overcome the above problem. After normalization and fusion alarms, vulnerability alerts from the host were verified [80].

The CA correlation analysis also utilizes warnings in effect to query associated alerts, CVE objects, and CAPEC items to predict real attackers' purposes. Rebuilding a series of KG alert scenarios employed the DARPA 2000 dataset for framework performance evaluation by comparing the total of remaining alerts after using KG for correlation analysis [9]. A theory associated multiple steps' CAs with IDS's warnings [81]. The consequential association analysis CSKG algorithm handles CS attack events and graphically displays the air-ground integrated network's attack scenario. The CSKG holds five-entry tuples: (attack, event, alarm, relation, and rule). The association study calculated the coincidence degree among collected events' sequences and those attacked in the KG.

Simulations can prove the algorithm's practicality by comprehending the space-ground integration network and experimental limits. Manual log investigation rarely scales, resulting in a lack of understanding and transparency regarding issues. A configurable framework for automated KG building from raw log messages was developed to address this issue [82]. Enabling semantic analysis of log data fills a major gap and provides KG builders with several data sources. In Ref. [67], ML is used for KGs to improve IDS-generated alarms in current industrial systems, making them more helpful for human operators.

13.5.5 Smart Decision-Making

Current CS assessments aim at personal experience and poor intelligence. Improving CTI assessment is a critical issue. KG technology makes studying the CS decision model and enhancing CTI assessment beneficial. Introducing KG-reliant intelligent decision-making research situations like CA generation strategy and security policy validation is crucial.

Attack Strategy Generation: An invader's perspective on CA techniques can reveal security issues and provide solutions. A KG recommender CA in Ref. [83] contrasts CyGraph's query-based technique. A six-tuple KG construction schema based on four open databases (CVE, CWE, MSF, and CAPEC) is included. This collaborative filtering characterizes node differences using meta-path, a recommendation list generator that calculates path correlation scores with node vectors. ML feature extraction and heterogeneous information network meta-path construction provide a CA entity recommendation algorithm in the second phase. This KG can search and recommend new CTI intelligently. This approach predicts vulnerability weaknesses better than content-based search recommendations. It uses natural language vulnerability descriptions to forecast and recommend CA patterns. A knowledge-driven CA strategy generation system [84] may manage several industrial control network vulnerabilities from an attacker's standpoint. The method includes vulnerability exploitation KG, industrial control network graphics, and knowledge reasoning principles. Security experts recommend using the attack procedure to find device-level CA routes. Initially, CA techniques can examine several vulnerabilities on device-level nodes. A full CA graphical algorithm exploits the sequence for all device vulnerabilities and connects device-level nodes consistent with the firewall and other protective device access restrictions. This KG generated CA pathways from numerous small-scale control network vulnerabilities. Adding CTIs necessitates additional CA techniques as KG expands, especially the most cost-effective ones.

Security Policy Validation: Its ontological, heuristic, workflow, and process layers enable logical analysis, CTI analysis, and CPS security policy validation [85].

The architecture is validated, and an event-driven engine for intelligence graph traversal is prototyped via scenarios describing the most typical CTs in digital banking. However, this framework only supports digital banking apps and does not provide datasets.

13.5.6 Vulnerability Prediction and Supervision

Several use cases elucidate various CSKG analytic traits in vulnerability prediction and supervision. In security operations, managing, categorizing, quantifying, and prioritizing a system's weaknesses is a vital precondition for CT elimination to successfully protect valuable resources.

KGs allow advanced knowledge about managing massive vulnerability records by organizing them in a structured ontological format. Another SEPSES KG scenario [48] is a query supporting security analysts by relating organizational asset information to a nonstop updated stream of notorious susceptibilities. A "CS vulnerability ontology" (CVO) is a theoretical model that represents formal knowledge vulnerability within the controlling domain [57], utilizing the CVO to propose a "cyber intelligence alert" (CIA) structure to send cyber alarms about forthcoming vulnerabilities and countermeasures. Its components embrace the vulnerability repository, exposure mapper, "social media intelligence extractor-tagger" (SMIET), CVO, RDF converter, the "cyber intelligence ontology" (CIO), and cyber warnings rules engine. An industrial CSKG was stored in Neo4j [57, 86] grounded on Internet vulnerabilities to investigate, query, and envisage temporal, spatial, and correlation dimensions.

CyGraph correlated incursion alarms to notorious vulnerability paths and suggested the best actions for reacting to attacks. CyGraph forms a query-centered predictive model of potential attack paths and dangerous vulnerabilities. As formerly said, a CSKG employing CWE [74] could estimate absent relations and typical CWEs' consequences through a translation-based, descriptive CT representation for the knowledge-learning scheme. To discover hidden relationships among vulnerabilities, the intelligent flow of the CWE Chain's samples [39] requires an automatic analysis query-based model and demonstrated KG vulnerability (VulKG) employing vulnerability data (NVD, CVE, CPE, and CWE). Yet, the example could partially replace security experts' analysis and labeling work under specific scenarios with the operator previously identifying the query objective. A malware KG, MalKG [53], is the first OO-automated KG with CTI for effectively running sparse or erroneous threat information manually curating the MT3K benchmark dataset. It demonstrated the prediction of MalKG's capabilities utilizing two use cases. One of the usage scenarios forecasts and sorts all potential vulnerabilities or CVEs from impacted SW by comprehensively utilizing facts from the network environment, malware, and KG. An exposure exploitation KG can integrate and extract multi-dimensional domain knowledge [84]. KG attack strategies enhance widespread vulnerability abuse and flexible response performance by occupying each device's corresponding node, displaying industrial network feasibility.

Similarly, chain reasoning and confidence appraisal studies [9] supported vulnerability labeling and latent relations' discovery between CWEs. Similarity matching via source code level graphs judges the resemblances between the target node and the vulnerability database node. This tactic offers new insights into susceptibility mining, expanding relations in KGs aiming at vulnerability to identify alternatives with similar consequences [9].

13.5.7 Malware Acknowledgment and Analysis

KGs can evaluate and recognize malware. A graph-centered malware rank inference MalRank algorithm appears in Ref. [87] to infer a node malignity score from its correlations to other KG entities, e.g., conjoint name servers or IP ranges through a KG modeling global observed entities' associations in proxy and IDS logs, boosted by CTI and "OO intelligence" (OSINT). CT detection is formulated in the "security information and event management" (SIEM) milieu as a large-scale graph inferential problem. Real-world data experiments from a global enterprise's SIEM showed that MalRank conserves a high detection rate, outshining its predecessor, i.e., belief propagation, in accuracy and efficiency.

Moreover, this approach effectively identifies previously unknown malicious entities like IP addresses and domain names. Along with the past informed application scenarios, MalKG could also handle the malware attribution scenario [53, 88]. As an illustration, given a newly learned malware, the expert must build a malware's origination fingerprint by assembling good features, viz. campaign, author, and other things. MalKG automates the malware features' prediction, e.g., the newly revealed malware may partake in similarities with disclosed malware from a particular APT group. APT hacker teams' profiling and automatic attribution can be realized by mining key CTI elements and dynamic behavioral reasoning [53, 78]. The key solution establishes a unified language to designate different APT organizations' behaviors and traits to build a KB about APT organizations without disclosing related research details.

13.5.8 Physical System Connection

The CSKG uses BD analysis and graph mining to intensely scrutinize the information and the physical layers coupling relationship in the industrial control systems and grasp decision-making, risk prediction, accident analysis, CA identification, and other assisted traits and automated processing.

CS analytic capabilities in MITRE's CSA method CyGraph from Refs. [56] and [68] comprise a simple network design with underlying connectivities amid routers, switches, firewalls, and hosts. The internal network possesses three defense domains (i.e., mission client terminals, DMZ, and data center). The outer firewall guards the in-house network from the exterior and watches the crucial data center servers. The KG was built with firewall rules and vulnerability scan results based on the information on the network topology. A typical internal network model with six elements verifies the design's effectiveness [49, 70], where the firewall insulates the intranet router from the Internet. The FTP server and hosts are connected to the router directly. A network example of generating penetration paths [29] contains an Internet host, a DMZ with a web server, and three subnets. The hacker is an Internet host. Constructing a proper experimental network setting could aid in demonstrating approaches' effects and reproducing CA and defensive processes [89].

Exploring the control network systems' security is also essential. An HW prototype comes from the industrial systems' design, integrating ICT and OT elements. The network displays main traffic flows afterward [67]. A CT assessment for IoT terminals employing KG sensed and measured the CS risks and CTs of massive IoT terminals in real time [60, 90] but lacked a suitable network for evaluation. The domain KG may analyze multiple vulnerabilities in the control network to generate CA strategies [84]. The target network topology possesses the Internet, a router, two firewalls, an enterprise network, plus Ethernet. One firewall shields all local network assets. The other goes between the Ethernet and the enterprise network. The router connects the first firewall with the enterprise network. The second firewall plus the industrial Ethernet go after. The enterprise network assets are an admin host, web server, and printer. Some sensing peripherals (e.g., oximeters, valves, and flow meters) are connected to the Ethernet.

A "demilitarized zone" (DMZ) is an Internet subnet coupled via a router. A firewall isolates each subnet, and the hackers usually start Internet offensive actions so that investigators adapt firewalls to (i) tackle intricate networks by varying or adding devices, (ii) outspreading subnets, or (iii) altering connection mechanisms. The network topology renders the environment, inserting SW and HW into each node, securing protection measures and existing exposures.

13.5.9 Supplementary Reasoning Tasks

SE is a CA type wherein the hacker exploits human weaknesses through SE [91] and poses a severe CT SE threat's barriers [92], calling for ontological development and assessment criteria as per applications. The ontology affords a formal, explicit knowledge schema to comprehend, analyze, reuse, and assign SE domain information via KG.

Today's Internet has a significant amount of fake CS intelligence. A system can filter out information to get provenance information and represent it for CTI treatment [90]. This rationale enhances the existing CSKG model to encompass CTI and fused provenance graphs with CSKG reasoning to enforce information preservation and credibility, besides rejecting the rest. Besides, including provenance classes in the CSKG schema can give more evidence about the data source.

A KG embedding predicts within- and across-type dealings for SW security entities appears in Ref. [93]. Finding missing relationships among entities supports analysts in enriching SW security evidence. Albeit, this CSKG is not OO, so one could not read its details. In Ref. [78], several other CSKG application scenarios and two conventional reasoning approaches exist. Despite some limitations in stating satisfactory particulars, the application scenarios, for instance, CT modeling, APT-CT hunting, intelligent safekeeping, cyberspace valuation/mapping, supply chain safety, and CPS defense, were outlined [78]. Two reasoning technologies are established on CSKG: (a) relational via graph representation learning and (b) multi-relational schemes through NNs.

13.6 Discussion and Future Trends on CSKG

It has been possible to use KGs in many knowledge-driven CS tasks:

Additional OO Datasets: This is needed because the current ones do not solve all problems. Creating a CSKB dataset for development tasks can include environmental assets, attributions, existing topologies, and behavioral data (e.g., alarms and logs). Annotated CS datasets are essential for training or testing IE models, including pre-training or prompt-based language models. Present datasets could not handle this task productively, having various drawbacks: First, most datasets target only one IE task (entity mining), seldom for two or more; second, owing to different ontologies and research targets, the entities' and relations' kinds are different. Third, existing datasets rely on English, which cannot meet the multi-language requirement; and last, manually interpreting the corpus continues as the primary initial data for the vertical model. New multi-language CS IE datasets require extensive and reliable data investigation. A statement paper and standard annotation should accompany these anticipated datasets. Semi-supervised or unsupervised extraction and prompt-based generating methods can reduce the need for an annotated vertical corpus in the annotated process.

Dynamic Construction: Established KG frameworks for top-down [94] and bottom-up [95] approaches can build huge KBs. The first prevails in CS (creating an ontology schema first, then extracting corpus knowledge from it), primarily regarding expert knowledge. Ontology learning, or automated ontology construction technology, is still needed to capture new knowledge throughout ontology updates. Traditional KGs focus on deterministic, static entities, relations, attributions, etc. The KG investigations and prerequisites for field applications will incorporate event and dynamic knowledge akin to conditional relationships, temporal information, causal evidence, and event subordination linkages. Building a CS event temporal KG will require further work to represent CS event knowledge and facilitate relevant logical reasoning.

Application Scenarios [9]**:** Despite stable CSKG creation methods, no one supports a unified OO KG. KGs are helpful but incomplete, redundant, and ambiguous, resulting in uninformative query responses. Different conditions require constant KG rebuilding. The KG's automated reasoning ability is underutilized, and its use to tackle CS practical problems like KG completion is unclear. More research and reasoning investigations are needed to gain knowledge. The semantic mismatch between CSKG and logs limits its usage in CA path examination. Filling this semantic gap with necessary knowledge allows the semantic link between CSKG and log. To identify dangers and network CSA, the CSKG must engage more with the network's internal awareness, notably the CPS, and use its automated reasoning and association analysis skills.

Evaluation Criteria: CSKG applications across most CS functions in defensive and offensive circumstances are still developing. KG evaluation standards are lacking. Researchers often assess IE model correctness, precision, and F1-score values. "Mean rank" (MR), "mean reciprocal rank" (MRR), plus "Hits@n", can test the triple prediction model's logic, disclose the KG's query, and deliver visualization capabilities in instances entailing queries [9]. These are not thorough examinations of KG's notions, as no one can deem a KG superior in certain scenarios.

The IoT has enticed interest lately since it helps consumers enhance their lifestyles and professionally keep up with CPS technology breakthroughs. IoT edge devices vary in technology and storage file formats. These devices must authenticate each other before delivering data by exploiting highly secure mutual authentication. Mutual authentication is crucial to peer-to-peer communication. These resource-constrained devices authenticate with locked session keys. Successful authentication authorizes a device to access shared resources. Data privacy breaches can affect confidentiality and integrity. Thus, devices seeking data transmission must be validated. Although blockchain and AI ameliorate security extensively, this work focuses on AI alone. In future works, blockchain can store validated session keys for network devices decentralizedly. Blockchain helps stabilize edge devices during low battery and guarantees cloud and fog computing access [96–99]. Albeit AI learns and adapts to threats better with new key management technologies to improve security, the discussed designs will benefit from blockchain [97–99]. This manuscript analyzes contemporary security trends and traditional essential security procedures, bringing a thorough quality analysis on authentication and session keys, merging SW and HW entities, and AI-based CS authentication.

13.7 Conclusion

This chapter overviewed various works about "artificial intelligence" (AI) for "cybersecurity knowledge graph" (CSKG) in assorted application scenarios, presenting a succinct CSKG background, underlying concepts, and construction technologies. Then, several openly available datasets for building CSKGs, their IE tasks, and their downsides are exemplified. Next, a comparative revision of different AI designs for CS was carried out, elaborating on recent CSKG scenarios' progress. Security managers can count on KG to naturally comprehend security intelligence, network situations, and entity relationships. Then, security entities' attributes were discovered, which could function as a groundwork for understanding CS knowledge, analyzing CS data, and finding attack patterns and abnormal traits related to cyberattacks.

References

1 Kumar, K. and Pande, B.P. (2022). Applications of machine learning techniques in the realm of cybersecurity. *Cyber Security and Digital Forensics* 2022: 295–315.

2 Estrela, V.V., Saotome, O., Loschi, H.J. et al. (2018). Emergency response cyber-physical framework for landslide avoidance with sustainable electronics. *Technologies* 6: 42. https://doi.org/10.3390/technologies6020042.

3 Liebetrau, T. (2022). Cyber conflict short of war: a European strategic vacuum. *European Security* 1–20.

4 Estrela, V.V., Jumani, A.K., Laghari, A.A. et al. (2023). Internet of medical things (IoMT) layers for medical cyber-physical systems. In: *Intelligent Healthcare Systems* (ed. V.V. Estrela) chap. 3, 45–65. London: CRC Press.

5 Estrela, V.V., Grata, E.G.H., Deshpande, A. et al. (2023). In-body devices and sensors communication – how implantables, ingestibles, and injectables interact with the internet. In: *Intelligent Healthcare Systems* (ed. V.V. Estrela) chap. 12. London: CRC Press.

6 Oruma, S.O., Sánchez-Gordón, M., Palacios, R.C. et al. (2022). A systematic review on social robots in public spaces: threat landscape and attack surface. *Computers* 11: 181.

7 Deshpande, A., Estrela, V.V., and Razmjooy, N. (2021). *Computational Intelligence Methods for Super-Resolution in Image Processing Applications.* Zurich: Springer Nature. https://doi.org/10.1007/978-3-030-67921-7.

8 Hemanth, J. and Estrela, V.V. (2017). Deep learning for image processing applications. In: *Advances in Parallel Computing*, vol. 31. Amsterdam: IOS Press ISSN: 978-1-61499-822-8. https://www.iospress.nl/book/deep-learning-for-imageprocessing-applications.

9 Alowaidi, M.A., Sharma, S., Alenizi, A., and Bhardwaj, S. (2023). Integrating artificial intelligence in cyber security for cyber-physical systems. *Electronic Research Archive* 31 (4): 1876–1896.

10 Sriavstava, R., Singh, P., and Chhabra, H. (2020). Review on cyber security intrusion detection: using methods of machine learning and data mining. In: *Internet of Things and Big Data Applications*, 121–132. Cham: Springer.

11 Deshpande, A., Estrela, V.V., and Patavardhan, P. (2021). The DCT-CNN-ResNet50 architecture to classify brain tumours with super-resolution, convolutional neural network, and the ResNet50. *Neuroscience Informatics* 1 (4): 100013. ISSN 2772-5286.

12 Perdisci, R., Ariu, D., Fogla, P. et al. (2009). McPAD: a multiple classifier system for accurate payload-based anomaly detection. *Computer Networks: The International Journal of Computer and Telecommunications Networking* 53 (6): 864–881.

13 Xue, R., Tang, P., and Fang, S. (2022). Prediction of computer network security situation based on association rules mining. *Wireless Communications and Mobile Computing* 2022: 2794889.

14 Zeng, Z.R., Peng, W., Zeng, D. et al. (2022). Intrusion detection framework based on causal reasoning for DDoS. *Journal of Information Security and Applications* 65: 103124.

15 Sikos, L.F., Philp, D., Howard, C. et al. (2019). Knowledge representation of network semantics for reasoning-powered cyber-situational awareness. In: *AI in Cybersecurity*, 19–45. Cham: Springer.

16 Rastogi, N., Dutta, S., Zaki, M.J. et al. (2020). Malont: an ontology for malware threat intelligence. In: *International Workshop on Deployable Machine Learning for Security Defense*, 28–44. Cham: Springer.

17 Zhao, J., Yan, Q., Li, J. et al. (2020). TIMiner: automatically extracting and analyzing categorized cyber threat intelligence from social data. *Computers & Security* 95: 101867.

18 Bouarroudj, W., Boufaida, Z., and Bellatreche, L. (2022). Named entity disambiguation in short texts over knowledge graphs. *Knowledge and Information Systems* 64: 325–351.

19 Ji, S., Pan, S., Cambria, E. et al. (2021). A survey on knowledge graphs: representation, acquisition, and applications. *IEEE Transactions on Neural Networks and Learning Systems* 33 (2): 494–514.

20 Sikos, L.F. (2023). Cybersecurity knowledge graphs. *Knowledge and Information Systems* 65: 3511–3531.

21 Zhang, K. and Liu, J. (2020). Review on the application of knowledge graph in cyber security assessment. In: *IOP Conference Series: Materials Science and Engineering*. IOP Publishing. https://doi.org/10.1088/1757-899X/768/5/052103.

22 Sikos, L.F., Stumptner, M., Mayer, W. et al. (2018). Representing network knowledge using provenance-aware formalisms for cyber-situational awareness. *Procedia Computer Science* 126: 29–38.

23 Lassila, Ora, and Ralph R. Swick. *Resource Description Framework (RDF) Model and Syntax Specification, W3C, 22 Feb*. 1999. http://w3.org/TR/1999/REC-rdf-syntax-19990222.

24 Singh, A.K., Mishra, A., Shekhar, S., and Chakraborty, A. (2019). From strings to things: knowledge-enabled VQA model that can read and reason. In: *Proc. 2019 IEEE/CVF International Conference on Computer Vision (ICCV)*, 4601–4611.

25 Yang, Y.J., Xu, B., Hu, J.W. et al. (2018). Accurate and efficient method for constructing domain knowledge graph. *Ruan Jian Xue Bao/Journal of Software* 29 (10): 2931–2947.

26 Syed, Z., Padia, A., Finin, T. et al. (2016). UCO: a unified cybersecurity ontology. In: *Proc. Workshops at the thirtieth AAAI Conference on Artificial Intelligence*.

27 Ding, Y., Wu, R., and Zhang, X. (2019). Ontology-based knowledge representation for malware individuals and families. *Computers & Security* 87: 101574.

28 Jian, G. and An, W. (2020). Research on ontology-based network threat intelligence analysis technology. *Computer Engineering and Applications* 56 (11): 112–117.

29 Wang, S., Wang, J.H., Tang, G.M. et al. (2019). Intelligent and efficient method for optimal penetration path generation. *Journal of Computer Research and Development* 56: 929–941.

30 Ammi, M., Adedugbe, O.A., Al-Harby, F.M., and Benkhelifa, E. (2022). Taxonomical challenges for cyber incident response threat intelligence: a review. *International Journal of Cloud Applications and Computing* 12: 1–14.

31 Kanna, K., Estrela, V.V., and Rodrigues, J.J.P.C. (2021). *Cyber Security and Digital Forensics – Proc. ICCSDF 2021*. Zurich: Springer Nature. https://doi.org/10.1007/978-981-16-3961-6.

32 Sanagavarapu L M, Iyer V, Reddy R. *A Deep Learning Approach for Ontology Enrichment from Unstructured Text*. arXiv preprint arXiv:2112.08554, 2021.

33 Li, M., Li, Y., and Lin, M. (2021). Review of transfer learning for named entity recognition. *Journal of Frontiers of Computer Science and Technology* 15 (2): 206.

34 Li, J., Ye, D., and Shang, S. (2019). Adversarial transfer for named entity boundary detection with pointer networks. *IJCA - International Journal of Computer Applications* 5053–5059.

35 Zhou, P. et al. (2016). Attention-based bidirectional long short-term memory networks for relation classification. In: *Proc. 54th Annual Meeting of the Association for Computational Linguistics*, vol. 2: Short chapters, 207–212.

36 Vashishth S, Joshi R, Prayaga S S, et al. *RESIDE: Improving Distantly-Supervised Neural Relation Extraction using Side Information*. 2018.

37 Lin, Y., Shen, S., Liu, Z. et al. (2016). Neural relation extraction with selective attention over instances. In: *Proc. 54th Annual Meeting of the Association for Computational Linguistics*, vol. 1: Long Chapters, 2124–2133.

38 Fu, T.-J., Li, P.-H., and Ma, W.-Y. (2019). GraphRel: modeling text as relational graphs for joint entity and relation extraction. In: *Proc. 57th Annual Meeting of the Association for Computational Linguistics*, 1409–1418.

39 Guo, Y., Liu, Z., Huang, C. et al. (2021). CyberRel: joint entity and relation extraction for cybersecurity concepts. In: *Proc. Int'l Conference on Information and Communications Security*, 447–463. Cham: Springer.

40 Mitamura, T., Liu, Z., and Hovy, E.H. (2015). Overview of TAC KBP 2015 event nugget track. In: *Text Analysis Conference*. National Institute of Standards and Technology.

41 Walker, C., Strassel, S., Medero, J., and Maeda, K. (2006). ACE 2005 multilingual training corpus. Technical report. In: . Linguistic Data Consortium.

42 Sevgili O, Shelmanov A, Arkhipov M, et al. *Neural Entity Linking: A Survey of Models Based on Deep Learning*. arXiv preprint arXiv:2006.00575, 2020.

43 Chen, X., Jia, S., and Xiang, Y. (2020). A review: knowledge reasoning over knowledge graph. *Expert Systems with Applications* 141: 112948.

44 Li, X., Yifeng, L., Haixia, Z., and Kezhen, H. (2021). Key technologies of cyber security knowledge graph. *Frontiers of Data and Computing* 3 (3): 9–18.

45 MITRE. Mitre. https://www.mitre.org, 20 Mar. 2023.

46 US-CERT Security Operations Center. National Vulnerability Database, https://nvd.nist.gov, 20 Mar. 2023.

47 MITRE. Common Attack Pattern Enumeration and Classification. https://capec.mitre.org, 23 Mar. 2023.

48 Kiesling, E., Ekelhart, A., Kurniawan, K. et al. (2019). The SEPSES knowledge graph: an integrated resource for cybersecurity. In: *International Semantic Web Conference*, 198–214. Cham: Springer.

49 Sun Nan. *CWE-Knowledge-Graph-Based-Twitter-Data-Analysis-for-Cybersecurity*. https://github.com/nansunsun/CWE-Knowledge-Graph-Based-Twitter-Data-Analysis-forCybersecurity, 21 Jan. 2023.

50 Wang Di. *CyberSecurity Knowledge Graph*. https://github.com/HoloLen/CyberSecurity_Knowledge_graph, 12 May 2023.

51 Cheng Xingqi. *Visualization Web Page of Vulnerability Knowledge Graph*. https://cinnqi.github.io/Neo4j-D3-VKG. 10 May 2023.

52 Sarhan, I. and Spruit, M. (2021). Open-CYKG: an open cyber threat intelligence knowledge graph. *Knowledge-Based Systems* 233: 107524.

53 Rastogi, N, Dutta, S, Christian, R, et al. (2021). *Predicting Malware Threat Intelligence Using KGs*. arXiv preprint arXiv:2102.05571.

54 Zhang, R. and Li, W. (2021). An intelligent security operation technology system framework AISecOps. *Frontiers of Data and Computing* 3 (3): 32–47.

55 Zenglin, X., Yongpan, S., Lirong, H. et al. (2016). Review on knowledge graph techniques. *Journal of University of Electronic Science and Technology of China* 4: 589–606.

56 Noel, S., Harley, E., Tam, K.H. et al. (2016). CyGraph: graph-based analytics and visualization for cybersecurity. In: *Handbook of Statistics*, vol. 35, 117–167. Elsevier.

57 Syed, R. (2020). Cybersecurity vulnerability management: a conceptual ontology and cyber intelligence alert system. *Information & Management* 57 (6): 103334.

58 Wu, S., Zhang, Y., and Cao, W. (2017). Network security assessment using a semantic reasoning and graph-based approach. *Computers and Electrical Engineering* 64: 96–109.

59 Philpot M. *Cyber Intelligence Ontology*, https://github.com/daedafusion/cyber-ontology, 18 Oct. 2015.

60 Pang, T., Song, Y., and Shen, Q. (2021). Research on security threat assessment for power IoT terminal based on knowledge graph. In: *Proc. 5th Inf. Technology, Networking, Electronic and Automation Control Conf. (ITNEC)*, vol. 5, 1717–1721. IEEE.

61 FireEye. (2018). *Common Vulnerability Scoring System*. https://www.fireeye.com/content/dam/collateral/en/mtrends-2018.pdf

62 Narayanan, S.N., Ganesan, A., Joshi, K. et al. (2018). Early detection of cybersecurity threats using collaborative cognition. In: *Proc. 4th International Conference on Collaboration and Internet Computing (CIC)*, 354–363. IEEE.

63 Gao, P., Shao, F., Liu, X. et al. (2021). Enabling efficient cyber threat hunting with cyber threat intelligence. In: *Proc. 37th International Conference on Data Engineering (ICDE)*, 193–204. IEEE.

64 SENKI, *Open Source Threat Intelligence Feeds*, https://www.senki.org/operators-securitytoolkit/open-source-threat-intelligence-feeds, 28 Aug. 2020.

65 Jian, S., Lu, Z., Du, D. et al. (2020). Overview of network intrusion detection technology. *Journal of Cybersecurity* 5 (4): 96–122.

66 Liu, F., Li, K., and Song, F. (2021). Distributed DDoS attacks malicious behavior knowledge base construction. *Telecommunications Science* 37 (11): 17–32.

67 Garrido, J.S., Dold, D., and Frank, J. Machine learning on knowledge graphs for context-aware security monitoring. In: *2021 IEEE International Conf. Cyber Security and Resilience (CSR)*, vol. 2021, 55–60. IEEE.

68 Noel S, Harley E, Tam K H, et al. *Big-Data Architecture for Cyber Attack Graphs Representing Security Relationships in NoSQL Graph Databases*. 2015.

69 Vukotic, A., Watt, N., Abedrabbo, T. et al. (2015). *Neo4j in action*. Shelter Island: Manning.

70 Ye, Z., Guo, Y., Li, T. et al. (2019). Extended attack graph generation method based on knowledge graph. *Computer Science* 46 (12): 165–173.

71 Ruohonen, J. (2019). A look at the time delays in CVSS vulnerability scoring. *Applied Computing and Informatics* 15 (2): 129–135.

72 Zhu, Z., Jiang, R., Jia, Y. et al. (2018). Cyber security knowledge graph-based cyber attack attribution framework for space-ground integration information network. In: *Proc. 18th Int'l Conf. Comm. Technology (ICCT)*, 870–874. IEEE.

73 Xue, J. (7 Sept. 2025). *Attack attribution: Provenance graph construction technology based on causation*. NSFOCUS. http://blog.nsfocus.net/attack-investigation-0907.

74 Han, Z., Li, X., Liu, H. et al. (2018). Deepweak: reasoning common software weaknesses via knowledge graph embedding. In: *Proc. 25th Int'l Conference on Software Analysis, Evolution and Reengineering (SANER)*, 456–466. IEEE.

75 Mitre. *Common Weakness Enumeration*, 28 Feb. 2022, https://cwe.mitre.org.

76 Alsaheel, A., Nan, Y., Ma, S. et al. (2021). ATLAS: a sequence-based learning approach for attack investigation. In: *Proc. 30th USENIX Security Symposium (USENIX Security 21)*, 3005–3022.

77 Kovalenko, O., Wimmer, M., Sabou, M. et al. (2015). Modeling automationml: semantic web technologies vs. model-driven engineering/. In: *220th IEEE Conf. Emerging Technologies & Factory Automation (ETFA)*, 1–4. IEEE.

78 NEFOCUS (5 Jan. 2023). *Security Knowledge Graph Technology White Chapter*. NSFOCUS. www.nsfocus.com.cn/html/2022/92_0105/166.html.

79 Xue, J. (17 Sept. 2023). *Attack Reasoning: Dilemma of Application of Security Knowledge Graph*. NSFOCUS. http://blog.nsfocus.net/stucco-cyber.

80 Wang, W., Jiang, R., Jia, Y. et al. (2017). KGBIAC: knowledge graph-based intelligent alert correlation framework. In: *Proc. Int'l Symposium on Cyberspace Safety and Security*, 523–530. Cham: Springer.

81 Qi, Y., Jiang, R., Jia, Y. et al. (2018). Association analysis algorithm based on knowledge graph for space-ground integrated network. In: *Proc. IEEE 18th Int'l Conference on Communication Technology (ICCT)*, 222–226. IEEE.

82 Ekelhart A, Ekaputra F J, Kiesling E. *Automated Knowledge Graph Construction From Raw Log Data*. 2020.

83 Ou, Y., Zhou, T., and Zhu, J. Recommendation of cyber attack method based on knowledge Graph. In: *2020 Int'l Conf. Computer Eng. And Intelligent Control (ICCEIC)*, vol. 2020, 60–65. IEEE.

84 Chen, X., Shen, W., and Yang, G. (2021). Automatic generation of attack strategy for multiple vulnerabilities based on domain knowledge graph/. In: *Proc. IECON 2021–47th Annual Conference of the IEEE Industrial Electronics Society*, 1–6. IEEE.

85 Vassilev, V., Sowinski-Mydlarz, V., Gasiorowski, P. et al. (2021). Intelligence graphs for threat intelligence and security policy validation of cyber systems. In: *Proc. Int'l Conf. Art. Intell. and Appl*, 125–139. Singapore: Springer.

86 Tao, Y., Jia, X., and Wu, Y. (2020). A research method of industrial internet security vulnerabilities based on knowledge graph. *Network Security Protection Technology* 39 (1): 6–13.

87 Najafi, P., Mühle, A., Pünter, W. et al. (2019). MalRank: a measure of maliciousness in SIEM based knowledge graphs. In: *Proc. 35th Annual Computer Security Applications Conference*, 417–429.

88 Dutta S, Rastogi N, Yee D, et al. *Malware Knowledge Graph Generation*. arXiv preprint arXiv:2102.05583, 2021.

89 Sun, C., Hu, H., Yang, Y. et al. (2022). Prediction method of 0-day attack path based on cyber defense knowledge graph. *Chinese Journal of Network and Information Security* 8 (01): 151–166.

90 Mitra, S., Piplai, A., Mittal, S. et al. (2021). Combating fake cyber threat intelligence using provenance in cybersecurity knowledge graphs. In: *2021 IEEE Int'l Conf. Big Data (Big Data)*, vol. 2021, 3316–3323. IEEE.

91 Wang, Z., Sun, L., and Zhu, H. (2020). Defining social engineering in cybersecurity. *IEEE Access* 8: 85094–85115.

92 Wang, Z., Zhu, H., Liu, P. et al. (2021). Social engineering in cybersecurity: a domain ontology and knowledge graph application examples. *Cybersecurity* 4 (1): 1–21.

93 Xiao, H., Xing, Z., Li, X. et al. (2019). Embedding and predicting software security entity relationships: a knowledge graph based approach. In: *International Conf. Neural Information Processing*, 50–63. Cham: Springer.

94 Shang, H., Jiang, R., Li, A. et al. (2017). A framework to construct knowledge base for cyber security. In: *IEEE 2nd International Conf. Data Science in Cyberspace (DSC)*, vol. 2017, 242–248. IEEE.

95 Liu, Q., Li, Y., Duan, H. et al. (2016). Knowledge graph construction techniques. *Journal of Computer Research and Development* 53 (3): 582–600.

96 Khan, A.A., Laghari, A., Gadekallu, T.R. et al. (2022). A drone-based data management and optimization using metaheuristic algorithms and blockchain smart contracts in a secure fog environment. *Computers and Electrical Engineering* 102: 108234.

97 Laghari, A.A., Zhang, X., Shaikh, Z.A. et al. (2023). A review on quality of experience (QoE) in cloud computing. *Journal of Reliable Intelligent Environments*. https://doi.org/10.1007/s40860-023-00210-y.

98 Khan, A.A., Laghari, A.A., Shaikh, A. et al. (2021). A blockchain security module for brain-computer interface (BCI) with multimedia life cycle framework (MLCF). *Neuroscience Informatics* 100030. https://doi.org/10.1016/j.neuri.2021.100030.

99 Attkan, A. and Ranga, V. (2022). Cyber-physical security for IoT networks: a comprehensive review on traditional, blockchain and artificial intelligence based key-security. *Complex & Intelligent Systems* 8: 3559–3591.

14

Security in Blockchain-Based Smart Cyber-Physical Applications Relying on Wireless Sensor and Actuators Networks

Maria A. de Jesus[1], Asif A. Laghari[2], Abdullah A. Khan[3], Awais Khan Jumani[4], Mohammad Shabaz[5], Anand Deshpande[6], R. Jenice Aroma[7], Kumudha Raimond[8], and Asiya Khan[9]

[1]*Department of Telecommunications, Federal Fluminense University (UFF), RJ, Niterói, Brazil*
[2]*Sindh Madresstul Islam University, Karachi, Sindh, Pakistan*
[3]*Research Lab of Artificial Intelligence and Information Security, Faculty of Computing, Science and Information Technology, Benazir Bhutto Shaheed University, Karachi, Sindh, Pakistan*
[4]*Department of Computer Science, Sindh Madressa-tul-Islam University, Karachi, Sindh, Pakistan*
[5]*Chitkara University Institute of Engineering and Technology, Chitkara University, Rajpura, Punjab, India*
[6]*Electronics and Communication Engineering, Angadi Institute of Technology and Management, Belagavi, India*
[7]*Department of CSE, Karunya Institute of Technology and Sciences, Karunya University, Coimbatore, India*
[8]*Department of Computer Science and Engineering, Karunya Institute of Technology and Sciences, Coimbatore, India*
[9]*School of Engineering, Computing and Mathematics (Faculty of Science and Engineering), University of Plymouth, Plymouth, UK*

14.1 Introduction

A "business sector" can be any potential application field, such as banking, agribusiness, disaster relief, etc. Nowadays, the "cyber-physical system" (CPS) rationale [1–4], i.e., a framework placing together computation (aka virtualized building blocks) with physical (real) processes whose conduct depends on the computational and physical parts. Within a CPS, devices can exchange information and intermingle with the physical realm through sensors and actuators that observe and control the hardware (HW) and software (SW) processes in a feedback loop. The amalgamation of sensing, actuation, computation, and communication competencies expands the overall performance, security, and reliability. This set of circumstances brings to mind "cybersecurity" (CS) concerns for CPSs, the "Internet of Things" (IoT) gadgets and the "extended IoT"

Applying Artificial Intelligence in Cybersecurity Analytics and Cyber Threat Detection, First Edition.
Edited by Shilpa Mahajan, Mehak Khurana, and Vania Vieira Estrela.

(XIoT) that are an integral growing part of significant business sectors related to infrastructures, governments, and quotidian life [5, 6]. This chapter implies that CS is the practice of safeguarding against unwanted assaults on HW, servers, mobile devices, "information and communication technologies" (ICT) systems, networks, SW, and data [6–8].

Today, a knowledge sector may encompass many issues, including local face-to-face care or amenities, faraway databank access, laboratory analysis, online public awareness, and administrative business tasks [9]. In contrast, inspecting and controlling facilitates service control and aids service suppliers in helping the public outside the business' tangible facility, properly tracking stakeholders' aftermaths, ongoing superior services, and identifying at-risk folks. It also enables participants to maintain contact with their providers, comply with schedules, and mend trust and wellness processes. Instead, persons in remote areas lack access to modern services due to technology and staff deficiencies. Real-time observation and well-being of all participants (stakeholders), real environments, and other ignored stakeholders, be it a person, animal, or small area. IoT-based "general CPS ontology" (GCPSO) management may rely on mobile devices, terminals, or other technology that affords constructive and preventive remote interventions [10], accomplishing emergent individuals'/businesses' demands and high operational costs. It interconnects accessible assets and delivers smart, safe, and inexpensive services.

The IoT is a mainly physical technology system, e.g., buildings, in-body, on-body, and out-body gadgets, administration facilities, research centers, and local face-to-face services, in which full people's information access is assured through the Internet. Such up-and-coming technologies assist advancement in modernization due to Internet and computing HW developments. The "general intelligent blockchain CS CPS" (GIBCS-CPS) centers on a structure that employs participants' resources, including reliable information, multimedia coordination, and records retrieval blended with possible remote decision-making and control [6–8]. The IoT integration in inspecting and control systems has impediments owing to "big data" (BD) and the obligation for encryption protocols to inhibit people's records from leaking [11]. Any malicious individual's or corporation's intervention contrariwise will expose and manipulate participant's data in any fashion with serious repercussions, even demises [12, 13].

A secure, real-time monitoring and control system must confront previous matters, maximizing emergent security advantages plus ICT. A "wireless sensor and actuator (or actor) network" (WSAN) designates wireless communication via devices holding (i) sensors to monitor ecological and physical conditions pertaining to individuals, areas, or objects and (ii) multiple actuators, such as servomechanisms, motors, valves, drug-delivering units, and drones, to perform actions. WSANs can gather facts from the region of interest, aka application (i.e., ecology-related settings, trading markets, automated buildings, agribusinesses, live beings bodies, harvests, etc.) to control the indispensable entity's traits undergoing inspection. WSANs comprehend paramount IoT and Industry 4.0 forming elements for creating intelligent businesses, environments, agrarian locales, cities, medical scenarios, etc. [14–19]. An effective WSAN installation calls for subjugating many hindrances and delivering reliable services. These comprise the dynamic and intelligent supervision of sensors and actuators, the asset-limited network nodes' nature, and the continuous, robust, and secure data exchange between HW sections.

WSAN's distinctive control/data decoupling tackles remote observation and efficient application sector devices' control. Conversely, blockchain technology preserves the participant's history records, and sensors acquire information securely and confidentially without alteration prospects. For this reason, WSANs [13] and blockchain sub-systems [20, 21] within the target CPS can be a directly positive effect solution. This chapter investigates an efficient and reliable GCPSO to inhibit any insider/outsider intruder from inoculating data, falsifying data, violating participants' secrecy, or even instigating a "denial of service" (DoS) "cyberattack" (aka "cyber threat" (CT)) against the GCPSO [4, 20, 21]. The GIBCS-CPS also offers a modular trust management implementation founded on blockchain technology, CS defenses, and decision-making benefits from these technologies from the GCPSO perspective. The recommended GIBCS-CPS boosts priorities and manages concerns concerning trust. Simultaneously, it defends various monitoring and control system components while protecting stakeholders' privacy by fashioning a secure environment where separate security modules coexist to warrant a consistent GCPSO.

Conversely, several person-centered solutions emphasize "knowledge domain bases" (KDBs) management, which involves all individual-related records, comprising the protection and trust facets of data, HW, and SW [22, 23]. Ideally, the network, monitoring, and control must require fewer improvements than the participants' side. This rationale can cause undesired situations, principally with remote work, owing to the minimization of stakeholders' physical contact, dislocation time, and stress, among other actors. This chapter establishes the minimum HW/SW framework for protected, trusted remote checking and control of CPS and partakers' processes as follows:

- A remote, real-time, and protected stakeholders' monitoring and control architecture via blockchain and WSAN,
- A scalable, flexible structure that can start/ turn off any module while sustaining other modules' functionalities, and
- An efficient, lightweight "trust management scheme" (TMS) for monitoring and controlling a business sector.

Numerous algorithms' input data make up valuable features. However, Internet data are limitless, and exploiting their authorization can be tricky, occasioning extremely difficult-to-handle data verification scenarios in complex CPSs. So, designs that assist in robustifying data storage, processing, and sharing in-depth operations across Internet environments are essential. These designs produce a more genuine, secure BD cyberspace and improve algorithms on various information sources.

The chapter is outlined as follows: Section 14.2 presents relevant works on CPSs with WSANs, blockchain, and their hybridization. The planned GIBCS-CPS architecture and design goals appear in Section 14.3. The TMS [4] details are depicted in Section 14.4. Blockchain incorporation in GIBCS-CPS occurs in Section 14.5. Performance is pondered in Section 14.6. To close, Section 14.7 brings in conclusions.

14.2 Methodology

Demand for business sector facilities with remote and local treatment units necessitates CPS upgrading with pros and cons, banking on three relevant schemes: WSANs, blockchain, and hybrid strategies.

14.2.1 WSAN-Centered Solutions

A WSAN infrastructure embraces many developing paradigms, mixing sensing, computation, and control, affecting real-time physical process control and realization [24–26]. Multiple quality products with superior freedom at a constant price will be available to customers worldwide. To address expanding human, machine, and product interconnectivity concerns, all manufacturers require autonomous interaction and highly robust local and global interconnectivity across their systems and sub-systems. WSANs' benefits help streamline operations management. WSANs can be inexpensive, easily deployable, and flexible, making them better by decentralizing autonomous task decision-making and lessening human interaction. Independence helps varied sectors supporting intelligent systems and processes, improving production dependability and profits. These networks undertake noise, fading, hotness, dust, multipath consequences, and electromagnetic (EM) interference at multiple stack protocol layers, disrupting "quality of service" (QoS)-aware data delivery [24–30]. Diverse low-power standards and remedies have eliminated obstacles. IEEE 802.15.4 enhancements fulfill utilization expectations [31], becoming part of most standards and answers, e.g., ZigBee [32], THREAD [33], WirelessHART [34], Z-WAVE [4], ISA [35], 6LoWPAN [36], LoRa [37], and WIA-PA [38]. These advances have increased a WSAN's safety, time-critical operation, and automation [39]. Ample work addressed designing and building efficient "medium access control" (MAC) protocols to improve network speed and QoS [40]. MAC affects dependability, scalability, low latency, energy efficiency, and security.

14.2.1.1 Benefits

Cost drop: The main operational and capital expenditures result from rapid installation, effortless repairs, trouble-free system reconfigurations, etc., while saving time.

Flexible architecture/design: Wireless solutions can malleably handle rigid, fixed specific processes, viz robots and gyratory equipment, in dangerous zones and extreme temperatures.

Safety: Wirelessness translates to remotely reconfiguring and upholding processes and systems, preventing humans from being in hazardous locations. Likewise, mechanical failures are a common problem, which affects reliability and causes applications' downtime. Wireless solutions are less prone to deterioration failures, making them safer and less inclined to failures.

14.2.1.2 Challenges

WSANs bring nontrivial challenges demanding serious remediation efforts. The imperfect, error-prone wireless medium causes packet losses (PLs) and variable delays. Although wired networks have losses, WSANs have more caveats because of fluctuating channel conditions, narrow spectrum, multipath broadcast, and fading. Besides, an important issue is efficiently exploiting and accessing shared wireless mediums, which the MAC sublayer runs as a data link layer part. An inept MAC strategy can squander rare communication assets. The most critical challenges appear below.

Packet losses: Channel impairments cause PLs in wireless interactions due to collisions, multipath fading, and small channel achievements. Buffer overflow yields congestion, which wastes packets in transit. Packet reordering follows a long transmission time, triggering packet dropouts.

Variable delay: WSANs have random delays and insert time uncertainties within sampled, encoded, and diffused data hitting the target for decoding on the receiver, which adds delay. Retransmissions are frequent, with poor link quality, boosting delay and energy intake. A decisive performance indicator is the delay, which should have minimum variability and adequate upper bound to avoid adverse application QoS impacts.

Data rate: The limited channel bandwidth constraints the number of communication network medium devices. Hence, an efficient protocol may minimize the overhead.

All previous imperfections mentioned above may degrade performance. Thus, effective protocols can counterbalance these losses and lessen adverse effects.

Today's nodes have more memory, processing power, and extended battery life. In most usages, sensing, actuation, and control are also imperative. Sensors acquire data, and actuators send certain data-centered control decisions as commands to adjust a CPS part.

14.2.1.3 WSANs' Structure

Because actuation is vital in controlling processes and systems, the trend is integrating sensors, actuators, and their respective controllers to attain sensing and actuating node tasks. Actuators act in the physical environment and possess networking skills like reception, broadcasting, processing, and dispatching data. A robot may perform in the physical environment through assorted actuators. Yet, from a networking viewpoint, a robot may be deemed a single networking object (or actuator). Consequently, an actuator may contain many actuators, encompassing heterogeneous tools. A WSAN is a distributed hybrid, heterogeneous sensor/actuator structure whose sensors directly communicate with actuators. Actuators can also converse among themselves. Hence, WSANs encompass sensor-to-actuator and actuator-to-actuator interactions via single-hop or multihop broadcasts. WSAN can perform sensing, data fusion, acting properly in the physical environment thanks to decision-making, and collaborate distributedly. Actuators are rich in computational, communication, and battery power resources. They may perform sensing tasks for local corrections, strictly restricting trustworthiness, predictability, and availability and requiring a sink or gateway to observe the overall network.

14.2.1.4 Characteristics of WSAN

Generally, actuation is more complex than sensing. Depending on the application, an immediate response to a sensor input may be required, further imposing certain real-time constraints. WSANs are characterized by some of the following unique features.

Real-time guarantee: This requirement interchangeably deals with latency and delay bound, i.e., strict timing constraints are involved between sensing and acting. As soon as data is detected, it should trigger actuators. If the required data encounters latency and the actuation command is performed late, it makes data less effective, meaning sensing data must be valid when acting.

Reliable coordination: Sensors communicate among themselves and also with actuators. Thus, sensors-to-actuator and actuator-to-actuator coordinations are involved in selecting the suitable actuator for the action through metrics (viz existing energy, distance, location, coverage, etc.) These coordinations are essential to maintain reliability, self-organization, and network QoS. Still, at the same time, they impose new challenges on networking to provide robust and delay-tolerant protocols and solutions.

Traffic differentiation: The environment is heterogeneous due to resource-constrained sensors and resource-rich devices like actuators. Therefore, efficient resource allocation and utilization techniques need to be developed. Energy efficiency for sensor nodes is a big concern but less concerning for actuators. Moreover, actuating messages are more delay-sensitive than standard sensor measurements, so message priority differs. Heterogeneity must be exploited cleverly in protocol design so that application QoS requirements and constrained resources of the sensors are not at stack.

14.2.1.5 WSANs Applications

Application necessities vary regarding criticality, reliability, timeliness, and importance of data in detail.

- **Safety systems**: These are always critical and require immediate action during emergencies (i.e., in need of real-time communication), are highly delay-sensitive, and entail low latency and outstanding reliability. Nonetheless, in terms of bandwidth requirements, they tend to have moderate bandwidth.
- **Control systems**: They can be closed-loop (CL), open-loop (OL), and process control systems [41]. Generally, CL systems observe processes and act as per decision, being generally autonomous and not involving humans in the loop. OL structures do not possess feedback and call for persons in the loop, i.e., humans, to make adjustments. Each control arrangement imposes different delay constraints, e.g., CL is more fault-finding than OL control. Process control systems can tolerate some delays.
- **Alerting systems**: These regular events or alert systems result from continuous observing that indicates short-term operational costs at different stages of SW or HW.
- **Predictive maintenance and automatic fault detection**: This crucial trait helps anticipate a failure instigated by surveillance and possible automatic maintenance via advanced procedures resulting from sudden machine shutdowns that lead to impromptu downtime and massive losses. So, a reliable WSAN can estimate machine faults precisely and jointly to evade worst-case situations.
- **Monitoring systems**: These include checking process variables, equipment condition, structural health, etc., to continuously gather data from an essential sector for long durations, analyses, and make better decisions. These systems cover nearly every application's aspect.

14.2.1.6 WSAN Requirements

Reliability: Link quality varies in the unreliable wireless medium, and quality in both bidirectional link ways differs. Poor link quality can wane broadcast and create latency, worsening on-time control decisions and leading to system letdowns and financial losses. The reliability can be handled at different levels. As an illustration, it can be modeled by an energy efficiency function that depicts the network lifecycle satisfactorily and consistently throughout that epoch. Reliability (packet reception rate) should exceed a threshold to assure a certain reliability level without degrading processes' and systems' efforts.

Packet priority and heterogeneity: The real world calls for heterogeneousity. Sensing measurements, controlling commands, and actuation tasks engender different generated packets. Each traffic has a different treatment priority. Thus, assigning packet priority warrants some degree of timely performance. Selected actions require prompt execution, albeit others can endure a certain flexibility level for execution, as CL systems, actuation, and control commands are more indispensable than sensor data. Accordingly, the system responds appropriately to faults when a priority difference level is embedded in the protocol.

Energy effectiveness/power consumption: Energy replacements for battery-powered nodes are nearly unmanageable, especially in inaccessible areas. Nevertheless, energy efficiency is also a significant concern, e.g., reliability and latency. Augmenting reliability expands energy efficiency, leading to low packet reception rate and latency to the energy consumption detriment. Therefore, careful tradeoffs must be handled under existing metrics that estimate and analyze compromises, leading to robust and flexible protocol development.

Adaptation: Often, control traffic requirements change dynamically for different process controller states. Altering the wireless medium and network topologies imposes further necessities. Communication protocols cope with dynamic traffic by adapting their parameters per control requirements and the medium.

Scalability: It denotes a system's capability to scale well or deliver high flexibility, supporting modifications adaptively for adding and removing nodes or functionalities without degrading performance. A WSAN may require too many nodes. Then, communication protocols' scalability must comply with such a scenario. Yet, scalable MAC protocols' development is a nontrivial and challenging task. Existing standards like WirtelessHART and ISA100.11a chiefly rely on "time division multiple access" (TDMA) protocols, constraining the participating nodes' total while simultaneously satisfying QoS requirements. Therefore, WSANs require protocols supporting scalability at different protocol stack layers to achieve better performance.

Multihop communication: Large-scale network deployments usually span over a large area. So, many sensor nodes are deployed at different locations, with sensor nodes transmitting their data and relaying data of nodes located multiple hops from the sink. Therefore, multihop communication remains an inherent share of such scenarios, allowing further flexibility in adding new nodes in the current network in case of plant structural changes. It also adds redundancy. In primary communication path failure, nodes can utilize alternative paths to reach sinks. However, this also imposes challenges of selecting a particular relay node if multiple relay nodes exist to not overload a specific path and warrant timely data delivery with better routing and mobility administration.

Scalability and network control in Ref. [42] use a WSAN controller to track traffic flows and assure network/ device traffic rule exchange. The quantity of controllers (the main factor in business sector sub-CPS-WSAN amalgamations) must be carefully planned [43–45]. A mathematical model uses convex optimization to find the ideal number of controllers for a WBAN framework, pondering latency, controllers, and WSAN-enabled switches [13, 14]. A GCPSO uses a security-integrated monitoring and control system to offer stakeholder services reliably and minimize risks. The heterogeneous structure of WSANs demands a method to supply QoS-improved services [46]. Still, this work will not address this. WSAN deployment was recommended for bandwidth and real-time data communications.

14.2.2 Blockchain-Based Solutions

Since Bitcoin's debut, several blockchain variants have permitted businesses to exploit new technologies to gather, process, and analyze stakeholder data. Distributed identification and permission control use blockchain-enabled deployment with a comprehensive security policy view [47]. A hypothetical blockchain use in business has been extensively examined in Refs. [48, 49] to identify flaws and future research, mainly in blockchain deployment costs. Performance, architectures, and standards were supplanted with security and privacy compliance.

Similarly, Refs. [50, 51] have systematically reviewed trendy business sector applications, covering security, privacy, and data analyses/sharing via blockchain, besides critical conceptions, including identity supervision, data encryption, storage, access control, and "smart contracts" (SCs). An e-health CPS data privacy and network security prevented unauthorized access by a KDB distribution network utilizing a blockchain, mobile cloud platform, and the open "Interplanetary File System" (IPFS) [52]. Their deployment fallouts are promising and offer a feasible securing data transfer method on mobile clouds with performance ameliorations in trivial access organization, network latency, and safety through elevated privacy and security thresholds.

Blockchain's back-end transaction logging could help third parties, and cryptographically verified platforms maintain confidence. Business decentralization has emerged in the business sector. Although limited, well-defined cryptographical and mathematical methods like hashing enable blockchain's developing ledger to be tamper-proof, safe, and unchangeable [53, 54].

Blockchain uses "consensus algorithms" (CAs) to validate and link blocks. Famous blockchain networks Bitcoin and Ethereum had insecure proof-of-work (PoW) CA [55]. CTs boosted blockchain security research. Later, blockchain 2.0 focuses on SCs [56, 57], or the law of code [58] may eliminate trusted third parties. Ethereum and Hyperledger Fabric, with chain codes [59, 60], became popular SC blockchains. Ethereum uses PoW as CA but has no restrictions, unlike Bitcoin. SCs cannot just work in finance [56]. CS still has room for improvement [61].

Blockchain-based CS applications are analyzed, showing the increase in networking adoption in various domains and encompassing IoT [62]. According to Ref. [63], blockchain technologies can protect shared data and provide data trust for anything "as a service." The causes and symptoms of vulnerabilities follow.

Broken access control (AC): It limits stakeholders' access, restricting their resources despite assigned permissions. AC failure commonly means stakeholders performing business functions requiring different consents than the ones set, among other activities. Errors also lead to unauthorized records disclosure, alteration, or destruction. "AC vulnerabilities" (ACV) include:

(1) Allowing all participants access to resources intended for specific roles, stakeholders, or authorization groups violates least privilege.
(2) Bypassing access control checks with URL, internal application state, or HTML page modifications. API attack tools can bypass access regulation checks.
(3) No API controls (e.g., "PUT," "POST," or "DELETE").
(4) Privilege elevation, where an attacker can log in as a user without executing administrative tasks from a lower-privilege account.

Prevention entails limited resources' access with AC, working with a trusted server where the invader cannot alter data. Protection methodologies follow:

(1) Access should be repudiated by default, excluding if the element is a public resource.
(2) Use AC tools again throughout the application.
(3) Impose application business bounds.
(4) Deactivate web servers' directory listings.
(5) Rate-restrained API and controller permission.

Cryptographic failures (CFs): They can compromise systems or expose sensitive data due to cryptography shortcomings. Credit card numbers and personally identifiable information need further protection. The data type determines protection techniques and compliance with information privacy rules like the EU "General Data Protection Regulation" (GDPR) [64]. Common CFs are:

(1) Unenforced browser encryption without HTTP security headers.
(2) Server certificate trust chain invalid.
(3) FTP, SMTP, and HTTP browser protocols communicate data clearly.
(4) Using or disregarding weak cryptographic techniques and protocols in legacy code.

CF prevention depends on application functioning and data type. There are several facets to data protection. Preventing includes:

(1) Classify application-processed, transferred, or stored data. Classify sensitive data by privacy, commercial, or regulatory requirements.
(2) Store only necessary data and trash after the action.
(3) Encrypt all data at rest and transmission.
(4) Avoid sending sensitive data over obsolete protocols.

Injection: Source-code examination can detect cross-site scripting, SQL injection, XML injection, and others. Automation can find vulnerabilities by checking all parameters and data inputs. Applications are injection-prone when:

(1) User data is accepted without validation, sanitization, or filtering.
(2) Sensitive data is extracted from hostile data.
(3) Executing prevention.

Prevention of injection attempts requires separating queries and actions from data:

(1) Include interpreter special characters in escape syntax.
(2) Query controls prevent unexpected inputs from acting unofficially.
(3) Use safe APIs for prepared statements with parameterized queries apart from the interpreter.

Insecure design: It is not an insecure implementation, albeit a design can have imperfections, occasioning vulnerabilities. Unsafe designs do not ameliorate during performance because they lack suitable security controls. Failing to accurately assess SW or HW risks associated with the design leads to insufficient safekeeping. A security culture employs impenetrable design policies to appraise CTs and confirm the code follows the rules and is verified against notorious attack schemes. Prevention embraces strategies that foster a safe development culture:

(1) Application security professionals' partnerships can estimate and design controls through a secure development lifecycle.

(2) Ready-to-use components for secure design patterns.
(3) Resourceful CT modeling respects access controls, critical authentication, essential data flows, and business logic.

Security misconfiguration: Besides other factors, an array of improperly configured controls may contribute to application vulnerability. Some common caveats:

(1) Wrongly configured cloud services permissions.
(2) Enabling unnecessary features leads to redundant opened ports, services, or erroneously elevated privileges.
(3) Default account login credentials may be unchangeable.

A thorough, robust security configuration process starts repeatable precautionary actions across systems and is somewhat automated as below:

(1) Establishing a repeatable security strengthening strategy, ideally through automation, to protect new environments properly with every deployment.
(2) Only use what is necessary. Uninstall or eliminate extra features and components.
(3) Install an automated process to appraise security across environments.

Vulnerable and outdated constituents: Unpatched legacy tools still in production after discovering and disclosing vulnerabilities can be a significant risk. Applications are in danger when not running the latest SW version. The application may be susceptible if a library or component version is used despite being unreliable. Non-scanned components for vulnerabilities may also face risk. Launching a patch-management process can alleviate the outbreak potential by terminating vulnerabilities before they turn into an issue, such as:

(1) Eradicating unused or superfluous libraries, constituents, frameworks, documentation, and archives.
(2) Continual surveillance and server- and client-flank components' inventory.
(3) Utilizing only sanctioned libraries and sources over protected links.
(4) Unsupported legacy libraries and components.

Identification and authentication failures: Here, stakeholders' identities, authentications, and session data are not settled before one can get into systems and data. Reasons that may jeopardize applications due to these failures consist of weak passwords, inadequately hashed, plain-text data password warehousing, and letting bots perform automated CAs, viz credential stuffing, and brute-force. Prevention via secure passwords for storage and retrieval may involve:

(1) Multi-factor authentication implementation.
(2) Circumvention of default credentials in deployments (especially for administrative accounts).
(3) Limited account enumeration exposure.

SW and data integrity failures: Trusting data and SW updates without testing their integrity allows invaders to issue malware employing the SW supply chain in seemingly legitimate SW updates. Numerous systems use automated updates without integrity verification. Prevention begins with confirmation and includes:

(1) Applying digital signatures or other authentication forms to get SW updates ensures they have come from credible sources and arrived intact.
(2) Verification if third-party libraries and other reliances are from authentic sources.
(3) Verify that third-party assets share no vulnerabilities by automated security tools and attend to the SW supply chain.

Security logging and monitoring failures: Targets are audit logs and monitoring throughout an outbreak. Security watching and records are paramount to discovering and mitigating active breaches. Letdowns happen when:

(1) Logging does not record high-value transactions, login tries, or failed attempts.
(2) Mistakes and warnings engender unclear, scant, or no log entries.
(3) APIs/applications are not examined for suspicious undertakings.
(4) Security logs exist only locally.
(5) Applications cannot spot CTs to issue timely "attacks in progress alerts."

Prevention aims at permitting security logging and checking across applications. Designers should guarantee appropriate security controls, such as

(1) Login, entrance control, and server-side corroboration failures should relate to a logged stakeholder's context to ensure that malign and suspicious activities are preserved long enough for analysis.
(2) Logs should be made in a suitable format for log supervision tools to read.
(3) Permit surveillance and alerts for distrustful activities.
(4) Embrace an incident reaction and mitigation plan.

"Server-side request forgery" (SSRF): It handles weaknesses within stakeholder-convenience structures at application and network levels. SSRF flaws occur once web applications fetch stakeholder-requested remote assets without validating the destination. Specific requests can go to the application via an unforeseen source. Applications ordinarily get hold of URLs for easier end-users task-switching (often within the application) while accessing other features over the fetched URL. Cumulative cloud/fog architectures' complexity means SSRF happens at a higher frequency. Protected segmented networks separate remote resources and block other non-essential traffic by employing "deny-by-default" policies. SSRF schemes should take in the following:

(1) Data input must be sanitized, validated, and filtered.
(2) Deactivation of HTTP server-level redirection.

(3) Warranting server responses arrive as expected, so unprocessed server reactions should never reach a stakeholder.

New vulnerability variants: They emphasize application data tendencies with extra training benefits for companies concentrating on particular CWEs for programming languages or frameworks actively utilized.

(1) **Insecure design**: It contains design and infrastructural flaws and risks. Distinguished from other exposures, insecure design cannot be amended through correct implementation.
(2) **SW/data entry failures**: They contain risks of accepting SW updates without corroborating integrity, focusing on the hypothesis that updates can have permanent trust.
(3) **"Server-side request forgery" (SSRF)**: Risks arise from URL fetching from an application to a different one at the stakeholder's request without confirming the URL's truthfulness. This server-side defenselessness is risky since fake requests can bypass CS schemes like VPNs, firewalls, or other access controls.

14.2.3 Hybrid Solutions

Security enhances data privacy and scalability; thus, stakeholders combine "WSAN with blockchain" (WSANB) in the business sector [65–68]. This chapter's focal point is the breakdown of current blockchain deployments in WSANs that endorse integrity, confidentiality, and network infrastructure accessibility. This will help determine the potential of adding blockchain into WSAN architecture for security and privacy [41, 69–74].

Using a blockchain-based WSAN data chain, providing a distributed trustworthy record of WSAN data, and breaking the isolation of multi-vendor devices for fault recovery will reduce network failure recovery expenses via Ethereum and OpendayLight [75]. In Ref. [76], a general blockchain-based WSAN framework addressed the centralized control plane issue by merging the control plane and application layer into one major component and adding security features to obtain blockchain-improved distributed controller security. A blockchain-based collaborative "distributed DoS" (DDoS) CT prevention solution employing SCs to enable WSAN domain collaboration and convey DDoS outbreak information reliably, effectively, and decentralizedly appeared in Ref. [77] (Figure 14.1).

14.3 GIBCS: An Overview

Figure 14.2 exhibits the GIBCS-CPS design, which views local and remote business stakeholders. Participants can use terminals, cellphones, or other intelligent devices to access back-end (data access layer) devices, viz servers, mainframes,

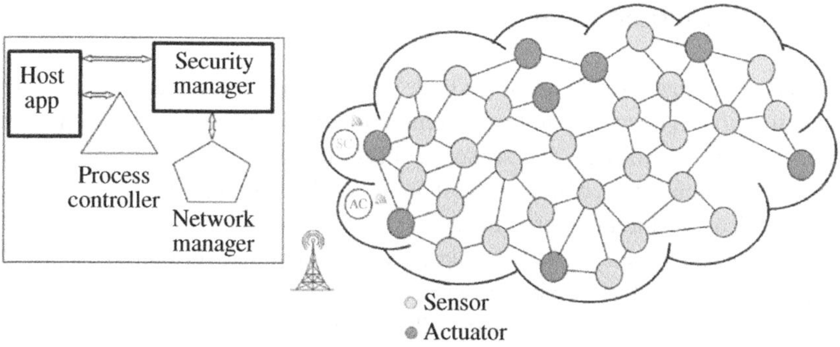

Figure 14.1 General WSAN architecture. A sensor and actuator network with a sink amalgamates the network manager, security supervision, controller, and application. SC: Sensor controller. AC: Actuator controller.

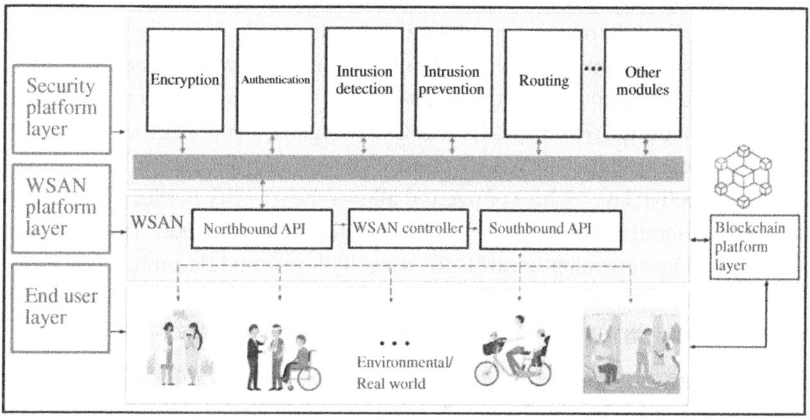

Figure 14.2 GIBCS-CPS different layers.

databanks, and others that provide data services. The back end encompasses SW modules, devices, and computers not visible to users. Design must decouple client issues from the front-end (presentation layer), back-end SW, physical infrastructure, or HW. The WSAN regulates these gateways by distributing non-selective security policies from WSAN controllers.

Data routing rules will be saved on the smartphone. Back-end components include the GCPSO controller, database, and client application that monitors the mobile app and sensors. The proposed design's architecture is shown in Figure 14.2. This architecture has four layers:

1. User Layer;
2. SDN Layer;
3. Security Layer;

14.4 Blockchain Layer

User layer: The gateway (edge or fog node) mobile app coordinates sensor-target database traffic. The trusted authority sends rules and policies to the mobile app via the GCPSO controller. The sensors collect vital data from participants and send it to the mobile app, which routes them depending on smartphone app guidelines. Dedicated modules authenticate and authorize mobile applications and sensors in the security layer. The mobile app acts as a conduit between sensors and target datasets. The trusted authority sends rules and policies to the mobile app via the GCPSO controller. The sensors collect vital participant data and send information to the mobile app, which does routing as per smartphone app guidelines. Security modules handle mobile app and sensor authentication/ authorization.

WSAN layer: The GIBCS-CPS architecture core layer is the WSAN. A NBI allows communication between a given level and higher-level components in the same network. In contrast, a southbound interface (SBI) does the reverse, i.e., permits communication among a particular component and lower-level parts. Controllers and northbound/southbound APIs are the main WSAN network components. Southbound APIs in the GIBCS-CPS design will connect the mobile app to the WSAN controller. The WSAN controller uses northbound APIs to implement the protective layer. This connection allows the security platform's modules to access southbound APIs on all WSAN controller-linked nodes (mobile apps and sensors). The controller controls the security layer module-mobile app interactions. Additionally, the controller has its apps and services. This GIBCS-CPS architecture features routing, which identifies and conveys sensor data.

Security layer: The security integration layer connects and orchestrates security modules. Figure 14.3 depicts the GCPSO security and privacy components.

Blockchain layer: The design utilizes permissioned blockchain to securely and quickly connect system actors. It has two phases:

- The first phase documents approved actions, system actors log in, and use dedicated interfaces (APIs). It may include sensitive information.
- In the second, blockchain-supported infrastructure domain miners will add information to the blockchain by unraveling the PoW procedure. Blockchain nodes that can add data are the ones containing only miners. The blockchain is not updated if a miner cannot solve the PoW CA routine.

14.4.1 WSAN-Based Network Model

14.4.1.1 WSAN Overview

Figure 14.3 illustrates WSAN splitting the network into data, control, and application planes. Data planes send and receive network communication. Traffic

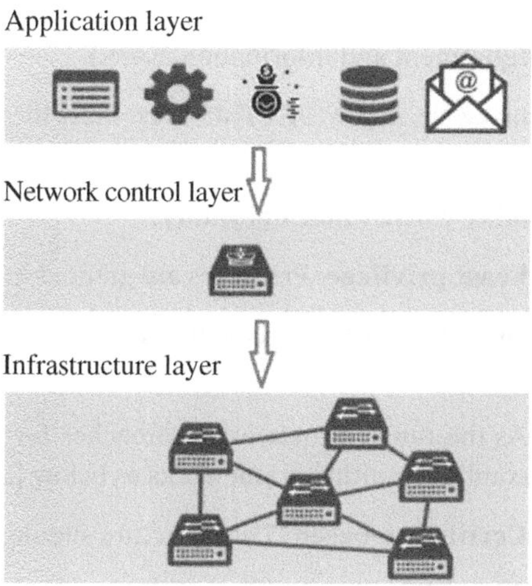

Figure 14.3 WSAN architecture. Application layer: physical HW, virtual machines, virtual hosts. Network control layer: regulates the network. Infrastructure layers: programmable switches.

transfer decisions are made at the control plane. The device plane stores WSAN programs.

WSAN applications may disseminate their SW and HW statistics and inbound connections to the northbound controller interface. Applications can also notify the controller of network management commands akin to flow rule addition or removal and are designed to achieve specific purposes, employing controller data and other sources to decide if the network should be altered. Applications receive only the control plane permissions (such as read, write, notification, and target device ID) from the controller's access control sub-system.

14.4.1.2 Problem Statement

Altering and controlling network status with different applications is a paramount WSAN feature. Supporting third-party growth undermines confidence. Third-party apps represent a CT since trusted SW modules are hard to determine. Policies in the WSAN allow network applications to directly alter WSAN-reliant networks [78]. Many WSAN controllers necessitate authentication, sanction, and logging aptitudes. When third-party applications contact a northbound interface (NBI), administrators assume the same as the network applications' controller. Applications can misuse policies to leak data or destroy specialized networks, causing widespread damage. The confidence management system for the NBI of the WSAN controller performs business sector monitoring. This strategy should address trust management characteristics [79].

Dynamicity: The confidence level should vary throughout a user's interaction with an application.

Content dependency: The application's skill to win confidence may rest on the target task.

Subjectivity: The trust management system should consider WSAN features (e.g., equipment and information assets).

Likewise, any WSAN TMS must meet the criteria and adhere to these principles:

Proof of identity: Nodes involved in a communication must authenticate each other when/where obligatory.

Least privilege: Privileges are granted in line with the request.

Inspect and log: Incidents must be scrutinized and reported aptly for security motives.

As the range of network approaches for TMS is broad, a possible solution is to combine multiple frameworks as below [80].

Certificate-based: This structure should provide authentication.

Policy-based: A framework must discern permissible acts for applications.

Behavior-based: This arrangement tracks and analyzes application activities to assign a confidence rating.

14.5 Trust Management

The suggested TSM for a WSAN-based domain platform concentrates on the WSAN architecture, which is the communication part of the business sector. The recommended architecture establishes trust between the control layer and network applications. Figure 14.4 illustrates the framework linking applications to the WSAN architecture's control layer. The structure is made up of five elements depicted next.

14.5.1 Authentication Module

Application requests for control plane network modifications trigger the framework's authentication with control plane challenges credentials following the submission. The controller allows or refuses network service after confirming application credentials. This text will not discuss authentication because it needs further detail, but it emphasizes CS.

14.5.2 Authorization Module

It controls two groups of app permissions. One set includes necessary rights that, if misused, might have profound effects, while the other covers non-critical rights.

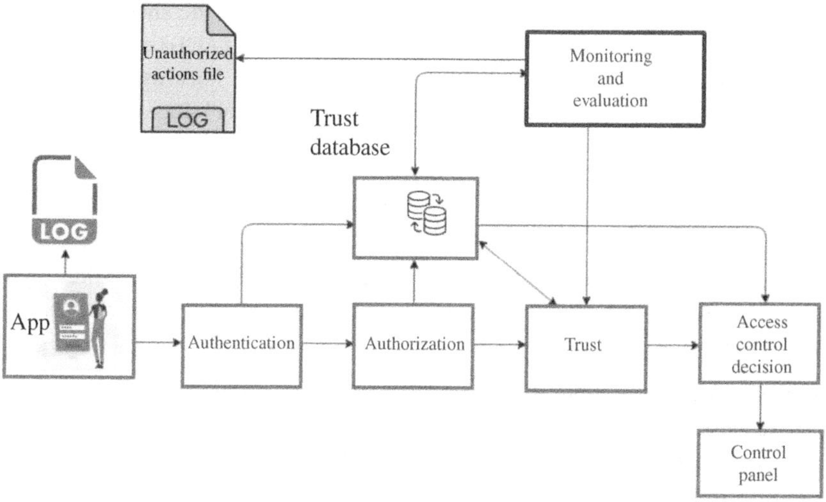

Figure 14.4 Trust management modules and interactions.

The "trust database module" (TDM) tracks all permissions. The functions they perform divide apps into two types. Security programs come first and foremost. Applications without security priority are second. CS applications can limit a static administrator's network security policy in reaction to new run-time CTs, including malevolent traffic, contaminated internal resources, blacklist-worthy external entities, and dangerous aggregate traffic patterns.

14.5.3 Trust Database Module

The TDM is a data storage constituent that keeps track of all characteristics and values needed for the framework's assessments and determinations. Both functions consult the database for warehoused data. The network administrator arbitrarily determines the values allotted to several network applications. The TDM computes a permissions-requesting program's trust value (TV) that depends on four elements [81, 82].

(1) **Reputation sub-system**: It assesses historical interactions between nodes.
(2) **Operational risk sub-system**: The network parts affected by the application may be missing.
(3) **Information risk sub-system**: It handles possible knowledge disclosure losses.
(4) **Privacy level sub-system**: The network traffic device perceived by the WSAN controller.

The TDM gauges the TV, employing some constants and the above variables. The display, i.e., TV, is sent to the "access control decision" (ACD) module. Users will have interfaces to count appropriate and significant hazards and set two "threshold TVs" (TTVs), which are "acceptable" and "crucial" since risk variables vary by network.

14.5.4 Access Decision Control (ACD)

This segment assigns the calculated TV from the trust section to one of the zones itemized beneath. The ACD module governs the application's trustworthiness by checking this TV.

Critical zone: If an application's confidence level remains deficient, it should cease work and cut off;

Surveillance zone: For a medium-level confidence application, decisions must address the "monitoring and evaluation" (ME) module, aka MEM;

Trusted zone: For a high-level confidence application, it works with the MEM that habitually observes it.

The application's confidence level drops as the TV value falls. The MEM decisions are founded on observations.

14.5.5 Monitoring and Evaluation Module (MEM)

Controller-network application relationships should be frequently evaluated. The MEM monitors the ACD module actions and checks trustworthy regions' log files for incorrect activity requests. The module surveils the region corresponding to the application log files and reports to the WSAN controller administrator.

Assessing the application's behavior helps manage and adjust its "reputation value" (RP). The MEM evaluation process has positive users' defined constants A, B, and C. If the program requests illegal rights, this module lowers RP. If no deviant occurrences are found, it may boost RP.

14.6 Blockchain for Secure Monitoring Back-End

Bitcoin possesses a reward mechanism in PoW, where the vulnerable proof-of-work CA is responsible for most of these CTs. In many cases, Bitcoin was also found vulnerable to other CTs, including DoS [83] and bypassing the authentication [84, 85]. Ethereum conquered many of these security concerns, albeit somewhat weak. The crowdfunded "decentralized autonomous organization" (DAO) [84] project on the Ethereum blockchain was a renowned blockchain application. However, the outbreak on DAO later led the Ethereum to split into the Ethereum and Ethereum Classic. Several SCs were also vulnerable, and such incidents have continued.

It brought new thoughts, leading to a rapid blockchain security enhancement. Lots of advances were advised in the traditional PoW as a CA by developing new alternative CTs [86] like proof-of-stack (PoS), which does not require mining and reduces environmental losses as in PoW. Previous research strengthened these blockchains and focused on security aspects [87, 88].

Blockchain-founded surveillance within CPSs is an auspicious ICT development that can handle data gathering with security and privacy caveats throughout stakeholders' scrutiny. All monitoring procedures relate to the beforehand computed TV. They are afterward encrypted and held in the blockchain, warranting the system's CS.

A miner's (like a WSAN controller's) block comes, and the "blockchain domain server" verifies the nonce's legitimacy before adding it to the blockchain. However, one server can receive many blocks. Therefore, the blockchain may fork. A distributed CA should fix this problem. Servers can fork or add blocks. The branch with the most servers grows fastest. The longest one becomes the network's distributed CA, while the others are deleted. The servers will also save their blocks in erased forks and add them to the blockchain later. This strategy ensures every server has an identical blockchain.

The fallouts from numerous investigations point to the fact that previous CTs inspire blockchain research in CS domains. However, several CT prevention methods have been introduced [89] to quickly curb uncovered vulnerabilities to stop or reduce the CT impact. Then, these works have been centered on analyzing the reasons for different CTs and alleviating them to mend the affected blockchain network. Besides, CTs' data from several business sectors can aid in estimating relationships among CTs on new blockchain networks.

The CVEs from the preceding years have consistently augmented the number of vulnerabilities, which calls for research about estimating more exposures and preparing solutions before new attacks to increase upcoming blockchains' safety. FL can also help more effectually with this purpose. Likewise, efforts may ensue in discovering the best risk assessment methodology in blockchain tools. Along with the research on developing technical solutions for possible CT detection and risk assessment in forthcoming blockchains, fresh work should look at the finest tactics for application security and evaluation.

Blockchains' CS and accompanying risk assessment must be prioritized for many potential network CTs. The "Common Vulnerability Scoring System" (CVSS) can prioritize faraway code execution to uncover vulnerabilities by scoring them. Due to a temporal mismatch between vulnerability discovery and score assignment, methods to help with this have been developed. Sorting risk assessment steps to suitably address blockchain CTs becomes a notable struggle, and the blockchain application domain affects vulnerability occurrence. Due to these reasons, risk assessment methods must be studied, and best practices must be defined for most blockchain networks' diversity. The goal should also prioritize vulnerability testing for good and logical reasons.

ML approaches for estimating highly possible attacks for dedicated blockchains can be developed due to a noticeable growth in the subsequent CS domain through more protected electronic cash dealings or cryptocurrencies to plenty of application domains. Several ML-based approaches have been introduced to detect attacks like DDoS. Federated learning (FL) [90, 91] and blockchain and FL influence go beyond financial services to expand the privacy, security, and trust of CPSs. Metaverse and digital twins can help improve the service ecosystems. Finally, unraveling future challenges has demanded insights from businesses and investigators, owning to progress in scalability and integration. This will intensify the network complexity and escalate the CA scope even further. Detecting and mitigating possible attacks in such situations also requires more advanced steps. Hence, ML possibilities should be analyzed for dynamic risk assessment and CT hunting early in blockchain-centered solutions. Hybrid architectures are also in trend, aiming to successfully manage transactions' on- and off-chain processing. Novel solutions might also be scalable, utilizing ML to resolve and accomplish off-chain processing.

14.7 Blockchain-Enabled Cybersecurity: Discussion and Future Directions

Furthermore, WSANs support communication with more adaptability and control over observed and controlled devices. This integrated platform and in-built applications can alleviate the GCPSO's functionality and security. The GIBCS-CPS can provide efficient GCPSO checking operations with negligible energy intake and overhead, which is paramount to the business sector [92]. Future work may add more architectural functionalities, such as crafting a user-friendly interface to simplify tasks, perform distant actions in emergencies, and predict unfavorable situations.

Improving CS measures, building a safe online environment, and ensuring the quick availability of information simultaneously seem to be an ever-lasting challenge. Unfortunately, despite these technical advancements, many previous works indicate that the overall blockchain network is still prone to CTs [93–95]. Vulnerable CAs can create some CTs, ultimately disturbing every blockchain network part. The "Common Vulnerabilities and Exposures" (CVE) comprises a database and system [96–100] for publicly sharing information on CS defenselessness.

The ranking of vulnerabilities includes various variables, including online application data analysis by individuals and organizations. Companies/organizations can receive contributing data or keep it anonymous. Data sources include bug bounty programs, safety consultancies, and vendors. Supporters provide the data period, web application count, and MITRE "common weakness enumerations" (CWEs). Contributors must disclose core CWE application numbers. Totaling all tested apps and comparing them to CWE-affected applications yields the incidence rate. The top results are ranked based on application and security professionals' surveys to analyze vulnerabilities' fundamental causes from symptoms wherever possible.

Early detection and mitigation of possible CAs is advantageous to ensure proper security for existing and upcoming blockchains. Due to preexistent CT vectors' close relation, selected blockchains' sub-parts could be highly susceptible to attacks, requiring different designs for blockchain modeling and its applications. An intelligent modeling approach not only understands these issues but also unlocks the doors for even more or similar applications [56].

14.8 Conclusions

Business sector monitoring and remediation systems are handy for mentoring and assessing stakeholders' well-being. In addition, they expose stakeholders to computer hacking risks. The "general intelligent blockchain CS CPS" (GIBCS-CPS) centers on a structure that employs participants' resources, including reliable information, multimedia coordination, and records retrieval blended with possible remote decision-making and control supporting IoT integration, "BD" and protocols to inhibit people's records from leaking.

Cloud and fog computing usage equips blockchain with a flexible and cost-effective service by on-demand resource sharing, bringing together extra security risks. The combination of improved CPSs relying on blockchain allows for continuously evaluating attack surface changes consistent with the cloud/fog environments. Dynamic qualities give defenders a tactical gain against threats. Still, when gauging the architecture effectiveness, the character of traditional security evaluation methods becomes unstable, especially when merging multiple ICT elements and techniques. Hence, there is a lack of standard ways to quantitatively appraise such frameworks' effectiveness.

Additionally, a hierarchical architecture allows utilizing each network layer separately for the effectiveness appraisal of each circumstance. The GIBCS-CPS helps grasp and enlist relationships between the CS traits of blockchain, many types of vulnerabilities, and other caveats [101–103]. Prospect research dimensions concerning cybersecurity and blockchain are also debated.

The GIBCS-CPS fortifies all parts of a generic business sector's control, surveillance, and drawbacks' remediation of systemic components. It also conserves stakeholders' privacy by erecting diverse security modules to function together and, conditional to blockchain technology, to defend the "general CPS ontology" (GCPSO).

References

1 Rani, S., Mishra, R.K., Usman, M. et al. (2021). Amalgamation of advanced technologies for sustainable development of smart city environment: a review. *IEEE Access* 9: 150060–150087.

2 Ying, Z., Ma, M., Zhao, Z. et al. (2022). A reputation-based leader election scheme for opportunistic autonomous vehicle platoon. *IEEE Transactions on Vehicular Technology* 71: 3519–3532.

3 Estrela, V.V., Saotome, O., Loschi, H.J. et al. (2018). Emergency response cyber-physical framework for landslide avoidance with sustainable electronics. *Technologies* 6: 42. https://doi.org/10.3390/technologies6020042.

4 Barka, E., Dahmane, S., Kerrache, C.A. et al. (2021). STHM: a secured and trusted healthcare monitoring architecture using SDN and Blockchain. *Electronics* 10: 1787. https://doi.org/10.3390/electronics10151787.

5 Estrela, V.V., Deshpande, A., Lopes, R.T. et al. (2023). The building blocks of health 4.0–internet of things, big data with cloud and fog computing. In: *Intelligent Healthcare Systems* (ed. V.V. Estrela), 24–44. London, UK: CRC Press Chapter 2.

6 Yaga, D., Mell, P., Roby, N., and Scarfone, K. (2018). *Draft Blockchain Technology Overview (NISTIR-8202)*, 59. National Institute of Standard and Technology.

7 Azmoodeh, A., Dehghantanha, A., Conti, M., and Choo, K.-K.R. (2018). Detecting crypto-ransomware in IoT networks based on energy consumption footprint. *Journal of Ambient Intelligence and Humanized Computing* 9 (4): 1141–1152.

8 Mittal, A., Gupta, M., Chaturvedi, M. et al. (2021). Cybersecurity enhancement through blockchain training (CEBT) – a serious game approach. *International Journal of Information Management Data Insights* 1 (1): 100001. https://doi.org/10.1016/j.jjimei.2020.100001.

9 Albahri, A., Alwan, J.K., Taha, Z.K. et al. (2021). IoT-based telemedicine for disease prevention and health promotion: state-of-the-art. *Journal of Network and Computer Applications* 173: 102873.

10 Philip, N.Y., Rodrigues, J.J.P.C., Wang, H. et al. (2021). Internet of Things for in-home health monitoring systems: current advances, challenges and future directions. *IEEE Journal on Selected Areas in Communications* 39: 300–310.

11 Verma, N., Singh, S., and Prasad, D. (2021). A review on existing IoT architecture and communication protocols used in healthcare monitoring system. *Journal of The Institution of Engineers (India): Series B* 103: 245–257.

12 Almalki, F.A. and Othman, S.B. (2021). EPPDA: an efficient and privacy-preserving data aggregation scheme with authentication and authorization for IoT-based healthcare applications. *Wireless Communications and Mobile Computing, Hindawi* 1–5594159. 18.

13 Shreya, S., Chatterjee, K., and Singh, A.K. (2022). A smart secure healthcare monitoring system with Internet of Medical Things. *Computers and Electrical Engineering* 101: 107969.

14 Nair, G.N., Fagnani, F., Zampieri, S., and Evans, R.J. (2007). Feedback control under data rate constraints: an overview. *Proceedings of the IEEE* 95 (1): 108–137.

15 Faheem, M., Abbas, M.Z., Tuna, G., and Gungor, V.C. (2015). Edhrp: energy efficient event driven hybrid routing protocol for densely deployed wireless sensor networks. *Journal of Network and Computer Applications* 58: 309–326.

16 Tuna, G. and Gungor, V.C. (2017). A survey on deployment techniques, localization algorithms, and research challenges for underwater acoustic sensor networks. *International Journal of Communication Systems* 30 (17): e3350.

17 Faheem, M., Tuna, G., and Gungor, V.C. (2017). LRP: link quality-aware queue-based spectral clustering routing protocol for underwater acoustic sensor networks. *International Journal of Communication Systems* 30 (12).

18 Römer, K. (2004). Tracking real-world phenomena with smart dust. In: *European Workshop on Wireless Sensor Networks*, 28–43. Heidelberg: Springer.

19 Wang, X., Wang, S., and Bi, D. (2009). Distributed visual-target-surveillance system in wireless sensor networks. *IEEE Transactions on Systems, Man, and Cybernetics. Part B, Cybernetics* 39 (5): 1134–1146.

20 Khanna, K., Estrela, V.V., and Rodrigues, J.J.P.C. (ed.) (2021). *Cyber Security and Digital Forensics – Proc. ICCSDF 2021. Lecture Notes on Data Engineering and Communications Technologies*. Singapore: Springer. https://doi.org/10.1007/978-981-16-3961-6.

21 Lv, P., Wang, L., Zhu, H. et al. (2019). An IOT-oriented privacy-preserving publish/subscribe model over blockchains. *IEEE Access* 7: 41309–41314.

22 Mayer, A.H., da Costa, C.A., and Righi, R.D.R. (2020). Electronic health records in a blockchain: A systematic review. *Health Informatics Journal* 26: 1273–1288.

23 Fatokun, T., Nag, A., and Sharma, S. (2021). Towards a blockchain assisted patient owned system for electronic health records. *Electronics* 10: 580.

24 Nayak, A., Stojmenovic, I. (2010). *Wireless Sensor and Actuator Networks: Algorithms and Protocols for Scalable Coordination and Data Communication*. https://doi.org/10.1002/9780470570517.

25 Raza, S., Faheem, M., and Guenes, M. (2019). Industrial wireless sensor and actuator networks in industry 4.0: exploring requirements, protocols, and challenges – a MAC survey. *International Journal of Communication Systems* 32.

26 Nikoukar, A., Abboud, M., Samadi, B. et al. (2018). Empirical analysis and modeling of Bluetooth low-energy (BLE) advertisement channels. In: *Proc. 17th Annual Mediterranean ad hoc Networking Workshop (MED-HOC-NET)*, 1–6. Capri, Italy: IEEE.

27 Zhu, H., Li, M., Chlamtac, I., and Prabhakaran, B. (2004). A survey of quality of service in IEEE 802.11 networks. *IEEE Wireless Communications* 11 (4): 6–14.

28 Laghari, A.A., Khan, A., He, H. et al. (2020). Quality of experience (QoE) and quality of service (QoS) in UAV systems. In: *Imaging and Sensing for Unmanned Aircraft Systems*, vols. 2 and 10 (ed. V.V. Estrela, J. Hemanth, O. Saotome, et al.), 213–242. London, UK: IET. https://doi.org/10.1049/PBCE120G_ch10.

29 Baloch, J.A., Jumani, A.K., Laghari, A.A. et al. (2021). A preliminary study on quality of experience assessment of compressed audio file format. In: *2021 IEEE URUCON*, 161–165. https://doi.org/10.1109/URUCON53396.2021.9647114.

30 Laghari, A.A., Zhang, X., Shaikh, Z.A. et al. (2023). A review on quality of experience (QoE) in cloud computing. *Journal of Reliable Intelligent Environments*. https://doi.org/10.1007/s40860-023-00210-y.

31 IEEE Standard for Low-Rate Wireless Networks (2016). *IEEE Std 802.15.4-2015 (Revision of IEEE Std 802.15.4-2011)*, 1–709.

32 *ZigBee Alliance*. http://www.zigbee.org/, Last accessed 02-06-2023. 2023.

33 *Thread Group*. http://www.threadgroup.org/, Last accessed 10-05-2023. 16. Z-wave Alliance. http://www.z-wave.com/, Last accessed 11-07-2023, 2023.

34 *FieldComm Group*. https://fieldcommgroup.org/, Last accessed 19-05-2023, 2023.

35 *The International Society of Automation – ISA*. https://www.isa.org/, Last accessed 20-08-2023, 2023.

36 Kushalnagar N, Montenegro G, Schumacher C. *Ipv6 Over Low-Power Wireless Personal Area Networks (6lowpans): Overview, Assumptions, Problem Statement, and Goals*; 2007. RFC 4919, RFC Editor, http://www.rfc-editor.org/rfc/rfc4919.txt.

37 *LoRa Alliance*. https://www.lora-alliance.org/, Last accessed 24-04-2023; 2023.

38 *Industrial Automation Process Automation (WIA-PA).* http://www.industrialwireless.cn/en/06.asp, Last accessed 11-08-2023; 2023.

39 Wang, C., Bi, Z., and Da Xu, L. (2014). IoT and cloud computing in automation of assembly modeling systems. *IEEE Transactions on Industrial Informatics* 10 (2): 1426–1434.

40 Sadeghi, R., Barraca, J.P., and Aguiar, R.L. (2017). A survey on cooperative MAC protocols in IEEE 802.11 wireless networks. *Wireless Personal Communications* 95 (2): 1469–1493.

41 Ploplys, N.J., Kawka, P., and Alleyne, A. (2004). Closed-loop control over wireless networks. *IEEE Control Systems* 24 (3): 58–71.

42 Isravel, D.P., Silas, S., and Rajsingh, E.B. (2021). SDN-based traffic management for personalized ambient assisted living healthcare system. In: *Intelligence in Big Data Technologies – Beyond the Hype* (ed. J.D. Peter, S.L. Fernandes, and A.H. Alavi), 379–388. Singapore: Springer.

43 Hasan, K., Ahmed, K., Biswas, K. et al. (2020). Control plane optimisation for an SDN-Based WBAN framework to support healthcare applications. *Sensors* 20: 4200.

44 Arshaghi, A., Razmjooy, N., Estrela, V.V. et al. (2020). Image transmission in UAV MIMO UWB-OSTBC system over Rayleigh channel using multiple description coding (MDC). In: *Imaging and Sensing for Unmanned Aircraft Systems*, vols. 2 and 4 (ed. V.V. Estrela, J. Hemanth, O. Saotome, et al.), 67–90. London, UK: IET. https://doi.org/10.1049/PBCE120G_ch4.

45 Razmjooy, N., Deshpande, A., Khalilpour, M. et al. (2021). Optimal bidding strategy for power market based on improved world cup optimization algorithm. In: *Metaheuristics and Optimization in Computer and Electrical Engineering. Lecture Notes in Electrical Engineering*, vol. 696 (ed. N. Razmjooy, M. Ashourian, and Z. Foroozandeh). Cham: Springer. https://doi.org/10.1007/978-3-030-56689-0_7.

46 Jnr, B.A., Nweke, L.O., and Al-Sharafi, M.A. (2020). Applying software-defined networking to support telemedicine health consultation during and post Covid-19 era. *Health Technology* 2190–7196.

47 Esposito, C., Ficco, M., and Gupta, B.B. (2021). Blockchain-based authentication and authorization for smart city applications. *Information Processing and Management* 58: 102468.

48 Hölbl, M., Kompara, M., Kamišalić, A., and Nemec Zlatolas, L. (2018). A systematic review of the use of blockchain in healthcare. *Symmetry* 10: 470.

49 Vazirani, A.A., O'Donoghue, O., Brindley, D., and Meinert, E. (2019). Implementing blockchains for efficient health care: systematic review. *Journal of Medical Internet Research* 21: e12439.

50 Agbo, C.C., Mahmoud, Q.H., and Eklund, J.M. (2019). Blockchain technology in healthcare: a systematic review. *Healthcare* 7: 56.

51 Jin, H., Luo, Y., Li, P., and Mathew, J. (2019). A review of secure and privacy-preserving medical data sharing. *IEEE Access* 7: 61656–61669.

52 Nguyen, D.C., Pathirana, P.N., Ding, M., and Seneviratne, A. (2019). Blockchain for secure EHRs sharing of mobile cloud based E-health systems. *IEEE Access* 7: 66792–66806.

53 Ali Syed, T., Alzahrani, A., Jan, S. et al. (2019). A comparative analysis of blockchain architecture and its applications: problems and recommendations. *IEEE Access* 7: 176838–176869. https://doi.org/10.1109/ACCESS.2019.2957660.

54 Lee, N.-Y., Yang, J., Onik, M.M.H., and Kim, C.-S. (2019). Modifiable public blockchains using truncated hashing and sidechains. *IEEE Access* 7: 173571–173582. https://doi.org/10.1109/AC-CESS.2019.2956628.

55 Gupta, C. and Mahajan, A. (2020). Evaluation of proof-of-work consensus algorithm for blockchain networks. In: *Proc. 11th International Conference on Computing, Communication and Networking Technologies (ICCCNT)*, 1–7. https://doi.org/10.1109/ICC-CNT49239.2020.9225676.

56 Ferreira da Silva, C. and Moro, S. (2021). Blockchain technology as an enabler of consumer trust: a text mining literature analysis. *Telematics and Informatics* 60: 101593. https://doi.org/10.1016/j.tele.2021.101593.

57 Ferreira, A. (2021). Regulating smart contracts: legal revolution or simply evolution? *Telecommunications Policy* 45 (2): 102081. https://doi.org/10.1016/j.telpol.2020.102081.

58 Filippi, P. D., Hassan, S. (2018). *Blockchain Technology as a Regulatory Technology: From Code is Law to Law is Code*. CoRR, abs/1801.02507. http://arxiv.org/abs/1801.02507.

59 Pancari, S., Rashid, A., Zheng, J. et al. (2023). A systematic comparison between the ethereum and hyperledger fabric blockchain platforms for attribute-based access control in smart home IoT environments. *Sensors (Basel, Switzerland)* 23.

60 Dinh, T.T.A., Liu, R., Zhang, M. et al. (2018). Untangling blockchain: a data processing view of blockchain systems. *IEEE Transactions on Knowledge and Data Engineering* 30 (7): 1366–1385. https://doi.org/10.1109/TKDE.2017.2781227.

61 Li, Y. and Liu, Q. (2021). A comprehensive review study of cyber-attacks and cyber security; emerging trends and recent developments. *Energy Reports* 7: 8176–8186. https://doi.org/10.1016/j.egyr.2021.08.126.

62 Taylor, P.J., Dargahi, T., Dehghantanha, A. et al. (2020). A systematic literature review of blockchain cyber security. *Digital Communications and Networks* 6 (2): 147–156.

63 Lomotey, R.K., Kumi, S., and Deters, R. (2022). Data trusts as a service: providing a platform for multi-party data sharing. *International Journal of*

Information Management Data Insights 2 (1): 100075. https://doi.org/10.1016/j.jjimei.2022.100075.

64 Tamburri, D.A. (2020). Design principles for the general data protection regulation (GDPR): a formal concept analysis and its evaluation. *Information Systems* 91: 101469. https://doi.org/10.1016/j.is.2019.101469.

65 Parra, L., Sendra, S., Lloret, J., and Rodrigues, J.J. (2017). Design and deployment of a smart system for data gathering in aquaculture tanks using wireless sensor networks. *International Journal of Communication Systems* 30 (16): e3335.

66 Ghayvat, H., Mukhopadhyay, S., Gui, X., and Suryadevara, N. (2015). WSN- and IoT-based smart homes and their extension to smart buildings. *Sensors* 15 (5): 10350–10379.

67 Mukherjee, S., Dolui, K., and Datta, S.K. (2014). Patient health management system using e-health monitoring architecture. In: *Proc. 2014 IEEE International Advance Computing Conference (IACC)*, 400–405. Palladam, India: IEEE.

68 Saneja, B. and Rani, R. (2017). An efficient approach for outlier detection in big sensor data of health care. *International Journal of Communication Systems* 30 (17): e3352.

69 Elkamel, R. and Cherif, A. (2017). Energy-efficient routing protocol to improve energy consumption in wireless sensors networks. *International Journal of Communication Systems* 30 (17): 1–9.

70 Wang, Q. and Jiang, J. (2016). Comparative examination on architecture and protocol of industrial wireless sensor network standards. *IEEE Communication Surveys and Tutorials* 18 (3): 2197–2219.

71 Civerchia, F., Bocchino, S., Salvadori, C. et al. (2017). Industrial Internet of Things monitoring solution for advanced predictive maintenance applications. *Journal of Industrial Information Integration* 7: 4–12.

72 Swain, R.R., Khilar, P.M., and Dash, T. (2018). Fault diagnosis and its prediction in wireless sensor networks using regressional learning to achieve fault tolerance. *International Journal of Communication Systems* 31 (14): e3769.

73 Raza, M., Aslam, N., Le-Minh, H. et al. (2018). A critical analysis of research potential, challenges, and future directives in industrial wireless sensor networks. *IEEE Communication Surveys and Tutorials* 20 (1): 39–95.

74 Alharbi, T. (2020). Deployment of blockchain technology in software defined networks: a survey. *IEEE Access* 8: 9146–9156.

75 Xue, C., Xu, N., and Bo, Y. (2019). Research on key technologies of software-defined network based on blockchain. In: *Proceedings of the 2019 IEEE International Conference on Service-Oriented System Engineering (SOSE), San Francisco, CA, USA, 4–9 April*, 239–2394.

76 Wenjuan, L., Weizhi, M., Zhiqiang, L., and Man-Ho, A. (2020). Towards blockchain-based software-defined networking: security challenges and solutions. *IEICE Transactions on Information and Systems* E103.D: 196–203.

77 El Houda, Z.A., Hafid, A., and Khoukhi, L. (2019). Co-IoT: a collaborative DDoS mitigation scheme in IoT environment based on blockchain using SDN. In: *Proceedings of the 2019 IEEE Global Communications Conference (GLOBECOM), Waikoloa, HI, USA, 9–13 December*, 1–6.

78 Canini, M., Venzano, D., Peresini, P. et al. (2012). A "nice" way to test openflow applications. In: *Proceedings of the 9th USENIX Conference on Networked Systems Design and Implementation, San Jose, CA, USA, 25–27 April.*

79 Loschi, H.J., Estrela, V.V., Hemanth, D.J. et al. (2020). Communications requirements, video streaming, communications links and networked UAVs. In: *Imaging and Sensing for Unmanned Aircraft Systems*, vols. 2 and 6 (ed. V.V. Estrela, J. Hemanth, O. Saotome, et al.), 113–132. London, UK: IET https://doi.org/10.1049/PBCE120G_ch6.

80 Yan, Z. (2013). *Trust Management in Mobile Environments: Autonomic and Usable Models*, 1ee. Hershey, PA, USA: IGI Global.

81 Burikova, S., Lee, J., Hussain, R. et al. (2019). A trust management framework for software defined networks-based Internet of Things. In: *Proc. 10th Annual Information Technology, Electronics and Mobile Communication Conference (IEMCON), 17–19 October 2019*, 0325–0331. Vancouver, BC, Canada: IEEE.

82 Yang, Z., Yang, K., Lei, L. et al. (2018). Blockchain-based decentralized trust management in vehicular networks. *IEEE Internet of Things Journal* 6: 1495–1505.

83 Baek, U.-J., Ji, S.-H., Park, J.T. et al. (2019). DDoS attack detection on bitcoin ecosystem using deep learning. In: *Proc. 20th Asia-Pacific Network Operations and Management Symposium (APNOMS)*, 1–4. https://doi.org/10.23919/APNOMS.2019.8892837.

84 Zhao, X., Chen, Z., Chen, X. et al. (2017). The DAO attack paradoxes in propositional logic. In: *4th Int'l Conf. Systems and Informatics (ICSAI)*, 1743–1746. https://doi.org/10.1109/ICSAI.2017.8248566.

85 Singh, S., Hosen, A.S.M.S., and Yoon, B. (2021). Blockchain security attacks, challenges, and solutions for the future distributed IoT network. *IEEE Access* 9: 13938–13959. https://doi.org/10.1109/ACCESS.2021.3051602.

86 Estrela, V.V., de Jesus, M.A., Intorne, A.C. et al. (2023). Blockchain technology enabling better services in the healthcare domain. In: *Intelligent Healthcare Systems* (ed. V.V. Estrela), 135–158. London, UK: CRC Press Chapter 7.

87 Khan, A.A., Laghari, A., Gadekallu, T.R. et al. (2022). A drone-based data management and optimization using metaheuristic algorithms and blockchain smart contracts in a secure fog environment. *Computers and Electrical Engineering* 102: 108234.

88 Khan, A.A., Laghari, A.A., Shaikh, A. et al. (2021). A blockchain security module for brain-computer interface (BCI) with multimedia life cycle framework (MLCF). *Neuroscience Informatics* 100030. https://doi.org/10.1016/j.neuri.2021.100030.

89 Pawar, S. and Palivela, D.H. (2022). LCCI: a framework for least cybersecurity controls to be implemented for small and medium enterprises (SMEs). *International Journal of Information Management Data Insights* 2 (1): 100080. https://doi.org/10.1016/j.jjimei.2022.100080.

90 Kim, H., Park, J., Bennis, M., and Kim, S. (2018). Blockchained on-device federated learning. *IEEE Communications Letters* 24: 1279–1283.

91 Chatterjee, P., Das, D., and Rawat, D.B. (2023). Next generation financial services: role of blockchain enabled federated learning and metaverse. In: *Proc. 2023 23rd International Symposium on Cluster, Cloud and Internet Computing Workshops (CCGridW)*, 69–74. IEEE/ACM.

92 Nikoukar, A., Raza, S., Poole, A. et al. (2018). Low-power wireless for the Internet of Things: standards and applications. *IEEE Access* 6: 67893–67926.

93 Chen, Y., Chen, H., Zhang, Y. et al. (2022). A survey on blockchain systems: attacks, defenses, and privacy preservation. *High-Confidence Computing* 2 (2): 100048. https://doi.org/10.1016/j.hcc.2021.100048.

94 Christen, P., Schnell, R., Ranbaduge, T., and Vidanage, A. (2022). A critique and attack on "blockchain-based privacy-preserving record linkage". *Information Systems* 108: 101930. https://doi.org/10.1016/j.is.2021.101930.

95 Wang, H., Wang, Y., Cao, Z. et al. (2019). An overview of blockchain security analysis. In: *Cyber Security* (ed. X. Yun, W. Wen, B. Lang, et al.), 55–72. Singapore: Springer Singapore.

96 Prakash, R. and AnoopV., S., Asharaf, S. (2022). Blockchain technology for cybersecurity: a text mining literature analysis. *International Journal of Information Management Data Insights* 2: 100112.

97 CVE (1999). *Mitre Attack*. https://cve.mitre.org/cgi-bin/cvekey.cgi.

98 Kushwaha, S.S., Joshi, S., Singh, D. et al. (2022). Systematic review of security vulnerabilities in Ethereum blockchain smart contract. *IEEE Access* 10: 6605–6621. https://doi.org/10.1109/ACCESS.2021.3140091.

99 Nair, P.R. and Dorai, D.R. (2021). Evaluation of performance and security of proof of work and proof of stake using blockchain. In: *Proc. Third International Conf. Intelligent Communication Technologies and Virtual Mobile Networks (ICICV)*, 279–283. https://doi.org/10.1109/ICICV50876.2021.9388487.

100 Lyu, Y., Le-Cong, T., Kang, H.J. et al. (2023). CHRONOS: time-aware zero-shot identification of libraries from vulnerability reports. In: *Proc.*

45th International Conference on Software Engineering (ICSE), 1033–1045. IEEE/ACM.

101 Alwan, A.A., Ciupala, M.A., Brimicombe, A.J. et al. (2022). Data quality challenges in large-scale cyber-physical systems: a systematic review. *Information Systems* 105: 101951. https://doi.org/10.1016/j.is.2021.101951.

102 Monteiro, A.C.B., Franca, R.P., Estrela, V.V. et al. (2020). UAV-CPSs as a test bed for new technologies and a primer to Industry 5.0. In: *Imaging and Sensing for Unmanned Aircraft Systems*, vols. 2 and 1 (ed. V.V. Estrela, J. Hemanth, O. Saotome, et al.), 1–22. London, UK: IET. https://doi.org/10.1049/PBCE120G_ch1.

103 Liu, Y., Lu, Q., Yu, G. et al. (2022). Defining blockchain governance principles: a comprehensive framework. *Information Systems* 102090. https://doi.org/10.1016/j.is.2022.102090.

15

Leveraging Deep Learning Techniques for Securing the Internet of Things in the Age of Big Data

Keshav Kaushik

School of Computer Science, University of Petroleum and Energy Studies, Dehradun, Uttarakhand, India

15.1 Introduction to the IoT Security

The Internet of Things (IoT), which allows common gadgets to be connected to the internet and communicate with one another, has completely changed how we engage with technology. IoT devices generate vast amounts of data, providing businesses and consumers with unprecedented opportunities to collect, analyze, and gain insights from this data. However, this increased connectivity and data generation also pose significant challenges for organizations, requiring them to adopt new approaches to manage, store, and analyze IoT data. The emergence of big data has further amplified the importance of IoT in modern society. Big data refers to the collection, processing, and analysis of large and complex datasets that cannot be processed using traditional data processing techniques. IoT devices generate massive amounts of data, including sensor data, telemetry data, and user-generated data. This data can be used to gain insights into consumer behavior, product usage, and operational efficiency, among other things.

However, the volume, velocity, and variety of data generated by IoT devices present significant challenges for data storage, processing, and analysis. Traditional data processing techniques are often insufficient to handle the massive scale and complexity of IoT data, requiring organizations to adopt new approaches, including big data analytics. The combination of IoT and big data has created a new paradigm that offers unprecedented opportunities for innovation, growth, and insights. However, this combination also poses significant challenges, including data privacy, security, and compliance. As the number of IoT devices continues to grow, so does the potential for cyber threats and data breaches, making IoT security a top priority for organizations.

The importance of IoT security in big data cannot be overstated. IoT devices generate vast amounts of data that are collected and analyzed to gain insights and

Applying Artificial Intelligence in Cybersecurity Analytics and Cyber Threat Detection, First Edition.
Edited by Shilpa Mahajan, Mehak Khurana, and Vania Vieira Estrela.

improve operational efficiency. However, this data also contains sensitive and personal information that must be protected from cyber threats. IoT devices are often connected to critical infrastructure, such as energy grids, transportation systems, and healthcare facilities [1]. An attack on these devices can result in significant financial, operational, and reputational damage. Additionally, as the number of connected devices increases, so does the attack surface, making it more challenging to protect IoT systems from cyber threats. Moreover, the data generated by IoT devices is often unstructured and complex, making it difficult for traditional security methods to detect and mitigate threats. The sheer volume, velocity, and variety of data generated by IoT devices pose significant challenges for security teams, requiring them to adopt new approaches and technologies to address these challenges.

Therefore, ensuring the security of IoT devices and the data they generate is critical to maintaining the integrity and trustworthiness of IoT systems [2]. Failure to protect IoT devices and data can result in severe consequences for businesses, consumers, and society as a whole. As a result, IoT security is a top priority for organizations, and the use of big data analytics and deep learning (DL) approaches is essential to address the unique security challenges posed by IoT in the big data era.

The emergence of the IoT has created new opportunities for businesses [3] to collect and analyze data, but it has also posted significant challenges for IoT security. The sheer volume, velocity, and variety of data generated by IoT devices have made it more difficult for organizations to protect their IoT systems from cyber threats. Figure 15.1 shows some of the significant big data challenges in IoT security.

- **Data collection and processing**: IoT devices generate vast amounts of data in real time, which must be collected, processed, and analyzed. The sheer volume of data generated by IoT devices makes it difficult for organizations to manage and process this data effectively.
- **Data privacy and compliance**: IoT devices collect sensitive and personal information, making it critical to ensure that this data is handled securely and in compliance with relevant data privacy regulations. However, ensuring data privacy [4] and compliance is a challenging task due to the massive amounts of data generated by IoT devices.
- **Data storage and management**: As the volume of data generated by IoT devices continues to grow, organizations must find ways to store and manage this data efficiently. This requires the adoption of new storage and management approaches, including distributed storage and cloud-based solutions.
- **Real-time analysis**: IoT devices generate data in real-time, which requires real-time analysis and response to prevent cyber threats. However, traditional

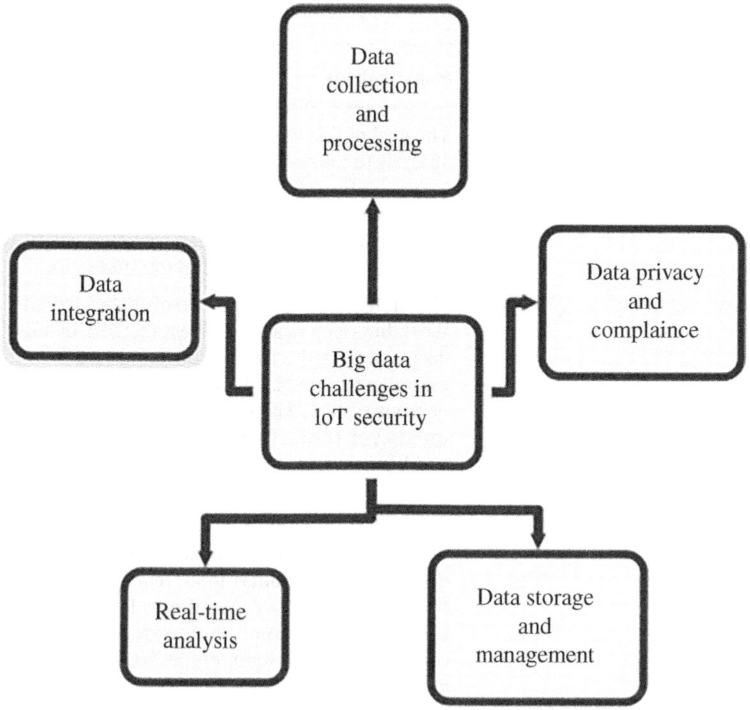

Figure 15.1 Big data challenges in IoT security.

security methods are often insufficient to address real-time analysis and response requirements.

- **Data integration**: IoT devices generate data from different sources and in different formats, making it difficult to integrate this data with existing IT systems. Integration challenges can lead to data silos, making it difficult to gain a complete understanding of IoT systems.

Addressing these big data challenges is critical to ensuring the security of IoT devices and the data they generate. The use of big data analytics and DL approaches can help organizations overcome these challenges and improve the security of IoT systems [5]. There are various DL approaches that can be used to enhance IoT security. These approaches are based on machine learning algorithms that enable the identification of potential cyber threats and help prevent them from causing damage. Some of the different DL approaches for IoT security include:

- **Deep neural networks (DNNs)** are a subset of neural networks that may be trained to spot patterns in data. These networks may be utilized to find IoT data abnormalities that could be signs of a cyber danger.

Table 15.1 below shows the Comparative Analysis of related work around deep learning, IoT, and big data.

Table 15.1 Comparative analysis of related work around deep learning, IoT, and big data.

References	A	B	C	D	Major findings
[8]	√	√	√	×	The goal of this project is to employ big data analysis to make smart cities' data processing more secure and effective. The study uses distributed parallelism and deep learning methods to deal with the massive volumes of multi-source data gathered in the smart city
[9]	√	√	√	×	The architecture proposed in this paper, called Wearable Deep Learning (WearableDL), blends deep learning, the Internet of Things, and wearable technology. It is inspired by the human nervous system. The spinal cord represents the Internet of Things (IoT) for cloud computing and big data flow/transfer, while the peripheral sensory and motor nerves represent wearable technology as edge devices for big data gathering
[10]	√	√	×	√	This paper proposes a deep learning model for diagnosing gallbladder stones using big data from the medical IoT. As gallbladder stones become more common worldwide, the stones can be classified into four types based on their chemical composition
[11]	√	√	×	×	The conceptual framework for cyber-physical manufacturing systems is presented in this study and is based on a literature review. The World Economic Forum, Capgemini, Microsoft, Omdia, PwC, and Software AG are just a few of the sources that the framework uses data from. This study examines and quantifies the relationship between deep learning, industrial big data analytics, and smart process planning as they relate to sustainability
[12]	√	√	×	×	In order to improve large data feature learning and feature fusion, this study suggests a deep learning model called tensor deep learning (TDL). TDL converts vector space data to tensor space and utilizes tensors to describe the complexity of multisource heterogeneous data. The average square sum error component of the output layer reconstruction error is changed to the tensor distance in order to better grasp the data distribution. A high-order back-propagation approach is also suggested in the study to train the model's parameters

(continued)

Table 15.1 (Continued)

References	A	B	C	D	Major findings
[13]	√	√	×	×	In order to obtain high classification accuracy for identifying assaults in distributed systems, the study introduces a Distributed Attack Detection Model (DADEM) that blends deep learning with Big Data analytics. As a result of its superior performance over other algorithms including logistic regression, KNN, ID3 decision tree, CART, and SVM, the sequential deep learning model is chosen as the classification engine. The suggested model obtains a classification accuracy of 99.64% and 99.98% for two separate datasets. A strategy is also put out for improving the model to lessen overhead in a limited setting like IoT
[14]	√	√	√	×	The paper provides an overview of how deep learning is used in the IoT domain to process large amounts of data. It describes the characteristics and requirements of IoT and explains why deep learning a good choice for IoT implementation is
[15]					In order to guarantee the secrecy and integrity of collaborative DL in IoT, BlockDeepNet is a secure deep learning (DL) strategy for the IoT that integrates DL with blockchain. To prevent privacy leaks, collaborative DL is used at the device level, while blockchain is used to assure security. Higher accuracy for DL may be attained by BlockDeepNet with tolerable latency and computational overhead of blockchain operation

A: deep learning; B: machine learning; C: Internet of Things; D: big data.

- **Convolutional neural networks (CNNs)** are a type of neural network that can be used to analyze visual data, such as images and videos. In IoT security, CNNs can be used to analyze security camera footage and detect potential threats.
- **Recurrent neural networks (RNNs)** are a subset of neural networks that are good at analyzing sequential data, which makes them ideal for IoT security. They may be used to find possible cyber dangers by tracking trends in IoT data over time.
- **GANs (generative adversarial networks)** are a class of neural network that can create new data by learning from old data. They may be used to produce fake data that can be tested to see how well IoT security mechanisms work.

- **Autoencoders**: Autoencoders are a type of neural network that can be used to detect anomalies in data. In IoT security, they can be used to detect abnormal patterns in sensor data that may indicate a cyber threat.

These DL approaches can help organizations detect potential cyber threats in IoT data and prevent them from causing damage. By leveraging the power of machine learning algorithms, organizations can improve the security of IoT systems and protect sensitive data from cyber threats.

In this chapter, we will explore the use of DL approaches for IoT security in the big data era. We will discuss the challenges of IoT security, including the growing number of connected devices, the complexity of IoT systems, and the need to protect sensitive data. We will also provide an overview of various DL techniques and architectures that can be used for IoT security, including anomaly detection, intrusion detection, malware detection, and attack attribution. Additionally, we will discuss the use of big data platforms for IoT security data analysis and provide examples of real-world applications of DL for IoT security.

15.2 Role of Deep Learning in IoT Security

As the number of connected devices continues to rise, DL's role in IoT security is becoming more and more crucial. DL algorithms may be used to evaluate massive volumes of data generated by IoT devices in real time, spot possible security problems, and take the necessary precautions to stop them. DL can evaluate complicated data patterns that could be challenging to find with conventional security methods, which is one of its primary advantages in IoT security. As an illustration, DL algorithms may examine network data and spot odd patterns that could point to the presence of a botnet or a cyberattack. Similar to how sensor data may be analyzed, DL algorithms can be used to spot abnormalities that could be signs of security concerns. DL's capacity to instantly react to new threats is another benefit for IoT security. DL algorithms are capable of learning to recognize new security dangers as they appear by being educated on massive volumes of data. By doing so, businesses may keep ahead of cyber threats and safeguard IoT devices from constantly emerging security vulnerabilities.

Additionally, DL may be utilized to enhance the precision and effectiveness of current security systems. For example, DL algorithms can be used to enhance intrusion detection systems by identifying patterns that may indicate a cyberattack. Similarly, DL techniques can be used to improve the accuracy of malware detection systems by identifying common patterns that may indicate the presence of malware on an IoT device.

In addition to these benefits, DL can also be used to protect sensitive data generated by IoT devices. Privacy-preserving techniques, such as federated learning, can be used to train DL algorithms on encrypted data without compromising the privacy of the underlying data. This can help organizations protect sensitive data, such as personal information and medical data, generated by various types of IoT devices. The role of DL in IoT security is critical for protecting IoT devices and sensitive data from cyber threats. DL techniques can be used to analyze large amounts of complex data in real time, identify potential security threats, and take appropriate measures to prevent them. The use of DL in IoT security can help organizations improve the accuracy and efficiency of existing security solutions and adapt to new and evolving security risks.

DL techniques have been increasingly popular in recent years because of their capacity to evaluate vast volumes of complicated data and spot patterns that conventional security solutions can find challenging to notice. DL techniques have grown more crucial around IoT security since IoT devices produce enormous volumes of data that need real-time analysis to stop cyberattacks. Figure 15.2 shows the DL techniques that are commonly used for IoT security.

- **Anomaly detection**: Anomaly detection is a technique that can be used to identify data patterns that deviate significantly from the normal behavior of IoT devices. DL algorithms can be trained on large amounts of data to identify unusual data patterns and flag them as potential security threats. Anomaly detection can be applied to various IoT devices, such as sensors, cameras, and connected vehicles.
- **Intrusion detection**: Intrusion detection is a technique that can be used to identify and respond to cyberattacks on IoT devices. DL algorithms can analyze network traffic and identify unusual patterns that may indicate a cyberattack. Intrusion detection can be used to protect IoT devices from various types of attacks, such as denial-of-service attacks and man-in-the-middle attacks.
- **Malware detection**: Malware detection is a technique that can be used to identify malicious software that may be present on IoT devices. DL algorithms can be trained on malware samples to identify common patterns that may indicate the presence of malware on an IoT device. Malware detection can be applied to various types of IoT devices, such as routers, cameras, and smart home devices [6].
- **Botnet detection**: Botnet detection is a technique that can be used to identify and respond to botnets that may be present on IoT devices. Botnets are networks of compromised devices that can be used to launch cyberattacks on other devices or networks. DL algorithms can analyze network traffic to identify patterns that may indicate the presence of a botnet.
- **Attack attribution**: Attack attribution is a technique that can be used to identify the source of a cyberattack on an IoT device. DL algorithms can analyze network traffic and identify patterns that may be associated with a particular attacker or group of attackers. Attack attribution can help organizations identify

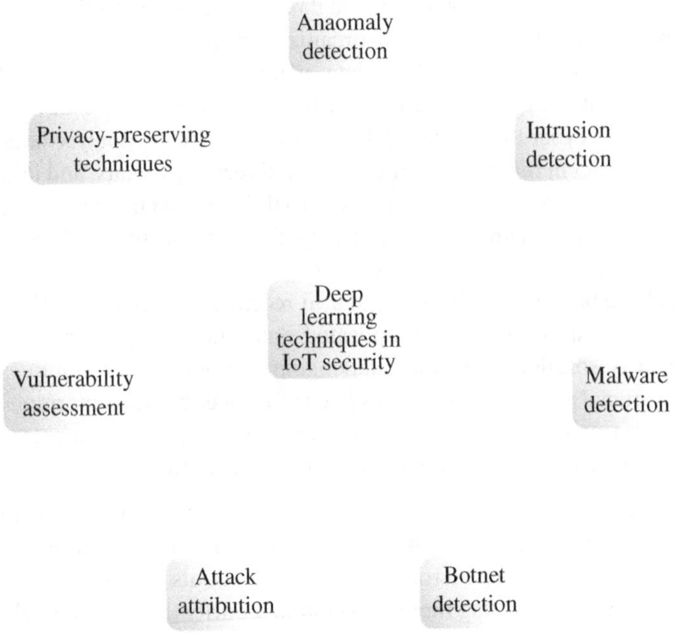

Figure 15.2 Deep learning techniques in IoT security.

the source of cyberattacks and take appropriate measures to prevent future attacks.

- **Vulnerability assessment**: Vulnerability assessment is a technique that can be used to identify vulnerabilities in IoT devices and networks. DL algorithms can analyze network traffic and identify patterns that may indicate vulnerabilities in IoT devices. Vulnerability assessment can help organizations identify potential security risks and take appropriate measures to address them.
- **Privacy-preserving techniques**: Privacy-preserving techniques are a set of techniques that can be used to protect sensitive data generated by IoT devices. DL algorithms can be trained on encrypted data to analyze patterns without accessing the underlying data. Privacy-preserving techniques can be used to protect sensitive data, such as personal information and medical data, generated by various types of IoT devices.

DL techniques are becoming increasingly important for IoT security due to their ability to analyze large amounts of complex data in real time. Organizations can use these techniques to protect IoT devices from various types of cyber threats, such as malware, botnets, and cyberattacks. The use of DL techniques can help organizations improve the security of IoT devices and protect sensitive data from cyber threats.

15.3 Deep Learning Architecture for IoT Security

DL architectures for IoT security typically involve several layers of neural networks that are trained on large amounts of data to identify patterns and anomalies that may indicate potential security threats. The architecture may differ depending on the specific use case and data type, but some common components include:

- Input layer: This layer receives data from IoT devices, which could include sensor data, network traffic, or other types of data.
- Hidden layers: These layers consist of multiple neural networks that process and analyze the input data to identify patterns and anomalies. The number of hidden layers can vary depending on the complexity of the data and the desired level of accuracy.
- Output layer: This layer produces the final output of the DL model, which could be a prediction, classification, or anomaly detection.

There are several DL architectures that are commonly used in IoT security, including:

CNNs are a subset of DL algorithms that are frequently employed in the analysis of images and videos. However, they may also be used to analyze other forms of data, such as sensor data produced by IoT devices.

CNNs are created to find patterns in data by extracting features from convolutional filters. Small sections of the input data are subjected to these filters one at a time, and the resulting feature maps are processed by further layers of neural networks to find increasingly intricate patterns. The capacity of CNNs to automatically learn features from data, without the need for manual feature engineering, is one of its main advantages. They are therefore suitable for high-dimensional and complicated data, such as time-series data or photographs.

CNNs typically consist of several layers, including:

- Layer that uses convolutional filters to extract features from the input data is known as the convolutional layer. Throughout the training process, the filters are picked up.
- The pooling layer preserves the most crucial characteristics while reducing the dimensionality of the feature maps produced by the convolutional layer.
- Convolutional and pooling layer output is processed by the fully connected layer to get a final prediction or classification.

CNNs have been effectively used for a variety of IoT security tasks, including virus detection using audio and video as well as image-based intrusion detection. They are especially helpful for applications involving the analysis of plenty of visual data, such CCTV video or satellite photos.

- **RNNs** are a type of DL algorithm that are commonly used for sequential data, such as time-series or text data. Unlike traditional feedforward neural networks, RNNs can handle variable-length inputs and maintain internal state, making them well-suited for tasks that involve analyzing sequences of data. RNNs process input data one timestep at a time, where each timestep corresponds to one element in the sequence. At each timestep, the RNN updates its internal state based on the current input and the previous state. This allows the network to capture information about the sequence history and use it to make predictions about future elements in the sequence.

One of the key advantages of RNNs is their ability to model temporal dependencies in data, making them well-suited for tasks such as language modeling, speech recognition, and time-series prediction. In addition, RNNs can be used in combination with other types of DL algorithms, such as CNNs, to process sequential data with complex spatial and temporal patterns.

RNNs come in several different forms, including:

- Simple RNNs: The simplest form of RNN, which uses a single recurrent layer to process input sequences.
- Long short-term memory (LSTM) networks: A more complex form of RNN that includes additional memory cells and gates, allowing them to better capture long-term dependencies in data.
- Gated recurrent units (GRUs): A simplified version of LSTM networks that are faster to train and require fewer parameters.

RNNs have been successfully applied to a wide range of IoT security tasks, including time-series anomaly detection, malware detection, and intrusion detection. They are particularly useful for tasks that involve analyzing sequential data, such as sensor data generated by IoT devices over time. RNNs are a powerful DL algorithm that can handle variable-length inputs and maintain internal state, making them well-suited for tasks that involve analyzing sequences of data. They can be used in combination with other types of DL algorithms to process sequential data with complex spatial and temporal patterns. RNNs have been successfully applied to a wide range of IoT security tasks, particularly those involving sequential data.

- **Autoencoders** are a kind of neural network called an autoencoder that is frequently employed for unsupervised learning tasks including dimensionality reduction and feature extraction. The goal of autoencoders is to learn a compressed representation of the input data with the least amount of information lost during encoding and decoding.

  An encoder network and a decoder network are the two major components of an autoencoder. The input data is received by the encoder network, which transforms it into a compressed representation, or "latent space," that has less dimensions than the original data. The decoder network then uses the compressed representation to map it back to the original data in an effort to properly recreate the input. The difference between the input data and the output of the decoder network is measured and used to train autoencoders. A compressed representation of the input data that captures its most crucial aspects is learned by the autoencoder by minimizing this loss.

Autoencoders have the potential to learn intricate data representations in an unsupervised fashion without the requirement for labeled training data, which is one of its main advantages. As a result, they are highly suited for jobs that require examining and analyzing huge databases, such as text or picture data. Numerous IoT security tasks, such as virus identification, intrusion detection, and anomaly detection, have been successfully completed using autoencoders. They are especially beneficial for jobs involving the analysis of large-scale data, such as sensor data produced by IoT devices.

In order to handle complicated and high-dimensional data with spatial and temporal patterns, autoencoders can also be used in conjunction with other DL methods, such as CNNs or RNNs. A potent DL method called an autoencoder can learn intricate data representations without the use of labeled training data. They work effectively for jobs that require examining and analyzing huge datasets, especially when the data is high dimensional. In order to analyze complicated and high-dimensional data, autoencoders may be combined with other DL algorithms. They have been effectively employed for a variety of IoT security applications.

- A generator network and a discriminator network make up the two neural networks that make up the DL method known as GANs. GANs are employed in generative modeling, which entails developing a model that can produce fresh data that is comparable to an existing dataset. The generator network creates a fresh sample of data that is meant to be identical to the training data by receiving a random noise vector as input. The discriminator network receives a sample of data, either created by the generator network or taken from the training set, and attempts to identify whether it is real or fraudulent.

A technique known as adversarial training is used to train both the discriminator and generator networks simultaneously. While the discriminator network works to separate the created data from the genuine data, the generator network attempts to create data samples that would deceive it into categorizing them as real. The generator network gains the ability to produce increasingly realistic data samples as the training process goes on, tricking the discriminator network.

GANs have been applied to a variety of tasks, including the creation of literature, music, and images and videos. GANs may be used for tasks like producing synthetic data for training anomaly detection models or producing adversarial instances to evaluate the resilience of DL models in the context of IoT security.

Even for complicated datasets like photos or videos, GANs can produce realistic data samples that are comparable to the training data. This is one of its key advantages. GANs may be difficult to train, and they are prone to instability, which can cause mode collapse or other training issues. A potent DL approach called GANs may be applied to generative modeling tasks, such as the creation of images and videos. They have a variety of uses in IoT security, including producing synthetic data for training anomaly detection models and adversarial instances to evaluate the resilience of DL algorithms. While GANs can be challenging to train and prone to instability, they are a valuable tool for DL researchers and practitioners.

DL architecture for IoT security involves multiple layers of neural networks that are trained on large amounts of data to identify patterns and anomalies. The specific architecture may vary depending on the use case and data type, but commonly used architectures include CNNs, RNNs, autoencoders, and GANs. The use of DL in IoT security can help organizations identify and prevent potential security threats in real time.

15.4 Future Scope of Deep Learning in IoT Security

The future scope of DL in IoT security is vast and promising. With the rapid growth of IoT devices, there is an increasing need for robust and efficient security mechanisms to protect against cyberattacks. DL offers a range of techniques and algorithms that can help to address this challenge, and there are several areas where DL is expected to play an important role in the future of IoT security:

- Real-time detection and response: DL algorithms can be used to detect and respond to cyberattacks in real time, enabling IoT systems to rapidly adapt and defend against evolving threats.
- Enhanced privacy and data protection: DL can be used to develop new privacy-preserving techniques for IoT data, ensuring that sensitive data is protected even in the event of a breach.
- Improved anomaly detection: In IoT systems, DL algorithms can assist in increasing the efficacy and accuracy of anomaly detection while lowering the likelihood of false positives and false negatives.
- Adversarial machine learning: DL techniques can be used to develop robust machine learning [7] models that are resistant to adversarial attacks, ensuring that IoT systems remain secure even in the face of sophisticated attackers.
- Federated learning: Through the use of federated learning, many IoT devices may work together to train a machine learning model without disclosing private

information. This method may be used to create IoT security models that are more precise and effective.

Overall, the future of DL in IoT security looks bright, with new techniques and algorithms being developed and applied to address the complex and evolving security challenges posed by IoT systems. As the number of IoT devices continues to grow, DL will play an increasingly important role in ensuring the security and integrity of these systems.

15.5 Conclusion

IoT security is an important and challenging field that requires robust and efficient solutions to protect against cyberattacks. DL approaches have emerged as a promising tool for addressing the security challenges in IoT systems. In this chapter, we have discussed various DL techniques such as anomaly detection, intrusion detection, malware detection, botnet detection, attack attribution, vulnerability assessment, and privacy-preserving techniques. The role of DL in IoT security and the DL architectures such as CNNs, RNNs, autoencoders, and GANs are also discussed in this chapter. These architectures are capable of processing large amounts of data, extracting meaningful features, and detecting complex patterns in IoT systems. Moreover, the author highlighted the big data challenges in IoT security and how DL can help in addressing those challenges. DL algorithms can handle large amounts of data, learn from the data, and generalize the knowledge for new data, which is critical in IoT security, where the amount of data is constantly increasing. The future scope of DL in IoT security is also highlighted in this paper. With the rapid growth of IoT devices, DL is expected to play an increasingly important role in ensuring the security and integrity of these systems. Real-time detection and response, enhanced privacy and data protection, improved anomaly detection, adversarial machine learning, and federated learning are some of the promising areas where DL can make significant contributions to IoT security.

Ultimately, DL approaches offer a range of techniques and algorithms that can help address the complex and evolving security challenges posed by IoT systems. The future of DL in IoT security looks bright, with new techniques and algorithms being developed and applied to ensure the security and integrity of IoT systems.

References

1 Singh, K., Kaushik, K., and Ahatsham, & Shahare, V. (2020). Role and impact of wearables in IoT healthcare. *Advances in Intelligent Systems and Computing* 1090: 735–742. https://doi.org/10.1007/978-981-15-1480-7_67.

2 Kaushik, K. and Singh, K. (2020). Security and trust in IoT communications: role and impact. *Advances in Intelligent Systems and Computing* 989: 791–798. https://doi.org/10.1007/978-981-13-8618-3_81.

3 Kaushik, K. and Dahiya, S. (2018). Security and privacy in IoT based e-business and retail. In: *Proceedings of the 2018 International Conference on System Modeling and Advancement in Research Trends, SMART 2018*, 78–81. https://doi.org/10.1109/SYSMART.2018.8746961.

4 Vashisht, S., Gaba, S., Dahiya, S., and Kaushik, K. (2022). Security and privacy issues in IoT systems using blockchain. *Sustainable and Advanced Applications of Blockchain in Smart Computational Technologies* 113–127. https://doi.org/10.1201/9781003193425-8.

5 Kaushik, K. (2022). The role of IoT in the design of a security system. *Advancing Computational Intelligence Techniques for Security Systems Design* 39–50. https://doi.org/10.1201/9781003229704-3.

6 Bhardwaj, A., Kaushik, K., Bharany, S. et al. (2022). Comparison of IoT communication protocols using anomaly detection with security assessments of smart devices. *Processes* 10 (10): 1952. https://doi.org/10.3390/PR10101952.

7 Kaushik, K., Bhardwaj, A., Dahiya, S. et al. (2022). Multinomial naive bayesian classifier framework for systematic analysis of smart IoT devices. *Sensors* 22 (19): 7318. https://doi.org/10.3390/S22197318.

8 Li, X., Liu, H., Wang, W. et al. (2022). Big data analysis of the Internet of Things in the digital twins of smart city based on deep learning. *Future Generation Computer Systems* 128: 167–177. https://doi.org/10.1016/J.FUTURE.2021.10.006.

9 Dargazany, A.R., Stegagno, P., and Mankodiya, K. (2018). WearableDL: wearable Internet-of-Things and deep learning for big data analytics – concept, literature, and future. *Mobile Information Systems* 2018: https://doi.org/10.1155/2018/8125126.

10 Yao, C., Wu, S., Liu, Z., and Li, P. (2019). A deep learning model for predicting chemical composition of gallstones with big data in medical Internet of Things. *Future Generation Computer Systems* 94: 140–147. https://doi.org/10.1016/J.FUTURE.2018.11.011.

11 Throne, O. and Lazaroiu, G. (2020). Internet of Things-enabled sustainability, industrial big data analytics, and deep learning-assisted smart process planning in cyber-physical manufacturing systems. *Economics, Management, and Financial Markets* 15 (4): 49–58.

12 Wang, W. and Zhang, M. (2020). Tensor deep learning model for heterogeneous data fusion in Internet of Things. *IEEE Transactions on Emerging Topics in Computational Intelligence* 4: 32–41. https://doi.org/10.1109/TETCI.2018.2876568.

13 Ahmed, H. I., Nasr, A. A., Abdel-Mageid, S. M., & Aslan, H. K. 2021 DADEM: distributed attack detection model based on big data analytics for the enhancement of the security of Internet of Things (IoT). *International Journal of Ambient Computing and Intelligence (IJACI)*, 12(1), 114–139. https://doi.org/10.4018/IJACI.2021010105, https://Services.Igi-Global.Com/Resolvedoi/Resolve.Aspx?Doi=10.4018/IJACI.2021010105.

14 Tiwari, R., Sharma, N., Kaushik, I. et al. (2019). Evolution of IoT data analytics using deep learning. In: *Proceedings - 2019 International Conference on Computing, Communication, and Intelligent Systems, ICCCIS 2019, 2019-January*, 418–423. https://doi.org/10.1109/ICCCIS48478.2019.8974481.

15 Rathore, S., Pan, Y., and Park, J.H. (2019). BlockDeepNet: A blockchain-based secure deep learning for IoT network. *Sustainability* 11 (14): 3974. https://doi.org/10.3390/SU11143974.

Index

Applying Artificial Intelligence in Cybersecurity Analytics and Cyber Threat Detection, First Edition.
Edited by Shilpa Mahajan, Mehak Khurana, and Vania Vieira Estrela.

Printed and bound by CPI Group (UK) Ltd, Croydon, CR0 4YY
27/10/2024
14580673-0003